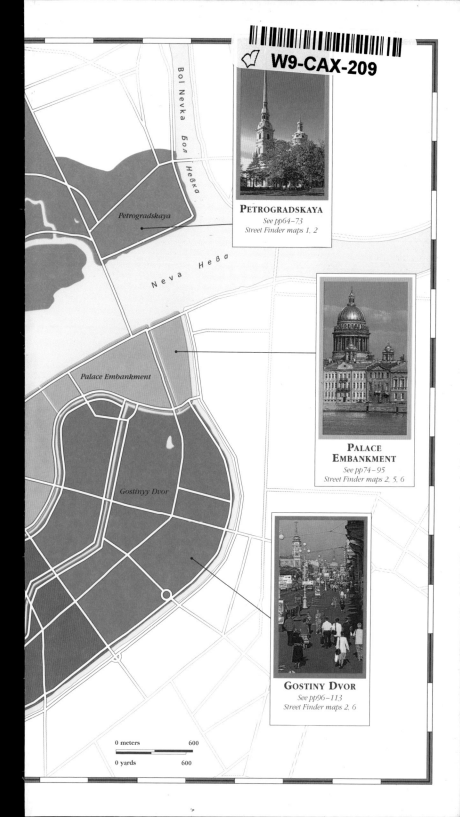

W9-CAX-209

PETROGRADSKAYA
See pp64–73
Street Finder maps 1, 2

PALACE EMBANKMENT
See pp74–95
Street Finder maps 2, 5, 6

GOSTINY DVOR
See pp96–113
Street Finder maps 2, 6

Petrogradskaya

Palace Embankment

Gostinyy Dvor

Bol Nevka

Бол Невка

Neva Нева

0 meters   600
0 yards   600

ST. PETERSBURG

EYEWITNESS *TRAVEL GUIDES*

ST. PETERSBURG

Main contributors:
CATHERINE PHILLIPS
CHRISTOPHER AND MELANIE RICE

DK

DK PUBLISHING, INC.

A DK PUBLISHING BOOK

PROJECT EDITOR Anna Streiffert
ART EDITOR Marisa Renzullo
EDITOR Ella Milroy
US EDITORS Mary Sutherland, Michael T. Wise
DESIGNERS Gillian Andrews, Carolyn Hewitson,
Paul Jackson, Elly King, Nicola Rodway
VISUALIZER Joy Fitzsimmons
MAP CO-ORDINATORS Emily Green, David Pugh

MANAGING EDITORS Fay Franklin, Georgina Matthews
MANAGING ART EDITOR Annette Jacobs
SENIOR MANAGING EDITOR Vivien Crump
DEPUTY ART DIRECTOR Gillian Allan

PRODUCTION Jo Blackmore, Anna Pauletti, David Proffit
PICTURE RESEARCH Brigitte Arora
DTP DESIGNER Sarah Martin, Pamela Shiels

MAIN CONTRIBUTORS
Catherine Phillips,
Christopher and Melanie Rice

MAPS
Rob Clynes, Maria Donnelly, Ewan Watson
(Colourmap Scanning Ltd)

PHOTOGRAPHERS
Demetrio Carrasco, John Heseltine

ILLUSTRATORS
Stephen Conlin, Maltings Partnership, Chris Orr & Associates,
Paul Weston
•

Text film output by Graphical Innovations, London
Reproduced by Colourscan, Singapore
Printed and bound in Italy by G. Canale

First American Edition, 1998
2 4 6 8 10 9 7 5 3 1

Published in the United States by
DK Publishing, Inc.,
95 Madison Avenue, New York, New York 10016

Copyright © 1998 Dorling Kindersley Limited, London
Visit us on the World Wide Web at htttp://www.dk.com

Library of Congress Cataloging-in-Publication Data
St. Petersburg.
p. cm. -- (Eyewitness travel guides)
ISBN 0-7894-3530-6
1. Saint Petersburg (Russia) -- Description and travel.
I. Series.
DK552.S69 1998   98-3673
914.7'210486 -- dc21   CIP

Floors are referred to throughout in accordance with American usage; i.e., the "first floor" is at ground level. Details such as telephone numbers, opening hours, prices, and travel information are correct at the time of going to press, but are liable to change. The publishers cannot accept responsibility for any consequences arising from the use of this book.

We would be delighted to receive any corrections and suggestions for incorporation in the next edition. Please write to: Senior Editor, Eyewitness Travel Guides, DK Publishing, Inc., 95 Madison Ave., New York, NY 10016.

CONTENTS

HOW TO USE
THIS GUIDE 6

Bronze model of ship, a symbol
of St. Petersburg

INTRODUCING
ST. PETERSBURG

PUTTING
ST. PETERSBURG
ON THE MAP 10

THE HISTORY OF
ST. PETERSBURG 16

ST. PETERSBURG
AT A GLANCE 32

ST. PETERSBURG
THROUGH THE YEAR 50

Petersburgers enjoying the snow
outside the Hermitage

ST. PETERSBURG
AREA BY AREA

VASILEVSKIY ISLAND 56

PETROGRADSKAYA 64

PALACE EMBANKMENT
74

Little Stable Bridge crossing the Moyka River

GETTING TO
ST. PETERSBURG
210

GETTING AROUND
ST. PETERSBURG 213

ST. PETERSBURG
STREET FINDER
222

GENERAL INDEX 238

GOSTINYY DVOR
96

SENNAYA PLOSHCHAD
114

FARTHER AFIELD
124

TWO GUIDED WALKS
132

BEYOND
ST. PETERSBURG
138

SHOPS AND MARKETS
186

ENTERTAINMENT IN
ST. PETERSBURG 192

Pelmeny, a meat or fish dumpling
dish originally from Siberia

15th-century icon of St. George
and the Dragon, Russian Museum

ACKNOWLEDGMENTS
250

PHRASE BOOK
AND
TRANSLITERATION
252

SURVIVAL GUIDE

PRACTICAL
INFORMATION
200

Golden statues of the Grand
Cascade at Peterhof

TRAVELERS'
NEEDS

WHERE TO STAY 166

RESTAURANTS AND
CAFÉS 174

St. Isaac's Cathedral, lavishly decorated inside with more than
40 different stones and minerals

HOW TO USE THIS GUIDE

THIS GUIDE WILL HELP you get the most from your visit to St. Petersburg, providing expert recommendations as well as detailed practical information. *Introducing St. Petersburg* maps the city and sets it in its geographical, historical, and cultural context, with a quick-reference timeline on the history pages giving the dates of Russia's rulers and significant events. *St. Petersburg at a Glance* is an overview of the city's main attractions. *St. Petersburg Area by Area* starts on page 54 and describes all the important sights, using maps, photographs, and illustrations. The sights are arranged in two groups: those in St. Petersburg's central districts and those a little farther afield. The guided walks reveal two characteristics of the city – its canals and its islands. *Beyond St. Petersburg* describes sights requiring one- or two-day excursions. Hotel, restaurant, shopping, and entertainment recommendations can be found in *Travelers' Needs*. The *Survival Guide* includes tips on everything from transportation and telephones to personal safety.

FINDING YOUR WAY AROUND THE SIGHTSEEING SECTION

Each of the seven sightseeing areas is color-coded for easy reference. Every chapter opens with an introduction to the area it covers, describing its history and character. For central districts, this is followed by a Street-by-Street map illustrating a particularly interesting part of the area; for sights beyond the city limits, by a regional map. A simple numbering system relates sights to the maps. Important sights are covered by several pages.

1 Introduction to the area
For easy reference, the sights are numbered and plotted on an area map, with metro stations shown where helpful. The key sights (great buildings, museums, and open-air sights) are listed by category.

A locator map shows where you are in relation to other areas of the city center.

Each area has color-coded thumb tabs.

Locator map

The area shaded in pink is shown in greater detail on the Street-by-Street map.

2 Street-by-Street map
This gives a bird's eye view of interesting and important parts of each sightseeing area, with accurate drawings of all the buildings within them. The numbering of the sights ties in with the preceding area map and with the fuller descriptions on the pages that follow.

A suggested route for a walk is shown in red.

St. Petersburg Area Map

The colored areas shown on this map (see pp14–15) are the five main sightseeing areas into which central St. Petersburg has been divided for this guide. Each is covered in a full chapter in the *St. Petersburg Area by Area* section (pp54–131). They are also shown on other maps throughout the book. In *St. Petersburg at a Glance* (pp32–49), for example, they help you locate the most interesting museums and palaces, or where to see the city's many delightfully designed bridges. The maps' colored borders match the colored thumb tabs on each page of the section.

Numbers refer to each sight's position on the area map and its place in the chapter.

Practical information lists all the information you need to visit every sight, including a map reference to the *Street Finder* maps (pp230–37).

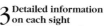

3 Detailed information on each sight
All the important sights are described individually. They are listed to follow the numbering on the area map at the start of the section. The key to the symbols summarizing practical information is on the back flap.

A Visitors' Checklist provides the practical information you will need to plan your visit.

Story boxes highlight unique aspects or historical connections of a particular sight.

4 St. Petersburg's major sights
These are given two or more full pages in the sightseeing area where they are found. Buildings of interesting architecture are dissected to reveal their interiors; museums and galleries have color-coded floor plans to help you find important exhibits.

Stars indicate the best features or works of art.

INTRODUCING
ST. PETERSBURG

PUTTING ST. PETERSBURG
ON THE MAP 10-15
THE HISTORY OF ST. PETERSBURG 16-31
ST. PETERSBURG AT A GLANCE 32-49
ST. PETERSBURG THROUGH THE YEAR 50-53

Putting St. Petersburg on the Map

THE RUSSIAN FEDERATION, or Russia as it is usually known, is the world's largest country, covering an area of 17.4 million sq km (6.7 million sq miles). Situated in its north-west corner, St. Petersburg is Russia's second city, with a population of just under five million. Once Russia's capital and known as its "Window on the West" *(see pp20–21)*, the city was built on the marshy lands where the Neva joins the Gulf of Finland. Of the 13 countries bordering Russia, Estonia, and Finland are St. Petersburg's closest neighbors.

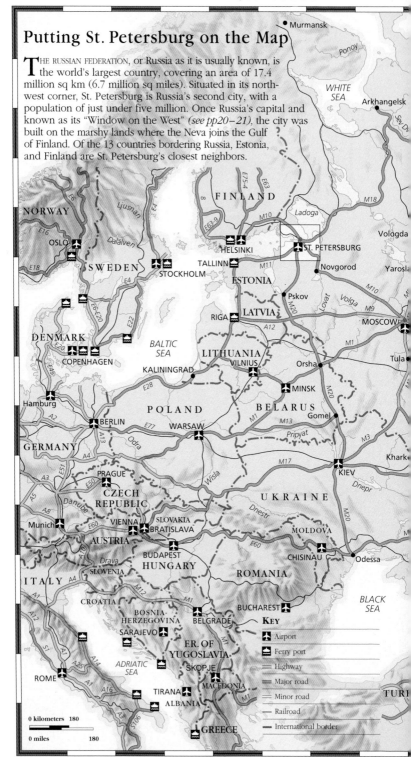

KEY

✈	Airport
⛴	Ferry port
▬	Highway
▬	Major road
—	Minor road
—	Railroad
⌁	International border

0 kilometers 180

0 miles 180

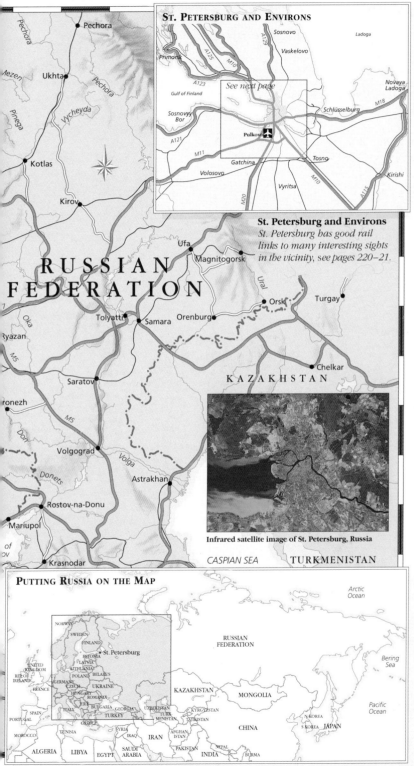

St. Petersburg and Environs

Pechora
Ukhta
Pechora
Pinega
Vycheyda
Mezen
Kotlas
Kirov
Ryazan
Oka

RUSSIAN
FEDERATION

Ufa
Magnitogorsk
Ural
Tolyatti
Samara
Orenburg
Orsk
Turgay

KAZAKHSTAN

Chelkar
Saratov
Volgograd
Volga
Astrakhan
Voronezh
Don
Donets
Rostov-na-Donu
Mariupol
of ov
Krasnodar

CASPIAN SEA   TURKMENISTAN

St. Petersburg and Environs

St. Petersburg has good rail links to many interesting sights in the vicinity, see pages 220–21.

ST. PETERSBURG AND ENVIRONS

Sosnovo
Ladoga
Vaskelovo
Primork
A129
A125
M10
Novaya Ladoga
Gulf of Finland
A123
See next page
Schlüsselburg
M18
Sosnovyy Bor
Pulkovo
A121
M11
Gatchina
Tosno
Kirishi
Volosovo
M10
A115
Vyritsa
M20

Infrared satellite image of St. Petersburg, Russia

PUTTING RUSSIA ON THE MAP

Arctic Ocean
NORWAY
SWEDEN
FINLAND
RUSSIAN FEDERATION
ESTONIA
St. Petersburg
LATVIA
Bering Sea
UNITED KINGDOM
LITHUANIA
REP OF IRELAND
POLAND
BELARUS
FRANCE
GERMANY
CZECH
UKRAINE
HUNGARY
ROMANIA
KAZAKHSTAN
MONGOLIA
Pacific Ocean
SPAIN
ITALY
BULGARIA
GEORGIA
UZBEKISTAN
KYRGYZSTAN
N.KOREA
PORTUGAL
GREECE
TURKEY
TURK MENISTAN
TAJIKISTAN
CHINA
S.KOREA JAPAN
MOROCCO
TUNISIA
SYRIA
IRAQ
AFGHAN ISTAN
ALGERIA
LIBYA
EGYPT
SAUDI ARABIA
IRAN
PAKISTAN
NEPAL
INDIA
BURMA

Greater St. Petersburg

ST. PETERSBURG'S FIRST BUILDINGS were situated on islands on the north side of the Neva but, as the city started to grow, the center moved south of the river. Today St. Petersburg spreads out over more than 40 islands, with high-rise suburbs sprawling almost all the way out to the imperial country palaces *(see pp146–59)*. The metro and suburban trains offer easy transportation to sights situated farther away from the city center *(see pp220–21)*.

Vyborg

Repino

Solnechnoe

Beloostrov

Beloostrov

Pesochnyy

Pesochnyy

Sestroretskiy Razliv

Sestroretsk

SESTRORETSK

Gorskaya

Kame

Sosnovyy Bor

Lisiy Nos

Konna

Lakht

KRONSTADT

Gulf of Finland
(Finskiy Zaliv)

Bolshaya Izhora

Malaya Izhora

A121

Oranienbaum

LOMONOSOV
ORANIENBAUM

PETERHOF

Novyy Petergof

STRELNA

Sosno

Polyar

Nizino

Vladimirovka

Chernaya

Petrovskoe

Razbegaevo

Annino

Gore

Gostilitsy

Zaborode

KRASNOE
SELO

M11

Ropsha

KEY

Central St. Petersburg	
Greater St. Petersburg	
Airport	
Train station	
Major road	
Minor road	
Railroad	

Gorki

Russko-Vysotskoe

Lagolovo

Villo

Villoz

M11

Kipen

Kuyduzi

Skvoritsy

Tayt

0 kilometers   3

0 miles   3

Gatchina

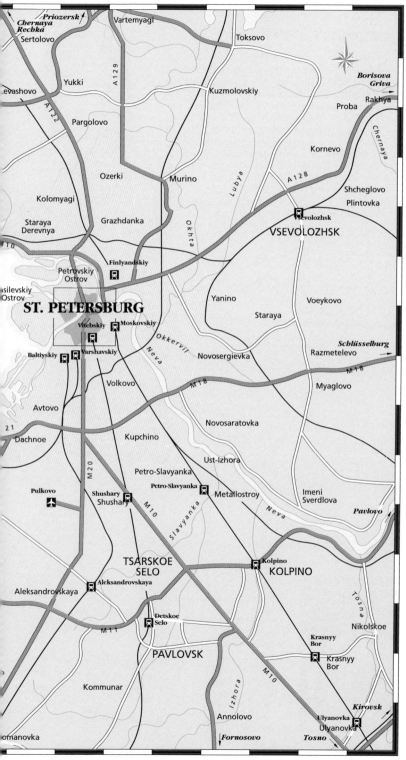

Central St. Petersburg

ST. PETERSBURG'S five central areas described in this book each have their own character, reflecting different sides of the city's past. The southern bank of the Neva, Palace Embankment, is lined with glorious, stately palaces. Gostinyy Dvor, to the east, has always been the commercial hub of the city, with shops, bars, and restaurants lining Nevskiy prospekt. To the west lies Sennaya Ploshchad, a mixture of romantic, tree-lined canals and reminders of the 19th-century lowlife of Dostoevsky's novels. Vasilevskiy Island, the largest in the city, combines a naval heritage with scholarly institutions. Petrogradskaya, to the north, is dominated by the Peter and Paul Fortress.

Vasilevskiy Island

Adorned with figures representing four great Russian rivers, the Rostral Columns (see p60) stand on the eastern tip of the island. From here there are sweeping views of the Neva and its embankments.

Petrogradskaya

Burial place of the Romanov tsars, the SS. Peter and Paul Cathedral (see p68) stands within the fortress where Peter the Great began building the city in 1703. Its tall gilded spire dominates the skyline of Petrogradskaya, an area otherwise characterized by many splendid Style-Moderne buildings.

Gostinyy Dvor

Nevskiy prospekt, the city's main artery, is crossed by waterways such as Moyka River (see p36), shown here. These intersections are bustling in the summer, with cafés on river boats and by the water's edge.

Palace Embankment

Part of the Hermitage, the former imperial Winter Palace (see pp92–3), dominates this grand waterfront with a burst of Baroque splendor. The embankment is lined with monuments from the famous Bronze Horseman (p78) to Peter the Great's modest Summer Palace (p95).

Sennaya Ploshchad

St. Petersburg's most famous theater, the Mariinskiy (see p119), is best known for its classical ballet. The surrounding area, with quiet streets lining its canals, is perfect for walks during the atmospheric White Nights.

0 meters   600

0 yards   600

KEY

- Major sight
- Main sight
- **M** Metro station
- River boat pier
- Police station
- Orthodox church

THE HISTORY OF
ST. PETERSBURG

FOUNDED IN 1703, *within ten years St. Petersburg had become capital of the vast Russian empire and quickly gained a reputation as one of Europe's most beautiful cities. In the 20th century it underwent three name changes, three revolutions, and a 900-day siege. For a city less than 300 years old, it has an amazing history.*

Some 850 years before St. Petersburg became capital of Russia, local Slavic tribes invited the Viking chieftain Rurik to rule them. His successor founded Kiev, which grew into a great princedom. In 988 Grand Prince Vladimir adopted Orthodox Christianity with profound consequences; Orthodoxy was to become a cornerstone of Russian identity. Paradoxically, Russia only emerged as a united entity during the 250-year domination of the Muslim Mongols. In 1237 these fierce tribes conquered all the principalities except Novgorod. In the 14th century the Mongols chose Moscow's power-hungry grand prince, Ivan I (1325–40), to collect tribute from other subjugated principalities. This sealed the fate of the Mongols, for, as Moscow thrived under their benevolence, she also became a real threat.

Ivan IV "the Terrible"

Mongol warriors in a 14th-century manuscript illustration

Within 50 years, an army led by Moscow's Grand Prince Dmitriy Donskoy won a first victory over the Mongols, and the idea of a Russian nation was born.

During the long reign of Ivan III (1462–1505) the Mongols were finally vanquished and Moscow's prestige increased. Ivan the Terrible (1533–84) was the first to be called "Tsar of All the Russias." Yet his reign, which began in glory, ended in disaster. Ivan killed his only heir, and the so-called Time of Troubles followed as Russia came under a succession of weak rulers and Polish usurpers invaded Moscow.

THE FIRST ROMANOVS

To end this strife, in 1613 the leading citizens chose Mikhail Romanov to be tsar, thus initiating the 300-year Romanov rule. Under Mikhail, Russia recovered from her upheavals, but his greatest legacy was his son Alexis. Intelligent and pious, Alexis modernized the state, encouraging an influx of foreign architects, codifying laws, and asserting the power of the state over the church.

TIMELINE

800	1000	1200	1400	1600
862 Rurik establishes Viking stronghold at Novgorod	**1147** Moscow is founded	**1480** Ivan III stops paying tribute to Mongols	**1605–13** Time of Troubles	*Boris Godunov*
863 Cyril and Methodius create early version of Cyrillic	**1462–1505** Reign of Ivan III			
988 Prince Vladimir converts to Orthodox Christianity	**1108** Town of Vladimir is founded	**1223** First Mongol raid	**1242** Alexander Nevsky defeats the Teutonic Knights	**1533–84** Reign of Ivan IV the Terrible	**1613** Mikhail Romanov becomes first tsar of the Romanov dynasty
		1240 Mongol rule established in Rus	**1598** Boris Godunov claims title of tsar after 12 years as regent	

PETER THE GREAT

The future Peter the Great, founder of St. Petersburg, was born during the transition from a medieval to a more modern state, After his father Alexis's death, Peter's childhood was overshadowed by rivalry between his mother's family, the Naryshkins, and that of his father's first wife, the Miloslavskiys. At ten, Peter ascended the throne, but the Streltsy Guards, influenced by the Miloslavskiys, started a revolt. As a result his half-brother Ivan became his co-tsar and Ivan's sister Sophia their regent. The memory of seeing his family killed caused his hatred of Moscow and distrust of its conservative, scheming society.

Peter the Great (1682–1725)

When Ivan died in 1696, the 24-year-old Peter had grown to a giant of a man with a stormy combination of willpower and energy. Long hours spent drilling toy soldiers developed into a full-scale reform of the Russian army. But Peter's dream was of a Russian navy. In 1697, he went on a European tour to study shipbuilding and other technologies. To everyone's dismay the young tsar spent more hours working at the docks than socializing at court. On his return to Russia he lost no time in enforcing westernizing reforms.

A NEW CAPITAL

It was Peter's determination to found a northern port with an unrestricted passage to the Baltic that led to war with Sweden, at the time one of the strongest countries in Europe. By May 1703 Peter had secured the Neva River and began to build the Peter and Paul Fortress and a shipyard opposite *(see pp20–21)*. Only an autocrat with Peter's drive could have succeeded in building a

View of St. Petersburg in the early 17th century, with the Admiralty shipyard to the left

TIMELINE

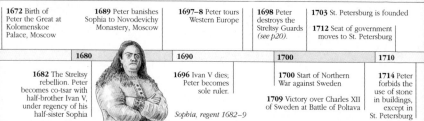

1672 Birth of Peter the Great at Kolomenskoe Palace, Moscow

1689 Peter banishes Sophia to Novodevichy Monastery, Moscow

1697–8 Peter tours Western Europe

1698 Peter destroys the Streltsy Guards *(see p20)*.

1703 St. Petersburg is founded

1712 Seat of government moves to St. Petersburg

1680   **1690**   **1700**   **1710**

1682 The Streltsy rebellion. Peter becomes co-tsar with half-brother Ivan V, under regency of his half-sister Sophia

1696 Ivan V dies; Peter becomes sole ruler.

Sophia, regent 1682–9

1700 Start of Northern War against Sweden

1709 Victory over Charles XII of Sweden at Battle of Poltava

1714 Peter forbids the use of stone in buildings, except in St. Petersburg

LIFE AT ELIZABETH'S COURT

When Elizabeth was not busy looking over architectural plans, she would lie around on her bed, gossiping with a group of ladies whose chief task was to tickle her feet. Her restless nature meant that her courtiers had to endure endless hunts and skating parties, and were required to keep her company at all hours. Her riotous cross-dressing masquerades were notorious, as was her vast wardrobe, allegedly containing over 15,000 dresses.

Tsarina Elizabeth going for a stroll at Tsarskoe Selo, surrounded by eager courtiers

city on this fetid bogland, where daylight and building materials were in short supply and disastrous floodings regular. More than 40,000 Swedish prisoners-of-war and peasants labored and perished here, their bones contributing to the city's foundations.

Whether or not it was always Peter's intention to make this his new capital, it became possible only after his decisive victory at Poltava in 1709 put an end to the Swedish threat. St. Petersburg was named capital of Russia in 1712, and by Peter's death in 1725 there were 40,000 inhabitants in the city and many more in the surrounding labor encampments.

WOMEN RULERS

For most of the rest of the 18th century Russia was ruled by women, whose taste did much to set the celebrated architectural tone of St. Petersburg.

During the brief reigns of Peter's wife Catherine I (1725–27) and his grandson Peter II (1727–30), the court abandoned this frontier city for the more comfortable life in Moscow. But when the throne passed to Anna, daughter of Peter's co-tsar Ivan, she decided to create a recognizably European court in St. Petersburg. Anna was 37 at the time and had spent most of her life in Germany. This was obvious in her choice of ministers and favorites, of whom many were German. Fashion and style, however, were imported from France and opera from Italy. Though she herself was serious, plain, and somewhat cruel, Anna did much to put the court on a footing with the most frivolous in Europe, as well as encouraging a flowering of civilization.

Tsarina Elizabeth, daughter of Peter the Great, was the ideal successor to this glittering court. Elizabeth was attractive, energetic, and cheerful, a combination that endeared her to almost everyone, especially the Guards who helped secure her place on the throne. She left the affairs of state to a series of well chosen advisors. The only element of seriousness lay in Elizabeth's perhaps surprising piety, which at times led her to retire temporarily into a convent. Her main legacy is the splendid Baroque architecture she commissioned, designed mainly by her favorite architect Rastrelli (see p93).

Elizabeth (1741–61)

1721 Peace of Nystad ends war with Sweden

1733 Cathedral of SS. Peter and Paul is finished after 12 years' work

1738 Russia's first ballet school is founded in St. Petersburg

1745 Tsarevich Peter marries the future Catherine the Great

1757 St. Petersburg Academy of Arts is founded

1717 Peter travels to Holland and France

1725 Catherine I is empress after death of Peter the Great

1730–40 Reign of Anna

1727–30 Reign of Peter II

1741 Ivan VI is deposed and Elizabeth comes to power supported by Guards' officers

Anna Ivanovna, daughter of Ivan V

1754 Rastrelli's Winter Palace is begun

A Window on the West

Determined to drag his country out of the medieval period, and inspired by the few westerners he met in Moscow, Peter the Great was the first tsar to travel to Western Europe. He returned with many ideas for reforms and architectural novelties for his new city. In 1710, when the Swedish threat was over, the reluctant imperial family and government were moved to this chilly, damp outpost. But Peter was adamant, and soon a rational street plan, stone buildings, and academies made St. Petersburg a thriving capital in which fashions and discoveries from Europe were tried out before filtering through to the rest of Russia.

EXTENT OF THE CITY

▨ 1712   ☐ Today

PLAN OF THE NEW CITY

This map of 1712 shows Peter's original plan for his capital, with Vasilevskiy Island as center. This was abandoned due to the hazards of crossing the Neva, and the city spread out around the Admiralty instead.

The Carpenter Tsar
During his 1698 tour of Europe, Peter (to the left in this picture) spent months at the Deptford Docks, laboring with his men to learn the basics of ship building.

Based on Amsterdam, the original city grid was meant to follow a strict network of canals, but this had to change (see p57).

Menshikov palace

New Fashions
Peter's desire to westernize Russia led to a rule forcing his courtiers to have their bushy beards shaved off.

THE STRELTSY REBELLION

As a result of a malicious rumor that Peter's relatives planned the murder of his half-brother Ivan, in 1682 the Streltsy Guard regiments invaded the Kremlin. A horrifying massacre took place in front of the 10-year old Peter, who saw his adviser and members of his family murdered. This traumatic event is probably what caused Peter's facial tic and certainly his wish to build another capital city. In 1698 he took a terrible revenge by torturing over a thousand Streltsy Guards to death.

Brutal murders in the Kremlin, 1682

The Battle of Poltava

The struggle with Sweden for control over the Baltic led to the Great Northern War. Nine years after the embarassing defeat at Narva, Peter the Great's army reforms bore fruit. In 1709 he won a decisive battle over Charles XII at Poltava, and thereby Russia's first victory over a major European power.

WHERE TO SEE PETER THE GREAT'S CITY

Some of the buildings from the early St. Petersburg still exist in the city center, including the rustic Peter the Great's Cabin *(p73)*, the Summer Palace *(p95)*, and the Baroque Menshikov Palace *(p62)*. Much of Peter and Paul Fortress *(pp66–7)* also dates from this time. It is also well worth visiting Monplaisir, Peter's first home at Peterhof *(pp146–7)*.

Peter the Great's workshop, the Summer Palace

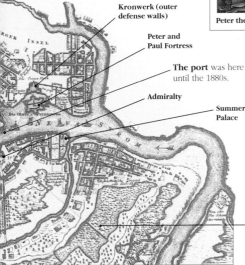

Kronwerk (outer defense walls)

Peter and Paul Fortress

The port was here until the 1880s.

Admiralty

Summer Palace

Wine Goblet

The tsar, who could hold his drink, enjoyed pressing alcohol on his guests until they passed out. This elegant crystal goblet belonged to his close friend Aleksandr Menshikov and is engraved with his coat of arms.

Marshy soil and a lack of local stone made construction difficult. Thousands of laborers died during the first stages.

Catherine I

After an unsuccessful first marriage, Peter was drawn to a Lithuanian girl who had followed the army back from the wars in 1704. Her healthy good looks were brought to the tsar's attention by Aleksandr Menshikov (see p62). Although only two daughters survived, their marriage was happy, and Catherine succeeded Peter as the first woman on Russia's throne.

Mice Bury the Cat

Colored woodcuts, lubki, *served as political cartoons in Peter's day. The tsar was always portrayed as a cat because of his moustache.*

CATHERINE THE GREAT

Catherine, a German princess, was chosen by Elizabeth as wife for her successor, the petty-minded Peter III. When Peter ascended the throne in 1761 Catherine had resided in Russia for 18 years and was fully fluent in Russian. She had made it her duty to steep herself in the Russian culture that she later came to adore. Six months into Peter's reign, Catherine and her allies in the Imperial Guard deposed the tsar. He was assassinated within days and she was crowned Catherine II.

Catherine the Great in 1762

By Catherine's death at the age of 67, her reputation as an enlightened leader *(see p24)* had been overshadowed by her illiberal reaction to the news of the French Revolution in 1789 and by scandalous rumors concerning her later love affairs. However, she left a country vastly enlarged after successful campaigns against Turkey and Poland.

WAR AND PEACE

During the Napoleonic Wars, under Catherine's grandson Alexander I, Russia finally took her place alongside the other great European powers.

Despite his part in the murder of his father Paul, much was expected of the handsome new tsar who was infected by the ideals of enlightened government. Russia was by now desperately in need of reform. Of particular concern was the plight of the peasantry, who were tied to the land in serfdom.

However, the necessities of war outweighed everything, and no inroads were made against the Russian autocracy during Alexander I's reign.

Determined to harness the wave of Russian patriotism, Alexander joined Britain and marched against Napoleon in Austria in 1805. After the crushing defeat at the battle of Austerlitz, however, the inexperienced tsar retreated, his army having lost 11,000 men.

At the Peace of Tilsit, signed in 1807, Napoleon divided Europe into French and Russian spheres, lulling Alexander into a false sense of security. In 1812 the French emperor invaded Russia, but was defeated by its size and climate. The Russian army followed his forces to Paris, taking part in the allied campaign that led Napoleon to abdicate in 1814. In celebration, Alexander commissioned a series of imposing public edifices in a fitting Empire style.

Murder of Paul I, 1801. Despite all his precautions, Catherine's unstable, paranoid son was murdered in a coup in his own fortified palace *(see p101)*

TIMELINE

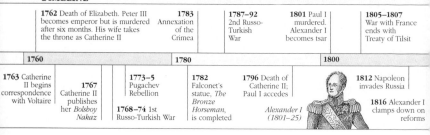

1762 Death of Elizabeth. Peter III becomes emperor but is murdered after six months. His wife takes the throne as Catherine II	**1783** Annexation of the Crimea	**1787–92** 2nd Russo-Turkish War	**1801** Paul I murdered. Alexander I becomes tsar	**1805–1807** War with France ends with Treaty of Tilsit
1760		**1780**		**1800**
1763 Catherine II begins correspondence with Voltaire	**1767** Catherine II publishes her *Bolshoy Nakaz*	**1773–5** Pugachev Rebellion **1768–74** 1st Russo-Turkish War	**1782** Falconet's statue, *The Bronze Horseman,* is completed	**1796** Death of Catherine II; Paul I accedes *Alexander I (1801–25)*	**1812** Napoleon invades Russia **1816** Alexander I clamps down on reforms

Decembrist rebels defeated by tsarist troops, 1825

THE DECEMBRIST REBELLION

Officers of the Russian army who had witnessed the freedoms of democratic Europe were frustrated by Alexander's failure to consider constitutional reform. When his stern brother Nicholas was declared tsar in 1825, these liberals rallied their soldiers to support the older brother Constantine, who had given up his rights to the throne, in the hope that he would be more open-minded. They made a stand on December 14th on what is now Decembrists' Square *(see p78)*. Troops loyal to the tsar were instructed to fire on the rebels, killing hundreds before the leaders surrendered. The new tsar, Nicholas I, treated them with the severity that was to become the hallmark of his reign. Five leading figures were hanged, and over a hundred exiled to Siberia.

A CITY OF RICH AND POOR

For much of the 19th century, a walk along Nevskiy prospekt offered a microcosm of an increasingly divided society. Striding past drunks, beggars, and prostitutes, the city's courtiers, cocky young officers, and leading citizens headed for shops selling imported fashionable accessories, or to the distinguished delicatessen Yeliseev's to buy caviar and champagne. They often lived above their means, mortgaging their serfs and lands to keep up with the astronomical costs of their luxurious lives. This was also a city in which the salary of a low ranking government clerk was never sufficient to feed a family. In the countryside, tension was growing among the serfs tied to the large estates of the aristocracy. With such blatant inequality, growing pressure for political reform was inevitable.

After the unrelenting autocracy of Nicholas I, the "Iron Tsar," liberals welcomed the reign of his fair-minded son Alexander II. In 1861, the tsar passed the Edict of Emancipation, abolishing serfdom, but requiring peasants to buy their land at far from advantageous terms. Thus industrialization finally took off as peasants flocked to the big cities to work in factories, only to be met by even worse living conditions.

THE NAPOLEONIC INVASION

Napoleon's Grand Army of 600,000 men reached Moscow in September 1812, after the victory at Borodino, but was defeated by the tactics of nonengagement devised by the great Russian hero General Kutuzov. Finding himself in a city abandoned by its rulers and set on fire by its people, and with the Russian winter ahead, Napoleon was forced into a retreat over the frozen countryside. He eventually reached the border, with only 30,000 men left alive.

French army retreating from Moscow 1812

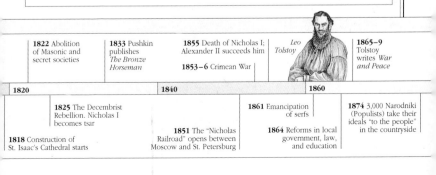

The Enlightened Empress

BORN A MINOR GERMAN PRINCESS, Catherine II was a learned and energetic woman. She recognized the importance of the great philosophers Voltaire and Diderot, with whom she corresponded. She bought collections of European art for the Hermitage *(see pp84–93)* and libraries for Russia's scholars, and talked much about reducing the burden on Russia's serfs. However, an uprising in the 1770s and news of the French Revolution in 1789 quelled her liberal notions and, when she died, the majority of Russians were just as badly off as before.

EXTENT OF THE CITY

■ *1790*   □ *Today*

Royal Guards Swear Allegiance
On June 28, 1762, Catherine usurped the throne of her unpopular husband Peter III in a palace coup. The guards regiments flocked to support her, and the tsar was assassinated on July 6.

The Temple alludes to Catherine's passion for Neo-Classical architecture.

The medal is presented to Count Orlov for his victory over the Turks at Chesma in 1770.

CATHERINE THE GREAT

Catherine II "the Great" (1762–96) pursued an expansionist foreign policy. Russia's first naval victory, leading to the annexation of the Crimea, is commemorated allegorically on this fabric.

Count Alexey Orlov, brother of Catherine's one-time lover Grigoriy, played an important role in her takeover of the throne.

Catherine's Instructions
In 1767 the 36-year-old Catherine published her 22-chapter Great Instruction (Bolshoy Nakaz). The book is a collection of ideas on which a reform of Russia's legal system was to be based.

Pretender Pugachev
The greatest threat to Catherine's reign was caused by the Cossack Pugachev, who claimed to be Peter III. He was arrested, but escaped to lead a widespread peasant uprising that broke out in 1773 and ended only with his execution in 1775.

The New Academy of Sciences
Catherine, who founded over 25 major academic institutions in Russia, also commissioned new buildings for those already existing. Quarenghi built the Neo-Classical Academy of Sciences in 1783–5.

Catherine is portrayed as Pallas Athena, goddess of wisdom and warfare, with her attributes of a shield and helmet.

WHERE TO SEE THE NEO-CLASSICAL CITY

Catherine had the Marble Palace (*see p94*) and the Tauride Palace (*p128*) erected for two of her lovers, and added the Small and Large Hermitage and the theater (*p84*) to the Winter Palace. Her architect Cameron designed the Cameron Gallery and the Agate Pavilion at Tsarskoe Selo (*p150*) and Pavlovsk Palace (*pp156–9*).

Grecian Hall at Pavlovsk, created by Charles Cameron in 1782–6

Empire-Style Vase (1790)
Porcelain was much prized at court. In 1744 the first Russian producer, the Imperial Porcelain Factory, opened in St. Petersburg.

The fabric, used for a screen, was made by the Pernons factory, Lyons, in 1770.

Mikhail Lomonosov
A philosopher, historian, linguist, and scientist, Lomonosov (1711–65) personified the intellectual enlightenment of 18th-century Russia (see p45). This sculpture of him as a boy by the seashore refers to his fisherman origins.

Grigoriy Potemkin (1739–91)
Of all her lovers, Catherine respected and admired Prince Potemkin the most. He was a successful general and an influential counselor. They remained friends until his death.

Alexander II was murdered by a revolutionary group in 1881. Tragically, he is said to have had the plans for a Russian parliament in his pocket

THE DEATH OF TSARIST RUSSIA
Pressure for reform had built up such a head of steam that in 1881, when still no radical changes had taken place, a revolutionary group murdered Alexander II. The reign of Alexander III was one of rabid reaction. The press was under strict censorship and the secret police more active than ever. But workers began to organize and opposition grew. Nicholas II took over a country on the verge of breakdown, in spite of the industrialization of the 1890's. The

unsuccessful war with Japan (1904–5) was followed by "Bloody Sunday." On January 9th, 1905, a peaceful demonstration carried a petition to the tsar only to be met by bullets. News of the massacre spread, and the 1905 Revolution broke out with strikes all over Russia. To avert further disaster, Nicholas II promised basic civil rights and an elected Duma (parliament), with the right to veto legislation. However, the tsar dissolved the parliament whenever it displeased him. This high-handed behavior, along with the royal family's unpopular friendship with Rasputin *(see p121)*, further damaged the Romanovs' reputation.

The outbreak of World War I brought a surge of patriotism that the tsar sought to ride. But, by late 1916, Russia had lost three and a half million men, morale at the front was low, and food supplies at home scarce.

Red Army badge

WORLD OF ART MOVEMENT

The oppressive political climate at the turn of the century did not prevent art from flourishing. A small group of St. Petersburg artists, including Bakst and Benois, grew into an influential creative movement under the inspired leadership of Sergey Diaghilev. Western art was introduced in their stylish *World of Art* magazine, while their stage designs and costumes for the Ballets Russes *(see p118)* brought Russian culture to the west.

Costume design by Leon Bakst, 1911

REVOLUTION AND CIVIL WAR
In February 1917 strikes broke out in the capital, now renamed Petrograd. The tsar was forced to abdicate, his family put under arrest, and a Provisional Government set up. But revolutionaries returning from exile organized themselves and, in October, an armed revolution overthrew the government *(see pp28–9)*.

TIMELINE

1881 Alexander II is assassinated by the "People's Will" group. Alexander III becomes tsar.

1902 Lenin publishes *What is to be Done?*

1898 Social-Democratic Workers' party is founded. Russian museum opens

The Romanov family in 1913

1913 300th anniversary Romanov ru

1880

1900

1881–2 Anti-semitic pogroms

1887 Lenin's brother is hanged for attempt on the tsar's life

1894 Alexander III dies, Nicholas II accedes

1903 Pro-violence Bolsheviks (under Lenin) secede from Social-Democratic Workers' party

1904–5 Russo-Japanese War

1905 The 1905 Revolution is followed by the inauguration of the first Duma in 1906

1914 Outbreak of WWI; St. Petersburg changes name to Petrograd

The leading Bolshevik party proved to be as careless of democracy as the tsar but, in March 1918, they kept their promise to take Russia out of the war. The army was desperately needed at home to fight the developing civil war.

The Bolsheviks (Reds) found themselves threatened by a diverse coalition of antirevolutionary groups that came to be known as the "Whites," initially supported by foreign intervention. It was the threat of the Whites' rallying opposition around the royal family that led to their execution in July 1918. But the Whites were a disparate force, and, by November 1920, the last troops had abandoned the struggle, leaving a devastated Soviet Russia to face two years of appalling famine. To manage, Lenin had to revise his aggressive "War Communism" nationalization project. His slightly milder New Economic Policy allowed for private enterprise.

The imperial palaces around St. Petersburg were totally destroyed by the Germans in World War II. This photo shows Pavlovsk (see pp156–9) in 1944

THE STALIN YEARS

In the five years after Lenin's death in 1924, Joseph Stalin used his position as General Secretary of the Communist Party to eliminate all rivals. He then established his long dictatorship.

The terror began in earnest with the collectivization of agriculture, which forced the peasants to give up all livestock, machinery, and land to collective farms. During this time, and in the ensuing famine of 1931–2, up to 10 million people are thought to have died.

Joseph Stalin on a propaganda poster from 1933

A first major purge of intellectuals took place in urban areas in 1928–9. Then, in December 1934, Sergey Kirov, the party leader in Leningrad, was assassin- ated on the secret orders of Stalin (see p72), but it was blamed on an anti-Stalinist cell. This became the catalyst for five years of purges throughout the country. By the time they were over, some 15 million people had been arrested, many sent to the Gulag (labor camps), and over a million executed.

Stalin's purge of the Red Army boded badly for World War II, for he had got rid of three quarters of his officers. When the Germans invaded Russia in 1941 they cut off Leningrad in less than three months, subjecting the city to a horrendous siege of 900 days (see p131) during which some 670,000 perished, most of them civilians. Leningrad came to be known as a "Hero City."

The Germans were eventually defeated, but the Russian people, who lost 20 million souls to the war, were subjected to renewed terror by Stalin, which lasted until his death in March 1953.

1917 The Russian Revolution *(see p29)*

1918 Civil War starts. Capital moves to Moscow

1920

1921 Lenin bans all opposition after the Kronstadt mutiny

1922 Stalin becomes General Secretary of the Party

1924 Lenin dies; Petrograd is named Leningrad

1925 Trotsky is expelled from the Politburo

1929 Collectivization of private land

1932 Socialist Realism is the only officially approved style in art

Sergey Kirov

1934 Leningrad Party Secretary Kirov is killed; Stalin's purges begin

1939 Nazi-Soviet pact

1940

1941 Nazis attack Russia; Siege of Leningrad starts

1942 First performance of Shostakovich's Seventh Symphony in besieged Leningrad

1944 The Siege ends

1947 The term "Cold War" is coined

The Russian Revolution

ST. PETERSBURG IS KNOWN as the cradle of the Russian Revolution, a central event in the history of the 20th century. After the 1917 February Revolution, which led to the abdication of Tsar Nicholas II, the Provisional Government declared a political amnesty. Exiled revolutionaries such as Lenin and Trotsky flooded into the city. By setting up a network of Workers' and Soldiers' Soviets, representative councils elected by the people, they established an alternative government. In October, when soldiers had deserted from the front in droves, the revolutionary leaders decided on the armed uprising that brought the Communists to power.

EXTENT OF THE CITY

■ *1917*   □ *Today*

Looting was tempting for the mob of sailors and soldiers, especially in the palace's well-stocked wine cellars.

The Ex-Tsar
Nicholas II, seen here clearing snow at Tsarskoe Selo during his house arrest in March 1917, was later taken with his family to Yekaterinburg, where they were murdered.

Soldier of the Red Guard

THE WINTER PALACE STORMING
Late on the evening of October 25, 1917, the battleship *Aurora (see p73)* fired some blank shots at the Winter Palace. The Red Guard, trained by Trotsky at the Smolnyy Institute, stormed the palace. Their aim was the arrest of the Provisional Government, unsuccessfully defended by 300 Cossacks.

The Cossacks, who defended the palace with some cadets and members of the Women's Battalion, were too few to offer any serious resistance.

Lenin, Leader of the People
A charismatic speaker, as shown in this painting by Victor Ivanov, Lenin returned from exile in April to lead the Revolution. By 1918, his Bolshevik faction had shown their determination to rule.

Revolutionary Plate
Various ceramics with revolutionary themes, mixed with touches of Russian folklore, were produced to celebrate every occasion, in this case, the Third International.

Leon Trotsky
The intellectual Trotsky played a leading military role in the Revolution. In 1927, during the power struggle after Lenin's death, he was exiled by Stalin. In 1940 he was murdered in Mexico by a Stalinist agent.

Propaganda
One hallmark of the Soviet regime was its powerful propaganda. Many a talented artist was employed to design posters spreading its message through striking graphics. War Communism during the Civil War (1918–20) was encouraged by posters such as this one, extolling the "pacifist Army of Workers."

Avant Garde Art
Even before 1917, Russia's artists had been in a state of revolution, producing the world's first truly abstract paintings. A great example of this new movement is Supremus No. 56, *painted in 1916 by Kazimir Malevich.*

Ministers of the Provisional Government tried to keep order but were arrested.

New Values
Traditions were radically altered by the Revolution; instead of church weddings, couples exchanged vows under the red flag. Loudly trumpeted sexual equality meant that women had to work twice as hard – at home and in the factories.

TIMELINE

1917 The February Revolution	**March** The tsar is persuaded to abdicate. Provisional Government is led by Prince Lvov	**October** Bolsheviks storm Winter Palace after signal from *Aurora* and expel Provisional Government	**March** Bolsheviks sign Brest-Litovsk peace treaty with Germany. Capital is moved to Moscow

1917	**1918**

July Kerensky becomes Prime Minister of Provisional Government	**1918 January** Trotsky becomes Commissar of War	**July** Start of Civil War. Tsar and family are murdered in prison at Yekaterinburg
Cruiser Aurora	**December** Lenin forms the CHEKA (secret police)	

The Washington Dove of Peace, a Russian caricature (1953) from the days of the Cold War

THAW AND STAGNATION

Three years after Stalin's death his successor Nikita Khrushchev denounced Stalin's crimes at the Twentieth Party Congress and the period known as "The Thaw" began. Political prisoners were released, and Solzhenitsyn's *One Day In the Life of Ivan Denisovich,* about life in the Gulag, was published.

In foreign affairs, things were not so liberal. Soviet tanks invaded Hungary in 1956 to prevent the country seceding from the Warsaw Pact and, in 1962,

Khrushchev's decision to put nuclear missiles in Cuba brought the world to the brink of nuclear war.

When Leonid Brezhnev took over in 1964, the intellectual climate froze once more and the persecution of political dissidents was stepped up. The first ten years of his regime were a time of relative plenty. But beneath the surface a vast black market and network of corruption were growing. The party apparatchiks, who benefited most from the corruption, had no interest in rocking the boat. When Brezhnev died in 1982, the politburo was determined to prevent the accession of a younger generation. He was followed by 68-year-old Yuriy Andropov and, when he died, 72-year-old Chernenko.

GLASNOST AND PERESTROIKA

Someone had to admit the bankruptcy of the antiquated system. But when 53-year-old Mikhail Gorbachev announced his policies of *glasnost* (openness) and *perestroika* (restructuring), when he took over in 1985, he had no idea what would follow. By the end of 1991 he was out of a job and the Soviet Union and its empire were no more.

Mikhail Gorbachev and George Bush

For the first time since 1917 the elections to the Congress of People's Deputies in 1989 contained an element of genuine choice, with rebels such as Boris Yeltsin and humanrights campaigner Andrey Sakharov winning seats. By autumn the

FIRST IN SPACE

It was under Khrushchev that the Soviet Union achieved its greatest coup against the West, launching the first Sputnik into space in 1957. That same year the dog Laika was the first living creature in space, aboard Sputnik II. She never came down again, but four years later Yuriy Gagarin made spectacular history as the first man in space, returning to a hero's welcome. The Soviets lost the race to put a man on the moon, but their space program worked as powerful propaganda, backing up the claims of politicians that Russia would soon catch up with and overtake the prosperity of the West.

Sputnik II and the space dog Laika, 1957

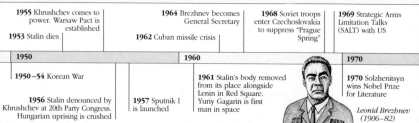

TIMELINE

1955 Khrushchev comes to power. Warsaw Pact is established	**1964** Brezhnev becomes General Secretary	**1968** Soviet troops enter Czechoslovakia to suppress "Prague Spring"	**1969** Strategic Arms Limitation Talks (SALT) with US
1953 Stalin dies	**1962** Cuban missile crisis		
1950	**1960**		**1970**
1950–54 Korean War	**1961** Stalin's body removed from its place alongside Lenin in Red Square. Yuriy Gagarin is first man in space		**1970** Solzhenitsyn wins Nobel Prize for Literature
1956 Stalin denounced by Khrushchev at 20th Party Congress. Hungarian uprising is crushed	**1957** Sputnik I is launched		*Leonid Brezhnev (1906–82)*

Demonstrations on Palace Square during the 1991 coup

ST. PETERSBURG TODAY

The economic reforms that Russia has undergone since 1991 have widened the gap between rich and poor. While some revel in the new opportunities for work and travel, others cry out for a return to Communism and the albeit limited social protection it offered. For many, freedom of speech outweighs the economic difficulties, although it too has brought problems, as highly dubious material including pornography and extreme right-wing propaganda is spreading.

The social problems are still being resolved, but increasing economic stability, including the monetary reform of 1998, has brought a flood of investment to the city, in everything from manufacturing to tourism. Meanwhile there has been a major religious revival, with churches used during the Soviet era as warehouses now being returned to their original purpose.

winds of change had blown through the Eastern bloc, country by country the people rising up against their pro-Soviet governments. In 1991, local elections bought nationalist candidates to power in the republics, and democrats in the major Russian local councils. Russia and the Baltic Republics seceded from the Soviet Union, while the people of Leningrad, always in the vanguard of progressive movement and now led by the reformist lecturer in law, Anatoly Sobchak, voted to restore the city's original name, St. Petersburg.

The new Russian State Emblem

With his great victory in the election for President of the Russian Republic, Yeltsin was able to deal the death blow to the Soviet Union. It came after the military coup against Gorbachev in August 1991, when Yeltsin's stand against the tanks in Moscow made him a hero. In St. Petersburg no tanks were on the street, but nonetheless Sobchak rallied supporters of democracy. When Gorbachev returned from house arrest, Yeltsin forced him to outlaw the Communist Party and, by the end of the year, the Soviet Union no longer existed.

A church wedding, popular again since religion has gained new importance among the young

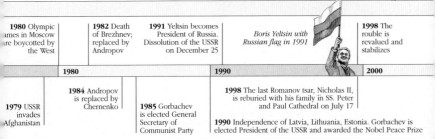

1979 USSR invades Afghanistan	1980 Olympic Games in Moscow are boycotted by the West	1982 Death of Brezhnev; replaced by Andropov	1984 Andropov is replaced by Chernenko	1985 Gorbachev is elected General Secretary of Communist Party	1991 Yeltsin becomes President of Russia. Dissolution of the USSR on December 25	1990 Independence of Latvia, Lithuania, Estonia. Gorbachev is elected President of the USSR and awarded the Nobel Peace Prize	1998 The last Romanov tsar, Nicholas II, is reburied with his family in SS. Peter and Paul Cathedral on July 17	1998 The rouble is revalued and stabilizes

Boris Yeltsin with Russian flag in 1991

1980   **1990**   **2000**

St. Petersburg at a Glance

Aᴄɪᴛʏ ʙᴜɪʟᴛ ᴏɴ ᴡᴀᴛᴇʀ, St. Petersburg offers beautiful scenery and a wide range of sights. The Peter and Paul Fortress *(see pp66–7)*, one of the city's first buildings, contrasts with Baroque monasteries and Neo-Classical palaces. The city's short but stormy history is reflected in many of its museums, which display everything from Catherine the Great's fine art collection in the Hermitage to memorabilia of the Revolution in the Kshesinskaya Mansion *(see p72)*.

To help you make the most of your stay, the following 12 pages are a time-saving guide to the best museums and palaces and the most interesting of the many bridges and waterways. The cultural figures that made St. Petersburg a city of importance are also featured. Below is a selection of sights that should not be missed by any visitor.

St. Petersburg's Top Ten Attractions

Russian Museum
See pp104–7

Mariinskiy Theater
See p119

Nevskiy Prospekt
See pp46–9

Church on Spilled Blood
See p100

The Hermitage
See pp84–93

Stieglitz Museum
See p127

St. Isaac's Cathedral
See pp80–81

SS. Peter and Paul Cathedral
See p68

Kazan Cathedral
See p111

Alexander Nevsky Monastery
See pp130–31

◁ **The Neo-Classical Kazan Cathedral with its impressive semicircle of granite columns**

St. Petersburg's Best: Bridges and Waterways

LIKE ITS WATERBOUND SISTERS, Amsterdam and Venice, St. Petersburg is built around a network of canals and rivers that are still the life-blood of the city. They contribute to its unique atmosphere by creating eerie mists that rise from the ice-laden waters in winter and, in summer, a glittering mirror of facades during the glowing sunsets and bright White Nights.

Bridges, necessary for communication between the islands, were also an excellent means to adorn the city with decorative sculptures, elaborate lampposts and wrought-iron work.

A walk or a boat trip *(see p134–5 and 218–19)* is the best way to enjoy them.

Winter Canal
Laid out in 1718–20, this narrow canal is crossed by three bridges and Yuriy Velten's Hermitage Theater foyer (1783–7).

Lieutenant Shmidt Bridge
Rebuilt in 1936–8, this bridge still retains its original cast-iron seahorse railings, designed by Bryullov.

Malaya Neva

Vasilevskiy Island

Bolshaya Neva

Palace Embankment

Moyka

Lion Bridge
One of the earliest of its kind, this pedestrian suspension bridge dates from 1825–6. Its cables are anchored inside four cast-iron lions, by sculptor Pavel Sokolov.

Sennaya Ploshchad

Kanal Griboedova

Fontanka

Egyptian Bridge
This bridge spanning the Fontanka was decorated in the Egyptian style fashionable at the time of its construction, in 1826.

| 0 meters | 500 |
| 0 yards | 500 |

Trinity Bridge
The ten-arched Trinity Bridge (1897–1903) is famous for its Style-Moderne lampposts and railing decorations, the work of the skillful French engineers Vincent Chabrol and René Patouillard.

Petrogradskaya

Neva

Swan Canal
This tree-lined canal (1711–19) leading out to the Neva is named after the swans that were once drawn to its peaceful waters.

Bridge Passage
Cleverly designed to span the confluence of the Moyka and the Griboedov, the Theater and Small Stable bridges were constructed by Traitteur and Adam in 1829–31.

Gostinyy Dvor

Anichkov Bridge
This three-span bridge, carrying Nevskiy prospekt across the Fontanka, was built in 1839–41. At each corner are Pyotr Klodt's impressive sculptures of men taming wild horses.

Lomonosov Bridge
The distinctive domed granite towers, built in 1785–7, originally contained the bridge's opening mechanism. The bridge was rebuilt in 1912, but the towers were kept.

Bank Bridge
Dating from the same time as the Lion Bridge, and designed by the same team, this bridge is adorned by four magnificent cast-iron griffons. Its name derives from the nearby former Assignment Bank.

Exploring St. Petersburg's Bridges and Waterways

A BOAT TRIP on St. Petersburg's canals and waterways is one of the highlights of any visit to the city. From the Anichkov Bridge the river boats (see p218) do a loop along the Neva, Fontanka, and Moyka Rivers, taking in many impressive bridges and landmarks. Alternatively, you can choose your own route to explore the city's rich architectural heritage by taking a water taxi (see p219). A pleasant wander along the embankments of the Griboedov Canal leads past imposing 19th-century apartment houses and fancifully decorated bridges. In the winter months you can walk on the frozen Neva.

> ### FINDING THE BRIDGES
>
> *Map references refer to the Street Finder on pp 230–37.*
>
> Alexander Nevsky Bridge **8 F3**
> Anichkov Bridge **7 42**
> Bank Bridge **6 ,E2**
> Egyptian Bridge **5 B5**
> Lantern Bridge **5 C2**
> Lieutenant Shmidt Bridge **5 B1**
> Lion Bridge **5 C3**
> Liteynyy Bridge **3 A3**
> Little Stable Bridge **2 F5**
> Lomonosov Bridge **6 F3**
> Palace Bridge **1 C5**
> Peter the Great Bridge **4 F5**
> Red Bridge **6 D2**
> St. Panteleymon's Bridge **2 F5**
> Singer's Bridge **2 E5**
> Theater Bridge **2 F5**
> Trinity Bridge **2 E4**

The ice-laden Neva River in front of the Peter and Paul Fortress

THE NEVA AND ITS BRANCHES

G REATEST OF St. Petersburg's numerous waterways, the Neva flows from Lake Ladoga in the east through the city to the Gulf of Finland, a distance of only 74 km (46 miles) in total. Vasilevskiy Island, one of more than 100 islands in the Neva delta, divides the river into two separate branches, Bolshaya (Great) Neva and Malaya (Small) Neva.

Icebound for at least four months of the year, the Neva usually shows the first signs of cracking in March. The official Opening of Navigation is announced by the port authority in mid-April. Until the Revolution the event was marked with great ceremony. The Commander of the Peter and Paul Fortress (see pp66–7), at the head of a naval flotilla, would scoop some icy water into a silver goblet that he presented to the tsar in the Winter Palace (see pp92–3).

RIVERS AND CANALS

I NSPIRED BY AMSTERDAM, Peter the Great kept the many streams of the delta as canals, which also helped to drain the swampy ground. As the city grew new ones were dug to improve the canal network.

The **Moyka** originally flowed from a swamp near the Field of Mars (see p94). In the 19th century the aristocracy lined its quays with impressive Neo-Classical mansions, which are still their main attraction. Canal boats and barges ply the 7-km (4-mile) long **Fontanka**, widest and busiest of the waterways, which was once the border of the city. These two rivers are linked by the **Kryukov Canal**, dug in the 18th century.

The **Griboedov Canal**, first known as the Catherine Canal in honor of Catherine the Great, was designed to move cargo from Sennaya Ploshchad. Today the atmosphere here is more tranquil. The stretch of water running south from the Lion Bridge is particularly picturesque. The narrowest

waterway is the **Winter Canal**, just to the east of the Winter Palace. Nearby is the delightful **Swan Canal**, which runs along the Summer Gardens (p95).

Steady industrial growth in the 19th century prompted the construction of a new canal, the **Obvodnyy**, in 1834, to take the increasing number of heavy cargo barges and supply water to the city outskirts.

NEVA BRIDGES

T HE MOST CENTRAL of the Neva bridges is the **Palace Bridge** (Dvortsovyy most). The present structure, built early in the 20th century, replaced a seasonal pontoon bridge that linked the mainland to Vasilevskiy Island.

View of the Moyka and its south bank, with a water taxi in foreground

Peter the Great Bridge, crossing the Neva near Smolnyy Institute

The other bridge to this island, **Lieutenant Shmidt Bridge** (most Leytenanta Shmidta, *see p63*), is named after a naval officer who led a rebellion of sailors of the Black Sea Fleet in 1905. The **Trinity Bridge** (Troitskiy most, *see p73*) was built in 1897–1903, in time for the city's bicentennial, by the French Batignolles company. At 582 m (1,910 ft), the Trinity Bridge was the Neva's longest, until the construction of the **Alexander Nevsky Bridge** (most Aleksandra Nevskovo) in the 1960s, which is some 900 m (2,950 ft). Between these two is the **Liteynyy Bridge** (Liteynyy most) built in 1874–9. In 1917, the city authorities tried to prevent rebel workers crossing the Neva from the Vyborg Side by raising the central bridge span. The tactic failed since the revolutionaries decided to cross on foot over the frozen ice.

Near the Smolnyy Institute is the **Peter the Great Bridge** (most Petra Velikovo), also known by its Soviet name Bolshoy Okhtinskiy most. It has a central drawbridge and distinctive steel twin arches, erected in 1909–11.

From April to November all Neva bridges are raised at night to allow ships to pass to and from the Volga *(see p201)*.

DECORATIVE BRIDGES

IN THE BEGINNING, wooden bridges spanned the canals and rivers of St. Petersburg. They were usually known by their color – red, blue, green, and so on. The **Red Bridge** (Krasnyy most) which carries Gorokhovaya ulitsa over the Moyka, has preserved its original name. Built in 1808–14, this iron bridge is decorated with picturesque lamps on four granite obelisks. Lamps are also a feature of the **Lantern Bridge** (Fonarnyy most) which crosses the Moyka river near to the Yusupov Palace *(see p120)*. Here the gilded lampposts are shaped to look like treble clefs. **Singer's Bridge** (Pevcheskiy most) at the other end of the Moyka takes its name from the choir of the nearby Glinka Capella. Its engineer, Yegor Adam, also designed the lace-like patterning of the railings.

At the junction where the Griboedov meets the Moyka is an interesting ensemble, formed by the wide **Theater Bridge** (Teatralnyy most) and

Lamppost, St. Panteleymon's Bridge

Small Stable Bridge (Malo-Konyushennyy most). The latter is cleverly designed to look like two bridges.

Among the more attractive bridges is Georg von Traitteur's pedestrian **Bank Bridge** (Bankovskiy most), crossing the Griboedov. Its cables are held up by two pairs of gold-winged griffins. The **Lion Bridge** (Lvinyy most), also by Traitteur, uses a similar device; in this case the suspension cables emerge from the open jaws of four proud lions.

St. Panteleymon's Bridge (Panteleymonovskiy most, *see p99*) spans the Fontanka near the Summer Gardens. It was Russia's first chain bridge (1823–4). The Empire-style decoration has survived and includes gilded fasces and double-headed eagles perched on laurel wreaths. Next to the Nevskiy prospekt, the **Anichkov Bridge** (Anichkovskiy most) is famous for its four vibrant bronze sculptures of wild horses and their powerful tamers, all of them in different positions. Farther down the Fontanka, framed by a handsome Neo-Classical square by Carlo Rossi, is the **Lomonosov Bridge** (most Lomonosova) with its unusual stone turrets. The **Egyptian Bridge** (Egipetskiy most) spans the Fontanka close to the Kryukov Canal. It is ornamented with bronze sphinxes and bridgeheads resembling the entrance to an Egyptian temple. Originally constructed in 1826, the bridge collapsed under the weight of a passing cavalry squadron but was rebuilt in 1955.

A CITY UNDER WATER

Peter the Great should have known it was a bad idea to found a city here. The first flood, just three months after he started the fortress in 1703, swept away his building materials. The water rises dangerously high on average once a year, but four floods, in 1777, 1824, 1924, and 1955, brought massive damage. In 1824 the whole city went under water and 462 buildings were totally destroyed. This inspired Pushkin's poem *The Bronze Horseman (see p78)*. Markers showing record water levels can be found by the Winter Canal and the Peter and Paul Fortress. In 1989 construction of a dam was begun to prevent future destruction.

A 19th-century illustration of one of the many floods in St. Petersburg

St. Petersburg's Best: Palaces and Museums

ST. PETERSBURG BOASTS more than 90 museums, many of them housed in palaces or other buildings of historical importance. Some are well known throughout the world, such as the Hermitage, which began as Catherine the Great's private collection of European art. Others, including the Russian Museum and the Summer Palace, highlight local art, history, and culture. Some of the most evocative museums are those commemorating the lives and work of famous artists, writers, and musicians. This selection represents the most interesting in each category.

The Hermitage
Now incorporating the breathtaking state rooms of the Winter Palace, the world-famous Hermitage holds nearly three million exhibits that range from Fine Arts to archaeological finds.

Petrogradsk

Malaya Neva

Vasilevskiy Island

Menshikov Palace
This grandiose Baroque palace on Vasilevskiy Island is testimony to the power of Peter the Great's friend and advisor, Prince Menshikov.

Bolshaya Neva

Palace Embankment

Sennaya Ploshchad

IMPERIAL COUNTRY PALACES

To escape the pressures of the capital, successive Russian rulers built sumptuous retreats in the rural hinterland of St. Petersburg. These offer a fascinating insight into the lifestyle of the Romanov dynasty.

Tsarskoe Selo's Catherine Palace was built by Rastrelli in a flamboyant Baroque style.

Peterhof's palace and pavilions are enhanced by the splendid cascades and fountains adorning the attractive grounds.

0 km	15
0 miles	15

Pavlovsk's Great Palace is set in an extensive naturalistic landscaped park, embellished with ponds, pavilions, and monuments.

Kshesinskaya Mansion
Built for a prima ballerina of the Mariinskiy Theater, this attractive Style-Moderne mansion now houses the Museum of Russian Political History, which contains souvenirs from the Revolution.

Summer Palace
Interiors and furniture, such as Peter the Great's original four-poster bed, give an idea of the tsar's relatively modest lifestyle.

Neva

Stieglitz Museum
A rich collection of applied art is displayed in Messmacher's magnificent building, which was inspired by palaces of the Italian Renaissance.

Gostinyy Dvor

Russian Museum
Carlo Rossi's Mikhaylovskiy Palace is the splendid setting for an outstanding collection of Russian art, ranging from medieval icons to contemporary paintings and sculptures. This semi-abstract work Blue Crest *by Vasily Kandinsky dates from 1917.*

Pushkin House-Museum
Period furnishings and personal belongings such as this inkstand re-create the atmosphere of Alexander Pushkin's last home.

0 meters   500

0 yards   500

Exploring St. Petersburg's Palaces and Museums

THE CITY'S PALACES range from imperial excess to the tasteful homes of the nobility, while art museums cover the fine and applied arts and folk crafts. The history of St. Petersburg, from its foundation as Peter the Great's "window on the West" to its role as the "cradle of the Revolution," is covered by a variety of museums, and its culture is documented in the apartments of writers, composers, and artists. More specialized interests, from locomotives and military paraphernalia to insects and whales, also find reflection in the wealth of museums.

Bedroom in the Chinese Palace (1760s), Oranienbaum

Peter the Great's Summer Palace overlooking the Fontanka

PALACES

THE FABULOUS WEALTH of imperial St. Petersburg is reflected in the magnificence of its palaces. No trip to the city would be complete without a visit to at least one of the spectacular out-of-town imperial summer residences, **Peterhof** *(see pp146–9)*, **Pavlovsk** *(see pp156–9)*, or the Catherine Palace *(see pp150–151)* at **Tsarskoe Selo**. These luxurious residences, built and added to in the last 200 years of Romanov rule, illustrate the extravagance of the imperial court and the wealth of the empire's natural resources. An abundance of gold, lapis lazuli, malachite, marble, and other precious minerals decorates many of the rich palace interiors. The palace parks and grounds are landscaped and filled with follies and monuments.

At the center of the city, the **Winter Palace** *(see pp92–93)* in the Hermitage epitomizes the opulence of the court, while Peter the Great's more intimate **Summer Palace** *(see p95)* makes a pleasing contrast. Peter's friend and counselor, Prince Alexander Menshikov, also built two sumptuous residences, the **Menshikov Palace** *(see p62)* on Vasilevskiy Island, and his summer country palace at **Oranienbaum** *(see p144)*.

Overlooking the Moyka River is the **Yusupov Palace** *(see p120)*, which is famed as the murder scene of Rasputin, the extraordinary peasant who exerted his malign influence over the Russian court.

For those in search of a tranquil setting, a pleasant day can be spent exploring the **Yelagin Palace** *(see p126)* and the island of the same name.

ART MUSEUMS

ONE OF THE WORLD'S greatest collections of Western art is housed in the **Hermitage** *(see pp84–93)*, which owns an astounding 2.8 million pieces of art. With collections ranging from Egyptian mummies to Scythian gold, Greek vases, Colombian emeralds, and a vast and dazzling array of Old Masters, Impressionist, and Post-Impressionist paintings, it is essential to be selective.

The **Russian Museum** *(see pp104–107)* is a showcase for Russian art, including the 20th-century avant-garde and the folk crafts that influenced it. Temporary exhibitions from its holdings are shown in the **Engineers' Castle** *(see p101)*, **Marble Palace** *(see p110)*, and **Stroganov Palace** *(see p112)*.

The **Academy of Arts** *(see p63)* exhibits work by past students as well as models of the city's notable buildings.

There are fascinating displays of applied arts from around the world in the **Stieglitz Museum** *(see p127)*, which includes ceramics, wood carving, ironwork, and embroidery. Its glass-roofed exhibition hall is equally impressive.

The Cyclist (1913) by Natalya Goncharova, Russian Museum

HISTORY MUSEUMS

ST. PETERSBURG's dramatic 300-year history is proudly recorded in a number of the city's museums. The **Cabin of Peter the Great** *(see p73)* was the earliest building constructed in the city, and it offers an intriguing insight into the surprisingly humble lifestyle of this tsar.

A group of historic sights lies within the Peter and Paul Fortress. The **Cathedral of SS. Peter and Paul** *(see p68)* houses the tombs of all but three of Russia's tsars since Peter the Great. The preserved cells of the grim **Trubetskoy Bastion** *(see p69)* act as a reminder of the hundreds of political prisoners confined within the fortress walls. In the **Commandant's House** *(see p69)*, the courthouse where prisoners were once interrogated, an exhibition looks at medieval settlements in the area, while the **Engineer's House** *(see p68)* focuses on daily life in St. Petersburg before the Revolution.

A wealth of revolutionary memorabilia, including Stalin-era posters and a huge propaganda stained-glass panel, can be found in the **Museum of Russian Political History**. The museum is located in the Kshesinskaya Mansion *(see p72)* that, in 1917, housed the Bolshevik headquarters. The **Cruiser Aurora** *(see p73)* also played a part in the Revolution, having fired a warning shot before the storming of the Winter Palace in October 1917.

For an impression of the prestigious pre-revolutionary school where poet Alexander Pushkin was a student, some of the classrooms of the **Lycée** at Tsarskoe Selo *(see p153)* have been restored to their 19th-century appearance.

On the southern outskirts of the city, in Victory Square *(see p131)*, the **Monument to the Heroic Defenders of Leningrad** poignantly evokes the Siege of Leningrad (1941–4) and acts as an important reminder of the great hardships endured by St. Petersburgers during World War II.

Office of Leningrad party secretary Sergey Kirov, Kirov Museum

SPECIAL INTEREST MUSEUMS

REMNANTS of Peter the Great's legendary "cabinet of curiosities" can be found in the city's oldest museum, the **Kunstkammer** *(see p60)*. Housed under the same roof is a **Museum of Anthropology and Ethnography**, displaying a large collection of artifacts from all over the world. For natural history, the **Zoological Museum** *(see p60)* encompasses most known life-forms, including a unique collection of mollusks and blue corals.

The **Naval Museum** *(see p60)* fascinates all ages with its model ships, small boats, figureheads, and flags, while the **Artillery Museum** *(see p82)* covers military hardware, from pikes to ballistic missiles. Train enthusiasts will find plenty to enjoy in the **Railway Museum** *(see p123)*, including an 1835 engine built for the Tsarskoe Selo railroad.

The **Museum of Musical Life** in the Sheremetev Palace *(see p129)* displays period

18th-century violin and score in Museum of Musical Life, Sheremetev Palace

instruments and explains the role of the Sheremetev family as leading music patrons in 19th-century St. Petersburg. Stage costumes, including the ones worn by the opera singer Fyodor Shalyapin, are on display alongside photos, set designs, and other ephemera in the **Theater Museum** on Ostrovskiy Square *(see p110)*.

HOUSE-MUSEUMS

A HANDFUL of evocative museums commemorates some of the city's most famous residents. Two lovingly preserved museums, the **Pushkin House Museum** *(see p113)* and the **Dostoevsky House-Museum** *(see p130)*, recapture something of the life and character of their former residents.

The **Anna Akhmatova Museum** in the former service quarters of the Sheremetev Palace *(see p129)* traces the dramatic life of the poetess who lived here for many years.

For an insight into the life of a powerful Communist official of the 1930s, visit the **Kirov Museum** *(see p72)*. The museum is devoted to the popular leader whose assassination on Stalin's orders initiated the Great Terror *(see p27)*.

Outside the city in **Repino** *(see p144)*, the house of the painter Ilya Repin is set in beautiful woodland on the Gulf of Finland.

Celebrated St. Petersburgers

As the residence of the Russian imperial family and court from the early 18th century, St. Petersburg was the focus of patronage and an almost boundless source of wealth. It was the perfect seedbed for creativity and the flowering of ideas. Institutions such as the Academy of Arts, the University, the Kunstkammer, and the Imperial School of Ballet trained generations of cultural figures and scientists to the highest standards. So successful were they that by the dawn of the 20th century, St. Petersburg had become one of the most important cultural centers in Europe.

Grigoriy Kozintsev
Director Kozintsev con-firmed his reputation in the West with his interpretation of Shakespeare's Hamlet (1964), made at Lenfilm (see p70).

Nikolai Gogol
A merciless satirist of St. Petersburg society, Gogol lived on Malaya Morskaya ulitsa (see p82) for three years.

Petrogradska

Malaya Neva

Vasilevskiy Island

Bolshaya Neva

Ilya Repin
This outstanding realist painter is seen here teaching life draw-ing at the Academy of Arts (see p63) where he was a professor.

Sennaya Ploshchad

Pyotr Tchaikovsky
Tchaikovsky graduated from the Conservatory (see p118) in 1865 and went on to com-pose his world-famous operas and ballets.

Anna Pavlova
A prima ballerina at the Mariinskiy Theater (see p121), Pavlova took Paris by storm in 1909 when she toured in Les Sylphides with the Ballets Russes.

Alexander Pushkin
The great poet, who sketched this self-portrait on a manuscript, died in the apartment that is now a museum (see p113).

Sergey Diaghilev
Driving force behind the Ballets Russes, Diaghilev also produced the World of Art *magazine in his apartment at 45 Liteynyy prospekt. He is shown here with Jean Cocteau (left).*

Neva

Palace Embankment

Anna Akhmatova
The poetess's most famous poem, Requiem, *is a powerful and moving indictment of the Stalinist regime. Akhmatova, seen here in a portrait by Nathan Altman, lived in the service quarters of the Sheremetev Palace (see p129).*

Gostinyy Dvor

Dmitriy Shostakovich
Shostakovich's Seventh Symphony *was broadcast live on the radio from the Great Hall of the Philharmonia (see p98) in August 1942, while the city was under siege. Many testified to its role in boosting the morale of the besieged citizens.*

Fyodor Dostoevsky
The novelist Dostoevsky lived for many years among the slums of Sennaya Ploshchad (see p122), which provided the setting for his greatest work, Crime and Punishment.

0 meters 500

0 yards 500

Remarkable St. Petersburgers

THE STREETS of St. Petersburg are redolent with literary and artistic associations. Fascinating art collections, house-museums, theaters, and concert halls evoke the memory of famous St. Petersburgers. The world of the 18th-century genius Lomonosov and 19th-century writers Pushkin and Dostoevsky can be imagined. So too, can the spirit of Russian ballet when dancers such as Anna Pavlova and Vaslaw Nijinsky thrilled the Mariinskiy audiences. During these early years of the 20th century, writers, musicians, dancers, and painters flocked to St. Petersburg, bringing with them a wealth of creativity.

Symbolist "Silver Age" poet, Andrei Bely (1880–1934)

WRITERS

CONSIDERED THE FATHER of modern Russian literature, **Alexander Pushkin** (1799–1837) was simultaneously intoxicated by St. Petersburg's beauty and sensitive to the underlying climate of political suspicion and intolerance that constrained writers in the wake of the Decembrist rebellion of 1825 *(see p22).* **Nikolai Gogol** (1809–52) responded to these constraints by satirizing the status quo. In *The Nose*, he targeted the city's bureaucrats with their inflated sense of self-worth and mind-numbing conformity.

Another aspect of the city altogether is revealed by **Fyodor Dostoevsky** (1821–81). His novel *Crime and Punishment*, one of more than 30 works set in the city, takes place against a backdrop of squalor in the notorious slums of Sennaya Ploshchad *(see p122).* The story of the murder of an old moneylender was based on a real crime, and the novel's publication in 1866 was blamed for a series of subsequent copycat killings.

Poetry, which flourished in the "Golden Age" of Pushkin, only regained its ascendancy over the novel in the "Silver Age" during the first decade of the 20th century. Some of the most exciting poets of the period, including **Aleksandr Blok** (1880–1921), **Andrei Bely**, and **Anna Akhmatova** (1889–1966), gathered at The Tower, an apartment overlooking the Tauride Gardens *(see p128).* Bely later wrote *Petersburg*, one of the earliest stream-of-consciousness novels.

Akhmatova is honored by a museum in the Sheremetev Palace *(see p129),* and one of her protégés, **Joseph Brodsky** (1940–96), went on to receive the Nobel Prize for literature in 1987. Brodsky became the bête-noire of the Leningrad literary establishment in the 1960s. The stubborn refusal of the authorities to publish his poetry, which they condemned as pessimistic and decadent, finally forced him to emigrate in 1972.

MUSICIANS

THE FIRST important composer to emerge from the nationalist movement was **Mikhail Glinka** (1804–57), the earliest composer of Russian opera. In 1862, the Conservatory *(see p120)* was founded by **Anton Rubinstein** (1829–94), and this became the focus of musical life in St. Petersburg. **Nikolai Rimsky-Korsakov** (1844–1908) taught here for 37 years, and together with composers such as **Modest Mussorgsky** (1839–81) and **Aleksandr Borodin** (1834–87), he formed "the mighty handful." They were a largely self-taught group aiming to develop a musical language based on Russian folk music and Slav traditions. Many of them wrote operas premiered at the Mariinskiy *(see p119).*

One of the musical geniuses of the 20th century was **Igor Stravinsky** (1882–1971). He spent much time abroad but, as works like *The Rite of Spring* testify, his cultural roots were firmly in his homeland.

The city's most important concert venue is the Great Hall of the Philharmonia *(see p194)* where **Pyotr Tchaikovsky**'s (1840–93) *Sixth Symphony* was premiered in 1893, and **Dmitriy Shostakovich**'s (1906–75) *Seventh Symphony*, his most famous work, was performed in 1942.

Portrait of composer Mikhail Glinka, painted by Ilya Repin in 1887

*The Circus (*1919) by Avant Garde
artist Marc Chagall

ARTISTS

FROM THE 18th century, the Academy of Arts *(see p63)* was the center of artistic life in St. Petersburg. **Dmitriy Levitskiy** (1735–1822), **Orest Kiprenskiy** (1782–1836), **Silvestr Shchedrin** (1791–1830), and Russia's first internationally recognised artist, **Karl Bryullov** (1799–1852), were all trained here.

In 1863, a group of students rebelled against the Academy and went on to establish the Wanderers movement *(see p106)*. To some extent the Academy and the Wanderers became reconciled when the most versatile of these artists, **Ilya Repin** (1844–1930), was appointed professor of painting at the Academy in 1893.

Five years later **Sergey Diaghilev** (1872–1929) and painter **Alexandre Benois** (1870–1960) launched the *World of Art* magazine *(see p107)*, proclaiming "Art for art's sake." Another collaborator, **Leon Bakst** (1866–1924), designed the most famous of the Ballets Russes costumes. Bakst also taught **Marc Chagall** (1889–1985), who later settled in France and had a profound impact on art in the West as well as in Russia. Other members of the Russian avant-garde include **Kazimir Malevich** (1878–1935) and **Pavel Filonov** (1883–1941).

Works by all of these artists can be seen at the Russian Museum *(see pp104–107)*.

DANCERS AND CHOREOGRAPHERS

THE SKILLS of Russian dancers are legendary, and the performances of the Mariinskiy (Kirov) Ballet Company continue to enthral audiences all over the world. Since 1836 the dancers have been trained at the former Imperial Ballet School *(see p112)*. In 1869–1903 the outstanding choreographer at the Mariinskiy was **Marius Petipa**. He inspired a generation of dancers including **Matilda Kshesinskaya** *(see p72)*, **Vaslaw Nijinsky** (1890–1950), and the legendary **Anna Pavlova** (1885–1931).

Petipa's successor, **Michel Fokine** (1880–1942), is famous as the principal choreographer of the Ballets Russes *(see p119)*. The Mariinskiy tradition was revived after the Revolution by another graduate of the Ballet School, **Agrippina Vaganova** (1879–1951). She paved the way for the modern generation of dancers including **Rudolf Nureyev** (1938–93) and, most recently, **Galina Mezentseva** and **Emil Faskhoutdinov**.

FILM DIRECTORS

THE LENFILM STUDIOS *(see p70)* were founded in 1918 on the site where the first Russian moving picture had been shown in 1896. In its heyday Lenfilm produced 15 movies a year. Its two most remarkable

Poster for *The Youth of Maxim* (1935) directed by Kozintsev

directors, **Grigoriy Kozintsev** (1905–73) and **Leonid Trauberg** (1902–90), first joined forces in 1922 and began making short experimental films. The pair then went on to direct *The New Babylon* (1929), remarkable for its montage and lighting effects, and *The Maxim Trilogy* (1935–39). Kozintsev's versions of *Hamlet* (1964) and *King Lear* (1970), with music composed by Shostakovich for both films, mark the height of his success in the West.

SCIENTISTS

The great polymath Mikhail Lomonosov

THE FOUNDATIONS of modern Russian science were laid in the 18th century by **Mikhail Lomonosov** (1711–65) *(see p61)*, who worked for over 20 years in the Kunstkammer *(see p60)*. His treatise, *Elementa Chymiae Mathematica*, published in 1741, anticipates Dalton's theory of the atomic structure of matter.

In 1869, **Dmitriy Mendeleev** (1834–1907), a professor of chemistry, compiled the Periodic Table of Elements.

Many people believe that the world's first radio signal was sent by **Aleksandr Popov** (1859–1906) from the laboratories of St. Petersburg University on March 24, 1896.

In 1904, the world-famous physiologist **Ivan Pavlov** (1849–1936) won the Nobel Prize for medicine for his theory of conditioned reflexes, which he demonstrated by experimenting on dogs and their hearing responses.

Nevskiy Prospekt
From the Admiralty to the Griboedov Canal

A PLEASANT STROLL ALONG this first stretch of St. Petersburg's main artery reveals a wealth of attractive buildings. A profusion of architectural styles ranges from the Baroque Stroganov Palace to the magnificent Neo-Classical Kazan Cathedral and the striking Style-Moderne House of Books. The stately avenue was once known as the "Street of Tolerance," referring to the group of churches of different denominations that were established here in the late 18th and early 19th centuries. *(See also p108.)*

Literary Café
Once called the Wolf and Beranger, this café was known for its fashionable clientele. Pushkin left from here for his fatal duel in 1837 (see p83).

The 1760s' apartment buildings at Nos. 8 and 10 are an example of early St. Petersburg Neo-Classicism.

Admiralty (p78)

Palace Square (p83) and the Hermitage (pp84–93)

ADMIRALTEYSKIY PROSPEKT

N E V S K I Y   P R O S P E K T

BOLSHAYA MORSKAYA ULITSA

MALAYA MORSKAYA ULITSA

BOLSHAYA MORSKAYA ULITSA

The Admiralty Gardens were laid out in 1872– 4. Near the fountain are busts of composer Mikhail Glinka, writer Nikolai Gogol, and poet Mikhail Lermontov.

St. Isaac's Cathedral (pp80–81) and Astoria Hotel (p79)

Aeroflot Building
Marian Peretyatkovich's severe granite building (1912) is uncharacteristic of the city's architecture. The upper stories were inspired by the Palazzo Medici in Florence, the arcades by the Doge's Palace, Venice.

ГРАЖДАНЕ!
ПРИ АРТОБСТРЕЛЕ
ЭТА СТОРОНА УЛИЦЫ
НАИБОЛЕЕ ОПАСНА

Sign at School No. 210
This school carries a sign, dating from the Blockade, warning "Citizens! This side of the street is more dangerous during artillery bombardment."

Barrikada Cinema
Now a movie theater, this handsome building was erected in 1768–71 for the city's police chief Nikolay Chicherin.

STAR SIGHT

★ **Kazan Cathedral**

0 meters	100
0 yards	100

Dutch Church Building
The Dutch church was housed behind the central Neo-Classical portico of Paul Jacot's seemingly secular building (1831–7). The elongated wings are still occupied by offices, flats, and shops.

LOCATOR MAP

Stroganov Palace
The façade of this splendid Baroque palace, one of the oldest buildings on the street (1753), is embellished with sculptural ornaments and the Stroganov coat of arms (see p112).

The Fashion House
Marian Lyalevich designed this building for Mertens Furriers in 1911–12. The impact of the Neo-Classical arches is heightened by the blue-tinged plate glass.

NAB REKI MOYKI

BOLSHAYA KONYUSHENNAYA UL

MALAYA KONYUSHENNAYA ULITSA

N E V S K I Y   P R O S P E K T

ULITSA PLEKHANOVA

KAZANSKIY MOST

KANAL GRIBOEDOVA

The House of Books
(Dom Knigi) was built for the Singer Sewing Machine Company in 1902–4 by Pavel Syuzor. The building, now a bookstore, is distinguished by a glass globe on a conical tower.

➤ **Continued** *(pp48–9)*

The Lutheran Church
(1833) was an important center for the evangelical community. Converted into a swimming pool during the Soviet era, it is once again open as a church *(see p112)*.

The Griboedov Canal,
originally known as the Catherine Canal, was renamed in 1923 after the 19th-century Russian playwright Aleksandr Griboedov.

★ Kazan Cathedral
Ninety-six Corinthian columns, arranged in four rows, form an extended arc facing Nevskiy prospekt. Andrey Voronikhin's design was inspired by Bernini's colonnade for St. Peter's in Rome. (See p111.)

Nevskiy Prospekt
From the Griboedov Canal to the Fontanka

NEVSKIY PROSPEKT has been the main focus for St. Petersburg's shopping and entertainment since the mid-18th century. As the prospekt continues toward the handsome Anichkov Bridge on the Fontanka River, there are growing numbers of cafés, bars, and restaurants, as well as three historic shopping arcades: the Silver Rows, Gostinyy Dvor, and Passazh. Bustling with life, this stretch of the avenue also has many sights of historic and architectural interest, including the Anichkov Palace.

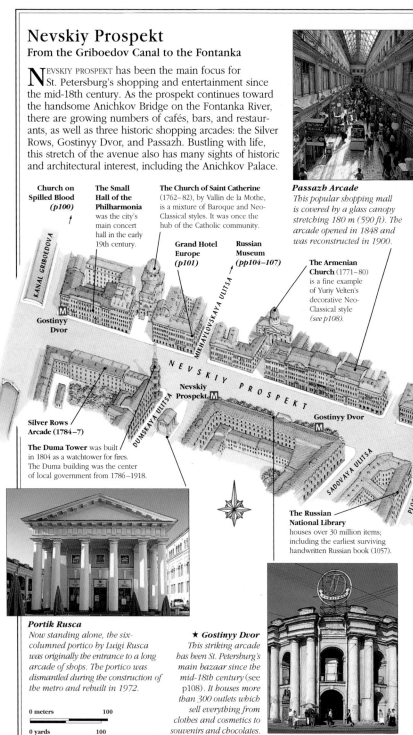

Church on Spilled Blood (p100)

The Small Hall of the Philharmonia was the city's main concert hall in the early 19th century.

The Church of Saint Catherine (1762–82), by Vallin de la Mothe, is a mixture of Baroque and Neo-Classical styles. It was once the hub of the Catholic community.

Grand Hotel Europe (p101)

Russian Museum (pp104–107)

Passazh Arcade
This popular shopping mall is covered by a glass canopy stretching 180 m (590 ft). The arcade opened in 1848 and was reconstructed in 1900.

The Armenian Church (1771–80) is a fine example of Yuriy Velten's decorative Neo-Classical style *(see p108).*

KANAL GRIBOEDOVA

Gostinyy Dvor Ⓜ

MIKHAYLOVSKAYA ULITSA

NEVSKIY PROSPEKT

Nevskiy Prospekt Ⓜ

DUMSKAYA ULITSA

Gostinyy Dvor Ⓜ

SADOVAYA ULITSA

PLOSH

Silver Rows Arcade (1784–7)

The Duma Tower was built in 1804 as a watchtower for fires. The Duma building was the center of local government from 1786–1918.

The Russian National Library houses over 30 million items; including the earliest surviving handwritten Russian book (1057).

Portik Rusca
Now standing alone, the six-columned portico by Luigi Rusca was originally the entrance to a long arcade of shops. The portico was dismantled during the construction of the metro and rebuilt in 1972.

| 0 meters | 100 |
| 0 yards | 100 |

★ *Gostinyy Dvor*
This striking arcade has been St. Petersburg's main bazaar since the mid-18th century (see p108). It houses more than 300 outlets which sell everything from clothes and cosmetics to souvenirs and chocolates.

★ Yeliseev's
Famous for its beautiful Style-Moderne decor, this building houses Yeliseev's delicatessen on the ground floor (see p109).

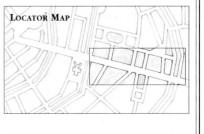

STAR SIGHTS

★ Yeliseev's

★ Gostinyy Dvor

Beloselskiy-Belozerskiy Palace
Now an exhibition and business center, this sumptuous palace was designed in Neo-Baroque style by Andrey Stakenschneider in 1847–8. The faded red facade is decorated with Corinthian pilasters and atlantes upholding balconies.

Quarenghi's Stalls were built in 1803–6 as trading rows. They were then handed over to the imperial chancellor and became known as the Cabinet.

Number 66 was occupied by the music publishers Bessel and Co. in the 19th century. Tchaikovsky was one of many composers who frequented their offices.

The Central District Tax Office has a Neo-Classical appearance, but was not built until the 1940s.

NEVSKIY PROSPEKT

OSTROVSKOVO

FONTANKA

ANICHKOV MOST

FONTANKA

Aleksandrinskiy Theater

A statue of Catherine the Great stands in Ostrovskiy Square *(see p110).*

The Anichkov Palace was first built as a present from Tsarina Elizabeth to her lover, Aleksey Razumovskiy. It later became the winter residence of the heir to the throne *(see p109).*

Moskovskiy railroad station

Anichkov Bridge
Four dynamic bronze statues of rearing horses and their tamers adorn this well-known landmark. They were designed in the 1840s by Pyotr Klodt (see p35).

ST. PETERSBURG THROUGH THE YEAR

WHATEVER THE weather, Russians are always ready to celebrate and consequently take their public holidays very seriously. Flowers have great symbolic significance, from mimosa for International Women's Day, to lilac to mark the beginning of summer. Every official holiday, as well as some local festivals such as City Day, are celebrated both in the center of town and in the many

Lilac, a symbol of summer

different districts, with regattas, balloon rides, and fireworks at night, when the torches on the Rostral Columns (see p60) are lit. Classical music is the central theme of a large number of festivals each year, attracting talented performers from all over the world. But even without an official holiday, Russian people love to get out and about, whether to ski or ice-skate in the winter months or gather mushrooms in late summer and autumn.

SPRING

SPRING HAS SET IN for good when the first sunbathers gather on the beaches outside the Peter and Paul Fortress (see pp66–7) and when, in early April after the waterways have thawed, the city's bridges open to allow ships through.

To warm themselves up after the months of cold, locals celebrate "maslennitsa," the making of pancakes (blini) prior to Lent. They then gather bunches of willow as a symbol of the approaching Palm Sunday. On the eve of Lent, "Forgiveness Sunday," it is common practice to ask forgiveness of those you might have offended during the year.

Once the snows have gone, the first trips to the dacha, or country house, are made to put the gardens in order.

Early sunbathers on the banks of the Peter and Paul Fortress

MARCH

International Women's Day (Mezhdunarodnyy den zhenshchin), Mar 8. Men rush around the city buying flowers for their womenfolk. It is a

Candles lighting up Russian Orthodox church during Easter service

tradition to say s prazdnikom (congratulations, on the holiday) to everyone. Theaters put on special performances and concerts and, however sexist it may seem to non-Russians, it is a very popular day.
From the Avant Garde to the Present (Ot avangarda do segodnya), mid-Mar. A celebration of 20th-century art and music in a city-wide festival.
Virtuosi 2000, late Mar/early Apr. Aspiring young musicians from all over the world come together to perform and compete on St. Petersburg's stages.
Easter Sunday (Paskha). The dates on which Lent and Easter fall change every year. On Easter Sunday, St. Petersburg churches are filled with worshippers, the evocative sound of ethereal music and chanting, and the smell of incense. Russians traditionally greet each other with Khristos voskres (Christ is risen), to which the reply is Voistine voskres (He is truly risen).

APRIL

Musical Spring in St. Petersburg (Muzikalnaya Vesna v Sankt-Peterburge), mid-Apr. As fur clothing and heavy boots are laid aside after the cold winter months, the public flock to concert halls throughout the city to hear St. Petersburg's talented classical musicians celebrate the disappearance of the last snows.
Cosmonauts' Day (Den Kosmonavtiki), Apr 12. Space exploration was one of the glories of the Soviet Union, and this occasion is celebrated with fireworks at 10pm.

MAY

Victory Day (Den Pobedy), May 9. After a rather somber ceremony at Piskarevskoe Cemetery (see p126), sharply-dressed veterans, festooned with medals and awards, fill Nevskiy prospekt (see pp46–9) and Palace Square (see p83) in commemoration of the Nazi surrender in 1945.
City Day (Den goroda), last week of May. To celebrate the day the city was founded, May 27, 1703, the City Day festival is packed full of events, from Peter the Great (see p18) look-alike contests to one of the most impressive fireworks displays to be held in the city all year. The manifold festivities all take place in and around the Peter and Paul Fortress (see pp66–7).

Proud war veteran on Victory Day

AVERAGE DAILY HOURS OF SUNSHINE

Hours
10 —
8 —
6 —
4 —
2 —
0 —
Jan Feb Mar Apr May Jun Jul Aug Sep Oct Nov Dec

Sunshine Hours

St. Petersburg's climate can vary dramatically from hot, sunny days and occasional heavy downpours during the summer months, to winters with sub-zero temperatures and snow. From mid-June to mid-July, it never gets dark. During the winter months the days are extremely short, but there can be days of bright sunshine.

SUMMER

ALILAC IN FLOWER is the real symbol that warm weather has set in, and there is an air of excitement once the Field of Mars *(see p94)* comes into bloom. Throughout the warm months, the city is deserted on weekends when people go off to their dachas usually situated around the pine forests northwest of the city.

St. Petersburg's main festive season is during the acclaimed White Nights in June, when the sun hardly sets and it never quite gets dark. Concerts, ballets, and other performances take place all over the city, which fills with thousands of visitors *(see p193)*. The most favored place to be at nighttime is on the embankments of the Neva, which are crowded with revelers watching the bridges being raised at 2am.

JUNE

Independence Day *(Den nezavisimosti)*, Jun 12. The day Russia became "independent"

of the Soviet Union is marked with fireworks at 10pm.

Trinity Sunday *(Troytsa)*, 50 days after Easter. Believers and atheists alike go to tidy the graves of their loved ones and raise a glass of vodka for their souls. Hundreds of special buses are added to get to cemeteries farther afield.

The White Nights Swing, Jazz Festival, mid-June. A large jam session supported by local and visiting musicians for anyone with an interest in jazz.

Stars of the White Nights, Classical Music Festival *(Zvezdy Belykh nochey)*, late Jun. This is the original White Nights festival, with first-class opera, classical music, and ballet concerts performed at all major venues.

White Nights, Rock Music Festival *(Belye nochi)*, late Jun. Numerous outdoor rock concerts are held at the Peter and Paul Fortress *(see pp66–7)* featuring a jamboree of both local bands and internationally known groups.

Festival of Festivals *(Festival-festivaley)*, last week in Jun. This is an international

Russian battleships moored on the Neva, Navy Day

noncompetitive film festival showing the best international films released over the past year. The festival attracts film stars from all over the world.

JULY

Handball on the Square *(Gandbol na Ploschadi)*, date variable. Palace Square *(see p83)* is transformed into a vast handball court for a day.

Volleyball by the Fortress *(Voleybol u Kreposti)*, date variable. Volleyball championships take place on the beach by the Peter and Paul Fortress *(see pp66–7)*.

Navy Day *(Den Voenno-Morskovo Flota)*, first Sun after Jul 22. The Neva resembles an enormous shipyard, with submarines and torpedo boats adorned with flags and bunting.

AUGUST

With schools on vacation and temperatures at their highest, most families escape to their dachas in the pine forests around the city. The majority of theater groups also go on tour, and many of the main theaters are closed.

Bridge opening in front of the Peter and Paul Fortress on a White Night

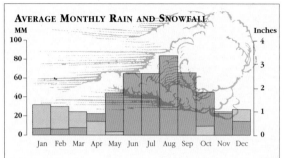

AVERAGE MONTHLY RAIN AND SNOWFALL

MM   Inches

Jan Feb Mar Apr May Jun Jul Aug Sep Oct Nov Dec

☐ Rainfall (from axis)

☐ Snowfall (from axis)

Rain and Snowfall Chart

St. Petersburg summers are humid and wet, but the downpours are a welcome relief from the summer heat. In winter frequent snowfalls build up to create enormous drifts, usually not thawing until late March.

AUTUMN

C ITY LIFE begins to gain pace as people return from their dachas and children begin to prepare for the start of school. In the last weeks of August, St. Petersburg is filled with posters heralding the start of a new school year, and shops are packed with parents frantically buying school supplies and clothes.

In September, when theaters re-open after the summer break, the city's cultural life resumes. The Mariinskiy (Kirov) returns from touring, and new plays and operas are premiered. October marks the start of the festival

Chanterelle mushrooms

season, with guest musicians and theater groups from all over the world taking part.

The crisp autumn weather is ideal for gathering mushrooms. Popular hunting spots can be found to the northwest of the city around Zelenogorsk and Repino *(see p144)*. Enthusiastic mushroom-gatherers rise early to hunt for chanterelles, oyster mushrooms, *podberyozoviki* (brown mushrooms), and *podosinoviki* (orange-cap boletes). The locals are skilled in identifying edible mushrooms but amateur pickers should be aware of the dangers of poisonous ones.

An activity with fewer potential side-effects might be a trip on the hydrofoil to Peterhof

Children dressed up for Teachers' Day, the first day of school

(see pp146–9) to see the playful fountains before they are switched off for the winter.

SEPTEMBER

Teachers' Day *(Den uchiteley)*, Sep 1. The city is full of children heading for their first day back at school, laden with flowers and gifts for their teachers.

OCTOBER

Theater Festival of the Baltic Countries *(Teatralnyy festival Baltiyskikh stran)*, Oct. Actors, clowns, and pantomime artists gather from the Baltic countries to perform in a few of the city's theaters with two weeks of antics.

Autumn in Tsarskoe Selo *(Osen v Tsarskom Sele)*, mid-Oct. A two-week festival of arts in the town of Tsarskoe Selo *(see pp150–53)*. Exhibitions, performance art, and concerts are held. Frequent buses are added to and from the city.

NOVEMBER

Sound Ways, Modern Music Festival *(Zvukovyye puti)*, mid-Nov. Catch up with the most avant-garde trends in Russian and European jazz and modern classical music.

Autumn colors in the park at Tsarskoe Selo

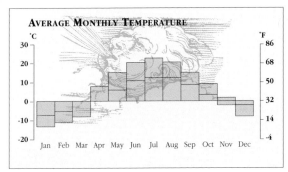

AVERAGE MONTHLY TEMPERATURE

Temperature Chart
St. Petersburg's climate is maritime and milder than might be expected. Summers are warm and often punctuated with hot days as early as May, though during the winter months temperatures often fall below freezing. St. Petersburg's average minimum and maximum temperatures throughout the year are shown in this chart.

WINTER

AS THE ICE thickens on the waters and the snow deepens, people head for the outdoors once more. Children's sleds are not expensive, and all other equipment can be rented. Cross-country skiing needs no lessons to make it fun. Tsarskoe Selo *(see pp150–53)* and Pavlovsk *(see pp156–9)* parks both provide ski and sled rental at the ski bases *(lyzhnaya baza)*. Skates can be rented for use in the rink at Moskovskiy Park Pobedy, by Moskovskaya metro in the southern suburbs.

The truly hardened members of the local "walruses" swimming club break the ice by the Peter and Paul Fortress *(see pp66–7)* every day to take an early morning dip. The less courageous are welcome to stand by and watch.

In the midst of winter activities come New Year and Christmas. New Year is the big holiday, while Christmas itself is celebrated according to the Orthodox calendar, on January 7. Many people also still celebrate Old New Year

Drilling a hole through the ice for wintertime fishing

Sledging on the frozen Neva outside the Hermitage *(see pp84–93)*

on January 14. Don't miss the traditional staging of the enchanting Christmas ballet, *The Nutcracker*, at the Mariinskiy Theater *(see p119)*.

DECEMBER

Constitution Day *(Den konstitutsii)*, Dec 12. When Yeltsin's new constitution replaced the Brezhnev version, a new constitution day replaced the old one. Fireworks are set off all over town at 10pm.
Musical Encounters in the Northern Palmyra *(Muzykalnyye vstrechi v Severnoy Palmire)*, Dec–Jan. This classical music festival is the last one of the year and is made even more magical by the outside backdrop of snowy streets and frozen waterways.
New Year's Eve *(Novyy god)*, Dec 31. Still the biggest holiday of the year, New Year's Eve is best celebrated with the local "champagne", Shampanskoye *(see p179)*. This is considered to be a family celebration, with people dressed as Grandfather Frost (the Russian equivalent of Santa Claus) and the Snow Maiden, the traditional bearers of gifts.

JANUARY

Russian Orthodox Christmas *(Rozhdestvo)*, Jan 7. Christmas is celebrated in a quieter fashion than Easter, with a traditional visit to an evening service on Christmas Eve (6th), when the church bells ring out all over the city.

FEBRUARY

Defenders of the Motherland Day *(Den zashchitnikov rodiny)*, Feb 23. The male equivalent of Women's Day. Men are congratulated and given flowers and presents.

PUBLIC HOLIDAYS

New Year's Day (Jan 1)
Russian Orthodox Christmas (Jan 7)
International Women's Day (Mar 8)
Russian Orthodox Easter (Mar/Apr)
Labor Day (May 1)
Victory Day (May 9)
Independence Day (Jun 12)
Constitution Day (Dec 12)

ST. PETERSBURG
AREA BY AREA

VASILEVSKIY ISLAND 56-63
PETROGRADSKAYA 64-73
PALACE EMBANKMENT 74-95
GOSTINYY DVOR 96-113
SENNAYA PLOSHCHAD 114-123
FARTHER AFIELD 124-131
TWO GUIDED WALKS 132-137

VASILEVSKIY ISLAND

I T WAS PETER THE GREAT'S intention that Vasilevskiy Island *(Vasilevskiy ostrov)*, the largest island in the Neva delta, was to be the administrative heart of his new capital. However, lack of access (the first permanent bridge was not built until 1850) and the hazards of floods and stormy crossings led to the abandonment of Peter's project, and the center grew up

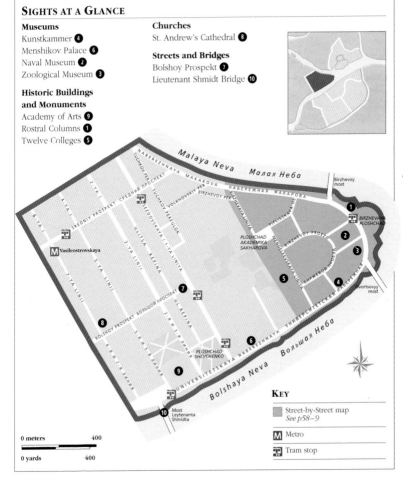

Allegorical sculpture of Neptune on the facade of the National Museum

across the river around the Admiralty *(see p60)* instead. The island's original street plan, based on canals that were never dug *(see p20)*, survives in the numbered streets known as lines *(linii)*, that run from north to south. The focal point of the island is at the east end with the fine ensemble of public buildings around the spit, or Strelka. The rest of the island developed with the spread of industrialization in the 19th century, and it became a middle-class haven. There was also a thriving German community here which is reflected in the several Lutheran churches. Today much of the island has a sedate air, with broad, tree-lined avenues, several museums, and some attractive 19th-century architecture.

SIGHTS AT A GLANCE

Museums
Kunstkammer ❹
Menshikov Palace ❻
Naval Museum ❷
Zoological Museum ❸

Historic Buildings and Monuments
Academy of Arts ❾
Rostral Columns ❶
Twelve Colleges ❺

Churches
St. Andrew's Cathedral ❽

Streets and Bridges
Bolshoy Prospekt ❼
Lieutenant Shmidt Bridge ❿

KEY

▨	Street-by-Street map See p58–9
Ⓜ	Metro
🚋	Tram stop

0 meters 400
0 yards 400

◁ **One of the two imposing 14th-century BC sphinxes situated in front of the Academy of Arts**

Street-by-Street: the Strelka

THE EASTERN END of Vasilevskiy Island is known as the Strelka, or "spit." Once St. Petersburg's main center of commerce, it has become an area of learning. The Academy of Sciences and St. Petersburg University are situated here, as are various museums, institutes, and libraries, housed in the former warehouses and customs buildings. The nautical theme is preserved in the Naval Museum and the two Rostral Columns. In front of these lighthouses is a lawn, a popular spot for newly married couples to have their pictures taken. From here there are views across the Neva toward the Peter and Paul Fortress *(see pp66–7)* and the Hermitage *(see pp84–93)*.

The Naval Museum and Rostral Columns from across the Neva

The Lomonosov Monument honors Mikhail Lomonosov (1711–65), who taught at the Academy of Sciences.

Twelve Colleges
Originally erected to house the 12 ministries of Peter the Great's government, they now form the main building of St. Petersburg University **5**

The Academy of Sciences was founded in 1724. The present building was constructed by Giacomo Quarenghi in 1783–5.

★ Kunstkammer
The Kunstkammer houses Peter the Great's collection of biological curiosities. Its tower, crowned by a sundial, is a St. Petersburg landmark **4**

MENDELEEVSKAYA LINIYA

BIRZHEVOY PROEZD

UNIVERSITETSKAYA NABEREZHNAYA

DVORTSOVYY MOST

Palace Embankment

Zoological Museum
With over 100,000 specimens the museum is one of the finest of its kind in the world. The exhibits include a set of stuffed animals that belonged to Peter the Great and a world-famous collection of mammoths **3**

STAR SIGHTS
★ Naval Museum
★ Kunstkammer

Academy of Sciences Library
was founded in 1714 with Peter the Great's personal book collection. It now has over 17 million volumes.

LOCATOR MAP
See Street Finder, map 1

The New Exchange Bazaar
was designed by Quarenghi in the early 19th century. At the time a busy market filled its Neo-Classical loggias. Today students have replaced the shoppers, as the building houses departments of the university.

The Institute of Russian Literature
was built in 1832 as the Customs House. It now includes a literary museum.

BIRZHEVOY MOST → Peter and Paul Fortress

★ **Naval Museum**
Among the museum's many fine model boats is the botik, also known as the "Grandfather of the Russian Navy," on which Peter the Great learned to sail ❷

Rostral Columns
Originally lighthouses guiding ships through the busy port of St. Petersburg, these imposing 32-m (105-ft) high columns are a distinctive feature of St. Petersburg's skyline. They are still lit for Navy Day (see p51) and other water festivals ❶

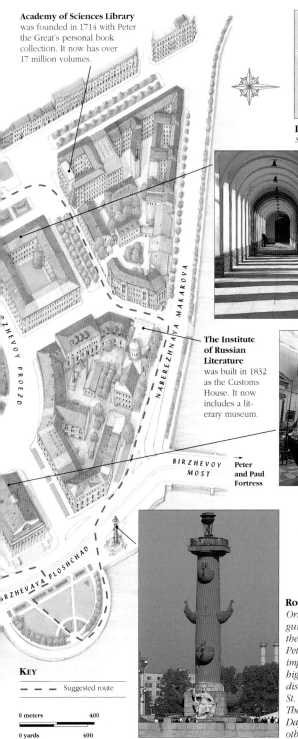

KEY

– – – Suggested route

0 meters   400
0 yards   400

Rostral Columns ❶

Ростральные колонны

Rostralnye kolonny

Birzhevaya ploshchad. **Map** 1 C5.
🚌 Э1, 7, 10, Э47, T128, 492.
🚎 1, 7, 10.

Situated on the Strelka in front of the Naval Museum, the twin russet-colored Rostral Columns were designed as lighthouses by Thomas de Thomon in 1810. During the 19th century the oil lamps were replaced by gas torches that are still lit on ceremonial occasions such as Navy Day *(see p51)*. Following a Roman custom, the columns are decorated with protruding ships' prows in celebration of naval victories. The monumental figures around the base represent four of Russia's great rivers, the Neva, Volga, Dnieper, and Volkhov.

Rostral Column on the Strelka

Naval Museum ❷

Центральный
Военно-Морской музей

Tsentralnyy Voenno-Morskoy muzey

Birzhevaya ploshchad 4. **Map** 1 C5.
📞 218 2502. 🚌 Э1, 7, 10, 47, Э47, T128, 492. 🚎 1, 7, 10.
🕐 10:30am–5:30pm Wed–Sun.
📷 🎫 English.

The former Stock Exchange *(birzha)* was built in 1805–10 as the focal point of the Strelka. The building was designed by the Swiss architect Thomas de Thomon and was modeled on one of the famous Greek temples at Paestum in Italy. Above the columned east facade is an allegorical sculpture featuring the sea god Neptune in a chariot drawn by sea horses; a reminder that maritime commerce was traditionally the lifeblood of this sea-oriented city.

The exchange was abandoned after the Revolution and in 1940 it was turned into a museum. Beneath the magnificent coffered ceiling of the spacious trading hall is an exhibition on the history of the Russian and Soviet navy from its origins under Peter the Great to the present day. A prime exhibit is the *botik*, the small, masted, wooden vessel on which Peter learned to sail. There is plenty of interest besides, from model ships and carved figureheads to uniforms, flags, and guided-missile submarines. There is also a superb diorama of the storming of the Winter Palace *(see pp28–9)* on the second floor landing.

The photographic displays around the hall concentrate on the revolutionary period. These were redesigned only in 1995 to present a more balanced view of events, such as the involvement of Western powers in World War II.

Neo-Classical facade of the Naval Museum, overlooking the Strelka

Zoological Museum ❸

Зоологический музей

Zoologicheskiy muzey

Universitetskaya naberezhnaya 1/3.
Map 1 C5. 📞 218 0112. 🚌 Э1, 7, 10, Э47, T128, 492. 🚎 1, 7, 10.
🕐 11am–5pm Sat–Thu. 📷 ♿
🎫 English.

Housed in a former customs warehouse designed by Giovanni Lucchini in 1826, this museum has one of the world's largest natural history collections containing more than 100,000 specimens. Some of the stuffed animals belonged to Peter the Great's Kunstkammer collection, including the horse he rode at the Battle of Poltava *(see p18)*.

Dioramas atmospherically recreate natural habitats for giant crabs, weasels, polar bears, and blue whales. The museum is famous for its collection of mammoths. The most prized carcass was exhumed from the frozen wastes of Siberia in 1902 and is almost 44,000 years old.

Weasel in the Zoological Museum

Kunstkammer ❹

Кунсткамера

Kunstkamera

Universitetskaya naberezhnaya 3.
Map 1 C5. 📞 218 1412. 🚌 Э1, 7, 10, Э47, T128, 492. 🚎 1, 7, 10.
🕐 11am–6pm Fri–Wed.
📷 🎫 English.

The delicate, sea green lantern tower of the Baroque Kunstkammer ("art chamber") is visible across this part of Vasilevskiy Island. The building, by Georg Mattarnovyy, was constructed in 1718–34 to exhibit Peter the Great's infamous Kunstkammer collection. While touring Holland in 1697 Peter attended the lectures of Frederik Ruysch (1638–1731),

The restrained Baroque facade of the Kunstkammer (1718–34), St. Petersburg's first museum

the most celebrated anatomist of his day. He was so impressed with Ruysch's collection of rarities that on a return visit in 1717 he purchased the entire collection of over 2,000 anatomical preparations. He transported it to St. Petersburg and exhibited it to a wide-eyed public, who were enticed by free glasses of vodka. At the time, Peter's collection also included bizarre, live exhibits of deformed or unusual people, including an hermaphrodite. This, Russia's first museum, also included a library, an anatomy theater, and an observatory.

Today the Kuntskammer houses the Museum of Anthropology and Ethnography, with the remnants of Peter's bizarre collection on display in the central rotunda. Included are the heart and skeleton of Peter's personal servant, "Bourgeois," a giant at 2.27 m (7.5 ft), and a cabinet of teeth extracted by the tsar, who was an enthusiastic amateur dentist. Most gruesome of all is the collection of pickled oddities that include Siamese twins and a two-headed sheep.

The halls surrounding the Kuntskammer collection contain exhibitions on the peoples of the world. Unfairly neglected by most foreign visitors, these old-fashioned displays present a vast and informative range of artifacts, from an Inuit kayak to Javanese shadow puppets.

Twelve Colleges ❺
Двенадцать коллегий
Dvenadtsat kollegiy

Universitetskaya naberezhnaya 7.
Map 1 C5. 🚌 *7, 47, 947, T128, 492.* 🚊 *10.* 🅾 *to public.*

THIS DISTINGUISHED Baroque building of red and white stuccoed brick is almost 400 m (1,300 ft) in length. It was intended for Peter the Great's newly streamlined administration of 12 colleges, or ministries. The single, uninterrupted facade was designed to symbolize the government's unity of purpose, while the unusual alignment, at right angles to the embankment, is explained by Peter's unrealized plan for a large

Mikhail Lomonosov (1711–65)

A section of the west facade of Trezzini's Twelve Colleges

square with an unbroken view across the Strelka. Another popular theory is that Prince Menshikov changed the plan in Peter's absence so that the building would not encroach on his grounds. Domenico Trezzini won the competition for the design in 1723, but subsequent bureaucratic wrangling delayed its completion for 20 years. The building's function gradually changed, and in 1819 part of it was acquired by St. Petersburg University. A string of revolutionaries, including Lenin in 1891, were educated here. Among the famous Russian lecturers to teach here were the chemist Dmitriy Mendeleev (1834–1907) *(see p45)* and the physiologist Ivan Pavlov (1849–1936) *(see p45).*

Overlooking the Neva, outside the Twelve Colleges, is the handsome bronze statue of the great 18th-century polymath Mikhail Lomonosov (unveiled in 1986). The son of a fisherman, Lomonosov was the first Russian-born member of the nearby Academy of Sciences. A "universal genius," he wrote poetry, systematized Russian grammar, and was a pioneer in mathematics and the physical sciences. Thanks to his scientific discoveries, the art of porcelain, glass, and mosaic production began in Russia.

The southern facade of Prince Menshikov's 18th-century palace

Menshikov Palace ❻

Меншиковский дворец
Menshikovskiy dvorets

Universitetskaya naberezhnaya 15.
Map 5 B1. 🅲 *213 1112.* 🚌 *7, 47, 347, T128.* 🚋 *10.* ⭘ *10:30am–4:30pm Tue–Sun.* 🚻 *11.* ♿
🎦 *compulsory (English available).*

THE OCHER-PAINTED Baroque
Menshikov Palace, with
its carved pilasters, was one
of the earliest stone buildings
in St. Petersburg. Designed by
Giovanni Fontana and Gottfried Schädel for Prince
Menshikov, the palace was
completed in 1720. The
palace grounds originally extended north as far as the
Malaya Neva River.

Prince Menshikov entertained
here on a lavish scale, often
on behalf of Peter the Great,
who adopted the palace as a
pied-à-terre. Guests would

cross the Neva by boat and
arrive to the grand welcome
of a liveried orchestra.

The palace is now a branch
of the Hermitage *(see pp84–93)*, housing a collection of
early 18th-century Russian cul-
ture that successfully evokes
the spirit of the age and reveals the extent to which
Peter the Great's court was
influenced by Western tastes.

The conducted tour begins
on the ground floor; besides
the kitchen there are displays
of Peter's cabinet-making
tools, costumes, sturdy oak
chests, and compasses.
Adorning the vaulted hallway
are statues imported from
Italy that include a Roman
Apollo dating to the 2nd
century AD.

Upstairs, the secretary's
rooms are decorated with 17th-
century Dutch engravings of
Leyden, Utrecht, and Kraków.
A series of rooms are lined
with hand-painted blue and
white 18th-century Dutch
tiles. Tiles were not only
fashionable, but also
a practical means
of deterring flies
and dust.

In the tiled bed-
room of Varvara
(Menshikov's
sister-in-law and
confidante) is a
German four-
poster bed, with a
Turkish coverlet wo-
ven from cotton, silk, and
silver thread. Hanging behind
it is a 17th-century Flemish
tapestry.

Menshikov and Peter often
received guests in the Walnut
Study, which has Persian
walnut paneling and views of
the Neva. Paintings hang from
colored ribbons, as was the
fashion, including a late 17th-

century portrait of Peter the
Great by Dutch painter Jan
Weenix. The mirrors were a
novelty at that time, and such
displays of vanity were condemned by the Orthodox
Church.

The Great Hall, decorated
in gold and stucco, is where
balls and banquets were held.
On one famous occasion, it
was the setting for a "dwarfs'
wedding" that Menshikov
arranged for the amusement
of his royal master.

**The fine, Style-Moderne *apteka*,
just off Bolshoy prospekt**

Bolshoy Prospekt ❼

Большой проспект
Bolshoy prospekt

Map 1 A5. Ⓜ *Vasileostrovskaya.*

THIS IMPOSING AVENUE was
opened early in the 18th
century to connect Menshikov's
estate to the Gulf of Finland.
It was widened in the 1930s.

The mix of styles ranges
from the Neo-Classicism of St.
Catherine's Lutheran Church
(1768–71) at No. 1 to the
Troyekurov House (No. 13, 6-
ya liniya) in 17th-century
Petrine Baroque.

Other buildings of note include the arcaded St. Andrew's
food market (1789–90) and
two Style-Moderne edifices.
One of these is the former
pharmacy or *apteka* (1907–10)
around the corner on 7-ya
liniya, with its fine mosaics
and tiling, and the other,
Adolph Gaveman's Lutheran
orphanage at No. 55 (1908).

PRINCE MENSHIKOV

A leading advisor, com-
rade-in-arms, and
friend of Peter the
Great, Aleksandr
Menshikov
(1673–1729)
rose from hum-
ble origins to
his position as
the first governor
of St. Petersburg.
After Peter's death
in 1725, Menshikov
engineered the ascension
of Catherine I (Peter's wife,
and Menshikov's former
mistress) to the throne, thus
maintaining his power until
her demise. His notorious
extravagance and venality
eventually caught up with
him. Accused of treason,
he died in exile in 1729.

The Academy of Arts (1764 – 88) on the Neva embankment, an example of early Russian Neo-Classicism

St. Andrew's Cathedral ❽

Андреевский собор
Andreevskiy sobor

6-ya liniya 11. **Map** 5 B1.
Ⓜ *Vasileostrovskaya.* ♿

FIRST BUILT under the initiative of Peter the Great's second wife, Catherine I *(see p21),* who donated 3,000 roubles toward its construction, the original wooden church on this site was destroyed by fire.

The present Baroque church with its distinctive steeple-like bell tower was constructed by Aleksandr Vist in 1764–80. The most stunning feature of the interior is the elaborately carved 18th-century iconostasis, which incorporates icons from the original church.

The treasure of St. Andrew's Cathedral, its beautiful Baroque iconostasis

Situated next door is Giuseppe Trezzini's small Church of the Three Saints (1740–60), which is dedicated to SS. Basil the Great, John Chrysostom, and Gregory of Nazianzus.

Academy of Arts ❾

Академия Художеств
Akademiya Khudozhestv

Universitetskaya naberezhnaya 17. **Map** 5 B1. 🄲 213 3578. Ⓜ *Vasileostrovskaya.* ◯ 11am–6pm Wed–Sun. 🄰 🄲

FOUNDED in 1757 to train home-grown artists in the preferred Western styles and techniques of art, the Academy spawned a galaxy of talent, including the great painter Ilya Repin *(see p42)* and architects Andrey Zakharov (1761–1811) and Andrey Voronikhin (1759–1814).

The innate conservatism of the Academy tended to discourage innovation and experiment, and in 1863 a band of 14 students walked out of their final exams in protest. They went on to found a realist art movement and became known as the Wanderers or *peredvizhniki (see pp106–7).*

The imposing Academy, built between 1764–88 by Aleksandr Kokorinov and Vallin de la Mothe, is an example of the transition from Baroque to Neo-Classicism. Still an art school, it exhibits the work of students past and present, including canvases, plaster casts of famous sculptures, architectural drawings, and models of many of the city's notable buildings, such as the magnificent Smolnyy Convent *(see p128).*

The splendid Neo-Classical halls and galleries, though faded, retain something of their original grandeur. Of note are the Conference Hall on the first floor, with its ceiling painting by Vasiliy Shebuev, and the adjoining Raphael and Titian galleries, adorned with copies of Vatican frescoes.

Flanking the river stairs outside the Academy are two sphinxes from the 14th century BC. Discovered among the ruins of ancient Thebes in Egypt, they were installed here in 1832. The faces are thought to bear a likeness of the pharaoh Amenhotep III.

Lieutenant Shmidt Bridge ❿

Мост Лейтенанта Шмидта
Most Leytenanta Shmidta

Map 5 B2. 🚌 1, 5, 11, 31.

ORIGINALLY KNOWN as the Nicholas Bridge, this was the first permanent crossing of the Neva when it opened in 1850. The reconstruction of the bridge, which was carried out in 1936–8, incorporated Aleksandr Bryullov's original railings, fancifully decorated with sea horses and tridents.

The bridge commemorates Lieutenant Pyotr Shmidt, a sailor on the cruiser *Ochakov,* who led an uprising of the Black Sea fleet in 1905 and was executed shortly afterward.

PETROGRADSKAYA

THE CITY was founded on the northern banks of the Neva River in 1703, at the height of the Great Northern War *(see p18)*. Building began with the construction of a wooden fortress, and Petrogradskaya, or the Petrograd Side, soon became a marshy suburb of wooden cabins occupied by craftsmen working on Peter the Great's new city.

Nearby, the area around Trinity Square was originally a small merchants' quarter centered around a now demolished church and St. Petersburg's first stock exchange.

Detail on bridge to Peter and Paul Fortress

Petrogradskaya was sparsely populated until the late 1890s, when the construction of the Trinity Bridge made the area accessible from the city center. The bridge caused a housing boom at the height of a fashion for Style-Moderne architecture, which is still in evidence today. The population quadrupled, and the area became very popular with artists and professionals.

The highlight of the area, which is still largely residential, is the Peter and Paul Fortress with its cathedral, museums, and grim history.

SIGHTS AT A GLANCE

Museums
Artillery Museum **7**
Cabin of Peter the Great **13**
Commandant's House **4**
Cruiser Aurora **12**
Engineer's House **2**
Kirov Museum **10**
Kshesinskaya Mansion **11**
Trubetskoy Bastion **6**

Gates
Neva Gate **5**
Peter Gate **1**

Cathedrals
Cathedral of SS. Peter and Paul **3**

Streets, Squares and Parks
Aleksandrovskiy Park **8**
Kamennoostrovskiy Prospekt **9**
Trinity Square **14**

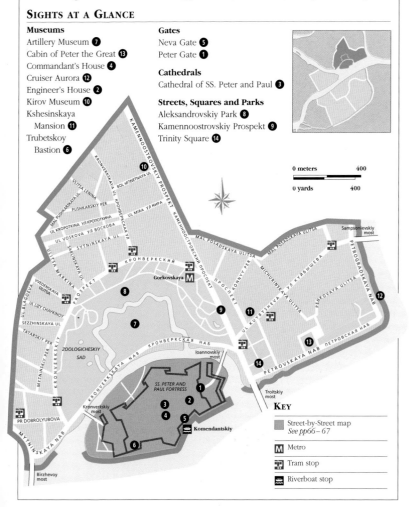

0 meters 400
0 yards 400

KEY

	Street-by-Street map See pp66–67
M	Metro
	Tram stop
	Riverboat stop

◁ **The Baroque Cathedral of SS. Peter and Paul in the Peter and Paul Fortress**

Street-by-Street: Peter and Paul Fortress

THE FOUNDING OF the Peter and Paul Fortress in 1703, on the orders of Peter the Great, is considered to mark the founding of the city itself. The fortress was first built in wood and was later replaced, section by section, in stone by Domenico Trezzini. Its history is a gruesome one, since hundreds of forced laborers died while building the fortress and its bastions were later used to guard and torture many political prisoners, including Peter's own son Alexis.

The cells where prisoners were once kept are open to the public, alongside a couple of museums and the magnificent cathedral that houses the tombs of the Romanovs.

The Archives of the War Ministry occupy the site of the "Secret House," a prison for political criminals in the 18th and 19th centuries.

Artillery Museum *(see p70)*

Kronverkskiy most

Zotov Bastion

Trubetskoy Bastion
From 1872–1921 the dark, damp, solitary-confinement cells in the bastion served as a grim prison for enemies of the state. Today, the bastion is open to visitors **6**

The Mint, founded in 1724, still produces ceremonial coins, medals, and badges.

The beach is popular in summer and in winter, when members of the "walruses" swimming club break the ice for an invigorating dip.

The Naryshkin Bastion (1725) is where the noon cannon is fired. The tradition began in 1873, stopped after the revolution, and was resumed in 1957.

Commandant's House
For 150 years this attractive Baroque house was the scene of interrogations and trials of political prisoners. It now houses a museum of local history **4**

Neva Gate
This riverside entrance, also known as "Death Gateway," leads to the Commandant's pier, from which prisoners embarked on their journey to execution or exile. The Neva River's flood levels (see p37) are recorded under the arch **10**

★ SS. Peter and Paul Cathedral

Marbled columns, glittering chandeliers, and painted decor combine with Ivan Zarudnyy's carved and gilded iconostasis to create a magnificent setting for the tombs of the Romanov monarchs ❸

The Boat House is now a souvenir shop.

Golovkin Bastion

The Grand Ducal burial vault is the last resting place of several grand dukes shot by the Bolsheviks in 1919 and of Grand Duke Vladimir, who died in exile in 1992.

LOCATOR MAP
See Street Finder, map 2

Peter Gate
The entrance to the fortress, by Domenico Trezzini, completed in 1718, features the Romanov double eagle with an emblem of St. George and the dragon ❶

STAR SIGHT

★ SS. Peter and Paul Cathedral

0 meters	100
0 yards	100

Ticket office

Ivan Gate, in the outer wall, was constructed from 1731–40.

Ioannovskiy most

Kamennoostrovskiy prospekt, Gorkovskaya Metro, and Trinity Bridge

This statue of Peter the Great is by Mikhail Chemiakin (1991).

Peter I Bastion

Engineer's House
This building, dating from 1748–9, houses temporary exhibitions of artifacts used in everyday life in St. Petersburg before the revolution ❷

KEY

– – – Suggested route

Peter Gate ❶
Петровские ворота
Petrovskie vorota

Petropavlovskaya krepost.
Map 2 E3. Ⓜ *Gorkovskaya.*

THE MAIN ENTRANCE to the
Peter and Paul Fortress is
through two contrasting arches.
The plain Neo-Renaissance
Ivan Gate (1730s) leads to the
more imposing Peter Gate
(1717–18), an ornate Baroque
structure with scrolled wings
and a rounded-gable pediment.
Domenico Trezzini redesigned
the Peter Gate, retaining Karl
Osner's expressively carved
bas-relief, which allegorizes
Peter the Great's victory over
Charles XII of Sweden *(see
p18)*. It depicts St. Peter
casting down the winged
sorcerer Simon Magus who
attempts to soar above him.

Peter Gate, entrance to fortress

Engineer's House ❷
Инженерный дом
Inzhenernyy dom

Petropavlovskaya krepost. **Map** 2 D3.
📞 *238 4540.* Ⓜ *Gorkovskaya.*
🕐 *11am–6pm Thu–Tue.* ♿
✒ *English.*

THE ENGINEER'S HOUSE, built
in 1748–9, has a changing
exhibition that gives a
fascinating glimpse of daily
life in St. Petersburg before
the Revolution. Architectural
backdrops and historical paintings give way to an engaging
miscellany of artifacts, ranging
from old shop fronts to model
boats, dueling pistols, court
costumes, and ball masks.
   In 1915 there were more
than 100 outlets selling musical instruments in the city,

**An accordion and organ surrounded by Style-
Moderne furniture, Engineer's House**

and the museum displays
an excellent collection that
includes phonographs,
symphoniums, and piano
accordions of the period.
   A section on vintage tech-
nology features Singer sewing
machines, typewriters, Bakelite
telephones, and box cameras.

Cathedral of
SS. Peter and Paul ❸
Петропавловский собор
Petropavlovskiy sobor

Petropavlovskaya krepost. **Map** 2 D4.
📞 *238 4540.* Ⓜ *Gorkovskaya.*
🕐 *11am–6pm Thu–Tue.* ♿
✒ *English.*

DOMENICO TREZZINI designed
this magnificent church
within the fortress in 1712.
Employed by Peter the Great,
who wished to turn his back
on traditional Russian church
architecture, Trezzini produced

a Baroque master-
piece of singular
elegance. The bell
tower was com-
pleted first to test
the foundations, and
this served as an
excellent viewpoint
from which Peter
could oversee the
construction work
of his new city. The
cathedral was com-
pleted in 1733, but
was badly damaged
by fire in 1756 when
the soaring 122-m
(400-ft) spire was struck by
lightning. The gilded needle
spire, crowned by a weather-
vane angel, remained the
tallest structure in St. Petersburg until the building of the
TV transmitter in the 1960s.
   The interior, with its glittering chandeliers, pink and
green Corinthian columns, and
overarching vaults, is also a
far cry from the traditional
Russian Orthodox church.
Even the iconostasis, culminating in a triumphal arch, is
a Baroque flight of fancy. This
masterpiece of gilded wood-
carving was designed by Ivan
Zarudnyy and executed in the
1720s by Moscow craftsmen.
   After Peter's death in 1725,
the cathedral became the last
resting place of the tsars. The
sarcophagi are all of a uniform
white Carrara marble, except
the tombs of Alexander II and
his wife Maria Alexandrovna,
which are carved from Altai

Cathedral of SS. Peter and Paul, with Dvortsovyy most in foreground

jasper and Ural rhodonite. Peter the Great's tomb, with a bronze bust often adorned with fresh flowers, lies to the right of the iconostasis.

The only tsars not buried here are Peter II, Ivan VI and, until recently, Nicholas II. In 1998 a controversial decision was taken to rebury the remains of the last Romanov tsar, his wife and children, and the servants that died together with them, in the cathedral.

The Grand Ducal Mausoleum, where relatives of the tsars are buried, was added to the northeast of the cathedral at the end of the 19th century.

Commandant's House ❹

Комендантский дом
Komendantskiy dom

Petropavlovskaya krepost. **Map** 2 D4.
📞 238 4540. Ⓜ *Gorkovskaya.*
🕐 11am–6pm Thu–Tue. 📷
🎫 English.

DATING FROM the 1740s, the plain brick, two-story Commandant's House served both as the residence of the fortress commander and as a courthouse. Over the years, political prisoners, including the Decembrist rebels *(see p23)*, were brought here for interrogation and sentencing.

The house is now a museum, with a ground-floor exhibition on medieval settlements in the St. Petersburg region, and temporary exhibitions upstairs.

Neva Gate ❺

Невские ворота
Nevskie vorota

Petropavlovskaya krepost. **Map** 2 E4.
Ⓜ *Gorkovskaya.*

THIS AUSTERE river entrance to the fortress was once known as the "Death Gate." Prisoners to be transported to the even more notorious Schlüsselburg Fortress (to the east of St. Petersburg) for capital punishment, or to a "living death" in penal servitude, were led down the granite steps and taken away by boat. The appropriately dour, gray gateway dates from

Neva Gate leading from the river into the Peter and Paul Fortress

1784–7 and is unornamented apart from an anchor in the pediment. In the archway, brass plaques mark record flood levels. The catastrophic inundation of November 1824 is the one commemorated in Pushkin's poem, *The Bronze Horseman (see p78).*

Trubetskoy Bastion ❻

Трубецкой бастион
Trubetskoy bastion

Petropavlovskaya krepost. **Map** 2 D4.
📞 238 4540. Ⓜ *Gorkovskaya.*
🕐 11am–6pm Thu–Tue. 📷
🎫 English.

PETER THE GREAT'S SON, the Tsarevich Alexis, was the first political prisoner to be detained in the grim fortress prison. Unjustly accused of treason in 1718 by his overbearing father, Alexis escaped abroad only to be lured back to Russia with the promise of

a pardon. Instead, he was tortured and beaten to death, almost certainly with Peter's consent and participation.

For the next 100 years prisoners were incarcerated in the much feared Secret House, since demolished. In 1872 a new prison building opened in the Trubetskoy Bastion; it has existed as a museum since 1924. On the ground floor there is a small exhibition of period photographs, prison uniforms, and a model of the guardroom. Upstairs are 69 isolation cells, restored to their original appearance, and downstairs there are two unlit punishment cells where the recalcitrant were locked up for 48 hours at a time. Once every two weeks, all detainees were taken to the Bath House for a delousing. Here prisoners were also put in irons before being taken off to penal servitude in Siberia.

POLITICAL PRISONERS

The fortress's sinister role as a prison for political activists continued until after the Revolution. Generations of rebels and anarchists were interrogated and imprisoned here,

Leon Trotsky (1879–1940) in the Trubetskoy Bastion

including Leon Trotsky in the wake of the 1905 Revolution. Other prominent detainees were the leading Decembrists in 1825 *(see p23)*, Dostoevsky in 1849 *(see p123)*, and, in 1874–6, the anarchist Prince Pyotr Kropotkin. In 1917 it was the turn first of the tsar's ministers, then of members of the Provisional Government. Then, during the Civil War, the Bolsheviks held hostage four Romanov grand dukes who were subsequently executed in 1919 *(see p27)*.

Rocket launcher in the courtyard of the Artillery Museum

Artillery Museum ❼

Музей Артиллерии
Muzey Artillerii

Kronverk. **Map** 2 D3. ☎ *232 0296.*
Ⓜ *Gorkovskaya.* ○ *11am–5pm
Wed–Sun.* ♿

THIS VAST, horseshoe-shaped
building of red brick stands
on the site of the Kronverk,
the outer fortifications of the
Peter and Paul Fortress *(see
pp66–67)*. Designed by Pyotr
Tamanskiy and constructed in
1849–60, the building was
originally used as the arsenal.

The museum boasts more
than 600 pieces of artillery
and military vehicles, including
tanks. There are uniforms,
regimental flags, muskets,
and small arms dating back
to medieval times, as well as
several rooms devoted to
World War II. A star exhibit
is the armored car in which
Lenin rode in triumph from
Finland Station *(see p126)* to
Kshesinskaya Mansion *(see
p72)* on April 3, 1917.

Aleksandrovskiy Park ❽

Александровский парк
Aleksandrovskiy park

Kronverkskiy prospekt. **Map** 2 D3.
Ⓜ *Gorkovskaya.* ♿

THE PARK'S UNIQUE character
as a center of popular
culture and entertainment was
established in 1900 with the
inauguration of the Nicholas
II People's House. This was
where pantomime artists, animal trainers, magicians, and
circus acts entertained the

crowds, while the more
serious-minded were drawn to
the lecture halls, reading
galleries, and tea rooms. The
pièce de résistance was the
domed Opera House (1911),
where the legendary bass
singer Fyodor Shalyapin gave
performances.

Today the Opera
House offers less
highbrow entertain-
ment, as its change
of name to Music Hall
suggests. The adjoin-
ing buildings, erected
in the late 1930s, in-
clude the innovative
Baltic House Theater
and the Planetarium.

The park still draws crowds
on summer weekends and
public holidays, although
some of the attractions,
especially the zoo, are now
rather shabby.

Kamennoostrovskiy Prospekt ❾

Каменноостровский проспект
Kamennoostrovskiy prospekt

Map 2 D2. Ⓜ *Gorkovskaya.*

DEVELOPED DURING the con-
struction boom of the late
1890s, this eye-catching avenue
is noted for its Style-Moderne
architecture. The first house,
at No. 1–3 (1899–1904), was
designed by one of the leading
proponents of the style, Fyodor
Lidval. The multitextured
facade, windows of contrasting
shapes and sizes, ornate iron
balconies, and fanciful carvings
are the most typical features
of this Russian version of Art
Nouveau. The neighboring

house (No. 5) was once occupied by Count Sergey Witte,
a leading industrialist who
negotiated the peace treaty
with Japan in 1905 *(see p26)*.

Situated just off the start of
the avenue is the city's only
mosque (1910–14). Designed
by Russian architects, its mina-
rets, majolica tiling, and rough
granite surfaces of the walls
are fully in keeping with the
surrounding Style-Moderne
architecture. The mosque
was, in fact, modeled on the
mausoleum of Tamerlane in
Samarkand and involved
Central Asian craftsmen.

At No. 10 is the tall portico
of the Leningrad Film Studios
(Lenfilm). It was on this site,
in May 1896, that the Lumière
brothers showed the first moving picture in Russia. Since its
founding in 1918, some of the
most innovative Soviet film
directors, such as Leonid Trauberg and Grigoriy
Kozintsev *(see p70)*,
have worked there.

At the intersection
with ulitsa Mira, each
house has individ-
ually designed
turrets, spires, reliefs,
and iron balconies,
forming a handsome
Style-Moderne
ensemble. Other buildings of
interest include No. 24
(1896–1912), with its red
brick majolica and terra-cotta
facade; No. 26–28, where
Sergey Kirov lived *(see p72)*;
and on the corner of Bolshoy
prospekt, the "Turreted House"
with its Neo-Gothic portal.

**Griffon, No. 1–3
Kamennoostrovskiy**

**Turreted House (1913–15),
Kamennoostrovskiy prospekt**

Style Moderne in St. Petersburg

Kshesinskaya Mansion railing detail

IN VOGUE throughout Europe from the 1890s to the 1900s, Art Nouveau marked a break with imitation of the past. The movement, known as Style Moderne in Russia, began in the decorative arts and was then reflected in architecture, where it led to an abundance of ornamental elements. Inspired by new industrial techniques, artists and architects made lavish use of natural stone and brick, wrought iron, stucco, colored glass, and ceramic tiles.

Dominated by sinuous and undulating lines, with a predominance of floral and vegetable elements, even traditional forms such as doors and windows are broken up, distorted, or given unexpected curves.

In fin-de-siècle St. Petersburg, the Style Moderne flourished as the city underwent a building boom, particularly on Petrogradskaya. The city became a showcase for the talents of such architects as Fyodor Lidval and Aleksandr von Gogen.

Kshesinskaya Mansion *reveals von Gogen's relatively severe version of Style Moderne. Asymmetrical in composition, it is enlivened with wrought iron and glazed tiles (see p72).*

Yeliseev's *is evidence of the skill of Gavriil Baranovskiy, who made excellent use of industrial techniques in the creation of large window spaces. The rich exterior detailing is matched by elegant fittings and chandeliers inside (see p109).*

28 Bolshaya Zelenina ulitsa *is one of the most outstanding examples of the use of stylized animal and fish motifs and a variety of surface decoration techniques. Fyodor von Postel's 1904–5 apartment house is reminiscent of the work of his contemporary, the Catalan architect Gaudí.*

1–3 Kamennoostrovskiy pr *is the work of St. Petersburg's master of Style Moderne, Fyodor Lidval. Delicate details such as floral and animal reliefs stand out against a background of discreetly elongated proportions and unusual window shapes.*

House of Books *(1910–14) reveals Pavel Syuzor's use of an unusually eclectic mix of architectural styles. Ornate Style-Moderne wrought-iron balconies and decorative wooden window frames combine with elements of Renaissance and Baroque Revivals.*

Portrait of Sergey Kirov made of feathers (1933–4), Kirov Museum

Kirov Museum ❿
Музей С. М. Кирова
Muzey S. M. Kirova

Kamennoostrovskiy prospekt 26–28, 4th floor. **Map** 2 D1. **C** *346 1481.* **M** *Petrogradskaya.* ○ *11am–5.30pm Thu–Tue.* 🎫

FROM 1926–36 this flat was home to one of Stalin's closest political associates, Sergey Kirov. As the charismatic first Secretary of the Leningrad Communist Party, Kirov soon gained national importance. His increasing popularity led Stalin to see him as a potential rival. On December 1, 1934, Kirov was gunned down at his office at the Smolnyy Institute *(see p128)* by Leonid Nikolaev, a party malcontent. Stalin used the assassination as an excuse to launch the Great Purges *(see p27)*, although most historians believe Stalin himself was behind Kirov's murder.

Kirov acquired the status of a martyr after his death, with countless buildings named in

his honor. His apartment has been preserved as it was in his lifetime. It is a unique example of the reverent, near cultlike status awarded Party leaders, with not only documents and photographs chronicling Kirov's political career, but a touching array of memorabilia including Kirov's shooting clothes and favorite books.

Kshesinskaya Mansion ⓫
Особняк М. Кшесинской
Osobnyak M Kshesinskoy

Ulitsa Kuybysheva 4. **Map** 2 E3. **C** *233 7052.* **M** *Gorkovskaya.* ○ *10am–5pm Fri–Wed.* 🎫 🎫

THIS REMARKABLE example of Style-Moderne architecture was commissioned for prima ballerina Matilda Kshesinskaya. Designed in 1904 by the court architect, AI Gogen, the building is almost playfully asymmetric with a single, octagonal tower. Most eye-catching of all are the many contrasting building materials with bands of pink and gray granite, cream-colored bricks, delicately ornamented iron railings, and majolica tiles.

The most impressive interior is the splendid recital hall with its pillared archway and palms. Nearby, the Kshesinskaya memorial room has some of the dancer's possessions, including sketches of Nicholas II.

In March 1917 the mansion was commandeered by the Bolsheviks and became their headquarters, and, on Lenin's return to Russia *(see p126)*, he addressed the crowds from the balcony facing the square.

The mansion, previously home to a museum glorifying the October Revolution, now houses a Museum of Russian Political History. On the first floor the Bolshevik Party secretariat and Lenin's office have been faithfully restored. Upstairs is a fascinating collection of memorabilia from the revolutionary era, including Communist posters, Nicholas II coronation mugs, and even a police file on Rasputin's murder *(see p121)*.

The final exhibition (ground floor), entitled "Democracy or Dictatorship?" traces Russia's troubled political history via documents, photographs, and artifacts, with a section on each of Russia's prerevolutionary political parties.

MATILDA KSHESINSKAYA

One of the finest prima ballerinas ever to grace the stage of the Mariinskiy Theater *(see p119)*, Matilda Kshesinskaya (1872–1971) graduated from the Imperial Ballet School *(see p118)* in 1890. She was equally famous for her celebrated affair with the tsarevich, later Tsar Nicholas II, which began soon after she graduated. Kshesinskaya emigrated to Paris in 1920 where she married the Grand Duke Andrey Vladimirovich, another member of the imperial family and the father of her 11-year old son. It was in Paris that she wrote her controversial memoirs, *Dancing in St. Petersburg*, which tells the tale of her affair with the last Russian tsar.

AI Gogen's elegant recital hall in the Kshesinskaya Mansion

The historic cruiser *Aurora* (1900), moored in front of the Neo-Baroque Nakhimov Naval Academy (1912)

Cruiser Aurora ⓬
Крейсер Аврора
Kreyser Avrora

Petrogradskaya naberezhnaya 4.
Map 2 F3. **C** 230 8440. **T** 6, 30,
54, 63. **O** 10:30am–4pm Tue–Thu,
Sat & Sun. **&** for a fee. Phone to book.

Aссording to the annals of the Revolution, at 9:40pm on October 25, 1917, the cruiser *Aurora* signaled the storming of the Winter Palace *(see p28)*, by firing a single blank round from its bow gun.

Completed in 1900, the vast cruiser was put into active service in 1903. It was later converted into a training ship, and at the start of the Siege of Leningrad *(see p27)* it was sunk to protect it from German forces. The ship was raised in 1944, 950 days later, and has been a museum since 1956. The famous gun, bell and the crew's quarters can be seen, along with an exhibition on the history of the *Aurora*.

Cabin of Peter the Great ⓭
Музей-домик Петра I
Muzey-domik Petra I

Petrovskaya naberezhnaya 6. **Map**
2 F3. **C** 232 4576. **M** Gorkovskaya.
O 10am–6pm Wed–Mon.
& **&** **&** English (book in adv).

Tнiс pine-log cabin was built for Peter the Great by his soldier-carpenters in just three days in 1703. Peter lived here for six years while overseeing the construction of his new city *(see pp20–21)*. Catherine the Great, ever eager to glorify Peter, had a protective brick shell erected round the cabin.

Marvelously evocative of the stark simplicity of Peter's lifestyle, there are only two rooms, both with period furnishings, and a hallway that doubled as a bedroom. Among Peter's personal possessions are a compass, frock coat, and his rowboat.

Adorning the steps outside are two statues of the mythical Shih Tze frog-lions, brought from Manchuria during the Russo-Japanese War *(see p26)*.

Trinity Square ⓮
Троицкая площадь
Troitskaya ploshchad

Map 2 E3. **M** Gorkovskaya.

Throughout the early 18th century, the whole of Petrogradskaya was known as Trinity Island. The name was derived from the Church of the Trinity (built in 1710; demolished 1930s) in Trinity Square, which formed the nucleus of the city's merchant quarter. Despite having no direct links to the mainland until the early 20th century, the area flourished with shops, a printing house, and the city's first stock exchange.

In the 1905 Revolution *(see p26)* the square witnessed one of the worst massacres of "Bloody Sunday" when 48 workers were killed by government troops. During the Communist era, the square became known as ploshchad Revolyutsii, commemorating those who had lost their lives.

From the square, across the widest point of the Neva, the Style-Moderne Trinity Bridge *(see p35)* stretches nearly 600 m (1,970 ft). Its construction led to a building boom in Petrogradskaya *(see p65)* and its completion in 1903 coincided with the city's bicentenary.

The ornate Trinity Bridge, crossing the Neva from Trinity Square

PALACE EMBANKMENT

Alexander Column, Palace Square

IN TERMS OF SHEER SCALE and grandeur, St. Petersburg's magnificent south waterfront has few equals. Its formidable granite quays, stretching over 2 km (1 mile) from the Senate building in the west to Peter the Great's Summer Palace in the east, and the surrounding area of stately aristocratic palaces and ornamental canal bridges are justly famous worldwide.

Every aspect of the city's history is juxtaposed in this rich area. Falconet's statue of Peter the Great, the Bronze Horseman, is an eloquent testimony to imperial ambition, while the square in which it stands is named in honor of the Decembrist rebels who retaliated against the tsarist regime in 1825. In Palace Square, Rastrelli's Winter Palace (part of the Hermitage) evokes the opulence of Imperial Russia, while the eternal Flame, flickering in the Field of Mars, is a more somber reminder of revolutionary sacrifice.

Dominating St. Petersburg's skyline are the magnificent dome of St. Isaac's Cathedral and the gilded spire of the Admiralty. Some of the best views can be appreciated by making a boat trip along the waterways (*see pp218–19*) or by strolling through the Summer Gardens.

SIGHTS AT A GLANCE

Palaces and Gardens
Marble Palace ⑭
Summer Gardens ⑯
Summer Palace ⑰

Museums
The Hermitage pp84–93 ⑫

Historical Buildings and Monuments
The Admiralty ①
The Bronze Horseman ③
Horseguards' Manège ④
House of Fabergé ⑨

Churches
St. Isaac's Cathedral pp80–81 ⑤

Streets and Squares
Decembrists' Square ②
Field of Mars ⑮
Malaya Morskaya Ulitsa ⑧
Millionaires' Street ⑬
Palace Square ⑪
St. Isaac's Square ⑥

Hotels and Cafés
Astoria Hotel ⑦
Literary Café ⑩

KEY

	Street-by-Street map See pp76–7
🚋	Tram stop
⛴	Riverboat stop

◁ **The golden dome of St. Isaac's Cathedral above elegant facades along the Neva**

Street-by-Street: St. Isaac's Square

Detail from the frieze on the Admiralty gate tower

THE HIGHLIGHT OF St. Isaac's Square is the imposing cathedral at its center, which opened in 1858 and is the fourth church to stand on this site. The cathedral, and subsequently the square, were named after St. Isaac of Dalmatia, because Peter the Great's birthday fell on this saint's day. The busy square, used as a market-place in the first half of the 19th century, is now at the heart of an area teeming with buildings and statues of historical and architectural interest. Among them are the Admiralty, the Mariinskiy Palace, and the Bronze Horseman.

Horseguards' Manège
Built in 1804–7 by Giacomo Quarenghi, this building housed the Life Guards' Mounted Regiment **4**

The Bronze Horseman
Etienne Falconet's magnificent statue of Peter the Great, his horse trampling the serpent of treason, captures the spirit of the city's uncompromising and willful founder **3**

Decembrists' Square
Dominating the western side of the square are Carlo Rossi's monumental Senate and Synod buildings, linked by a triumphal arch **2**

The Glory Columns, topped by bronze angels, were erected in 1845–6.

Myatlev House

★ **St. Isaac's Cathedral**
The magnificent golden dome of the cathedral is visible all across the city. 100kg (220lb) of gold leaf were needed to cover the dome's surface **5**

The Former German Embassy was designed by Peter Behrens in 1911–12.

ADMIRALTEYSKAYA NABEREZHNAYA

PROEZD DEKABRISTOV

UL YAKUBOVICHA

ISAAKIEVSK PLOSHCH

BOLSHAYA

MO

0 meters 100
0 yards 100

The Hermitage
and Winter Palace

LOCATOR MAP
See Street Finder maps 2, 5 & 6

The Admiralty

Sculptures and reliefs, celebrating the power of Russia's navy, decorate the Admiralty's façade. The archway of the main entrance is framed by nymphs carrying globes on their shoulders **1**

ADMIRALTEYSKIY PROSPEKT

GOROKHOVAYA UL

VOZNESENSKIY PROSPEKT

MAL MORSKAYA UL

Former Prince Lobanov-Rostovskiy Mansion is now a design institute. The lions in front of the arcade are by Italian sculptor Paolo Triscorni.

STAR SIGHT

★ **St. Isaac's Cathedral**

Nevskiy
prospekt

Astoria Hotel

The elegant ground-floor hallway of the Angleterre wing of the historic Astoria Hotel (see p173) reflects the major refurbishment undertaken in the early 1990s. Now under new management, the hotel enjoys an enviable location in the heart of the city **7**

The Former Ministry of State Property, designed by Nikolay Yefimov in 1844, is a fine example of Neo-Renaissance architecture.

MORSKAYA UL

REKI MOYKI

Siniy most *(see p79)*

The Mariinskiy Palace, named in honor of Maria, daughter of Nicholas I, now houses the St. Petersburg city hall.

St. Isaac's Square

Overlooking the square is Pyotr Klodt's statue of Tsar Nicholas I. The reliefs on the pedestal depict episodes from his reign. Tellingly, two of them show the suppression of rebellions **6**

KEY

- - - Suggested route

The Admiralty ❶
Адмиралтейство
Admiralteystvo

Admiralteyskaya naberezhnaya 2.
Map 5 C1 🚇 *7, Э47, T128.* 🚌 *1, 5, 7, 10, 17, 22.* 🚎 *31.* ◐ *to public.*

Having FOUNDED a city and built a fortress, Peter the Great's next priority was to create a Russian navy to guarantee access to the sea and dominance over Sweden.

The Admiralty began life as a fortified shipyard built on this site between 1704–11. Two years later, some 10,000 men were employed in building the first battleships of the embryonic Russian navy.

One of Russia's most inspired architects, Andrey Zakharov, began to rebuild the Admiralty in 1806. The remarkable facade is 407 m (1,335 ft) in length and is adorned with an abundance of sculptures and reliefs that document the glory of the Russian fleet. Zakharov retained some of the original features, including the central gate tower and spire, which he recast in Neo-Classical style with columned porticos and pavilions. The heightened spire was gilded and topped with a model frigate. This has become a symbol of the city, just like the trumpet-blowing pair of angels on the portals of the facade overlooking the Neva.

In the 1840s, shipbuilding was moved downstream, and the Admiralty was handed over to the Russian navy. It has been occupied by the Naval Engineering School since 1925.

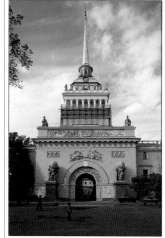

Tower and spire of the Admiralty (1806–23)

Decembrists' Square ❷
Площадь Декабристов
Ploshchad Dekabristov

Map 5 C1. 🚌 *T8, 10.* 🚎 *5, 22.*

The NAME of this square alludes to the momentous event in Russian history that took place here on December 14, 1825 *(see p23)*. During the inauguration of Nicholas I, liberal-minded army officers intent on imposing a constitutional monarchy attempted to stage a coup d'état in the square. After a confused standoff that lasted several hours, the rebel forces were routed with grapeshot by the new tsar and loyalist troops. Five of the ringleaders were later executed and 121 others

exiled to Siberia, effectively ending Russia's first revolution.

The imposing Neo-Classical buildings that command the western side of Decembrists' Square were intended to harmonize with the Admiralty. Designed by Carlo Rossi between 1829–34, they were the headquarters of two important institutions that were originally created by Peter the Great: the Supreme Court, or Senate, and the Holy Synod, which was responsible for the administration of the Orthodox Church. The two buildings, which now house historical archives, are linked to each other by a triumphal arch supported by Corinthian columns and decorated with a Neo-Classical frieze and a plethora of statuary.

The Bronze Horseman (1766–78)

The Bronze Horseman ❸
Медный Всадник
Mednyy Vsadnik

Ploshchad Dekabristov. **Map** 5 C1.
🚌 *T8, 10.* 🚎 *5, 22.*

The MAGNIFICENT equestrian statue of Peter the Great was unveiled in Decembrists' Square in 1782, as a tribute from Catherine the Great. The statue is known as The Bronze Horseman after Pushkin's famous poem. A French sculptor, Etienne Falconet, spent more than 12 years overseeing this ambitious project. The pedestal alone weighs

---

THE BRONZE HORSEMAN BY PUSHKIN

1956 stamp of Pushkin and the statue that inspired his poem

The famous statue of Peter the Great is brought to life in Alexander Pushkin's epic poem *The Bronze Horseman* (1833). In this haunting vision of the Great Flood of 1824 *(see p37)*, the hero is pursued through the mist-shrouded streets by the terrifying bronze statue. Pushkin's words evoke the domineering and implacable will for which the tsar was renowned: *"How terrible he was in the surrounding gloom! ... what strength was in him! And in that steed, what fire!"*

1,800 tons and was hewn from a single block of granite, which was hauled from the Gulf of Finland. It bears the simple inscription "To Peter I from Catherine II" in Latin and Russian. A serpent, symbolizing treason, is crushed beneath the horse's hooves.

Newlyweds often pose for photographs under the statue, which is meant to bring luck.

Horseguards' Manège ❹

Конногвардейский манеж
Konnogvardeyskiy manezh

Isaakievskaya ploshchad 1. **Map** 5 C2.
📞 *314 5959.* ⏰ *11am–7pm Fri–Wed.* 🚌 *T8, 10, 22, 39Э, 43.* 🚊 *5, 22.* 📷

T HE ENORMOUS INDOOR riding school of the Life Guards' Mounted Regiment was built by Giacomo Quarenghi in 1804–7 to resemble a Roman basilica. Two clues to the building's original function are the dynamic frieze of a horse race beneath the pediment and the statues on either side of the portico. The statues of the unclad twin sons of Zeus reining in wild horses are copies from the Quirinale Palace in Rome. The Holy Synod, scandalized by this display of nakedness so near to St. Isaac's Cathedral, ordered their removal. The statues were re-erected in 1954.

Next to the manège, which is now used for contemporary art exhibitions, are two marble pillars surmounted by bronze angels cast in Berlin, which were sent as a gift in 1840.

St. Isaac's Cathedral ❺

See pp80–81.

St. Isaac's Square ❻

Исаакиевская площадь
Issakievskaya ploshchad

Map 5 C2. 🚌 *T8, 10, 22, 39Э, 43.* 🚊 *5, 22.*

D OMINATED BY Auguste de Montferrand's majestic St. Isaac's Cathedral, this impressive square was created during the reign of Nicholas I,

St. Isaac's Cathedral, statue of St. Nicholas I and the Astoria, St. Isaac's Square

although a few of its earlier buildings date from the 18th century. The monument to Nicholas I at its center was also designed by Montferrand. Erected in 1859 and sculpted by Pyotr Klodt, it depicts the tsar in the uniform of one of Russia's most prestigious regiments, the Kavalergardskiy guards. The pedestal is embellished with allegorical sculptures of his daughters and his wife, who represent Faith, Wisdom, Justice, and Might.

On the western side of the square at No. 9, the Myatlev House is a Neo-Classical mansion, dating from the 1760s, that belonged to one of Russia's most illustrious families. The French encyclopedist, Denis Diderot, stayed here in 1773–4 following an invitation from Catherine the Great. In the 1920s it became the premises of the State Institute of Artistic Culture, where some of Russia's most influential avant-garde artists, including Kazimir Malevich and Vladimir Tatlin *(see p107),* worked.

The forbidding granite-faced building alongside is the former German embassy, designed in 1911–12 by the German architect Peter Behrens.

Across the 100-m (330-ft) wide Siniy most (Blue Bridge), which was the site of a serf market until 1861, the Mariinskiy Palace *(see p67)* dominates the southern end of the square.

Astoria Hotel ❼

Гостиница Астория
Gostinitsa Astoriya

Bolshaya Morskaya ulitsa 39. **Map** 6 D2. 📞 *210 5757.* 🚌 *T8, 10, 22, 39Э, 43.* 🚊 *5, 22.*
See Where to Stay p180.

N OW ONE OF St. Petersburg's leading hotels, the seven-story Astoria was designed by Fyodor Lidval in the Style Moderne *(see p71)* in 1910–12.

American writer John Reed, author of the famous eyewitness account of the Revolution *Ten Days that Shook the World,* was staying here when the Bolsheviks seized power.

In 1925, the poet Sergey Yesenin, husband of Isadora Duncan, hanged himself in the annex, after daubing the walls of his room with a farewell verse in his blood "To die is not new – but neither is it new to be alive."

The hotel's banqueting hall was to be the venue for Hitler's prematurely planned victory celebration, so sure was he that he would conquer the city.

Restored Style-Moderne foyer in the Astoria Hotel, on the eastern edge of St. Isaac's Square

St. Isaac's Cathedral ⑤

Исаакиевский собор
Isaakievskiy sobor

ST. ISAAC'S, one of the world's largest cathedrals, was designed in 1818 by the then unknown architect Auguste de Montferrand. The construction of the colossal building was a major engineering feat. Thousands of wooden piles were sunk into the marshy ground to support its 300,000-ton weight, and 48 huge columns were hauled into place. The cathedral opened in 1858 but was designated a museum of atheism during the Soviet era. Officially still a museum today, the church is filled with hundreds of impressive 19th-century works of art.

The Dome
From the dome there are panoramic views of the city that include the Admiralty (see p78) and the Hermitage (see pp84–93). Adorning the gilded dome are angels sculpted by Josef Hermann.

The mosaic icons on the iconostasis are by Bryullov, Neff, and Zhivago.

Angels with Torch
Ivan Vitali created many of the cathedral's sculptures, including the pairs of angels supporting gas torches that crown the four attic corners.

This chapel honors Alexander Nevsky, who defeated the Swedes in 1240 *(see p17).*

★ **Iconostasis**
Three rows of icons surround the royal doors through which a stained-glass window (1843) is visible. Above the doors is Pyotr Klodt's gilded sculpture, Christ in Majesty *(1859).*

The north pediment is ornamented with a bronze relief (1842–4) of the Resurrection, designed by François Lemaire.

Exit

Malachite and lapis lazuli columns frame the iconostasis. About 16,000 kg (35,280 lbs) of malachite decorate the cathedral.

St. Catherine's Chapel has an exquisite white marble iconostasis, crowned by a sculpted Resurrection (1850–4) by Nikolay Pimenov.

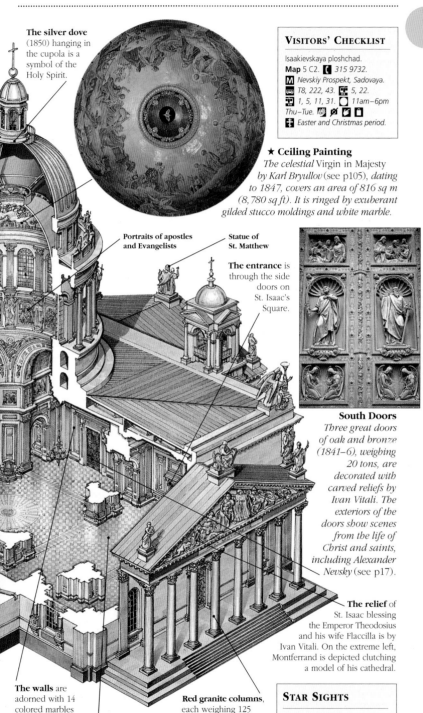

The silver dove (1850) hanging in the cupola is a symbol of the Holy Spirit.

VISITORS' CHECKLIST

Isaakievskaya ploshchad.
Map 5 C2. 315 9732.
Ⓜ *Nevskiy Prospekt, Sadovaya.*
T8, 222, 43. 5, 22.
1, 5, 11, 31. ⏱ 11am–6pm
Thu–Tue.
✝ *Easter and Christmas period.*

★ **Ceiling Painting**
The celestial Virgin in Majesty by Karl Bryullov (see p105), dating to 1847, covers an area of 816 sq m (8,780 sq ft). It is ringed by exuberant gilded stucco moldings and white marble.

Portraits of apostles and Evangelists

Statue of St. Matthew

The entrance is through the side doors on St. Isaac's Square.

South Doors
Three great doors of oak and bronze (1841–6), weighing 20 tons, are decorated with carved reliefs by Ivan Vitali. The exteriors of the doors show scenes from the life of Christ and saints, including Alexander Nevsky (see p17).

The relief of St. Isaac blessing the Emperor Theodosius and his wife Flaccilla is by Ivan Vitali. On the extreme left, Montferrand is depicted clutching a model of his cathedral.

The walls are adorned with 14 colored marbles and 43 other types of semi-precious stones and minerals.

The vast interior covers 4,000 sq m (43,000 sq ft).

Red granite columns, each weighing 125 tons, were transported from Finland by specially constructed ships.

STAR SIGHTS

★ **Iconostasis**

★ **Ceiling Painting**

Malaya Morskaya ulitsa with No. 13 in the middle

Malaya Morskaya Ulitsa ❽

Малая Морская улица
Malaya Morskaya ulitsa

Map 6 D1. 🚌 *10, Э10, 22, 43.* 🚎 *9, 22, 44.* 🚃 *31.*

Malaya morskaya ulitsa is sometimes still referred to as ulitsa Gogolya after the great prose writer, Nikolai Gogol (1809–52), who lived at No. 17 in 1833–6. It was here that Gogol wrote *The Diary of a Madman* and *The Nose*, two biting satires on the archetypal Petersburg bureaucrat "drowned by the trivial, meaningless labors at which he spends his useless life." Gogol's bitingly humorous, fantastical, and grotesque tales reveal a nightmarish and deeply pessimistic view of modern urban life.

The composer Pyotr Tchaikovsky *(see p42)* died in the top floor apartment of No. 13 shortly after the completion of his *Pathétique* symphony in November 1893. Officially he was supposed to have died of cholera, but it is commonly believed that he

committed suicide, due to pressure from Conservatory colleagues wishing to avoid a scandal after Tchaikovsky's alleged homosexual affair.

The house at No. 23 was occupied by the novelist Fyodor Dostoevsky *(see p44)* in 1848–9. It was here that he was arrested and charged with political conspiracy for his participation in the socialist Petrashevsky circle *(see p123)*. Today, the street manages to exude a 19th-century feel despite the many busy stores and businesses.

House of Fabergé ❾

Дом Фаберже
Dom Faberzhe

Bolshaya Morskaya ulitsa 24.
Map 6 D1. ⚫ *to public.* 🚌 *22, Э22, 43.* 🚎 *9, 22, 44.* 🚃 *31.*

The world-famous Fabergé jeweler's was established in Bolshaya Morskaya ulitsa in 1842 by Gustav Fabergé, of French Huguenot origin. It was not until the 1880s that his sons Carl and Agathon abandoned conventional jewelry making for intricate and exquisitely crafted *objets d'art* of a highly innovative design. Most famous of all their works are the imaginatively designed Easter eggs made for the tsars.

In 1900 Carl moved the business from No. 16–18 into custom-built premises at No. 24, where it remained until the Revolution. The exterior, designed by his relative Karl Schmidt, has striking triangular roof gables and multitextured stonework. The original showroom, with its squat red granite pillars, was on the ground floor. It is still a jeweler's, but with no connection to Fabergé. In the workshops above, boy apprentices were trained by master craftsmen in the arts of enameling, engraving, stone cutting, and jeweling.

In 1996, the 150th anniversary of Carl Fabergé's birth was marked by the unveiling of a memorial plaque at No. 24 and of a monument, designed by the sculptor Leonid Aristov and others, on the corner of Zamnevskiy prospekt and prospekt Energetikov.

FABERGÉ EGGS

In 1885 Alexander III commissioned the Fabergé brothers to create an Easter egg for Tsarina Maria Fyodorovna. Inside the shell of gold and white enamel was a beautifully sculpted golden hen. A tradition was established, and by the Revolution, there were 54 Fabergé Easter eggs, no two of which were alike. The *pièce de résistance* is the Siberian Railway Egg, commissioned by Nicholas II in 1900. It contains a miniature replica of the royal train, complete with ruby headlamps, rock crystal windows, and a clockwork engine. The Bonbonnière Egg was commissioned by Kelch, a wealthy industrialist, for his wife Varvara in 1903.

The Kelch Bonbonnière Egg

DEATH OF A POET

In November 1836 Pushkin received an anonymous letter awarding him the title of "Grand Master of the Most Serene Order of Cuckolds." It had been sent by Georges d'Anthès, a rogue cavalry officer who had been making overtures toward Pushkin's wife, the beauty and socialite Natalya Goncharova. Pushkin challenged d'Anthès to a duel and, on the afternoon of January 27, 1837, he met his

A Naumov's painting of Pushkin, fatally wounded after his duel

opponent in snow-bound woodland to the north of the city. D'Anthès fired first and Pushkin was mortally wounded. He died two days later, at 38. D'Anthès was later reduced to the ranks and banished from Russia.

Sign outside the Literary Café

Literary Café ⑩

Литературное сафе
Literaturnoe kafe

Nevskiy prospekt 18. **Map** 6 E1.
📞 312 6057. ⏱ noon–midnight.
Ⓜ *Nevskiy Prospekt.* ♿
See Restaurants and Cafés *p180*.

ALSO KNOWN AS the Café Wulf et Beranger after its original owners, this café is famous for its association with Alexander Pushkin, Russia's greatest poet *(see p43)*. It was here that Pushkin met his second, Konstantin Danzas, before setting out for his ill-fated duel with Baron d'Anthès. The café was a popular haunt for St. Petersburg writers from its beginning, frequented by Fyodor Dostoevsky and the poet Mikhail Lermontov (1814–41), among others.

Despite its hallowed literary importance and elegant setting, in Vasiliy Stasov's handsome building of 1815, the café itself does not merit the high prices.

Palace Square ⑪

Дворцовая площадь
Dvortsovaya ploshchad

Map 6 D1. 🚌 7, Э10, Э47.
🚊 1, 7, 10.

PALACE SQUARE has played a unique role in Russian history. Before the Revolution the square was the setting for colorful military parades, often led by the tsar on horseback. In January 1905, it was the scene of the massacre of "Bloody Sunday" *(see p26)* when gathered troops fired on thousands of unarmed demonstrators. Then, on November 7, 1917, Lenin's Bolshevik supporters secured the Revolution by attacking the Winter Palace *(see p28–9)* from the square, as well as its west side. Today it is still a favorite spot not only for political meetings but also for popular rock concerts *(see p51)*.

The resplendant square is the work of the inspired architect Carlo Rossi *(see p110)*. Facing the Winter Palace on its southern side is Rossi's magnificent General Staff Building (1819–29), the headquarters of the Russian army. Rossi demolished an entire block of houses to make room for it.

The two graceful, curving wings are connected by a triumphal double arch leading to Bolshaya Morskaya ulitsa. The arch is crowned by a lively sculpture of Victory in her chariot (1829), by Stepan Pimenov and Vasiliy Demut-Malinovskiy. Forming the eastern side of this striking architectural ensemble is the Guards Headquarters, designed by Aleksandr Bryullov in 1837–43. To the west lies the Admiralty *(see p78)*.

The Alexander Column in the center of the square is dedicated to Tsar Alexander I for his role in the triumph over Napoleon *(see pp22–3)*. On the pedestal are inscribed the words "To Alexander I, from a grateful Russia." The red granite pillar is balanced only by its immense 600-ton weight, making it the largest free-standing monument in the world. The column was designed by Auguste de Montferrand in 1829, and it took 2,400 soldiers and workmen two years to hew and transport the granite. It was actually erected in 1830–34. The column is surmounted by a bronze angel holding a cross, and together they stand 47 m (154 ft) high.

The Alexander Column and General Staff Building in Palace Square

The Hermitage ⑫

Эрмитаж
Hermitazh

O NE OF THE MOST FAMOUS museums in the world, the Hermitage
has a vast collection occupying a grand ensemble of
buildings. The most impressive is Rastrelli's Baroque Winter
Palace *(see pp92–3)*, to which Catherine the Great soon added
the more intimate Small Hermitage. In 1771–87, she erected the
Large Hermitage to house her rapidly growing collection of art.
The theater was built in 1785–7, and finally the New Hermitage
in 1839–51. The New and Large Hermitages were opened by
Nicholas I in 1852 as a public museum. Between 1918 and 1939,
after the establishment of Soviet power, the Winter Palace was
slowly incorporated into the Hermitage museum ensemble.

The New Hermitage
(1839–51) was
designed by Leo von
Klenze to form a
coherent part of the
Large Hermitage. It
is the only custom-
built museum within
the whole complex.

**Court
ministries**
were located
here until
the 1880s.

Atlantes
*Ten 5-m (16-ft) tall
granite atlantes hold up
what was the public
entrance to the Hermitage
museum from 1852 until
after the Revolution.*

A gallery spanning the
canal connects the theater
to the Large Hermitage and
forms the theater foyer.

The Winter Canal
(see p36)

**The Large
Hermitage** was
designed by Yuriy
Velten to house
Catherine's
paintings.

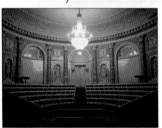

Theater
*During Catherine's reign, there
were regular performances held in
Quarenghi's theater. Today it hosts
exhibitions and concerts (see p194).*

★ Raphael Loggias
*Catherine was so impressed by engravings
of Raphael's frescoes in the Vatican that in
1787 she commissioned copies to be made
on canvas. Small alterations were made,
such as replacing the Pope's coat of arms
with the Romanov two-headed eagle.*

Hanging Gardens
This unusual raised garden is decorated with statues and fountains. During the Siege of Leningrad (see p27) Hermitage curators grew vegetables here.

The Small Hermitage
(1764–75), by Vallin de la Mothe and Yuriy Velten, served as Catherine's retreat from the bustle of the court.

VISITORS' CHECKLIST

Dvortsovaya nab 34–6. **Map** 2 D5.
📞 311 3465. 🚌 7,10, ⊃47,
T128. 🚎 1, 7,10. ⏰ 10:30am–
6pm Tue–Sat; 10.30am–5pm Sun.
Last adm 1 hour before closing.
📷 📹 in English (213 1112 to
book). ♿ 🚻 🎁

Winter Palace Facade
Rastrelli embellished the palace facades with 400 columns and 16 different window designs.

STAR SIGHTS

★ **Winter Palace State Rooms**

★ **Pavilion Hall**

★ **Raphael Loggias**

Palace Square

Main entrance

Neva River

The Winter Palace
(1754–62) was the official residence of the Imperial family until the Revolution.

★ **Pavilion Hall** (1850–8)
Andrey Stakenschneider's striking white marble and gold hall replaced Catherine's original interior. It houses Englishman James Cox's famous Peacock Clock (1772), previously owned by Catherine's lover Prince Potemkin, but now forming part of her collection.

★ **Winter Palace State Rooms**
The tsars spared no expense in decorating rooms such as the Hall of St. George. These rooms were not intended for private life, but to symbolize the power and wealth of imperial Russia.

The Hermitage Collections

CATHERINE THE GREAT purchased some of Western Europe's best collections between 1764 and 1774, acquiring over 2,500 paintings, 10,000 carved gems, 10,000 drawings, and a vast amount of silver and porcelain with which to adorn her palaces. None of her successors matched the quantity of her remarkable purchases. After the Revolution, the nationalization of both royal and private property brought more paintings and works of applied art, making the Hermitage one of the world's leading museums.

The Knights' Hall (1842–51) is used for displays of armor and weapons from the former imperial arsenal.

Stairs to ground floor

Raphael Loggias (*see p84*)

First floor

The Gallery of Ancient Painting (1842–51) is decorated with scenes from ancient literature. It houses a superb display of 19th-century European sculpture.

Ground floor

Special collection

The Hall of Twenty Columns (1842–51) is painted in Etruscan style.

The Litta Madonna (c.1491)
One of two works by Leonardo da Vinci in the museum, this masterpiece was admired by his contemporaries and was frequently copied.

STAR EXHIBITS

★ **Abraham's Sacrifice by Rembrandt**

★ **Ea Haere Ia Oe by Gauguin**

★ **La Danse by Matisse**

GALLERY GUIDE

Individual visitors enter from the Neva embankment, group tours from Palace Square. Start with the interiors of the Winter Palace state rooms on the first floor to get an overview of the museum. Select one or two topics of interest to concentrate on. 19th- and 20th-century European Art is best reached by either of the staircases on the Palace Square side of the Winter Palace.

★ **Abraham's Sacrifice** (1635)
In the 1630s Rembrandt was painting religious scenes in a High Baroque style, using dramatic and striking gestures rather than detail to convey his message.

Main entrance from the Neva embankment

Entrance for tours and guided groups

Second
floor

Stairs to
first floor

Stairs to
first floor

**The numismatic
collection** consists
of more than 90,000
coins and medals. Only
part of it is on display in
temporary exhibitions.

Stairs to
second floor

Stairs to
second floor,
numismatic
collection
only

★ **Ea Haere Ia Oe** (1893)
*This is one of the first paintings
Paul Gauguin did after he had
left France for Tahiti. His desire
to escape convention and
artificiality found expression
in his innovative use of
primitive art as
inspiration.*

★ **La Danse** (1910)
*Henri Matisse used strong tones of three
colors – blue, green, and red – to heighten
the drama and concentration of the
figures, totally lost in their dance.*

KEY TO FLOOR PLAN

☐	**Prehistoric:** Rooms 11–24, 26, 33
☐	**Classical:** 102, 107–117, 121, 127–131
☐	**Oriental:** 34–47, 55–66, 69, 100, 351–371, 381–397
☐	**Russian:** 147–153, 155–189, 190–198, 204, 260, 269–271, 282, 304–307
☐	**Italian and Spanish:** 207–223, 226–242
☐	**Flemish, Dutch, and German:** 243, 245–254, 258–259, 261–268
☐	**French and English:** 272–281, 283–287, 290–302
☐	**19th- and 20th-century European:** 314–325, 328–350
☐	**Temporary exhibition space**
☐	**Nonexhibition space**
☐	**No access**

Statue of Voltaire (1781)
*Catherine the Great corre-
sponded with Voltaire for over
15 years. She commissioned
Jean-Antoine Houdon's
marble statue, in which the
French writer is dressed in the
style of a Greek philosopher.*

The Winter Palace state
rooms *(see pp92–3)* contain
magnificent Russian and
European *objets d'art.*

Exploring the Hermitage Collections

IT IS IMPOSSIBLE to absorb the Hermitage's vast, encyclopedic collection in one or even two visits. Whether it be Scythian gold, antique vases, and cameos, or Iranian silver, every room has something to capture the eye. The furniture, applied art, portraits, and rich clothing of the imperial family went to make up the Russian section, which also includes the superb state rooms. The collection of European paintings was put together largely on the personal taste of the imperial family, while most of the 19th- and 20th-century European art, notably the Impressionists, Matisse, and Picasso, came from private collections after the Revolution. These are now regarded as the most popular exhibits.

Scythian gold stag dating from 7th–6th century BC

PREHISTORIC ART

PREHISTORIC artifacts found all over the former Russian Empire include pots, arrowheads, and sculptures from Paleolithic sites that date back nearly 24,000 years, and rich gold items from the time of the Scythian nomads living in the 7th–3rd centuries BC.

Peter the Great's famous Siberian collection of delicate gold work includes Scythian animal-style brooches, sword handles, and buckles. Objects continued to be discovered in Siberia, and, in 1897, a large, stylized stag, which once decorated an iron shield, was found at Kostromskaya. This is one of the few gold pieces not held in the Special Collection (for which a separate ticket is required), where most precious metals are concentrated.

Greek masters also worked for the Scythians, and from the Dnepr region came a late 5th-century BC comb decorated with naturalistic figures of Scythians fighting, as well as the late 4th-century BC Chertomlyk Vase with scenes of animal taming. Excavations

in the Altai, notably at Pazyryk in 1927–49, uncovered burials nearly 2,500 years old. Many perishable materials were preserved by the frozen land, including textiles, a burial cart, and even a man's heavily tatooed skin.

Gonzaga Cameo (285–246 BC), made in Alexandria

CLASSICAL ART

THE LARGE NUMBER of Greco-Roman marble sculptures range from the famous Tauride Venus of the 3rd century BC, acquired by Peter the Great in

1720, to Roman portrait busts. The smaller objects, however, are the real pride and joy of the Classical department.

The collection of red-figure Attic vases of the 6th–4th centuries BC is unequaled anywhere in the world. Exquisitely proportioned and with a lustrous shine, they are decorated with scenes of libation, episodes from the Trojan War, and in one case a famous image of the sighting of the first swallow (c.510 BC).

In the 4th and 3rd centuries BC, Tanagra was the center for the production of small, elegant terra-cotta figurines. They were discovered in the 19th century and became so popular that fakes were produced on a grand scale. The Russian ambassador in Athens, Pyotr Saburov, put his collection together in the 1880s before the copies appeared, making it unusually valuable.

Catherine the Great's true passion was for carved gems, which she bought en masse. In just ten years, she purchased some 10,000 pieces. The largest and most stunning gem in the Classical collection, however, is the Gonzaga Cameo, which was presented by Napoleon's ex-wife Josephine Beauharnais to Tsar Alexander I in 1814.

The Special Collection contains items of 5th-century gold jewelry made by Athenian craftsmen. They used a filigree technique for working gold so finely that the detail can only be seen properly through a magnifying glass.

ORIENTAL ART

THIS SELECTION of artifacts covers a wide range of cultures, from ancient Egypt and Assyria, through Byzantium, India, Iran, China, Japan, and the marvels of Uzbekistan and Tajikistan. The most complete sections are those where excavations were conducted by the Hermitage, mainly in China and Mongolia before the Revolution, and in Central Asia during the Soviet period.

Dating back to the 19th century BC, at the time of the Middle Egyptian Kingdom, is a seated porphyry portrait of

8th-century fresco of a wounded warrior from Tajikistan

Expeditions to Central Asia have produced carpets, bronzes, and wonderful glazed tiles. Uzbekistan and Tajikistan revealed marvelous complexes of 8th-century buildings at Varaksha, Adjina-Tepe, and Pendzhikent, which have been a source of beautiful frescoes, such as the one depicting the wounded warrior.

RUSSIAN ART

Although major Russian works of art were transferred from the Winter Palace to the Russian Museum *(see pp104–107)* in 1898, everything else that belonged to the imperial family was nationalized after the Revolution. This included anything from official portraits and thrones to looking glasses and petticoats. Over 300 items of apparel belonging to Peter the Great alone survive. Later, the department also began acquiring medieval Russian art, including icons and church utensils.

The tsars from Peter the Great onward invited foreign craftsmen and artists to train

Universal sundial (1714–19) from Peter the Great's collection

pharaoh Amenemhet III. The star of the Egyptian collection is an extremely rare, small, wooden statue of a standing man from the 15th century BC.

From the Far East – Japan, India, Indonesia, China, and Mongolia – comes an array of objects ranging from Buddhist sculptures and fabrics to a display of tiny netsukes (ivory toggles). Excavations at the cave temple of the Thousand Buddhas near Dun Huan in western China revealed 6th–10th-century icons, wall paintings, and plaster sculptures, including the lions that once guarded the cave. During the 13th-century Mongol invasion, the town of Hara-Hoto was destroyed and taken over by the surrounding desert. The sand preserved many usually perishable objects, from 12th-century silks to woodcuts.

From Byzantium come early secular items such as icons, religious utensils, and a 5th-century ivory diptych with scenes from a Roman circus.

Iran produced a large number of silver and bronze vessels, many of which were taken by medieval traders to Siberia and the Urals, where they were rediscovered by specialists in the 19th century. There is also a large collection of traditional Persian miniatures and a rich display of 19th-century Persian court portraits, which combine traditional elements with western oil painting, as in the *Portrait of Fatkh-Ali Shah* (1813–14).

locals. Peter studied with them, and his fascination for practical things is reflected in his large collection of sundials, instruments, and wood-turning lathes that includes the universal sundial by Master John Rowley. A bust by Bartolomeo Carlo Rastrelli (1723–30), however, portrays Peter as the mighty and cruel emperor, rather than the workman.

Russian artists were soon combining traditional art forms with European skills to create such intricate marvels as the openwork walrus ivory vase by Nikolay Vereshchagin (1798) and the large silver sarcophagus and memorial to Alexander Nevsky, truly Russian in scale (1747–52).

The gunsmiths of Tula (south of Moscow) perfected their technique to such an extent that they began producing unique furniture in steel inlaid with gilded bronze, such as the decorative, Empire-style dressing table set (1801).

The state interiors *(see pp92–3)* are the pride of the Russian department, revealing the work of Russian and foreign craftsmen from the mid-18th to the early 20th century. The discovery of large deposits of colored stones in the Urals inspired Russian artists to decorate whole rooms with malachite and to fill every corner of the Winter Palace with marble vases. It was through these rooms that the imperial family paraded on state occasions, greeting courtiers and ambassadors en route in the Field Marshals' Hall.

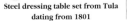

Steel dressing table set from Tula dating from 1801

ITALIAN AND SPANISH ART

THE DISPLAY of Italian art is superb. A few early works reveal the rise of the Renaissance in the 14th and 15th centuries and the styles then in vogue. Simone Martini's stiff *Madonna* (1340–44) contrasts with Fra Angelico's more humane fresco of the Virgin and Child (1424–30).

In the late 15th and early 16th century, artists disputed the merits of line, as practiced by the Florentine school, and the merits of color, virtue of the Venetians. The former can be seen in the *Litta Madonna* (c.1491) and the *Madonna Benois* (1478) by Leonardo da Vinci, a marble *Crouching Boy* by Michelangelo (c.1530), and two early portraits of the Virgin by Raphael (1502 and 1506). The Venetian school dominates with *Judith* by Giorgione (1478–1510) and an array of works by Titian, from his *Young Woman* (1530s) through to late, much darker works such as *St. Sebastian* (1570). Caravaggio's *A Young Man Playing a Lute* (1598) represents the northern schools.

Applied arts such as majolica and Venetian glass are the best way to appreciate later periods. The works of Antonio Canova, 18th-century sculptor (*Cupid and Psyche, The Three Graces*), also have a place of honor.

The Spanish collection on the other hand is more modest, but Spain's Golden-Age heroes can all be seen, from El Greco with *The Apostles Peter and Paul* (1587–92), through to Ribera, Murillo, and Zurbarán with *St. Lawrence* (1636). The portrait of a courtier, *Count Olivares*, painted c.1640 by Velázquez, contrasts with a much earlier genre scene of a peasant's breakfast (1617–18).

Venus and Cupid (1509) by Lucas Cranach the Elder

FLEMISH, DUTCH, AND GERMAN ART

THE SMALL COLLECTION of early paintings from the Netherlands includes a marvelous, jewel-like *Madonna and Child* (1430s) by the Master of Flemalle. He is thought to have been the teacher of Rogier van der Weyden, who is represented by *St. Luke Painting the Madonna* (c.1435).

Over 40 works by Rubens include religious subjects (*The Descent from the Cross*, 1617–18) and scenes from Classical mythology (*Perseus and Andromeda*, 1620–21), as well as landscapes and an immensely obese *Bacchus* (1636–40). His portraits, such as the *Infanta's Maid* (1625), reveal his common Flemish heritage with Van Dyck, whose paintings include a series of formal, full-length portraits and a dashing and romantic self-portrait from the late 1620s.

The Dutch section is rich in Rembrandts. Within a short period of time he produced the dramatic *Abraham's Sacrifice* (1635), the gentle *Flora* (1634), and the brilliant effects of *The Descent from the Cross* (1634). One of his last works was the *Return of the Prodigal Son* (1668–9), with an emotional depth unseen before.

Among the many small-genre paintings is Gerard Terborch's *Glass of Lemonade* from the mid-17th century. All the usual elements of a genre scene are imbued with psychological tension and heavy symbolism.

In the German collection, it is the works of Lucas Cranach the Elder that captivate the viewer. His *Venus and Cupid* (1509), the stylish *Portrait of a Woman in a Hat* (1526), and the tender *Virgin and Child Beneath an Apple Tree* reveal the varied aspects of his talent.

FRENCH AND ENGLISH ART

FRENCH ART was *de rigueur* for collectors in the 18th century, and this period is particularly well represented. Some major artists of the 17th century, including Louis Le Nain and the two brilliant and contrasting painters Claude Lorrain and Nicolas Poussin, are also exhibited. Catherine the Great had more sympathy for the naughtiness of later art, such as Antoine Watteau's elegant *Difficult Proposal*

A Young Man Playing a Lute, by Michelangelo Caravaggio (1573–1610)

Still Life with the Attributes of the Arts (1766), by Jean-Baptiste Chardin

(c.1716), *Stolen Kiss* (1780s) by Jean Honoré Fragonard, and several of François Boucher's fleshy and certainly far-from-virtuous heroines. At the same time, she bought *Still Life with Attributes of the Arts* (1766) by Chardin and, on the advice of Denis Diderot, Jean-Baptiste Greuze's moralizing *The Fruits of a Good Education* (1763). She also patronized sculptors, purchasing works by Etienne-Maurice Falconet (*Winter*, carved 1771) and Jean-Antoine Houdon (*Voltaire*, 1781).

Catherine also acquired English works, including a portrait of the philosopher John Locke (1697) by Sir Godfrey Kneller, who was also author of a portrait of Pyotr Potemkin (1682) in Russian 17th-century court dress. From Sir Joshua Reynolds Catherine commissioned *The Infant Hercules Strangling the Serpents* (1788). Her most daring purchase was of works by the still largely unknown Joseph Wright of Derby. *The Iron Forge* (1773) is a masterpiece of artificial lighting, but *Firework Display at the Castel Sant'Angelo* (1774–5) is a truly romantic fiery spectacle. She provided much work for English cabinet makers and carvers of cameos. She became one of Josiah Wedgwood's most prestigious clients, ordering the famous Green Frog Service for her Chesma Palace *(see p130).*

The Green Frog Service, Wedgwood (1773–4)

19TH- & 20TH-CENTURY EUROPEAN ART

ALTHOUGH THE royal family did not patronize the new movements in art in the 19th century, there were far-sighted private individuals whose collections were nationalized and entered the Hermitage after the 1917 Revolution. Thanks to them, the Barbizon school is represented by works such as Camille Corot's charming silvery *Landscape with a Lake*, French Romanticism by two richly-colored Moroccan scenes of the 1850s by Delacroix, and German Romanticism by Caspar David Friedrich's *On the Prow of the Ship* (1818–20).

Two collectors, Ivan Morozov and Sergey Shchukin, brought the Hermitage its superb array of Impressionist and Post-Impressionist paintings. Monet's art can be admired both in his early *Woman in a Garden* (1860s) and in the later, more exploratory *Waterloo Bridge, Effect of Mist* (1903). Renoir and Degas perpetually returned to women as subjects, as in Renoir's charming *Portrait of the Actress Jeanne Samary* (1878) and Degas's pastels of women washing (1880s–90s). Pissarro's *Boulevard Montmartre in Paris* (1897) is typical of his urban scenes, while Alfred Sisley painted weather effects and light in the French countryside.

A change in color and technique appeared as artists investigated new possibilities. Van Gogh used deeper tones in his *Women of Arles* (1888) and stronger brushstrokes in *Cottages* (1890). Gauguin turned to a different culture for inspiration, and his Tahitian period is represented by enigmatic works such as *Ea Haere Ia Oe* (1893). In *The Smoker* (c.1890–2) and *Mont Ste-Victoire* (1896–8), Cézanne introduced experiments with plane and surface that were to have a strong influence on the next generation.

Matisse played with both color and surface in the carpet-like effect of *The Red Room* (1908–9) and the flatness of the panels *La Musique* and *La Danse* (1909–10). His visit to Morocco introduced new light effects, as in *Arab Coffeehouse* (1913), but it was Picasso who took Cézanne's experiments one stage farther. In early works such as *Visit* (1902) from his Blue Period, Picasso concentrates on mood, but the surface destruction of the Cubist period of 1907–12, including *L'Homme aux Bras Croisés*, fills a whole room.

L'Homme aux Bras Croisés, painted by Pablo Picasso in 1909

The Winter Palace

PRECEDED BY three earlier versions on this site, the existing Winter Palace (1754–62) is a superb example of Russian Baroque. Built for Tsarina Elizabeth, this opulent winter residence was the finest achievement of Bartolomeo Rastrelli. Though the exterior has changed little, the interiors were altered by a number of architects and then largely restored after a fire gutted the palace in 1837. After the assassination of Alexander II in 1881, the imperial family rarely lived here. During World War I a field hospital was set up in the Nicholas Hall and other state rooms. Then, in July 1917, the Provisional Government took the palace as its headquarters, which led to its storming by the Bolsheviks (see pp28–9).

The 1812 Gallery
(1826) has portraits of Russian military heroes of the Napoleonic War, most by English artist George Dawe.

The Armorial Hall
(1839), with its vast gilded columns, covers over 800 sq m (8,600 sq ft). It now houses the European silver collection and a restored imperial carriage.

★ **Small Throne Room**
Dedicated in 1833 to the memory of Peter the Great, this room houses a silver-gilt English throne, made in 1731.

The Field Marshals' Hall
(1833) was the reception room where the devastating fire of 1837 broke out.

The Hall of St. George (1795) has monolithic columns and wall facings of Italian Carrara marble.

The Nicholas Hall, the largest room in the palace, was always used for the first ball of the season.

North facade overlooking the Neva

★ **Jordan Staircase**
This vast, sweeping staircase (1762) was Rastrelli's masterpiece. It was from here that the imperial family watched the Epiphany ceremony of baptism in the Neva, which celebrated Christ's baptism in the Jordan.

★ **Malachite Room**
Over two tons of ornamental stone were used in this sumptuous room (1839), which is decorated with malachite columns and vases, gilded doors and ceiling, and rich parquet flooring.

Alexander Hall
Architect Aleksandr Bryullov employed a mixture of Gothic vaulting and Neo-Classical stucco bas-reliefs of military themes in this reception room of 1837.

BARTOLOMEO RASTRELLI

The Italian architect Rastrelli (1700–71) came to Russia with his father in 1716 to work for Peter the Great. His rich Baroque style became highly fashionable and he was appointed Chief Court Architect in 1738. During Elizabeth's reign, Rastrelli designed several buildings, including the grandiose Winter Palace and impressive Smolnyy Convent *(see p128)*. Unlike Elizabeth, Catherine the Great preferred Classical simplicity, and Rastrelli retired in 1763, after she came to power.

The French Rooms, designed by Bryullov in 1839, house a collection of 18th-century French art.

The White Hall was decorated for the wedding of the future Alexander II in 1841.

South facade on Palace Square

Dark Corridor
The French and Flemish tapestries here include The Marriage of Emperor Constantine, *made in Paris in the 17th century to designs by Rubens.*

The Rotunda (1830) connected the private apartments in the west with the state apartments on the palace's north side.

West wing

The Gothic Library and other rooms in the northwest part of the palace were adapted to suit Nicholas II's bourgeois lifestyle. This wood-paneled library was created by Meltzer in 1894.

The Gold Drawing Room
Created in the 1850s, this room was extravagantly decorated in the 1870s with all-over gilding of walls and ceiling. It houses a display of Western European carved gems.

STAR FEATURES

★ **Small Throne Room**

★ **Malachite Room**

★ **Jordan Staircase**

Millionaires' Street ⓭
Миллионная улица
Millionnaya ulitsa

Map 2 E5. 🚊 *12, 53.*

MILLIONAIRES' STREET takes its name from the aristocrats and members of the imperial family who once lived in its opulent residences. Since the main facades and entrances overlook the river, some house numbers correspond to the embankment side.

On the eve of the Revolution, No. 26 (on the embankment) was the home of Grand Duke Vladimir Aleksandrovich, who was responsible for firing on peaceful demonstrators on Bloody Sunday *(see p26)*. His consort, Maria Pavlovna, was one of Russia's leading society hostesses who gave soirées and balls that eclipsed even those of the imperial court. The building (1867–72), which was designed by Aleksandr Rezanov in the style of the Florentine Renaissance, is now the House of Scholars.

Putyatin's house, at No. 12 Millionaires' Street, witnessed the end of the Romanov dynasty. It was here that Grand Duke Mikhail Aleksandrovich, Nicholas II's brother, signed the decree of abdication in March 1917. Next door, No. 10, was where French novelist Honoré de Balzac stayed in 1843, while courting his future wife, Countess Eveline Hanska. The mid-19th-century house was designed by Andrey Stakenschneider for his own use.

The delicately sculpted facade of No. 10 Millionaires' Street

Gala staircase of the Marble Palace

Marble Palace ⓮
Мраморный дворец
Mramornyy dvorets

Millionnaya ulitsa 5 (entrance from the Field of Mars). **Map** 2 E4. 📞 *314 3448.* 🚊 *12, 53.* ⏰ *10am–5pm Wed–Sun, 10am–4pm Mon.* 🎧 ✅ English.

THE MARBLE PALACE was built as a generous present from Catherine the Great to her lover Grigoriy Orlov, who had been instrumental in bringing her to power in 1762 *(see p22)*. An early example of Neo-Classical architecture, dating from 1768–85, the building is considered to be Antonio Rinaldi's masterpiece.

The palace takes its name from the many and varied types of marble used in its construction. Most of the interiors were reconstructed in the 1840s by Aleksandr Bryullov, although the gala staircase and the Marble Hall are Rinaldi's original work. The latter has marbled walls of gray, green, white, yellow, pink, and lapis lazuli, and a ceiling painting of the *Triumph of Venus* (1780s) by Stefano Torelli.

The palace, which housed a Lenin museum for 55 years, is now a branch of the Russian Museum *(see pp104–107)*. On display are works by foreign artists working in Russia and modern art bequeathed by the German collectors Peter and Irene Ludwig. Their collection includes a Picasso, *Large Heads* (1969), and work by post-war artists Jean-Michel Basquiat, Andy Warhol, Ilya Kabakov, and Roy Lichtenstein.

In front of the palace stands an unusual equestrian statue of Alexander III by Prince Pavel Trubetskoy. Unveiled on ploshchad Vosstaniya in 1911, the ridiculed statue was removed from its original site in 1937 and its vast pedestal was cut up to create statues of new heroes, such as Lenin.

Field of Mars ⓯
Марсово Поле
Marsovo Pole

Map 2 F5. 🚌 *25, 46, 134.* 🚊 *2, 12, 32, 34, 53, 54.*

ONCE A VAST marshy expanse, this area was drained during the 19th century and used for military maneuvers and parades, fairs, and other festivities. It was appropriately named after Mars, the Roman god of war. Between 1917 and 1923 the area, by then a sandy expanse, was nicknamed the "Petersburg Sahara." It was landscaped and transformed into a war memorial. The granite *Monument to Revolutionary Fighters* (1917–19), by Lev Rudnev, and the Eternal Flame (1957) commemorate the victims of the Revolutions of 1917 and the Civil War *(see p27)*.

The west of the square is dominated by an imposing Neo-Classical building

Eternal Flame, Field of Mars

erected by Vasiliy Stasov in 1817–19. This was formerly the barracks of the Pavlovskiy Guards, which were founded by Tsar Paul I in 1796. The military-obsessed tsar is said to have recruited only guardsmen with snub noses like his own. The Pavlovskiy officers were among the first to turn against the tsarist government in the 1917 Revolution *(see pp28–9)*.

Today the huge square is a popular spot for locals in the bright spring evenings, when it is alive with lilac blossoms.

Summer Gardens **16**
Летний сад
Letniy sad

Letniy Sad. **Map** 2 F4. 🚌 *46, 134.*
🚊 *2, 12, 32, 34, 54.* ⏰ *8am–8pm daily (May–Oct: 8am–10pm).*
⚫ *mid–end-Apr.* ♿

IN 1704 Peter the Great commissioned these beautiful gardens, which were among the first in the city. Designed by a Frenchman in the style of Versailles, the allées were planted with imported elms and oaks and adorned with fountains, pavilions, and some 250 Italian statues dating from the 17th and 18th centuries. A flood in 1777 destroyed most of the Summer Gardens, and the English-style garden that exists today is largely the result of Catherine the Great's more sober tastes. A splendid feature is the fine filigree iron grille (1771–84) along the Neva embankment, created by Yuriy Velten and Pyotr Yegorov.

For a century the Summer Gardens were an exclusive preserve of the nobility. When the gardens were opened to "respectably dressed members of the public" by Nicholas I, two Neo-Classical pavilions, the Tea House and the Coffee House, were erected overlooking the Fontanka. These are now used for temporary exhibitions of art by modern St. Petersburg artists.

Nearby, the bronze statue of Ivan Krylov, Russia's most famous writer of fables, is a favorite with Russian children. It was sculpted by Pyotr Klodt in 1854 with charming bas-reliefs on the pedestal depicting animals from his fables.

Ivan Krylov's statue amid autumn foliage in the Summer Gardens

Summer Palace **17**
Летний дворец
Letniy dvorets

Naberezhnaya Kutuzova. **Map** 2 F4.
📞 *314 0374.* ⏰ *11am–7pm daily.*
⚫ *Nov 11–Apr 30.* 🚌 *46, 134.*
🚊 *2, 12, 32, 34, 54.* 📷

BUILT FOR Peter the Great, the modest two-story Summer Palace is the oldest stone building in the city. It was designed in the Dutch style by Domenico Trezzini and was completed in 1714. The celebrated Prussian sculptor Andreas Schlüter created the delightful maritime bas-reliefs (1713), which are an allegorical commentary on Russia's naval triumphs under Peter the Great's stewardship.

Grander than his wooden cabin (*see p73*), Peter's second St. Petersburg residence is still by no means comparable to the magnificent palaces built by his successors.

On the ground floor, the reception room is hung with portraits of the tsar and his ministers and contains Peter's oak Admiralty Chair. The tsar's bedroom has its original four-poster bed with a coverlet of Chinese silk, and an 18th-century ceiling painting showing the triumph of Morpheus, the god of sleep. Next door is the woodshop, which contains some original Russian lathes as well as an elaborately carved wooden meteorological instrument, designed in Dresden in 1714.

The palace boasted the city's first plumbing system with water piped directly into the kitchen. The original black marble sink can still be seen, along with the beautifully tiled kitchen stove and an array of early 18th-century cooking utensils. The kitchen opens onto the exquisite dining room, imaginatively refurbished to convey an atmosphere of domesticity. It was used only for small family gatherings since major banquets were held at the Menshikov Palace (*see p62*).

An original staircase leads up to the first floor and the more lavish suite of Peter's second wife, Catherine. The throne in the aptly named Throne Room is ornamented with Nereids and other sea deities. The glass cupboards in the Green Room once displayed Peter's fascinating collection of curiosities before it was transferred to the Kunstkammer (*see p60*).

The remarkable stove in the Summer Palace's tiled kitchen

GOSTINYY DVOR

THE GREAT BAZAAR, Gostinyy Dvor, was the commercial heart of St. Petersburg at the beginning of the 18th century, and today it still hums with activity. A profusion of smaller retail outlets soon appeared on and around Nevskiy prospekt. Thriving communities of foreign merchants and businessmen also took up residence in the neighborhood.

Until the mid-19th century, shops in this area catered almost exclusively to the luxury side of the market, fulfilling the limitless demand, created by the royal and aristocratic households, for gold and silverware, jewelry, and haute couture. Increasing commercial and financial activity created a new middle class of business entrepreneurs. By the Revolution, banks proliferated around Nevskiy prospekt, their imposing new offices introducing diverse architectural styles to a largely Neo-Classical setting. Today the wheels of capitalism are turning again and Nevskiy prospekt still attracts a wealthy clientele. In contrast to the bustling commercial atmosphere of much of the area is the calm oasis of Arts Square, with the Russian Museum and other institutions that act as a reminder of the city's rich cultural life.

Statues on facade of the Russian Museum

SIGHTS AT A GLANCE

Churches
Armenian Church **7**
Church on Spilled Blood p100 **1**
Kazan Cathedral **15**
Lutheran Church **17**

Museums
Engineers' Castle **2**
Pushkin House-Museum **19**
Russian Museum pp104–107 **3**

Streets and Squares
Arts Square **4**
Nevskiy Prospekt **6**
Ostrovskiy Square **11**
Ulitsa Zodchevo Rossi **12**

Markets and Shops
Apraksin Market **14**
Gostinyy Dvor **8**
Yeliseev's **9**

Palaces
Anichkov Palace **10**
Stroganov Palace **16**
Vorontsov Palace **13**

Hotels
Grand Hotel Europe **5**

Historic Buildings
Glinka Capella **18**
Imperial Stables **20**

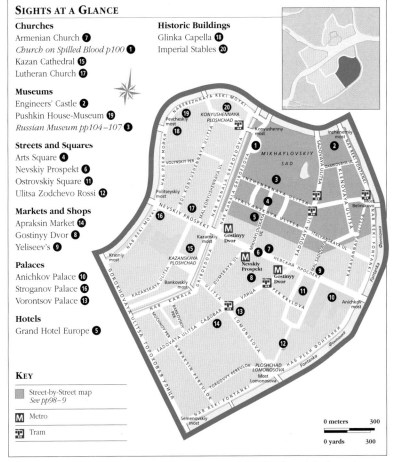

KEY

	Street-by-Street map See pp98–9
M	Metro
🚊	Tram

0 meters	300
0 yards	300

◁ **The busy Nevskiy prospekt, with the Duma tower on the left and the Admiralty in the background**

Street-by-Street: Around Arts Square

Peter the Great statue

THE APTLY NAMED Arts Square, one of Carlo Rossi's finest creations, is surrounded by buildings revealing the city's impressive cultural heritage. The grand palace housing the Russian Museum is flanked by theaters and the Philharmonia concert hall. Behind it are the leafy Mikhaylovskiy Gardens, a haunt of St. Petersburg's intellectuals. The gardens stretch down to the beautiful Moyka River, which together with two other waterways, the Griboedov and Fontanka, creates a shimmering frame for this picturesque area.

★ Church on Spilled Blood
Colorful mosaics and elaborate stone carving are the main features of the church's exterior, which emulates traditional 17th-century Russian style **1**

Mikhaylovskiy Gardens

NABEREZHNAYA REKI MOYK

MOYK

★ Russian Museum
Located in Rossi's Mikhaylovskiy Palace, this famous gallery boasts a fabulous collection of Russian painting, sculpture, and applied art. The grand staircase and White Hall are original features **3**

KANAL GRIBOEDOVA

NAB KANALA GRIBOEDOVA

INZHENERNAYA ULITSA

ITALYANSKAYA ULITSA

Statue of Pushkin (1957)

Nevskiy prospekt

Arts Square
The square's present name derives from the number of cultural institutions situated here. On the western side, the Mussorgsky Theater of Opera and Ballet opened in 1833 **4**

The Great Hall of the Philharmonia is one of the major concert venues in St. Petersburg *(see p194).*

Grand Hotel Europe
This famous St. Petersburg hotel was constructed by Ludwig Fontana in 1873–5. Mighty atlantes adorn its eclectic facade, which stretches all the way down to Nevskiy prospekt **5**

The Panteleymon Bridge was rebuilt in 1907–8 to support the new tramway, but it retains its original Empire-style decor by Lev Ilyin *(see p37)*.

Locator Map
See Street Finder map 6

The bird statue, cast in 1995 by Rezo Gabriadze, refers to a popular rhyme about vodka drinking.

Statue of Peter the Great (1747)

Engineers' Castle
Originally built for Paul I in 1797–1801, this castle was acquired by the Guards Corps of Engineers in 1823. Today it forms part of the Russian Museum and displays historical portraits ❷

STAR SIGHTS

★ **Russian Museum**

★ **Church on Spilled Blood**

KEY

— — — Suggested route

0 meters   100

0 yards   100

Museum of Hygiene, with macabre displays of preserved human organs, was established in 1919 to teach the public about health and hygiene.

The Circus or *"tsirk,"* advertised by a colorful neon sign, began performing in the 19th century when it was known as the Ciniselli Circus. It still offers traditional performances *(see p193)* in its original venue by the Fontanka.

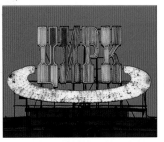

Map labels:
NAB. REKI FONTANKA
ZAMKOVAYA ULITSA
FONTANKA
INZHENERNAYA ULITSA
KLENOVAYA ALLEYA
KARAVANNAYA ULITSA
PLOSHCHAD BELINSKOVO
SADOVAYA ULITSA
MANEZHNAYA PLOSHCHAD
Nevskiy prospekt

Church on Spilled Blood ①

Храм Спас-на-Крови

Khram Spas-na-Krovi

VISITORS' CHECKLIST

Konyushennaya ploshchad. **Map** 2 E5. **☎** 315 1636. **Ⓜ** *Nevskiy Prospekt, Gostinyy Dvor.* **▨** *12, 53.* **◘** *11am–6pm Thu–Tue (last ticket sold 5:30pm).* 🎫 🚫 📷 🚻 🏛

THE CHURCH ON SPILLED BLOOD was built on the spot where Tsar Alexander II was murdered on March 1, 1881 *(see p26)*. In 1883 his successor, Alexander III, launched a competition for a permanent memorial. The winning design, in the Russian Revival style favored by the tsar himself, was by Alfred Parland and Ignatiy Malyshev. The foundation stone was laid in October 1883, but the building took almost a quarter of a century to complete.

A riot of color, the overall effect of the church is created by the imaginative juxtaposition of materials. Inside, more than 20 types of minerals, including jasper, rhodonite, porphyry, and Italian marble are lavished on the mosaics of the iconostasis, icon cases, canopy, and floor. The interior is temporarily open but might close for more restoration.

Mosaic Tympanum
Mosaic panels showing scenes from the New Testament adorn the exterior. They were based on designs by artists such as Viktor Vasnetsov and Mikhail Nesterov.

The tent-roofed steeple is 81 m (265 ft) high.

Coat of Arms
The 144 mosaic coats of arms on the bell tower represent the regions, towns, and provinces of the Russian empire. They were intended to reflect the grief shared by all Russians in the wake of Alexander's assassination.

Intricate Detailing
The flamboyant Russian Revival style of the exterior provides a dramatic contrast to the Neo-Classical and Baroque architecture that dominates the center of St. Petersburg.

Jeweler's enamel was used to cover the 1,000 sq m (10,760 sq ft) surface of the five domes.

Glazed ceramic tiles enliven the facade.

Mosaic portraits of the saints are set in tiers of *kokoshniki* gables. Almost 7,000 sq m (75,300 sq ft) of mosaics embellish the church's extravagant exterior.

Twenty dark red plaques of Norwegian granite are engraved in gilt letters with the most outstanding events of Alexander II's reign (1855–81). Among the historic events recorded are the emancipation of the serfs in 1861 and the conquest of Central Asia (1860–81).

Window Frames
The windows are flanked by carved columns of ornate Estonian marble. The casings are in the form of double and triple kokoshniki *(tiered decorative arches).*

South facade of the Engineer's Castle and statue of Peter the Great

Engineers' Castle ➋
Инженерный замок
Inzhenernyy zamok

Sadovaya ulitsa 2. **Map** 2 F5.
📞 210 4173. 🚌 46, 134, T74.
🚊 2, 12, 34, 54. ⏰ 10am–6pm
Wed–Mon. 📷 🎫 English.

T HE IMPOSING red brick castle overlooking the Moyka and Fontanka Rivers was originally named Mikhaylovskiy Castle. It was erected in 1797–1801 by Vasiliy Bazhenov and Vincenzo Brenna for Tsar Paul I. The tsar's obsessive fear of being assassinated led him to surround his new residence with moats and drawbridges, and to build a secret underground passage to the barracks on the Field of Mars *(see p94)*. All these precautions proved futile, and after living in his fortified castle for just 40 days, Paul fell victim to a military conspiracy that resulted in his murder *(see p22)*.

In 1823 the fortress was acquired by the Guards Corps of Engineers and was given its current name. The school's most famous graduate was Dostoevsky *(see p123)*. Today the castle serves as a branch of the nearby Russian Museum.

Paintings of the city's prominent citizens are hung in the portrait gallery, and there is a display on the building's military associations. The Church of the Archangel Michael can be accessed via the exhibition and is a good example of Brenna's Neo-Classical style.

In front of the castle stands a bronze statue of Peter the Great on horseback, designed by Bartolomeo Carlo Rastrelli and cast in 1747.

Russian Museum ➌
See pp104–107.

Arts Square ➍
Площадь Искусств
Ploshchad Iskusstv

Map 6 F1. Ⓜ *Nevskiy Prospekt, Gostinyy Dvor.*

S EVERAL OF THE CITY'S leading cultural institutions are located on this imposing Neo-Classical square, hence its name. The attractive square was designed by Carlo Rossi in the early 19th century to harmonize with the magnificent Mikhaylovskiy Palace (now the Russian Museum), which stands on its northern side.

On the opposite side of the square is the Great Hall of the St. Petersburg Philharmonia, also known as the Shostakovich Hall *(see p43)*. This is where the Philharmonic Orchestra has been based since the 1920s *(see p194)*. Constructed by

Paul Jacot in 1834–9, it started as a Nobles' Club where concerts were held. Among the works premiered here were Beethoven's *Missa Solemnis* in 1824 and Tchaikovsky's *(see p45) Pathétique* in 1893.

On the square's western side is the Mussorgsky Theater of Opera and Ballet *(see p194)*, rebuilt by Albert Kavos in the mid-19th century. In the center of the square is a sculpture of one of Russia's greatest literary figures, Alexander Pushkin *(see p44)*. The statue was executed by leading post-war sculptor Mikhail Anikushin.

Grand Hotel Europe's elegant Style-Moderne restaurant *(see p181)*

Grand Hotel Europe ➎
Гранд Отель Европа
Grand Otel Evropa

Mikhaylovskaya ulitsa 1/7. **Map** 6 F1.
📞 119 6000. Ⓜ *Nevskiy Prospekt, Gostinyy Dvor.* ♿ *See Where to Stay p173.*

O NE OF RUSSIA'S most famous hotels, the ornate Grand Hotel Europe (1873–5) was designed by Ludwig Fontana. The building owes much of its character to alterations made in the 1910s by Style-Moderne architect Fyodor Lidval.

Before the Revolution, the hotel's magnificent restaurant was a favorite rendezvous for members of the diplomatic corps and secret police. In the 1970s, the hotel café became a popular meeting place for young intellectuals and artists.

Pushkin's statue in front of the Russian Museum, Arts Square

The Church on Spilled Blood, a magical reminder of old Russia ▷

Russian Museum ❸

Русский Музей
Russkiy Muzey

Tʜɪs ᴍᴜsᴇᴜᴍ is housed in the Mikhaylovskiy Palace, one of Carlo Rossi's finest Neo-Classical creations, built in 1819–25 for Grand Duke Mikhail Pavlovich. Alexander III's plans to create a public museum were realized by his son, Nicholas II, when the Russian Museum opened here in 1898. Today, the museum holds one of the world's greatest collections of Russian art.

Stairs to ground floor

The Benois Wing, named after its main architect Leonty Benois, was added in 1913–19.

Stairs to ground floor

Room 79 usually displays paintings by avant-garde artists such as Chagall, Malevich, and Kandinsky.

Entrance to temporary exhibitions

Ticket office

★ **Mother** (1915)
The peasant woman in Kuzma Petrov-Vodkin's painting represents the future, while her Madonna-like pose echoes the Italian Renaissance.

Portrait of Sergey Diaghilev (1906)
Leon Bakst's painting reveals the determination and vitality of the famous impresario and founder of the Ballets Russes. Bakst also designed costumes for the Ballets (see p119).

STAR EXHIBITS

- ★ **The Last Day of Pompeii by Bryullov**
- ★ **Mother by Petrov-Vodkin**
- ★ **Barge Haulers on the Volga by Repin**

Stairs to first floor of Benois Wing

GALLERY GUIDE

The main entrance on Arts Square leads to the ticket office in the basement. The exhibition starts on the first floor. It is arranged chronologically in numbered rooms starting with icons in Room 1. It continues on the ground floor of the main building and Rossi Wing, ending with modern art on the first floor of the Benois Wing.

Folk-art Toy (1930s)
This clay toy from Dykomovo is part of the colorful selection of folk art that also includes lacquer boxes, painted ceramics, and textiles.

★ **The Last Day of Pompeii** (1833)
Karl Bryullov's Classical subject embodies the aesthetic principles of the Academy of Arts. This vivid depiction of the eruption of Vesuvius won him the Grand Prix at the Paris Salon.

VISITORS' CHECKLIST

Inzhenernaya ulitsa 4. **Map** 6 F1.
311 1465. M *Nevskiy Pros-pekt, Gostinyy Dvor.* Э1, 7, T8, 22, Э22, 43, Э47, T128. 1, 5, 7, 10, 22. 2, 5, 12, 14, 34, 54. 10am–5pm Mon; 10am–6pm Wed–Sun (last ticket an hour before closing). *Elevators/ ramps being added.* *English* (tel: 315 3565). *English.*

★ **Barge Haulers on the Volga** (1870–73)
Ilya Repin was the most famous member of the Wanderers, a group of artists dedicated to social realism and Russian themes. His powerful indictment of forced labor imbues the oppressed victims with somber dignity.

The White Hall contains original Empire-style furniture by Carlo Rossi.

Rossi Wing

Stairs to ground floor

Start of exhibition

Entrances from basement ticket office

A Meal in the Monastery (1865–76)
Vasiliy Perov's politically motivated canvas exposes the hypocrisy of the Orthodox clergy, with the juxta-position of good and evil, rich and poor, false piety and true faith.

The portico of eight Corinthian columns is the central feature of Rossi's facade. Behind is a frieze of Classical figures, designed by Rossi and executed by Demut-Malinovskiy.

Stairs to first floor

The main entrance is through a small door that leads to the basement with a ticket office, a cloakroom, toilets, and a café.

KEY

☐ Icons
☐ 1700–1860
☐ The Wanderers and Fin de Siècle
☐ 20th-century art
☐ Folk art
☐ Temporary exhibitions
☐ Nonexhibition space

Exploring the Russian Museum

Housing one of the world's greatest collections of Russian art, the museum originally housed officially approved works from the Academy of Arts *(see p63)*. When the museum was nationalized after the Revolution, art was transferred from palaces, churches, and private collections. By the 1930s, Socialist Realism had become state policy, and avant-garde works were stored away, to re-emerge with the advent of *perestroika* in the 1980s.

Portrait of E I Nelidova (1773),
by Dmitriy Levitskiy

The Angel with the Golden Hair, **an icon from the early 12th century**

Icons

The museum's fine collection begins with icons dating from the 12th–17th centuries. Russian icons derive from the Orthodox tradition and thus, just like Byzantine icons, tend to be somber, marked by an absence of movement and a remote, mystic characterization of the saints. A superb example is one of the earliest icons, *The Angel with the Golden Hair,* in which the large, expressive eyes and delicate modeling of the archangel Gabriel's face convey a sense of ethereal grace.

The Novgorod School *(see p163)* encouraged a much bolder and brighter style with a greater sense of drama and movement. And yet it is the poetically expressive and technically refined work of Andrey Rublev (c.1340–c.1430) that is considered by many to mark the pinnacle of Russian icon painting.

1700–1860

The first secular portraits (which owed much to the static quality of the icons) appeared in the second half of the 17th century. However, it was under Peter the Great that Russian painting fully cast off from its Byzantine moorings. Peter himself was the first patron to send young artists, often serfs, to study abroad. Secular art gained momentum in 1757 with the establishment of the Academy of Arts *(see p63)*, which placed a heavy emphasis on Classical and mythological subjects.

European influence permeates the work of Russia's first important portrait painters, Ivan Nikitin (1688–1741) and Andrey Matveev (1701–39). The art of portraiture matured with Dmitriy Levitskiy (1735–1822), among whose best-known works is a series of portraits of noble girls from the Smolnyy Institute.

Russian landscape painting was stimulated by the Romantic movement and in particular artists who sought inspiration abroad, including Silvestr Shchedrin (1791–1830) and Fyodor Matveev (1758–1826).

Ivan Aivazovskiy's (1817–1900) vast marine paintings, however, have something purely Russian in their scale and mood. Romanticism also influenced history painters such as Karl Bryullov (1799–1852), as in his depiction of *The Last Day of Pompeii.*

The Wanderers and Fin de Siècle

In 1863 a group of students led by Ivan Kramskoy (1837–87) rebelled against the Academy of Arts. Seven years later they went on to set up the Association of Traveling Art Exhibitions, and came to be known as the Wanderers *(Peredvizhniki)* or Itinerants. They demanded that painting be more socially relevant and were fundamentally committed to Russian subject matter.

The most versatile of the Wanderers was Ilya Repin *(see p43)*, whose bold canvas

Knight at the Crossroads (1882), by Viktor Vasnetsov

The Six-Winged Seraph (1904), by Mikhail Vrubel

Barge Haulers on the Volga combines a powerful attack on forced labor with a romantic view of the Russian people. *A Meal in the Monastery* by Vasiliy Perov (1833–82) is a satirical and equally effective attack on social injustice.

The nationalist element led history painters such as Nikolay Ge (1831–94) and Vasiliy Surikov (1848–1916) to turn to Russian history for inspiration, treating their subjects with a new psychological acuity, as in Ge's canvas of 1871–2, in which Peter the Great interrogates his sullenly resistant son.

The general Slavic revival also breathed new life into landscape painting, concentrating on the beauties of the Russian countryside. The master of the genre was Isaak Levitan (1860–1900), whose *Golden Autumn Village,* dated 1889, is almost Impressionist in style, a sign perhaps that the ascendancy of the Wanderers was coming to an end.

Viktor Vasnetsov (1848–1926) turned to Russia's heroic, and often legendary, pre-European past in realistically painted canvases such as the *Knight at the Crossroads.* A haunting metaphor for Russia's uncertain future, the painting reveals that Vasnetsov was unable to avoid the fin-de-siècle melancholy and mysticism that was so potently expressed in the work of the next up-and-coming generation of artists, notably the Symbolists.

20TH-CENTURY ART

THE DARK, brooding canvases of Symbolist Mikhail Vrubel (1856–1910) combine Russian and religious themes with a more international outlook. Vrubel used color and form to depict emotion and in *The Six-Winged Seraph* he employs a broken, vibrant surface to express tension.

Another major contribution to 20th-century art was the "World of Art" movement, founded by Alexandre Benois and Sergey Diaghilev in the 1890s *(see p26).* It rejected the notion of "socially useful art" in favor of a new tenet, "art pure and unfettered," and also opened up Russian painting to Western influences. Many members of the group,

Portrait of the Director Vsevolod Meyerhold (1916), Boris Grigorev

including Benois and Leon Bakst, designed stage sets and costumes for Diaghilev's Ballets Russes *(see p119).*

The Russian avant-garde grew out of these local influences, plus the art of Cézanne, Picasso, and Matisse. Mikhail Larionov (1881–1964) and Natalya Goncharova (1881–1962) both made brilliant use of Russian folk art as inspiration for primitivist works such as Goncharova's *Bleaching Canvas* (1908). They often altered their style in response to changing stimuli and later turned to Futurism's cult of the machine, as in Goncharova's *Cyclist* (1913) *(see p40).*

The link between innovation in painting and the arts in general at this time is strikingly depicted in Boris Grigorev's angular portrait of Meyerhold, himself renowned for his radical approach to theater.

Kazimir Malevich's (1878–1935) fascination with the juxtaposition of simple geometric shapes inspired the Suprematist movement. Vasily Kandinsky (1866–1944), a leading member of Munich's Blaue Reiter group, was also a key figure in the growth of Russian abstract art.

Marc Chagall (1887–1985), El Lissitskiy (1890–1941), and Alexander Rodchenko (1891–1956) are also represented.

Due to the high demand for the loan of avant-garde works abroad, a changing selection by the major artists is on display.

FOLK ART

FOLK ART became a strong influence on the development of modern Russian art in the 1860s, when the wealthy industrialist and patron Savva Mamontov established an artists' colony at Abramtsevo, near Moscow. Vasiliy Polenov (1844–1927), Ilya Repin and Viktor Vasnetsov were among the painters encouraged to work alongside, and learn from, the serf craftsmen on the estate. The museum's collection of folk art is wonderfully diverse and includes exquisitely embroidered tapestries, traditional headdresses, painted tiles, porcelain toys, and lacquered spoons and dishes.

Nevskiy Prospekt ❻
Невский проспект
Nevskiy prospekt

Map 6 D1–8 D3. Ⓜ *Nevskiy Prospekt, Gostinyy Dvor. See also pp46–9.*

Russia's most famous street, Nevskiy prospekt, is also St. Petersburg's main thoroughfare and artery. In the 1830s, the novelist Nikolai Gogol *(see p42)* declared with great pride: "There is nothing finer than Nevskiy Avenue… in St. Petersburg it is everything… is there anything more gay, more brilliant, more resplendent than this beautiful street of our capital?" In this respect very little has actually changed, for Nevskiy prospekt's intrinsic "all-power-ful" value still prevails today.

Laid out in the early days of the city, it was first known as the Great Perspective Road, running 4.5 km (3 miles) from the Admiralty *(see p78)* to the Alexander Nevsky Monastery *(see pp130–31)*. In spite of roaming wolves and uncontrollable flooding from the Neva *(see p37)* which made the avenue navigable in 1721, fine mansions, such as the Stroganov Palace *(see p116)* soon started to appear. Shops and bazaars, catering to the nobility, and inns for traveling merchants followed. A magnet pulling rich and poor alike, by the mid-18th century the avenue had become the place to see and be seen, to meet for gossip, business, and pleasure.

Today, the street still teems with people until late into the night throughout the year. Many of the city's sights are close to the stretch between the Admiralty and Anichkov Bridge *(see pp46–7)*. Some of the best shops *(see pp186–7)* can be found around Gostinyy dvor and Passazh arcade. Nevskiy prospekt also offers a wealth of cultural interest: the Small Philharmonia concert hall *(see p194)*, the exclusive Grand Hotel Europe *(see p101)*, the city's national library, and a variety of museums, churches, shops, movie theaters, and eateries. All this attracts people from all over town.

Armenian Church portico (1771–9)

Armenian Church ❼
Армянская церковь
Armyanskaya tserkov

Nevskiy prospekt 40–42. **Map** 6 F1. Ⓜ *Gostinyy Dvor.* ◯ 9am–10pm.

Yuriy Velten designed the beautiful blue and white Armenian Church of St. Catherine, with its Neo-Classical portico and single cupola. The church, which opened in 1780, was financed by a wealthy Armenian businessman called Ioakim Lazarev, who acquired the money from the sale of a Persian diamond that Count Grigoriy Orlov purchased for Catherine the Great *(see p22)*.

Closed in 1930, the building has now been returned to the Armenian community, and visitors are welcome to attend a service or view the restoration work that is under way.

Gostinyy Dvor ❽
Гостиный двор
Gostinyy dvor

Nevskiy pr 35. **Map** 6 F2. 📞 312 4165. Ⓜ *Gostinyy Dvor.* ◯ 10am–9pm Mon–Sat, 11am–6pm Sun.

The term *gostinyy dvor* originally meant a coaching inn, but as trade developed around the inns, with traveling merchants setting up their stalls, it later came to mean "trading rows." The original wooden structure of this *gostinyy dvor* was destroyed by fire in 1736. Twenty years later, Bartolomeo Rastrelli

View along the bustle of Nevskiy prospekt, the hub of St. Petersburg

designed a new building but the project proved too costly and ambitious. Building recommenced in 1761 and continued until 1785. Vallin de la Mothe created the striking sequence of columned arcades and massive porticos. The prominent yellow building forms an irregular quadrangle that is bounded on one side by Nevskiy prospekt. The combined length of its facades is nearly 1 km (3,300 ft).

In the 19th century the gallery became a fashionable promenade where more than 5,000 people were employed. Serious damage during the Siege of Leningrad *(see p27)* led to major reconstruction, making it more like a modern department store. Even now, with all the changes, it has retained its layout of "stalls" of individual trading units. Today it includes branches of foreign stores and a wide range of goods, making it the city's most important store *(see p187)*.

Style-Moderne stained-glass windows in Yeliseev's food store

Columned arcades, Gostinyy dvor

Yeliseev's

Елисеевский гастроном
Yeliseevskiy gastronom

Nevskiy prospekt 56. **Map** 6 F1.
[311 9323. M *Gostinyy Dvor.*
O *9am–9pm Mon–Fri, 10am–9pm Sat, 10am–7pm Sun.* ● *Public holidays.*

THE SUCCESSFUL Yeliseev dynasty was founded by Pyotr Yeliseev, an ambitious peasant who, in 1813, opened a wine shop on Nevskiy prospekt. By the turn of the century his grandsons owned a chocolate factory, numerous houses, inns and this famous food store. Housed in the city's most opulent Style-Moderne building, designed by Gavriil Baranovskiy in 1901–3, it is adorned with bronzes, heroic sculptures, and huge windows. The equally impressive interior, with its stained-glass windows, marble counters, and crystal chandeliers, steals the attention from the delicacies on sale *(see p190)*. A plaque by the main door honors the grandsons.

Anichkov Palace

Аничков дворец
Anichkov dvorets

Nevskiy prospekt 39. **Map** 7 A2.
M *Gostinyy Dvor.* ● *to public except for special events.*

IN THE EARLY days, the broad Fontanka river was lined by palaces accessible mainly by boat. One of them was the Anichkov Palace (1741–50), remodeled in Baroque style in 1754. The palace was a gift from Tsarina Elizabeth to her lover Aleksey Razumovskiy. It was named after Lieutenant Colonel Mikhail Anichkov, who set up camp on this site at the time of the founding of the city. Over the years the palace was rebuilt and altered many times, according to the tastes of each successive owner. After Razumovskiy's death, Catherine the Great in turn gave the building to her lover, Prince Potemkin *(see p25)*. In the early 19th century, Neo-Classical details were added by Carlo Rossi.

The palace then became the traditional winter residence of the heir to the throne. When Alexander III became tsar in 1881, however, he continued to live here, rather than move to the Winter Palace as was customary. After his death, his widow Maria Fyodorovna stayed on until the Revolution.

The palace originally had large gardens to the west but these were curtailed in 1816 when Ostrovskiy Square *(see p110)* was created and two Neo-Classical pavilions were added. The elegant colonnaded building overlooking the Fontanka to the east had been another addition to the palace, commissioned by Giacomo Quarenghi in 1803–5. It was initially built as an arcade where goods from the imperial factories were stored before being allocated to the palaces. Later it was converted into government offices.

Quarenghi's addition to the Anichkov Palace from Nevskiy prospekt

Porticoed facade of Aleksandrinskiy Theater (1828–32), Ostrovskiy Square

Ostrovskiy Square ⓫
Площадь Островского
Ploshchad Ostrovskovo

Map 6 F2. **M** *Gostinyy Dvor.* **Russian National Library** ⬤ *to foreigners unless special permission is obtained.* **Theater Museum** ◻ *11am–6pm Thu–Mon; noon–7pm Wed.* ⬤ *public hols.* 🎫 ✔

O NE OF RUSSIA'S most brilliant and prolific architects, Carlo Rossi, created this early 19th-century square, which is now named in honor of the prominent dramatist Aleksandr Ostrovskiy (1823–86).

The focal point of the square is the elegant Aleksandrinskiy Theater *(see p194)*, designed in the Neo-Classical style that Rossi favored. The portico of six Corinthian columns is crowned with a chariot of Apollo by Stepan Pimenov.

The building was the new home to Russia's oldest theater company, set up in 1756. Plays premiered here included Nikolai Gogol's *The Inspector General* (1836) and Anton Chekhov's *The Seagull* (1901). In Soviet times the theater was renamed the Pushkin Theater.

In the garden just in front of the theater is a monument to Catherine the Great, surprisingly the only one to be found in St. Petersburg. It was designed principally by Mikhail Mikeshin and unveiled in 1873. The statue depicts Catherine surrounded by states-men and other worthies and includes the female president (1783–96) of the Academy of Sciences, Princess Yekaterina Dashkova.

On the west side of the square, opposite the Anichkov Palace *(see p109)* is an elegant colonnade decorated with Classical sculptures. This is the extension of the Russian Library, made by Rossi in 1828–34. Founded in 1795, the library currently holds more than 28 million items. A prized possession is the personal library of the French philosopher Voltaire, which Catherine the Great purchased to show her appreciation of her sometime mentor and correspondent.

In the southeast corner of the square, at No. 6, is the Theater Museum, which traces the evolution of the Russian stage from its origins in mid-18th-century serf and imperial theaters. Amid the eclectic array of playbills, photographs, costumes, set designs, and other artifacts is the costume worn by the famous bass, Fyodor Shalyapin, in the opera *Boris Godunov*. There are also some bold and imaginative set designs by one of the great innovators of modern theater, the director Vsevolod Meyerhold (1874–1940).

Ulitsa Zodchevo Rossi ⓬
Улица Зодчего Росси
Ulitsa Zodchevo Rossi

Map 6 F2. **M** *Gostinyy Dvor.*

T HERE COULD BE no better memorial to Carlo Rossi than the near perfect architectural ensemble of identical arcades and colonnades forming Architect Rossi Street. The 22-m (72-ft) high buildings stand precisely 22 m (72 ft) apart and are 220 m (720 ft) in length. Viewed from ploshchad Lomonosova, the perspective hypnotically coaxes the eye towards the Aleksandrinskiy Theater.

At No. 2 is the home of the former Imperial School of Ballet, now named after the teacher Agrippina Vaganova (1879–1951), one of the few dancers not to emigrate after the Revolution. The school started in 1738 when Jean-Baptiste Landé began training orphans and palace servants' children to take part in court entertainment. It moved to its present quarters in 1836 and has since produced many of Russia's most celebrated dancers *(see p118)*, including Anna Pavlova and Rudolf Nureyev.

19th-century photograph of ulitsa Zodchevo Rossi (1828–34)

ARCHITECT CARLO ROSSI

Carlo Rossi (1775–1849) was one of the last great exponents of Neo-Classicism in St. Petersburg. He found an ideal client in Alexander I, who shared his belief in the use of architecture to express the power of the autocracy. By the time of his death, Rossi had created no fewer than 12 of St. Petersburg's impressive streets and 13 of its squares, including Palace Square *(see p83)*. Rossi's status as Alexander I's favorite architect encouraged rumors that Rossi was the offspring of an affair between Tsar Paul I and Rossi's Italian ballerina mother.

Central corpus of Vorontsov Palace

Vorontsov Palace ⑬

Воронцовский дворец
Vorontsovskiy dvorets

Sadovaya ulitsa 26. **Map** 6 F2.
⬤ *to public.* Ⓜ *Gostinyy Dvor,
Sennaya Ploshchad.*

T HE MOST EXCLUSIVE military
school in the Russian
empire, the Corps des Pages,
occupied the Vorontsov Palace
from 1810–1918. Among those
privileged enough to study
here were a number of the
Decembrists *(see pp22–3)* and
Prince Felix Yusupov *(see
p121)*. Today the palace houses
the Suvorov Military Academy.
Designed by Bartolomeo
Rastrelli *(see p93)*, the handsome palace that once stood in
its own extensive grounds
was built in 1749–57 for Prince
Mikhail Vorontsov, one of
Tsarina Elizabeth's leading
ministers. Rastrelli's graceful
wrought-iron railings are
among the earliest examples
of their kind in Russia.

Apraksin Market ⑭

Апраксин двор
Apraksin dvor

Sadovaya ulitsa. **Map** 6 E2.
Ⓜ *Gostinyy Dvor, Sennaya
Ploshchad.* ⃝ *9am–5pm.*

F OUNDED in the late 18th century, the market takes its
name from the Apraksin family
who owned the land it was
built on. When fire destroyed
the wooden stalls in 1862, the
arcade was erected. By 1900
there were more than 600
outlets selling everything from
food, wine, and spices to furs,
furniture, and haberdashery.
Today, stalls extend all the

way along Apraksin pereulok,
and in a yard *(see p187)*
behind the arcade, toys, car
parts, cigarettes, watches, TV
sets, alcohol, and leather jackets are sold.

Kazan Cathedral ⑮

Казанский собор
Kazanskiy sobor

Kazanskaya pl 2. **Map** 6 E1. ▐ *311
0495.* Ⓜ *Nevskiy Prospekt.* ⃝ *11am–
6pm Mon, Tue, Thu, Fri; noon–6pm
Sat; 12:30pm–6pm Sun.* ▮

O NE OF St. Peterburg's most
majestic churches, the
Kazan Cathedral was commissioned by Paul I and took over
a decade to build (1801–11).
The impressive design by serf
architect Andrey Voronikhin
was inspired by St. Peter's in
Rome. Its 111-m (364-ft) long,
curved colonnade disguises the
orientation of the building,
which runs parallel to Nevskiy
prospekt, conforming to a religious stipulation that the main
altar face east. Voronikhin originally intended to duplicate the
colonnade on the south side.
The cathedral is named after
the miracle-working icon of
Kazan, Mother of God, which

it once housed. The icon,
now in the Prince Vladimir
Cathedral on Petrogradskaya,
is said to have been responsible for delivering Moscow
from the Poles in 1612.
The interior decoration is
generally subdued. Its most
impressive features are the
great 80-m (262-ft) high dome
and the massive pink Finnish
granite columns with bronze
capitals and bases. The nave
still houses an exhibition on
Christianity that was set up
to supersede a museum of
atheism set up by the Communists during a time of
religious repression.
The cathedral's completion
coincided almost exactly with
the war against Napoleon *(see
p22)*. In 1813 Field Marshal
Mikhail Kutuzov (1745–1813),
who skillfully masterminded
the retreat from Moscow, was
buried here in the north chapel with full military honors.
Kutuzov has been immortal-
ized in Tolstoy's great novel
War and Peace (1865–9). His
statue and that of his comrade-
in-arms, Mikhail Barclay de
Tolly (1761–1818), both by
Boris Orlovskiy, have stood
in Kazanskaya ploshchad outside the cathedral since 1837.

Pink granite columns and mosaic floor in main nave, Kazan Cathedral

Stroganov Palace 🔟
Строгановский дворец
Stroganovskiy dvorets

Nevskiy prospekt 17. **Map** 6 E1.
🅼 *Nevskiy Prospekt.* 🅲 *311 8238.*
🅾 *for temporary exhibitions.* 🈳

Neo-Romanesque portal of the
Lutheran Church (1832–8)

THIS BAROQUE masterpiece was designed in 1752–4 by Bartolomeo Rastrelli *(see p93).* Commissioned by the enormously wealthy Count Sergey Stroganov, the palace was occupied by his descendants until the Revolution. The Stroganovs amassed their huge fortune through the monopoly they held on salt, which came from mines in their vast territories in the north.

The green and white palace, which overlooks both Nevskiy prospekt and the Moyka River, was one of the city's most impressive private residences. The magnificent river facade is decorated with Doric columns, cornices, pediments, and inventive window surrounds.

The Stroganovs were noted collectors of everything from Egyptian antiquities and Roman coins to icons and Old Masters. The palace was nationalized after the Revolution and then preserved for ten years as a museum of the life of the decadent aristocracy. When it was closed, some of the objects were auctioned in the West, and the rest were transferred

to the Hermitage *(see pp84–93).* The Russian Museum *(see pp104–107)* aims to revive the idea of a museum of noble life and, in the meantime, is opening rooms as restoration finishes, showing temporary exhibitions of objects relating to the Stroganov family.

Lutheran Church 🔟
Лютеранская церковь
Lyuteranskaya tserkov

Nevskiy prospekt 22–24. **Map** 6 E1.
🅼 *Nevskiy Prospekt.*

SET BACK a little from Nevskiy prospekt, the attractive, twin-towered Lutheran church is dedicated to St. Peter. Built in its present form during the

1830s, the church served St. Petersburg's ever-growing German community *(see p57).* The prize-winning design by Aleksandr Bryullov is in an unusual, Neo-Romanesque style.

From 1936 the church was used as a vegetable store until it was converted into a swimming pool in the late 1950s. The pool was carved out of the nave floor, the gallery lined with spectator benches, and there was a high diving board in the apse. The building has now been handed back to the German-Lutheran Church of Russia. Restoration is under way, but the church is open and has Sunday services.

Glinka Capella concert hall

Glinka Capella 🔟
Хоровая капелла имени
М. И. Глинки
*Khorovaya kapella imeni
MI Glinki*

Naberezhnaya reki Moyki 20. **Map**
2 E5. 🅲 *314 1058.* 🚌 *12, 53.*
🅾 *for concerts only.* 🈳 🚫
See Entertainment *p194.*

ENCLOSED WITHIN a courtyard off the Moyka River is this ocher-colored concert hall with a facade in the French Classical style of Louis XV. The Glinka Capella was designed by Leontiy Benois in 1887–9 as the residence of the Imperial Court Choir. Founded during the reign of Peter the Great, the choir is as old as the city itself. Former directors have include the distinguished Russian composers Mikhail Glinka (1804–57) and Nikolai Rimsky-Korsakov (1844–1908).

With its excellent acoustics Glinka Capella can claim to be one of the best concert halls in the world. Outside is Singers' Bridge *(Pevcheskiy most),* aptly named, which was designed by Yegor Adam in 1837–40.

Elaborate west facade of the Stroganov Palace overlooking the Moyka River

Personal effects in Pushkin's study, Pushkin House-Museum

than 4,500 volumes in a staggering 14 European and oriental languages. Among these are works by the authors whom Pushkin most admired, including Shakespeare, Byron, Heine, Dante, and Voltaire.

Pushkin House-Museum ⓳
Музей-квартира
А. С. Пушкина
Muzey-kvartira A.S. Pushkina

Naberezhnaya reki Moyki 12.
Map 2 E5. 311 3531. 12, 53.
11am–5pm Wed–Mon.
public hols.

EVERY YEAR on the anniversary of Alekander Pushkin's death (January 29, 1837), loyal devotees of Russia's greatest poet come to lay floral tributes outside his apartment. Pushkin was born in Moscow in 1799, but spent many years of his life in St. Petersburg, and the museum is one of several places in the city with which the poet is associated.

From the autumn of 1836 until his death, Pushkin lived in this opulent apartment overlooking the Moyka, with his wife Natalya, their four children, and Natalya's two sisters. It was here in the study that he bled to death after his duel with d'Anthès *(see p83).*

Some half dozen rooms on the first floor have been refurbished in Empire style. By far the most evocative is Pushkin's study, which is arranged exactly as it was when he died. On the writing table is an ivory letter opener given to the poet by his sister, a bronze handbell, and a treasured inkstand *(see p39).* Embellished with the figure of an Ethiopian boy, the inkstand is a reminder of Pushkin's great-grandfather, Abram Hannibal. Bought by the Russian ambassador in Constantinople as a slave in

1706, Hannibal served as a general under Peter the Great. He was the inspiration for the unfinished novel *The Negro of Peter the Great,* on which Pushkin was working at the time of his death.

On the wall in front of his desk is a Turkish saber presented to Pushkin in the Caucasus, where he had been exiled in 1820 for his radical views. Ironically it was there that he spent some of his happiest years. It was there, too, that he began his most famous work, *Eugene Onegin,* a novel in verse written in 1823–30.

The most impressive feature of the apartment is the poet's library, which contains more

Imperial Stables ⓴
Конюшенное Ведомство
Konyushennoe Vedomstvo

Konyushennaya ploshchad 1.
Map 2 E5. 12, 53.
Church daily.

THE LONG, salmon-colored building running parallel to the Moyka embankment is the former imperial stables. Originally built in the first part of the 18th century, the stables were reconstructed by Vasiliy Stasov in 1817–23.

The only part of the building open to the public lies behind the central section of the long south facade, crowned by a silver dome and cross. This is the church where Alekander Pushkin's funeral took place on February 1, 1837. Its Neo-Classical interior is in the form of a basilica and is decorated with yellow marble pillars. The gilded iconostasis of white wood is early 19th-century.

North facade of Imperial Stables (left) and Little Stable Bridge on the Moyka

SENNAYA PLOSHCHAD

T HE WESTERN PART of St. Petersburg is an area of contrasts, home to some of the city's wealthiest residences and most poverty-stricken dwellings. The palatial architecture along the English Quay is a world away from the decrepit living quarters around bustling Sennaya ploshchad, that have changed little since Dostoevsky (see p123) described them. In between lies the old maritime quarter, once inhabited by Peter the Great's shipwrights, many of whom were English. This area extended all the way from the New Holland warehouses to

Coat of arms on Yusupov Palace

St. Nicholas' Cathedral, which stands on the site of the naval parade ground. Theater Square has been a hub of entertainment since the mid-18th century. It is dominated by the prestigious Mariinskiy Theater and the Rimsky-Korsakov Conservatory, where many of Russia's greatest artists began their careers. Before 1917, the streets leading off the square were home to theater directors, actors, ballerinas, artists, and musicians. Today, performing artists are once more returning to live in this shady backwater, attracted by the peace of the tree-lined canals.

SIGHTS AT A GLANCE

Cathedrals
St. Nicholas' Cathedral ❷

Theaters
Mariinskiy Theater p119 ❶

Historic Buildings and Areas
Main Post Office ❼
New Holland ❺
Rimsky-Korsakov
   Conservatory ❸

Palaces
Yusupov Palace ❹

Streets and Squares
Bolshaya Morskaya Ulitsa ❽
The English Quay ❻
Sennaya Ploshchad ❾

Museums
Railroad Museum ❿

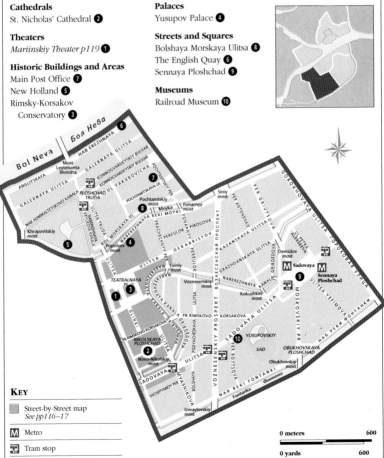

KEY

	Street-by-Street map
	See pp116–17
M	Metro
🚊	Tram stop

0 meters   600

0 yards   600

◁ **Gilded Baroque interior of the upper church of St. Nicholas' Cathedral**

Street-by-Street: Theater Square

THEATER SQUARE WAS ONCE known as Carousel Square and was frequently used as the site for fairs and festivals. During the 19th century, when St. Petersburg became the cultural capital of Russia, the Mariinskiy Theater and Rimsky-Korsakov Conservatory were established, and the neighborhood became home to many artists. Today, the tradition of entertainment is still thriving, and Theater Square remains a focal point for theatrical and musical life *(see p194).*

Atlas on prospekt Rimskovo-Korsakova

The tree-lined canal embankments and the gardens surrounding the beautiful St. Nicholas' Cathedral are enchanting places to stroll.

The Monument to Rimsky-Korsakov, who taught at the Conservatory for 37 years, was designed by Veniamin Bogolyubov and Vladimir Ingal and erected in 1952.

Yusupov Palace
Historic site of the gruesome murder of Rasputin (see p121), this grand palace belonged to the wealthy Yusupov family. Its opulent interiors include this Italian marble stair-case and a tiny Rococo theater ❹

Rimsky-Korsakov Conservatory
Tchaikovsky, Prokofiev, and Shostakovich (see p43) were among the talents nurtured by Russia's first conservatory, founded in 1862 by pianist and composer Anton Rubinstein ❸

Monument to Mikhail Glinka
(see p44)

★ **Mariinskiy Theater**
This theater has been home to the world-famous Mariinskiy (Kirov) Opera and Ballet Company since 1860. Hidden behind its imposing façade is the sumptuous auditorium where many of Russia's greatest dancers (see p118) have performed ❶

The Lion Bridge *(Lviny Most)* is one of a number of quaint and curious suspension bridges on the narrow, tree-lined Griboedov canal *(see p34).* These bridges are well-known meeting places, notably for romantic trysts.

LOCATOR MAP
See Street Finder, map 5

The House of Michel Fokine at No. 109 is where the renowned ballet master and choreographer lived before the Revolution.

STAR SIGHT

★ **Mariinskiy Theater**

The Benois House belonged to an artistic dynasty that included the cofounder of the World of Art movement, Alexandre Benois *(see p107).*

The Belfry, an elegant four-tiered structure with a gilded spire, was built to mark the main entrance to St. Nicholas' Cathedral.

St. Nicholas' Cathedral
A fine example of 18th-century Russian Baroque, the lofty upper church is richly decorated with icons, gilding, and this carved iconostasis. The lower church, beautifully lit with candles, is also open for worship ❷

KEY

– – – – Suggested route

NAB KANALA GRIBOEDOVA

SPEKT RIMSKOVO-KORSAKOVA

ULITSA MYASNIKOVA

KANAL GRIBOEDOVA

SADOVAYA ULITSA

The former Nicholas market, characterized by its long arcade and steep roof, was constructed in 1788–9. In the 19th century it became an unofficial labor exchange as many unemployed workers gathered here.

0 meters	100
0 yards	100

Ballet in St. Petersburg

Admired throughout the world, Russian ballet traces its origins back to 1738 when a French dancing master, Jean-Baptiste Landé, established a school in St. Petersburg to train the children of palace employees. The Imperial Ballet School, as it soon became known, flourished under a string of distinguished foreign teachers, culminating in Marius Petipa (1818–1910). Petipa first joined the school in 1847 as a principal dancer and later choreographed over 60 ballets, inspiring such famous dancers as Matilda Kshesinskaya *(see p72)*.

Matilda Kshesinskaya's ballet shoes

Following the 1905 revolution, a reaction against Classicism led to an increasing number of defections from the imperial theaters to the new private companies like Sergey Diaghilev's Ballets Russes. The dispersion of talent increased after the Bolsheviks seized power in 1917, and many artists went into exile abroad. Fortunately for Soviet Russia, the prima ballerina Agrippina Vaganova remained to train the next generation of dancers. St. Petersburg's Russian Ballet Academy now bears her name *(see p110)*.

Anna Pavlova's (1885–1931) most famous role, The Dying Swan, *was created especially for her by Michel Fokine. In 1912 Pavlova left Russia to form her own touring company, spreading her enthusiasm for ballet throughout Europe.*

Vaslaw Nijinsky (1890–1950) had one of his greatest roles as the golden slave in Schéhérazade, *which took Paris by storm in 1910. A principal of the Ballets Russes before World War I, he revolutionized male roles. His incomparable technical skills and expressive qualities influenced future generations of dancers.*

Rudolf Nureyev (1938–93), seen here in Sleeping Beauty *at the Mariinskiy, defected to the West in 1961. As both choreographer and dancer, Nureyev continued to enthral audiences for over 30 years until his death in 1993.*

The Mariinskiy Ballet, usually known abroad as the Kirov, is now reviving some of the original productions of the Ballets Russes, including their version of Giselle, *previously not shown in Russia.*

THE BALLETS RUSSES

The legendary touring company that revolutionized ballet between 1909 and 1929 was the brainchild of the impresario and art critic Sergey Diaghilev *(see p43)*. Diaghilev found a kindred spirit in the choreographer Michel Fokine, who shared his vision of a spectacle fusing music, ballet, and decor in a seamless artistic whole.

Diaghilev had the pick of dancers from the Mariinskiy, and, in 1909, he brought his Ballets Russes to Paris. The company went from strength to strength with successful tours worldwide.

Diaghilev's new company had a remarkable impact on the contemporary art world. The ballets of Fokine, prepared audiences for greater innovation and experiment. Exciting contributions from costume and set designers Leon Bakst and Alexandre Benois, the composer Igor Stravinsky, and the dancers Vaslaw Nijinsky, Anna Pavlova, and Tamara Karsavina all played a part in expanding artistic frontiers. After Diaghilev's death in 1929, the Ballets Russes fragmented but its ethos and traditions have been preserved in many of today's leading companies.

Early 20th-century program for the Ballets Russes

One of Russia's most important cultural institutions, the Mariinskiy Theater

Mariinskiy Theater ❶
Мариинский театр
Mariinskiy teatr

Teatralnaya ploshchad. **Map** 5 B3.
 114 1211. Э10, 22, 39Э, 43.
 1, 5, 11, 31, 42. for performances only (see pp194–5).

NAMED IN HONOR of Tsarina Maria Alexandrovna, wife of Alexander II, this theater is known abroad by its Soviet title, the Kirov, while at home it has reverted to its original name, the Mariinskiy Theater. The building was erected in 1860 by the architect Albert Kavos, who designed the Bolshoy Theater in Moscow. It stands on the site of an earlier theater that was destroyed by fire.

Imperial eagle on the royal box

In 1883–96, the Neo-Renaissance facade was remodeled by Viktor Schröter. The sumptuous pale blue and gold auditorium, where so many illustrious dancers have made their debut, creates a dazzling impression. Its architectural decoration of twisted columns, atlantes, cherubs, and cameo medallions has remained unchanged since the theater's completion, and the imperial eagles have recently been restored to the royal box. The ceiling painting of dancing girls and cupids by Italian artist Enrico Franchioli dates from c.1856, and the superb stage curtain was added during Russian ballet's golden age in 1914. Equally remarkable is the glittering festive lobby, decorated with fluted pilasters, bas-reliefs of Russian composers, and mirrored doors.

Although the Mariinskiy is better known abroad for its ballet company, it is also one of the country's leading opera houses. Most of the great 19th-century Russian operas were premiered here, including Mussorgsky's *Boris Godunov* (1874) and Tchaikovsky's *Queen of Spades* (1890). Shostakovich's highly controversial opera *Lady Macbeth of Mtsensk* also opened here in 1934. Widely acclaimed in St. Petersburg, this opera was rejected by Stalin and immediately dropped from the repertoire after the composer was denounced in a *Pravda* editorial entitled "Muddle instead of Music."

The Mariinskiy's luxuriant stage curtain, designed by Aleksandr Golovin in 1914

St. Nicholas' Cathedral ❷
Никольский собор
Nikolskiy sobor

Nikolskaya ploshchad. **Map** 5 C4.
🚋 *1, 5, 11, 42.* ⏰ *7am–noon, 4–7pm daily.*

THIS STUNNING Baroque cathedral by Savva Chevakinskiy, one of Russia's great 18th-century architects, was built in 1753–62. Founded for sailors and Admiralty employees housed in the neighborhood and named after Nicholas, the patron saint of sailors, the cathedral became known as the "Sailors' Church."

The beautiful exterior is decorated with white Corinthian pilasters and topped with five gilded cupolas. Nearby, within the cathedral's leafy grounds and overlooking the intersection of the Kryukov and Griboedov canals, is a slender, four-tiered bell tower crowned by a spire.

Following the Russian tradition, there are two churches within the cathedral. The lower church, intended for daily use, is lit by icon lamps, candles, and chandeliers, creating a magical effect. The icons (1755–7) are the work of the brothers Fedot and Menas Kolokolnikov. In total contrast, the upper church, used mainly on Sundays and festivals, has a brighter, airy feel and a typically Baroque exuberance, with gilt and stucco ornamentation and Italianate paintings.

The pale blue and white Baroque facade of St. Nicholas's Cathedral

Islamic arches and coffered ceiling in the Moorish Room, Yusupov Palace

The most impressive feature is the magnificent gilded iconostasis dating from 1755–60.

Rimsky-Korsakov Conservatory ❸
Консерватория имени Римского-Корсакова
Konservatoriya imeni Rimskovo-Korsakova

Teatralnaya ploshchad 3. **Map** 5 B3.
📞 *311 9977.* 🚎 *Э10, 22, 39Э, 43.* 🚋 *1, 5, 11, 31, 42.* ⏰ *for performances only.* 🎫 📷 *by appt.*

RUSSIA'S OLDEST music school, the conservatory was founded in 1862 by the piano virtuoso Anton Rubinstein (1829–94). The present building was designed in 1896 by Vladimir Nicolas.

Among those to graduate from the school before the Revolution were Tchaikovsky *(see p42)* and Sergey Prokofiev. In the Soviet years, the school continued to flourish, and the greatest musical figure to emerge from this era was composer Dmitriy Shostakovich (1906–75) *(see p43).*

In the courtyard outside the school are two statues. On the left, a 1952 memorial honors the school's influential teacher, Nikolai Rimsky-Korsakov, after whom the conservatory is now named. On the right, the statue of Mikhail Glinka (1906) by Robert Bach is a reminder that the conservatory stands on the original site where Russia's first opera, Glinka's *A Life for the Tsar,* was premiered in 1836 in the old Kamennyy (Stone) Theater.

Yusupov Palace ❹
Юсуповский дворец
Yusupovskiy dvorets

Naberezhnaya reki Moyki 94.
Map 5 B3. 📞 *314 8893.* 🚎 *22, 43.* 🚋 *1, 5, 11.* ⏰ *by appt noon–3pm daily.* 🎫

OVERLOOKING the Moyka, this yellow, colonnaded building (1760s) was designed by Vallin de la Mothe. The palace was acquired in 1830 by the aristocratic Yusupov family to house their superb collection of paintings. Major work was then carried out on the interior by Andrey Mikhaylov and Ippolito Monighetti.

The interiors, notable among them the exotic Moorish Room, with its fountain, colorful mosaics, and horseshoe arches, can be viewed by guided tour only. Separate tickets are needed for the tour of the cellars, which house an exhibition on Grigoriy Rasputin, the infamous "holy man," who was murdered here by Prince Felix Yusupov.

The elegant, Rococo-style family theater seats just 180, and attending a concert *(see p194)* is an experience in itself.

THE GRIM DEATH OF RASPUTIN

The Russian peasant and mystic Grigoriy Rasputin (1869–1916) exercised an extraordinarily powerful influence over the court and government of Russia *(see p26)*. The mysterious circumstances of his dramatic death on December 17, 1916 are infamous. Lured to Yusupov's palace on the pretext of a party, Rasputin was poisoned, then shot by Prince Felix Yusupov and left for dead. Returning to the scene the prince found Rasputin still alive, and a struggle ensued before Rasputin disappeared into the courtyard. Pursued by the conspirators, he was shot another three times and brutally battered before being dumped in the river. When his corpse was found three days later, clinging to the supports of a bridge, water in his lungs indicated death by drowning.

New Holland ❺

Новая Голландия
Novaya Gollandiya

Naberezhnaya reki Moyki 103. **Map** 5 B3. 🚌 *22, 43.* 🚎 *1, 5, 11, 31, 42.*

CREATED when the Kryukov canal was constructed between the Moyka and Neva rivers in 1719, this triangular island was originally used for storing ship timber. The name is in honor of the Dutch shipbuilders who inspired Peter the Great's naval ambitions.

In 1765, the original wooden warehouses were rebuilt in red brick by Savva Chevakinskiy. At the same time Vallin de la Mothe designed the austere but romantic arch facing the Moyka, which creates an atmospheric entrance to the timber yard. Barges would pass through the arch and into a turning basin beyond, then return loaded with timber

Vallin de la Mothe's impressive arch on the Moyka, leading into New Holland

along the canals towards the Admiralty shipyards. Today the overgrown and hard-to-reach island holds a certain charm in its isolation.

The English Quay ❻

Английская набережная
Angliyskaya naberezhnaya

Map 5 A2. 🚎 *1, 5, 11, 31.*

THE FIRST English merchants settled here in the 1730s, followed by a huge influx of craftsmen, architects, artists, innkeepers, and factory owners. In the 1760s the first English church opened, and the embankment came to be known in the 19th century as the English Quay. By the end of the century the area boasted a string of riverside mansions and was one of the city's most fashionable addresses. It has some fine views of the river and several impressive buildings. On naval holidays, ships richly decorated with flags line the shore.

The Neo-Classical mansion (1770s) at No. 10 was the fic-

tional setting for the debutante ball of Natasha Rostova, heroine of Tolstoy's epic novel *War and Peace*. It contrasts with the rusticated facade of No. 28, built in Florentine Renaissance style for the banking family of the barons von Derviz in the 1890s. No. 28 was later occupied by Grand Duke Andrey Vladimirovich, lover of ballet dancer Matilda Kshesinskaya *(see p72)*, and in 1917 it served as headquarters for the Socialist-Revolutionary Party. Its history took a peculiar turn when it became a Palace of Weddings, or registry office. A little farther along, at No. 32, is an elegant edifice built by Quarenghi in 1782–3.

Set back on ploshchad Truda is the palace of Grand Duke Nikolai Nikolaevich (son of Nicholas I), built in 1853–61 by Andrey Stakenschneider. In 1894 it became a school for young ladies of the nobility, but one of the first acts of the 1917 Bolshevik government was to hand it over to the unions, who still partly own it.

No. 44 is the Rumyantsev House, built in 1826–7. It was intended to be a museum for the private collection of Nikolay Rumyantsev, which he bequeathed to the nation. The collection was moved to Moscow in 1861, where the library now forms the basis of the Russian State Library. No. 56 is the former English church, an imposing Neo-Classical building by Quarenghi, dating from 1814.

Quarenghi's grand porticoed facade, at No. 32 on the English Quay

Main Post Office ❼
Главпочтамт
Glavpochtamt

Pochtamtskaya ulitsa 9. **Map** 5 C2.
📞 *312 8302.* 🚌 *T8, 22, 43.* 🚊 *5, 22.* ⏰ *9am–7:45pm Mon–Sat, 10am–5:45pm Sun.* ⬤ *public hols.*

THE MOST REMARKABLE feature of the Main Post Office is the arched gallery spanning Pochtamtskaya ulitsa. Built as an extension to Nikolay Lvov's main building, the gallery was added by Albert Kavos in 1859. Under the *Pochtamt* (Post Office) sign on the arch is a clock showing the time in major cities around the world.

Inside the post office, behind Lvov's porticoed Neo-Classical facade of 1782–9, is a splendid Style-Moderne hall characterized by decorative ironwork and a glass ceiling over the vast, tiled floor space. The hall was created in the early 20th century when a roof was constructed over what was originally the courtyard stables.

Porticoed facade, Main Post Office

Bolshaya Morskaya Ulitsa ❽
Большая Морская улица
Bolshaya Morskaya ulitsa

Map 5 C2. 🚌 *22, 43.*

ALWAYS ONE of St. Petersburg's most fashionable streets, shady Bolshaya Morskaya ulitsa is the choice of the artistic elite to this day. It has some exceedingly handsome 19th-century mansions hidden away between St. Isaac's Square *(see p79)* and Pochtamtskiy most.

Stone atlas at No. 43 Bolshaya Morskaya ulitsa (1840)

The mansion at No. 61 was built by Albert Kavos in the 1840s for the St. Petersburg Stage Coach Company. No. 52, nearby, was acquired by the Russian Union of Architects in 1932. Built by Aleksandr Pel in 1835–6, it was formerly the residence of the celebrated patron of the arts Aleksandr Polovtsov, who built up the impressive collection of the Stieglitz Museum *(see p127)*. The striking late 19th-century interiors with mahogany paneling, tapestries, and carved ceilings were designed by Maximilian Mesmacher and Nikolay Brullo and can be admired from the Nikolay restaurant *(see p180)*.

Just across the street, No. 47 is a particularly fine example of Style-Moderne architecture with sculpted stone rosettes,

delicate iron tracery, and a beautiful mosaic frieze of pink flowers. This is the work of Mikhail Geisler and Boris Guslistiy, dating from 1901–2. It was in this mansion that the celebrated émigré novelist Vladimir Nabokov (1899–1977) grew up, and there are plans to open a museum to him. Admired for his linguisitic ingenuity in both English and Russian, Nabokov hit the headlines across the world with the publication of *Lolita*, his *succès de scandale* of 1959.

Next door at No. 45 is the Union of Composers, the former home of socialite Princess Gagarina who lived here in the 1870s. The mansion was reconstructed in the 1840s by Auguste-Ricard de Montferrand, and it retains elements of the original 18th-century building.

Montferrand also built the former residence of millionaire industrialist Pyotr Demidov at No. 43. A mass of Renaissance and Baroque elements, with atlantes, vases, winged glories, and rustication, the facade also has Demidov's coat of arms.

Sennaya Ploshchad ❾
Сенная площадь
Sennaya ploshchad

Map 6 D3. Ⓜ *Sennaya Ploshchad, Sadovaya.*

CORRUGATED KIOSKS fill the center of this vast square, which is one of the oldest in the city. The local traders, seen by some as the guardians of *perestroika* and by others as a blot on the landscape, sell everything from chocolates and soft drinks to flowers, staples, and vodka. The square's name, meaning Haymarket, derives from the original market of livestock and fodder, which opened here in the 1730s.

Style-Moderne mosaic frieze at No. 47 Bolshaya Morskaya ulitsa (1901–2)

FYODOR DOSTOEVSKY

One of Russia's greatest writers, Fyodor Dostoevsky *(see pp43–4)* was born in 1821 in Moscow but spent most of his adult life in St. Petersburg, where many of his novels and short stories are set. A defining moment in his life occurred in 1849 when he was arrested and charged with revolutionary conspiracy. After eight months of solitary confinement in the Peter and Paul Fortress *(see pp66–7),* Dostoevsky and 21 other "conspirators" from the socialist Petrashevsky Circle were subjected to a macabre mock execution before being exiled to hard labor in Siberia until 1859. The sinister experience is recalled in his novel *The Idiot* (1868). He died in 1881.

The oldest building, at the center of the square, is the former guardhouse, a single-story Neo-Classical building with a columned portico, which dates to 1818–20. The guardsmen's duties ranged from supervising the traders to flogging serfs, mostly for minor misdemeanors. By that time the neighborhood had become synonymous with dirt, squalor, crime, and vice. At No. 3 is the site of "Vyazemskiy's Monastery," the nickname for a notorious tenement overrun with pubs, gambling dens, and brothels in the 1850s and '60s.

This was the squalid world so vividly evoked in Fyodor Dostoevsky's masterpiece *Crime and Punishment.* As the

Guardhouse and 1950s apartments in bustling Sennaya ploshchad

contemptuous hero of the novel, Raskolnikov, wanders around the market, he absorbs the "heat in the street.... the airlessness, the bustle and the plaster, scaffolding, bricks and dust.... that special St. Petersburg stench.... and the numerous drunken men" which "completed the revolting misery of the picture." The novel was finished in 1866 while Dostoevsky was living at Alonkin's House, (No. 7 Przhevalskovo ulitsa), to the west of the square.

During the Soviet era the square was given a new image, stallholders were banished, trees were planted, and it was optimistically renamed Peace Square (ploshchad Mira). The five-story, yellow and white apartments that surround the square today were also built then, in Stalin's version of Neo-Classicism. Sadly, in 1961, the square's most attractive monument, the Baroque Church of the Assumption, built in 1765, was torn down to make way for one of the city's earliest metro stations.

Railway Museum ❿
Музей железнодорожного транспорта
Muzey zheleznodorozhnovo transporta

Sadovaya ulitsa 50. **Map** 6 D4.
315 1476. Ⓜ *Sennaya Ploshchad, Sadovaya.* 🕐 *11am–5:30pm Sun–Thu.* 🈚 *on Sun and school hols.* 🎫 *English.*

MORE THAN 6,000 exhibits illustrate the history of the Russian railroad system since 1813. The most interesting sections of the museum deal with the earliest railroads, including Russia's first from Tsarskoe Selo to St. Petersburg, which began running in 1837, and the 650-km (404-mile) line from Moscow to St. Petersburg (1851).

Exhibits include models of the first Russian steam engine, built by the Cherepanovs in 1834, and an armored train used by Trotsky during the Civil War *(see p27).* An insight into luxury travel in the late tsarist period can be gained from the walk-through section of a first-class sleeping car with velvet upholstery and Style-Moderne decoration.

Model of 1830s engine for the Tsarskoe Selo railroad, Railway Museum

FARTHER AFIELD

WHILE THE majority of St. Petersburg's sights are centrally located, the outlying areas of the city have a number of places of architectural, cultural, and historical importance.

To the east is the Smolnyy district, taking its name from the tar yard that supplied the city's embryonic ship-building industry in the 18th century. The highlight of this area is Rastrelli's dazzling Baroque Smolnyy Convent. Nearby, the Smolnyy Institute is famed for its historic role as the Bolshevik headquarters during the October Revolution (see pp28–9).

Ceramic tile from 1770s stove, Stieglitz Museum

Southeast of the center lies the Alexander Nevsky Monastery where many of Russia's celebrated artists, architects, and composers are buried.

The southern suburbs offer a strikingly different perspective of the city, with rows of pompous 1930s–50s houses, a reminder that Stalin sought to destroy the city's historical heart by relocating the center from the old imperial district to the area around Moskovskaya ploshchad. The south also has the Chesma Church and the 1970s Victory Monument, a memorial to the suffering of St. Petersburgers during the Siege of Leningrad.

SIGHTS AT A GLANCE

Palaces
Sheremetev Palace ⑨
Tauride Palace ⑥
Yelagin Palace ①

Museums
Dostoevsky House-Museum ⑩
Stieglitz Museum ④

Churches
Alexander Nevsky Monastery ⑪
Cathedral of the
   Transfiguration ⑤
Chesma Church ⑫
Smolnyy Convent ⑦

Historic Buildings and Monuments
Finland Station ③
Piskarevskoe Memorial
   Cemetery ②
Smolnyy Institute ⑧
Victory Monument ⑬

KEY

▨	Central St. Petersburg
▨	Greater St. Petersburg
✈	Airport
▤	Train station
⛴	Ferry port
▬	Major road
=	Minor road

0 kilometers   3
0 miles   3

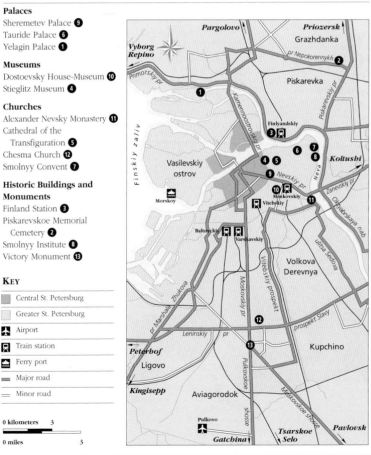

East facade of Yelagin Palace with Srednaya Nevka River in foreground

Yelagin Palace ❶

Елагин дворец

Yelagin dvorets

Yelagin ostrov 1. **[C** 239 0080. **M** *Chernaya Rechka.* **=** *71, 134.* **=** *34.* **=** *17, 26.* **○** *10am–6pm Wed–Sun.* 🖼 🚹 *to ground floor.* 🗹

O NE OF THE northernmost islands of St. Petersburg, Yelagin Island is named after a court official who built a palace here at the end of the 18th century. Alexander I then bought the island in 1817 for his mother, Maria Fyodorovna, and commissioned Carlo Rossi to rebuild the palace. The magnificent Neo-Classical palace (1818–22), enlivened on the east facade by a half rotunda flanked by Corinthian porticoes, is part of an ensemble that includes an orangery, a horseshoe-shaped stable block and porticoed kitchens.

The palace interior was destroyed by fire during World War II but is now undergoing restoration. The Oval Hall is resplendent with statuary and trompe l'oeils while the rooms leading from it are exquisitely decorated with stucco, faux marble, and painted friezes, executed by a collective of gifted artists and craftsmen.

Statue of Mother Russia (1956–60), Piskarevskoe Memorial Cemetery

In the Soviet period, the whole of the wooded island became the Central Park of Culture and Rest *(see pp136–7)*. Festivals and public entertainments are held here, and temporary exhibitions are put on in the palace's household quarters.

Piskarevskoe Memorial Cemetery ❷

Пискаревское мемориальное кладбище

Piskarevskoe memorialnoe kladbishche

Prospekt Nepokorennykh 74. **[C** 247 5716. **M** *Akademicheskaya.* **=** *Э71, T94, 123, 178, Э178.* **○** *10am–6pm daily.* 🚹 🗹

T HIS VAST, BLEAK cemetery is a most impressive memorial to the 670,000 Leningraders who died during the Siege of 1941–4 *(see p27)*. With diminishing food rations and no electricity, water, or heating, the citizens of Leningrad perished in vast numbers from starvation, cold, and disease. Thousands of corpses were dragged on sleds to collection points from which they were taken for burial in mass cemeteries on the outskirts of town. Piskarevskoe was the largest, with 490,000 burials.

Today the cemetery is a place of pilgrimage for those who lost relatives and friends during those desperate times. The memorial complex, designed by Yevgeniy Levinson and Aleksandr Vasiliev, opened in 1960, on the 15th anniversary of the end of the war. Two memorial halls, one of which contains an exhibition on the Siege, flank the stairs down to a 300-m (984-ft) long avenue, which culminates in a towering, heroic bronze statue of Mother Russia by Vera

Isayeva and Robert Taurit. On the wall behind are verses composed by Olga Bergholts, herself a survivor of the Siege. The funereal music broadcast over the whole cemetery adds to the somber atmosphere.

On either side of the avenue are 186 grassy mounds, each with a granite slab marking the year and indicating, with a red star or hammer and sickle, whether those interred were soldiers or civilians.

Locomotive 293, Finland Station

Finland Station ❸

Финляндский вокзал

Finlyandskiy vokzal

Ploshchad Lenina 6. **Map** 3 B3. **[C** 168 7687. **M** *Ploshchad Lenina.* See also p221.

O N THE NIGHT of April 3, 1917, the exiled Vladimir Lenin and his Bolshevik companions arrived at Finland Station after traveling from Switzerland on a sealed train. A triumphant reception awaited their return to Russia, and, on leaving the station, Lenin spoke to cheering crowds of soldiers, sailors, and workers. A statue erected outside the station in 1926 depicts Lenin delivering his speech.

The modern terminal was opened in the 1960s. On platform 5 there is a huge glass case containing Locomotive 293, which Lenin rode when fleeing the capital for a second time in July 1917. After spending the summer as a fugitive in Russian Finland, Lenin returned on the same train and spurred on the October Revolution *(see pp28–9)*.

Stieglitz Museum ❹

Музей Штиглица
Muzey Shtiglitsa

Solyanoy pereulok 13. **Map** 3 A5.
📞 *273 3258.* 🚌 *46, 134.* 🚎 *2, 34, 54.* ⭘ *11am–6pm (Oct–May: 11am–5pm) Tue–Sat.* 📷 📸

THE MILLIONAIRE industrialist Baron Aleksandr Stieglitz founded the Central School of Industrial Design in 1876. His aim was to train Russian students in applied arts and design by surrounding them with a collection of top quality original works for them to study.

19th-century crystal vase, Stieglitz Museum

With a large budget and the good taste of Stieglitz's son-in-law, Aleksandr Polovtsov *(see p122)*, the collection, unusual in covering both Western European and Oriental art, soon outgrew the school and in 1896 a Museum of Applied Arts opened next door. This magnificent building, designed by Maximilian Messmacher, was inspired by Italian Renaissance palaces. Inside, the halls and galleries were decorated in an impressive variety of national and period styles, echoing French and German Baroque and, above all, Italian Renaissance monuments, such as St. Mark's Library in Venice, the Raphael Loggias of the Vatican, and the Villa Madama, also in Rome.

After the Revolution the school was closed and the museum became a branch of the Hermitage *(see pp84–93)*. Serious damage to the building was inflicted during the siege of Leningrad *(see p27)*, and restoration continues. At the end of the war the school was revived to train gilders and carvers for the huge restoration program needed to repair the damaged city.

Situated on the ground floor, the exhibition features opulent displays of glassware, ceramics, and majolica, as well as porcelain from all the great European manufacturers. One room decorated in the style of the medieval Terem Palace in the Kremlin provides a superb backdrop for a collection of colorfully embroidered dresses and headgear made by Russian peasant women.

Some pieces of decorative metalwork including locks, keys, and craft tools, date back to the Middle Ages. The workmanship seen on the wooden furniture is breathtaking. The Neo-Gothic cabinet is a beautiful example. Its finely inlaid doors, depicting church naves in skillful perspective, open to reveal sculpted biblical scenes.

The guided tour concludes with a visit to the stunning Grand Exhibition Hall with its curving staircase of Italian marble and magnificent glass roof.

Cathedral of the Transfiguration ❺

Спасо-Преображенский собор
Spaso-Preobrazhenskiy sobor

Preobrazhenskaya ploshchad 1. **Map** 3 B5. 📞 *272 3662.* Ⓜ *Chernyshevskaya.* 🚌 *46, 134, 136, Э136.* 🚎 *49.* 🚎 *14, 90, 25.* ⭘ *8am–8pm daily.*

DESPITE ITS monumental Neo-Classicism, and the surrounding fence made of guns captured during the Russo-Turkish war *(see p22)*, Vasiliy Stasov's church has an intimate air as it nestles in its leafy square. The original church on this site was built by Tsarina Elizabeth to honor the Preobrazhenskiy Guards, but it was rebuilt after a fire in 1825. Today, the church is famous for its excellent choir, which is second only to that in the Alexander Nevsky Monastery *(see pp130–31)*.

Dolls in 17th–19th century Russian folk costumes, in front of the Terem Room, Stieglitz Museum

Tauride Palace ❻
Таврический дворец
Tavricheskiy dvorets

Shpalernaya ulitsa 47. **Map** 4 D4.
Ⓜ *Chernyshevskaya.* 🚌 *46, T74, 135, Э136.* ⚫ *to public.*

THIS FINELY proportioned palace by Ivan Starov was built in 1783–9 as a present from Catherine the Great to her influential lover Prince Grigoriy Potemkin *(see p25)*. Potemkin had successfully annexed the Crimea (Tauris) to Russia in 1783 and was given the title of Prince of Tauris, hence the palace's name.

Uncompromising in its lack of external ornamentation, the long, yellow building with its distinctive six-columned portico was one of Russia's first Neo-Classical designs. Sadly, the magnificent interiors have been badly damaged both by Catherine's son, Paul I, who turned the palace into a barracks, and by the many reconstructions undertaken.

The palace has played a vital role in 20th-century cultural and political life. In 1905, the impresario Sergey Diaghilev *(see p43)* organized the first ever exhibition of Russian 18th-century portraiture here. The following year the palace hosted Russia's first parliament, the State Duma. After the February Revolution of 1917 it became the seat of the Provisional Government, then the Petrograd Soviet of Workers' and Soldiers' Deputies. Today it is still a government building.

The lovely gardens, with winding streams, bridges, and an artificial lake, are among the city's most popular parks.

Facade of the Smolnyy Cathedral with adjacent convent buildings

Smolnyy Convent ❼
Смольный монастырь
Smolnyy monastyr

Ploshchad Rastrelli 3/1. **Map** 4 F4.
📞 *278 1461.* 🚌 *46, 58, 134, 136, Э136.* 🕐 *10am–5pm Fri–Wed.* ♿ 🎧 *English.*

THE CROWNING GLORY of this architectural ensemble is the stunning cathedral with its dome and four supporting cupolas topped by golden orbs.

As a symbol of her majesty, Tsarina Elizabeth founded the convent where many young noblewomen were to be educated. It was designed in 1748 by Bartolomeo Rastrelli *(see p93)*, who conceived a brilliant fusion of Russian and Western Baroque styles. Work advanced extremely slowly; 50,000 wooden piles were used to secure the foundations in the marshy soil, and the architect's model alone, now in the Academy of Arts *(see p63)*, took seven years to build.

Catherine the Great disliked Rastrelli's work and had little sympathy for the late Elizabeth. When she came to power in 1762, funding for the project stopped. It was only in 1835 that Nicholas I commissioned the Neo-Classical architect Vasiliy Stasov to complete the cathedral. His austere white interior contrasts dramatically with the luxuriant exterior.

Exhibitions and Sunday services are now held here, as are regular weekly concerts *(see p194)*. There are spectacular views of the city from the cathedral tower.

Smolnyy Institute ❽
Смольный Институт
Smolnyy Institut

Ploshchad Proletarskoy Diktatury.
Map 4 F4. 📞 *276 1461.* 🚌 *T8, 22, T26, 136.* 🚎 *5, 7, 11, 15, 16, 49.*
Lenin Museum 🕐 *10am–5pm Mon–Fri by appt only.* ♿ 🎧 *English.*

GIACOMO QUARENGHI considered this Neo-Classical building to be his masterpiece. Built in 1806–8 to house the school for young noblewomen, which had outgrown its premises at the Smolnyy Convent, the institute is famed for the part it played in the October Revolution *(see pp28–9)*.

It was from here, on October 25, 1917, that Lenin directed the Bolshevik coup d'état while the second All-Russian Congress of Soviets was convening simultaneously in the Assembly Hall. The Congress subsequently confirmed Lenin in power, and this became his seat of government until March 1918. With the Germans advancing and the outbreak of civil war *(see p27)*, the government left for Moscow, and the Institute was taken over by the Leningrad Communist Party. On December 1, 1934, the First

View of Tauride Gardens and the Tauride Palace beyond the lake

Isaak Brodskiy's 1927 painting of Lenin, Smolnyy Institute Assembly Hall

Secretary of the party, Sergey Kirov *(see p72)*, was assassinated here, an event that lit a slow fuse on Stalin's purges of the late 1930s *(see p27)*.

The rooms where Lenin lived and worked during the Revolution can be viewed by appointment. The rest of the institute now houses the Mayor's Office. The imperial eagle has replaced the hammer and sickle on the pediment, but the statue of Lenin outside has survived from 1927.

Sheremetev Palace ❾
Шереметьевский дворец
Sheremetevskiy dvorets

Naberezhnaya reki Fontanki 34. **Map** 7 A1. **C** 272 3898. **M** *Gostinyy Dvor.* **🚊** 3, 8, 15. **🚌** 5, 12, 14, 28, 34, 90. **⏰** noon–6pm Wed–Sun. 🚫 🎫

THE SHEREMETEV family lived on this site from 1712 – when the first palace was built here by Field Marshal Boris

Sheremetev – until the Revolution. The palace is also known as the Fountain House, or *Fontannyy dom*, after the many fountains that once adorned its grounds. The existing Baroque building dates essentially from the 1750s, when it was designed by Savva Chevakinskiy and Fyodor Argunov, although numerous later alterations were made.

Sheremetev's descendants were fabulously wealthy, at one time owning some 200,000 serfs. They were also among Russia's leading arts patrons, and the palace is now home to the Museum of Musical Life (*Muzey Muzikalnoy zhizhni*), which chronicles their contribution to music in the city. In the 18th and 19th centuries, serf composers, musicians, and actors from rural estates owned by the family performed in many concerts and plays at the palace. Among those to praise the fine Sheremetev choir was the composer Franz Liszt.

The museum's exhibits include a variety of period instruments and a number of scores, some of which are compositions by the Sheremetevs themselves.

One of Russia's greatest 20th-century poets, Anna Akhmatova, lived in one of the service buildings of the palace from 1933 to 1941 and then again between 1944 and 1954. Her flat is open to the public as the Anna Akhmatova Museum (*Muzey Anny Akhmatovoy*) and is reached through the courtyard of No. 53 Liteynyy prospekt. By the time she moved into the palace, it had been divided into dingy communal apartments. The rooms where she lived and worked display some of her personal possessions, which trace her intriguing life. Recordings of the poetess reading her own poems can also be heard.

ANNA AKHMATOVA

By 1914 Anna Akhmatova (1889–1966) was a leading light of Russia's "Silver Age" of poetry *(see p44)*. Tragedy gave her work a new dimension when first her husband was shot by the Bolsheviks, and then, in the 1930s, her son and her lover were arrested in Stalin's purges. Anna herself was placed under police surveillance and officially silenced for more than 15 years. Her most famous poem, *Requiem* (1935–61), inspired by her son's arrest, was written in fragments and distributed among friends to memorize. Anna was partially rehabilitated late in her life and received honorary awards abroad in 1965.

Pilastered facade of Sheremetev Palace on the Fontanka embankment

Dostoevsky House-Museum ⑩

Музей Достоевского
Muzey Dostoevskovo

Kuznechnyy pereulok 5/2. **Map** 7 B3.
🄲 *311 4031*. Ⓜ *Vladimirskaya.*
🚋 *16, 28, 34, 49, 90.* 🕐 *11am–6pm Tue–Sun.* 🚫 🖟

THIS EVOCATIVE museum was the final home of the famous Russian writer Fyodor Dostoevsky *(see p44)*, who lived here from 1878 until his death in 1881. Dostoevsky was then at the height of his fame, and it was here that he completed his last great novel, *The Brothers Karamazov*, in 1880. Gambling and debts, however, confined him to a fairly modest lifestyle in this five-room apartment.

Although Dostoevsky's public persona was dour and humorless, he was a devoted and affectionate husband and father. The delightful nursery contains a rocking horse, silhouettes of his children, and the book of fairy tales that he read aloud to them. In Dostoevsky's study are his writing desk and a reproduction of his favorite painting, Raphael's *Sistine Madonna*.

Chesma Church (1777–80), a very early example of Neo-Gothic in Russia

Chesma Church ⑫

Чесменская церковь
Chesmenskaya tserkov

Ulitsa Lensoveta 12. Ⓜ *Moskovskaya.*
🚌 *16.* 🚋 *29, 45.* 🕐 *10am–7pm daily.*

THERE IS LITTLE Russian about the highly unusual Chesma Church, which was designed by Yuriy Velten in 1777–80. Its fanciful terracotta-colored facade is decorated with thin vertical stripes of white molding that direct the eye upward to its zig-zagged crown and Neo-Gothic cupolas.

The name commemorates the great Russian naval victory over the Turks at Chesma in the Aegean in 1770. During the Communist era the church became a museum to the battle, but today the building is once again open as a church.

On the opposite side of ulitsa Lensoveta is the Neo-Gothic Chesma Palace (1774–77), formerly *Kekerekeksinen*, or Frog Marsh Palace. Also designed by Velten, it served as a staging post for Catherine the Great en route to Tsarskoe Selo *(see pp150–53)*. Wedgwood's famous dinner service with its frog emblem, now in the Hermitage *(see p91)*, was designed specially for the Chesma Palace.

The palace achieved notoriety when Rasputin's body lay in state here after his murder in 1916 *(see p121)*. Now substantially altered, it serves as a home for the elderly.

Alexander Nevsky Monastery ⑪

Александро-Невская лавра
Aleksandro-Nevskaya lavra

Ploshchad Aleksandra Nevskovo. **Map** 8 E4. 🄲 *274 2635*. Ⓜ *Ploshchad Aleksandra Nevskovo.* 🚌 *8, 58, T73.* 🚋 *1, 11, 14, 16, 22, 33.* 🚋 *7, 39, 44, 65.* **Cemeteries** 🕐 *10am–7pm Fri–Wed (10am–4pm Dec–Apr).* 🖟 *cemeteries only.* 🖟

FOUNDED BY Peter the Great in 1710, this monastery commemorates Alexander Nevsky, the prince of Novgorod, who defeated the Swedes on the Neva river in 1240. Peter himself had just defeated them, in 1709, in the course of the Great Northern War *(see p18)*.

From the entrance, a path runs between two large, walled cemeteries, then across a stream and into the main monastic complex. The earliest building, to the left of the gate, is the Church of the Annunciation (1717–22), designed by Domenico Trezzini. The church, currently closed to the public, was once the burial place for nonruling members of the Russian royal family. A series of red and white, mid-18th-century monastic buildings, including the Metropolitan's House (1755–8), surround the courtyard. Among the trees in the courtyard lie the graves of atheist Soviet scholars and leading Communists.

Dominating the essentially Baroque complex is the twin-towered and domed Neo-Classical Holy Trinity Cathedral, constructed by architect Ivan Starov in 1776–90. The wide nave inside is flanked by Corinthian columns with statues by Fedot Shubin. This leads to the impressive red agate and white marble iconostasis, that features copies of works by Van Dyck, Rubens, and others. To the right of the iconostasis is a silver reliquary that contains the remains of Alexander Nevsky, transferred

Dostoevsky's tombstone

Reliquary with Alexander Nevsky's remains, Trinity Cathedral

Victory Monument ⓭

Монумент Защитникам
Ленинграда

*Monument Zashchitnikam
Leningrada*

Ploshchad Pobedy. Ⓜ *Moskovskaya.*
🚌 *T2, 3, 11, 13, T13, T18, T20, 39,
Э39, 55, 64, 64A, T75, Э90, T90, 287,
Э287, 290, 431, 472, Э530.* **Memorial
Hall** ⭕ *10am–5pm Thu–Tue.* 🚹

ERECTED IN 1975 to coincide
with the 30th anniversary
of the end of World War II, this
somber memorial stands on the
site of a temporary triumphal
arch built to greet the returning
troops. Named the Monument
to the Heroic Defenders of
Leningrad, it commemorates

not only the estimated 670,000
victims of the Siege *(see p27)*,
but also the survivors. It was
designed by Sergey Speranskiy
and Valentin Kamenskiy and
sculpted by Mikhail Anikushin.
A 48-m (157-ft) high obelisk
of red granite rests near a vast,
circular enclosure that symbol-
izes the vicelike grip of the
siege. Heroic, larger-than-life
sculptures of soldiers, sailors,
and grieving mothers
surround the monument.

An underpass on Moskovskiy
prospekt leads to the gloomy,
subterranean Memorial Hall.
Here solemn music gives way
to the persistent beat of a
metronome, the wartime radio
signal, intended to represent

the city's defiant heartbeat.
The subdued lighting consists
of 900 dim, orange lamps,
one for each day of the Siege.
On the marble walls are tablets
inscribed with the names of
the 650 Heroes of the Soviet
Union who were awarded the
title after the war, and on the
far wall a mosaic depicts the
women of the city greeting
their soldier menfolk at the
end of the grim conflict.

Around the hall a small
display of artifacts, including
Shostakovich's violin *(see p43)*,
records the contribution of
different sections of the community to the war effort, and
an illuminated relief map
illustrates the battle lines.

Heroic partisans facing south towards the enemy during the Siege of Leningrad, detail of Victory Monument

to the previous church on
this site in 1724. Behind the
reliquary hangs a painting of
Nevsky, who has been venerated as a saint in Russia since
the mid-16th century.

Many of the nation's leading
cultural figures are buried in
the two monastic cemeteries
near the main entrance. The
city's oldest graveyard, the
Lazarus Cemetery, to the east,
contains the graves of the
polymath Mikhail Lomonosov
(see p45) and a number of
prominent architects, including
Andrey Zakharov, Thomas de
Thomon, Giacomo Quarenghi,
Carlo Rossi *(see p110)*, and
Andrey Voronikhin. Clustered
together along the northern
wall of the Tikhvin Cemetery
(to the west) are the tombs of
some of Russia's most famous
composers. Many of their
tombs are inscribed with musical motifs. Fyodor Dostoevsky
(see p44) is also buried here,
to the right of the entrance.

TOMBS OF INTEREST AT TIKHVIN CEMETERY

1 Mikhail Glinka
(Composer, 1804–57)
2 Ivan Krylov
(Poet, 1768–1844)
3 Marius Petipa
(Choreographer, 1818–1910)
4 Pyotr Klodt
(Sculptor, 1805–67)
5 Ivan Kramskoy
(Painter, 1837–87)
6 Pyotr Tchaikovsky
(Composer, 1840–93)

7 Modest Mussorgsky
(Composer, 1839–81)
8 Nikolai Rimsky-Korsakov
(Composer, 1844–1908)
9 Fyodor Dostoevsky
(Writer, 1821–81)

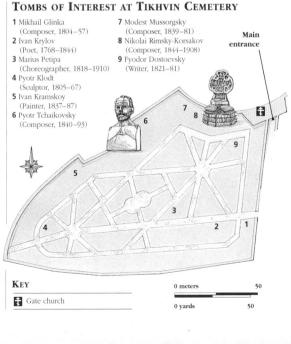

**Main
entrance**

KEY

🚹 Gate church

0 meters 50

0 yards 50

Two Guided Walks

S T. PETERSBURG IS a very manageable city to explore on foot, and many of its sights are best appreciated in this way. The two walks chosen present different sides of the city's character. However, since St. Petersburg is dominated by its location on a group of islands at the mouth of the Neva River, water plays a central part in both.

The first walk follows two of the many waterways, the Moyka River and the Griboedov Canal, that crisscross the heart of the city, presenting the magnificent scale of St. Petersburg as it was built in the 18th and 19th centuries. It shows the contrasts of rich palaces and overcrowded apartment houses, gilded bridges and the dilapidation of the area around Sennaya

19th-century urn on the steps of Yelagin Palace

ploshchad. An alternative way to appreciate the canals is to take a boat trip (see pp218–19), which delivers another perspective on the city's glorious historical buildings.

The second walk explores the world where Petersburgers have spent much of their free time since the 18th century. Yelagin and Kamenyy Islands, to the north of the center, were once the preserve of the rich, who spent the hot summers in the cool of their dachas, the marvelously varied architecture of which can still be admired today. The islands offer a calm retreat for all. Locals come to walk and row boats in summer, collect leaves in autumn, ski and skate in winter, or simply to breathe the fresh air in spring.

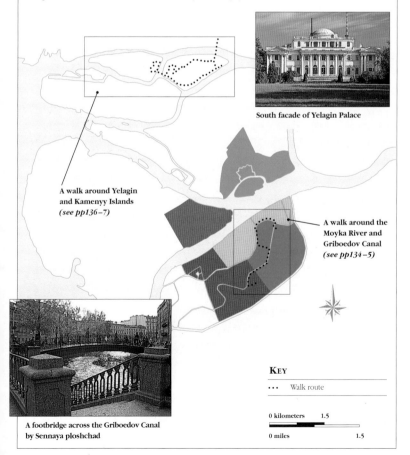

South facade of Yelagin Palace

A walk around Yelagin and Kamenyy Islands
(see pp136–7)

A walk around the Moyka River and Griboedov Canal
(see pp134–5)

A footbridge across the Griboedov Canal by Sennaya ploshchad

KEY

•••	Walk route

0 kilometers   1.5

0 miles   1.5

◁ **Peace and tranquillity enjoyed on one of the lakes of Yelagin Island**

A Walk along St. Petersburg's Waterways

A STROLL ALONG the embankments of the Moyka River and the Griboedov Canal is a chance to appreciate the history and splendid architecture of this beautiful city. The two waterways present interesting contrasts. The Moyka winds past the Imperial Summer and Winter Palaces and the lavish mansions of the aristocracy, while the Griboedov is lined with 19th-century apartments, once home to merchants, civil servants, and, toward Sennaya Ploshchad *(see p122)*, the working class. The walk also includes a short stretch of the majestic Nevskiy prospekt.

TIPS FOR WALKERS

Starting point: Church on Spilled Blood. *Length*: 5.8 km (3 miles). *Getting there*: Nevskiy Prospekt metro. *Stopping-off points*: Café Minutka, Nevskiy prospekt 20; Bistro Layma, nab kanala Griboedova 16.

View of the Church on Spilled Blood and the Griboedov canal

The Moyka River

Begin the walk at the recently restored Church on Spilled Blood ① *(see p100)*, built over the spot where Alexander II was assassinated in 1881 *(see p26)*. From here, walk around the church beside the park, crossing the canal bridge to Konyushennaya ploshchad. The square is embraced by the elongated facade of the former Imperial Stables ② *(see p113)*. Straddling the junction of the Griboedov Canal and the Moyka River are two cleverly linked bridges, the Malo-Konyushennyy most (Little Stable Bridge) and Teatralnyy most (Theater Bridge) *(see p37)*. Cross over these bridges to the north bank of the Moyka and the expansive facade of the Adamini House ③, designed by Domenico Adamini in 1823–7. Between 1916 and 1919 the basement was used

by an artists' and writers' club known as "The Bivouac of the Comedians." Visitors included the avant-garde theater director Vsevolod Meyerhold and the poets Aleksandr Blok and Anna Akhmatova *(see p44)*.

Turn left onto naberezhnaya reki Moyki and walk past the Round Market ④ built in 1790 by Giacomo Quarenghi, who had shopping arcades as one of his specialties. Continue along the embankment, passing Adam's Bolshoy Konyushennyy most (Great Stables Bridge) to Prince Abamelek-Lazarev's former mansion ⑤ built in 1913–15. The handsome facade, with Corinthian pilasters and graceful reliefs of dancing figures, is by Ivan Fomin. On the opposite bank is the 17th-century apartment house where Pushkin spent the last few months of his life. This is now a museum ⑥ *(see p113)*.

At the intersection of Millionaya ulitsa and the beautiful Winter Canal (Zimnyaya Kanavka) are the former barracks of the elite First Regiment of the Preobrazhenskiy Life-Guards. This prestigious corps was formed by Peter the Great in the 1690s.

General Staff Building

Quarenghi's arcaded Round Market (1790), overlooking the Moyka River

Sadovaya Ⓜ   Ⓜ Sennaya Pl

0 meters   300
0 yards   300

KEY

••• Tour route

Ⓜ Metro station

View of the tree-lined Griboedov Canal

Across the Winter Canal is the New Hermitage ⑦ *(see p84)*. Ten granite atlantes bear the weight of the elaborate porch. Returning to the Moyka, the route passes a green, three-story house ⑧, built by F. Demertsov for Alexander I's military advisor and sometime chief minister, Count Aleksey Arakcheev. The Moyka now makes a curve behind the majestic buildings of Palace Square *(see p83)* that also includes the Staff of the Guards Corps ⑨ and the huge crescent of Carlo Rossi's imposing yellow General Staff Building ⑩. Cross the Pevcheskiy most (Singers' Bridge) *(see p37)* ⑪ and follow the Moyka down to the Politseyskiy most (Police Bridge). The yellow building on the other side of the Moyka is the Literary Café ⑫, renowned as a meeting-place for writers in Pushkin's day *(see p83)*.

Nevskiy Prospekt

Turn left onto St. Petersburg's main street, where a range of architectural styles can be seen. On the left, the elegant facade of Paul Jacot's Dutch Church building ⑬ *(see p47)* hides rows of shops. Across the

road, the beautifully embellished facade of the Baroque Stroganov Palace ⑭ *(see p112)* contrasts starkly with the triple-arched glass frontage of the Style-Moderne Fashion House ⑮ *(see p47)*. The magnificent colonnaded forecourt of the Kazan Cathedral ⑯ *(see p111)* can be seen farther along.

The Griboedov Canal

Cross Nevskiy prospekt by the attractive Dom Knigi *(see p47)* and follow the Griboedov south. When you reach Georg von Traitteur's Bankovskiy most *(see p35)* ⑰, decorated with golden griffons, cross the canal and continue past the wrought-iron railings to the rear of the former Assignment Bank ⑱ (now occupied by an Economics University). Farther south the humped Kamennyy most (Stone Bridge) has survived since 1776 despite an attempt by the revolutionary group, Peoples' Will, to blow it up as Tsar Alexander II passed in his carriage. Across the Demidov most, on the corner of Kaznacheyskaya ulitsa ⑲ (No.1), is the apartment where Dostoevsky wrote *Notes from the House of the Dead* (1861). He was living on the same street when he wrote *Crime and Punishment*. Also with literary associations, the former Zverkov House ⑳ was where the novelist and dramatist Nikolai Gogol *(see p44)* lived in the 1830s.

The walk ends in Sennaya ploshchad *(see p122)*, where there are two metro stations.

Griffons on Bank Bridge (1826), Griboedov canal

Apartment where Dostoevsky lived, on the Griboedov Canal

A Walk around Kamennyy and Yelagin Islands

AN AREA OF ROLLING parkland, birch and lime groves, and fine river views, the northern islands of the Neva delta offer a retreat from city life. The imperial family built palaces on Kamennyy and Yelagin Islands at the end of the 18th century and were soon joined by wealthy aristocratic families. Before the Revolution, many government ministers, industrial magnates, and celebrities built themselves a dacha here. Today these neglected houses, some intimate, some palatial, in styles ranging from Neo-Gothic to Neo-Classical and Style Moderne, are being returned to their former glory by the new business elite.

Wooden facade of Dolgorukov Mansion

the fashionable architect, Vladimir Apyshkov, to build this splendid Style-Moderne mansion in 1913–14.

Continue west, and cross the canal bridge to reach the wooden Kamennoostrovskiy Theater ⑥, which took only 40 days to erect in 1827. Though in need of a coat of paint, its Neo-Classical portico, rebuilt by Albert Kavos in 1844, is still impressive. The banks of the Krestovka River, with views across to the boatyards of Krestovskiy Island, are ideal for a picnic. Return to the path and cross 1-y Yelagin most to Yelagin Island.

Yelagin Island

This island is an oasis of calm, popular with Petersburgers wishing to escape the city. A tollgate marks the entrance to the grounds of Carlo Rossi's

[Map with labels: 3-Y YELAGIN MOST, 2-Y Severnyy prub, 4-Y Severnyy prub, 5-Y Severnyy prub, Yelagin Palace, YELAGIN OSTROV, Srednaya Nevka, Средная Невка, 4-Y Fzhnyy prub, 3-Y Fzhnyy prub, TSENTRALNIY PARK KULTURIY I OTDYKHA IM KIROVA, 2-Y Fzhnyy prub, 2-Y YELAGIN MOST, 1-Y Fzhnyy prub]

South
Kamennyy Island

Begin at Chernaya Rechka metro station and head south to Bolshaya Nevka River, then crossing over to Kamennyy Island, an area of recreation and relaxation. Just across the main road is the small red-brick Church of St. John the Baptist ①, designed in Neo-Gothic style by Yuriy Velten in 1776–8. Nearby a yellow gateway leads to the grounds of Kamennoostrovskiy Palace ② (now a retirement home) from where Alexander I led the Russian campaign of 1812 against Napoleon *(see p26)*.

Follow Kamennoostrovskiy prospekt to the Malaya Nevka River, then turn right on to naberezhnaya Maloy Nevki where there is an imposing wooden mansion ③ at No. 11 with a white-columned portico. The Dolgorukov Mansion was built in 1831–2 by Smaragd Shustov for the Dolgorukovs,

one of Russia's oldest aristocratic families. The two sphinxes guarding the granite embankment date to 1824. From this point you can see across to Aptekarskiy or Apothecary's Island, named after the medicinal herb gardens founded by Peter the Great. St. Petersburg's Botanical Gardens are still located there. Continue along the path, which turns into naberezhnaya reki Krestovki. Standing in the middle of the path are the remains of Peter the Great's oak tree ④, said to have been planted by the tsar in 1718. The house on the left, toward the Malo-krestovskiy most, is the former home of Sergey Chaev ⑤, the chief engineer of the Trans-Siberian Railroad. Chaev commissioned

The tower of the Church of St. John the Baptist (1776–8)

Kamennoostrovskiy Theater (1827)

graceful Yelagin Palace ⑦ (see p126). The western spit of the island is ideal for viewing the often spectacular sunsets over the Gulf of Finland, especially during the White Nights (see p51). Across 2-y Yelagin most, leading south to Krestovskiy Island, are Petrovskiy Stadium and the Maritime Victory Park, and to the north, 3-y Yelagin most leads to Primorskiy prospekt and the Buddhist Temple, erected by Gavriil Baranovskiy in 1909–15 and inspired by traditional Tibetan architecture.

North Kamennyy Island

Return to Kamennyy Island across 1-y Yelagin most, taking the left fork on to Teatralnaya alleya from where you can see the former mansion of Aleksandr Polovtsov ⑧, minister of foreign affairs under Nicholas II. This splendid Neo-Classical mansion with Style-Moderne touches was built by Ivan Fomin in 1911–13. Leave Teatralnaya alleya and cut through the quiet and restful park, passing between the ponds and the canal. Near the junction with Bolshaya alleya are two more early 20th-century mansions. Follenveider's mansion ⑨ on the left, with its distinctive

Early 20th-century Polovtsov Mansion

tented tower, was designed by Roman Meltzer in 1904 and now belongs to the Danish consulate. Yevgeniya Gausvald's dacha ⑩ dates from 1898 and stands as one of the earliest Style-Moderne buildings in St. Petersburg. It was designed by Vasiliy Schöne and Vladimir Chagin.

Finally, the last stage of the walk leads along the 2-ya Berezovaya alleya, back to the starting point at Ushakovskiy most and Chernaya Rechka metro.

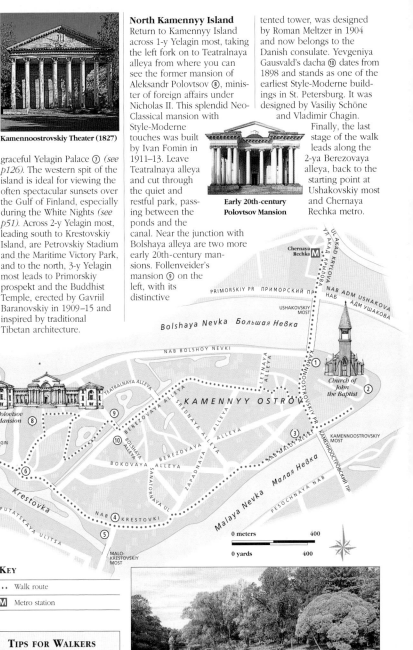

KEY

••• Walk route

Ⓜ Metro station

TIPS FOR WALKERS

Starting point: Chernaya Rechka metro station (see p215).
Length: 6 km (3.5 miles).
Stopping-off points: Café in former stables of Yelagin Palace (summer only) and plenty of places to picnic.

The tree-shrouded, grassy banks of the Krestovka River

BEYOND
ST. PETERSBURG

REPINO 144
ORANIENBAUM 144
GATCHINA 145
PETERHOF 146-149
TSARSKOE SELO 150-155
PAVLOVSK 156-159
NOVGOROD 160-163

BEYOND ST. PETERSBURG

THE COUNTRYSIDE *around St. Petersburg is typical of northwest Russia. Among its flat sweeps of land, pine forests, and lakes there are sights of cultural interest, including the imperial palaces and the walled medieval city of Novgorod. Venturing away from St. Petersburg allows a richer and deeper insight into this splendid land.*

Before St. Petersburg was founded in 1703, the surrounding landscape was a marshy and inhospitable wilderness inhabited by wolves. Nevertheless, the area from the Gulf of Finland to Lake Ladoga was of strategic importance for trading and thus one of the reasons for continuous wars between Sweden and Russia. At the time, the only city of importance here was Novgorod, an independent and quite wealthy principality *(see p17)*. It has retained its medieval atmosphere, so different from the imperial palaces adorning the countryside south of St. Petersburg. Each one reflects the taste of its owner. Peter the Great's fine residence, Peterhof, is dominated by water; the Gulf and the fountains mirror his maritime interest. Elizabeth wanted vibrant color and excess to

Muse of love and poetry, Pavlovsk

accommodate her extravagant balls, hence the grand Baroque palace at Tsarskoe Selo. Catherine the Great's love of intimacy led her to add private apartments to Tsarskoe Selo and the exquisite Chinese Palace at Oranienbaum. Paul I's military mania made him turn Gatchina into a castle, while his wife Maria Fyodorovna created a feminine, elegant residence at Pavlovsk. All the palaces except Oranienbaum suffered devastating damage during World War II *(see p27)*. A great deal of effort has been made at painstaking restoration over the last 50 years.

While the aristocracy indulged in their extravagances, the middle classes had more modest country houses. The comfortable dacha of the artist Repin, northwest of the city, gives visitors a feel of his more bohemian lifestyle.

The Novgorod Kremlin with the Cathedral of St. Sophia and its belfry

◁ The gilded maze of the main staircase at Peterhof's Grand Palace

Exploring St. Petersburg's Surroundings

MOST ST. PETERSBURGERS leave the city to spend time at their dacha or country house for weekends and holidays. But there are several ways of experiencing the countryside around St. Petersburg. There are many stunning imperial palaces, spread out like pearls in a necklace south of the city. Each one of them offers splendid interiors as well as beautifully laid out parks and gardens with lakes. Around the artist's studio at Repino is a more typical Baltic landscape, with pine and fir trees stretching down to the pebbly beaches of the Gulf of Finland.

Farther away to the south, the medieval town of Novgorod is a great representative of an old Russian city, complete with a walled kremlin and onion-domed churches.

Vyborg   P34

● PERVOMAYSKOE

ROSHCHINO

Vyborg
Primorsk   ZELENOGORSK

① REPINO

GULF OF FINLAND   SESTRORETSK

A121   KRONSTADT

SOSNOVYY BOR   Kovashi   ORANIENBAUM ②
③
PETERHOF   STRELNA

Ust-Luga

Kingisepp   KOPORE   KRASNOE SELO

M11   P38   GATCHINA

P40
VOLOSOVO   M20

← Kingisepp

Luga ↓

Facade of the Chinese Palace at Oranienbaum

GETTING AROUND

It is relatively easy to get to all of the imperial palaces, and to Repino, by suburban train or by taking a guided tour by bus *(see p200)*. Driving is less convenient, often taking longer than the train, and driving standards are variable. In the summer, the hydrofoil service is an alternative way to get to Peterhof *(see p221)*. Each of these sights can easily be visited in a day. Novgorod is situated farther away, however, so it makes sense to spend longer there. Mainline trains depart from Moscow train station *(see p221)* for Novgorod.

Coastal landscape along the Gulf of Finland

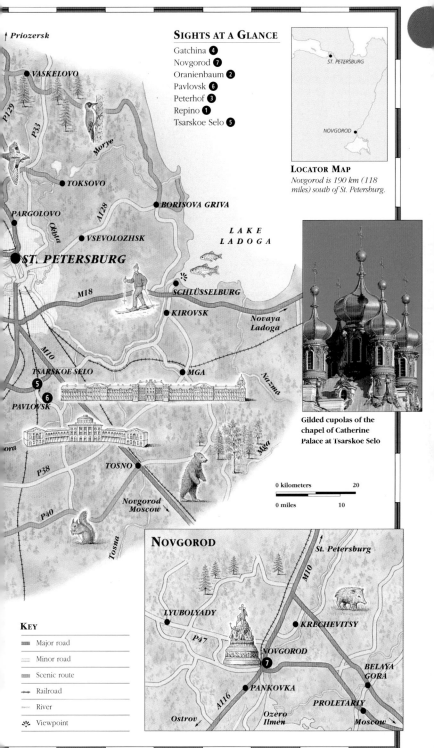

SIGHTS AT A GLANCE

Gatchina ❹
Novgorod ❼
Oranienbaum ❷
Pavlovsk ❻
Peterhof ❸
Repino ❶
Tsarskoe Selo ❺

LOCATOR MAP
Novgorod is 190 km (118 miles) south of St. Petersburg.

ST. PETERSBURG

NOVGOROD

† Priozersk

VASKELOVO

TOKSOVO

BORISOVA GRIVA

PARGOLOVO

VSEVOLOZHSK

LAKE LADOGA

ST. PETERSBURG

SCHLÜSSELBURG

KIROVSK

Novaya Ladoga

TSARSKOE SELO
❺
❻
PAVLOVSK

MGA

Gilded cupolas of the chapel of Catherine Palace at Tsarskoe Selo

TOSNO

Novgorod Moscow

| 0 kilometers | 20 |
| 0 miles | 10 |

NOVGOROD

St. Petersburg

LYUBOLYADY

KRECHEVITSY

NOVGOROD
❼

BELAYA GORA

PANKOVKA

PROLETARIY

Ostrov

Ozero Ilmen

Moscow

KEY

▬▬ Major road
▬▬ Minor road
▬▬ Scenic route
+++ Railroad
▬▬ River
☀ Viewpoint

Repino ❶
Репино
Repino

47 km (29 miles) NW of St. Petersburg. 🚉 *from Finland Station.* 🚌 *411 from Chernaya Rechka metro.* **Penaty,** Primorskoe shosse 411. 📞 *231 6828.* ⭕ *10:30am–6pm Wed–Mon (Oct–Apr: 10:30am–5pm).* 📷 ♿ *ground floor.*

O NLY ABOUT AN HOUR's drive from St. Petersburg on Primorskoe shosse, the northern coastal road, is a region of lakes, pine-scented forests, and sandy beaches. Among the green-painted dachas and sanatoriums is Repino, a resort named after one of Russia's greatest artists, Ilya Repin *(see p43)*, who lived here for over 30 years until his death in 1930 at age 86. His extraordinary dacha, with its steeply pitched glass roof and angled windows, was restored after damage in World War II and is now open as a museum.

Named Penaty in honor of the Roman household gods, Penates, the house was re-designed by Repin himself to accommodate all that an artist might need, including a glass-paneled veranda downstairs, which was used as a winter studio. On display in the first-floor studio are the artist's brushes and a number of his works, including an unfinished portrait of Pushkin *(see p44)* and Repin's last self-portrait.

Works by the artist adorn the dining room, including portraits of the singer Fyodor Shalyapin and writer Maxim Gorky, who were among Repin's many visitors. A specially constructed revolving dining table enabled guests to serve themselves and to store away their used

Studio of the eminent artist Ilya Repin at his home in Repino

dishes, since there were no servants. Anyone failing to follow this routine had to give an impromptu speech from the lectern in the corner.

In the garden, two small wooden follies are hidden among the trees, and Repin's grave is marked by a simple cross on the top of a hillock.

Oranienbaum ❷
Ораниенбаум
Oranienbaum

Oranienbaum, 40 km (25 miles) W of St. Petersburg. 📞 *422 4796.* 🚉 *from Baltic station.* **Grounds** ⭕ *9am–10pm (Oct–Apr: 9am–8pm).* **Palaces & Sliding Hill Pavilion** ⭕ *11am–5pm Mon, Wed–Sun (times vary slightly for individual buildings).* **Chinese Palace** ● *Oct–Apr.* 📷 📷

A S THE EXTRAVAGANT project of Peter the Great's closest friend and main political advisor, Aleksandr Menshikov *(see p62)*, Oranienbaum was far more ambitious in conception than Peter's palace at Peterhof *(see pp146–9)*, which lies just 12 km (7 miles) to the west.

The grandiose plan bankrupted Menshikov, and when he fell from grace in 1727, the estate entered the state treasury.

The Baroque appearance of Oranienbaum's Great Palace has changed little since it was constructed in 1710–25. Built by Gottfried Schädel and Giovanni-Maria Fontana, its sweeping wings culminate in two remarkable pavilions. Parts of the palace and the east (Japanese) pavilion are now open to the public.

From 1743 to 1761 the estate became the residence of the heir to the throne, the future Peter III, who built himself a miniature fortress with a small lake for his "navy" and a parade ground where he liked to play war games with soldiers. Peter also commissioned Antonio Rinaldi to build him a modest palace.

Peter's wife, Catherine (later Catherine the Great), abhorred her isolated existence here, but after Peter's murder *(see p22)* she recovered her spirits and created what she described as her "personal dacha." Built by Rinaldi in the 1760s and known as the Chinese Palace, it is famous for its fabulous Rococo interiors and voguish displays of chinoiserie.

The most unusual building at Oranienbaum is Rinaldi's Sliding Hill Pavilion, built in 1762 on Catherine's initiative. Wooden sledding hills were a common source of amusement among the Russian nobility. Catherine's visitors would climb the blue and white pavilion before descending by sled or toboggan along a roller-coaster run. The track, 500 m (1,640 ft) long, was originally flanked

Facade of Menshikov's Great Palace (1710–25), Oranienbaum

by a colonnade. Sadly, this collapsed in 1813, but there is a model in the pavilion.

A pleasant few hours can be spent wandering through the extensive grounds with their secluded paths, pine woods, ponds, and bridges.

Oranienbaum was the only palace in the area to escape German occupation during World War II (see p141). In 1948, the estate was renamed Lomonosov in honor of the famous 18th-century polymath (see p45) who established a glass and mosaic factory nearby. The complex has reverted to its original name, an allusion to the exotic orange trees

Austere central section of Gatchina palace

Paul I). Paul asked his favourite architect Vincenzo Brenna to re-fashion the palace to match his pronounced martial tastes. Brenna's large-scale alterations included the construction of an additional story and a moat with a drawbridge.

The next Romanov to spend any time here was Alexander III, who made it his permanent family residence in the late 19th century. The estate provided a safe and remote haven from the sporadic social unrest that was threatening the capital (see p26). The imperial family led a simple and secluded existence here. In keeping with the increasingly bourgeois tastes of the nobility in the whole of Europe, they scorned the state rooms, confining themselves instead to the cosy and more intimate servants' quarters.

In 1917, immediately after the Bolshevik party had seized power, the proclaimed leader of the Provisional Government,

Aleksandr Kerensky, fled to Gatchina where he made a last ditch attempt to rally his supporters. After a week, he deserted his troops and slipped away into exile (see p27).

After World War II, in which the palace was badly damaged, Gatchina was used for many years as a military academy. The lengthy and thorough restoration process is still under way. Of the restored rooms, the three most impressive are the Marble Dining Room, Paul I's gloomy bedroom at the top of one of Brenna's towers, and the magnificent White Ballroom. There is also a display of weaponry on the ground floor.

The delightful grounds are the wildest of all the palace parks. Among the attractions are the circular Temple of Venus (1792–3) on the secluded Island of Love and the Birch House (1790s). At first glance the latter appears to be nothing more than a pile of logs, but it actually conceals a suite of exquisite rooms.

The lake has boats for rent, and its clean water makes it an ideal spot for swimming in the summer. Since there are few facilities in the town itself, bring a picnic and enjoy the idyllic views and tranquillity.

Chinoiserie decorations in Catherine the Great's Chinese Palace, Oranienbaum

Peterhof ❸

See pp146–49.

Gatchina ❹
Гатчина
Gatchina

45 km (28 miles) SW of St. Petersburg. from Baltic Station. 431 from pl Pobedy. 8 271 13492. 10am–6pm Tue–Sun. English.

I N 1765, Catherine the Great presented the village of Gatchina to her lover, Prince Grigoriy Orlov. He commissioned Antonio Rinaldi to build a Neo-Classical palace that was completed in 1781. When Orlov died, two years later, Catherine transferred the estate to her son and heir Paul (later

Tsarskoe Selo ❺

See pp150–53.

Gatchina's sumptuous White Ballroom with its pseudo-Egyptian statues

Peterhof ❸

Петергоф
Petergof

WITH ITS COMMANDING views of the Baltic, Peterhof is a perfect expression of triumphalism. Originally designed by Jean Baptiste Le Blond, the Great Palace (1714–21) was transformed during the reign of Tsarina Elizabeth when Bartolomeo Rastrelli added a third story and wings with pavilions at each end. He tried to preserve Le Blond's early Baroque exterior, but redesigned the interiors, indulging his love for gilded Baroque decoration. Peterhof stands at the center of a magnificent landscaped park with both French and English gardens.

View from palace of Grand Cascade leading down to the Gulf of Finland

Neptune Fountain

Oak Fountain

Mezheumnyy Fountain

The Upper Gardens are framed by borders and hedges and punctuated with ornamental ponds.

The Imperial Suite

The imperial suite lies in the palace's east wing. Peter's Oak Study is one of the few rooms to have survive unaltered from Le Blond's design. Some of the oak panel designs are originals (1718–21) by Nicholas Pineau.

Cottage Palace

Orangery

Roman Fountain

★ The Grand Cascade

The dazzling cascade (1715–24) is a sequence of 37 gilded bronze sculptures, 64 fountains, and 142 water jets (see p149), descending from the terraces of the Great Palace to the Marine Canal and the sea.

Pyramid Fountain

Monplaisir

Adam Fountain

0 meters   25

0 yards   25

PETER THE GREAT'S PALACE

After his victory over the Swedes at Poltava in 1709, Peter the Great decided to build a palace "befitting to the very highest of monarchs." A visit to Versailles in 1717 furthered Peter's ambitions, and he employed more than 5,000 laborers, serfs, and soldiers, supported by architects, water-engineers, land-scape gardeners, and sculptors. Work proceeded at a frenetic pace from 1714 until Peterhof was officially opened in 1723.

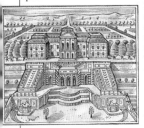

Le Blond's Great Palace was completed in 1721 and has changed considerably over the decades. Catherine the Great commissioned Yuriy Velten to redecorate some of Rastrelli's interiors in the 1770s, including the Throne Room and the Chesma Room.

Jean Baptiste Le Blond's original two-story Great Palace

VISITORS' CHECKLIST

Petrodvorets, 30 km (19 miles) W of St. Petersburg. **[** 427 9527. **[** from Baltic station (see p220) to Novyy Petergof. **[** Hermitage (May–Oct) (see p220). **Great Palace [** 10:30am–5pm Tue–Sun. **Other pavilions [** May–Sep: 10:30am–5pm Tue–Sun; Oct–Apr: 10.30am–4pm Sat & Sun. **Fountains [** May–Sep: 10am–6pm. **[** **[** **[** **[** **[** **[**

★ Main Staircase
Caryatids and gilded carvings adorn Rastrelli's glittering staircase. The ceiling fresco depicts Aurora and Genius chasing away the night.

Golden Hill Cascade

Marly and Hermitage

Eve Fountain

STAR FEATURES

★ Grand Cascade

★ Main Staircase

★ The State Rooms

Hydrofoil and Gulf of Finland

The Marine Canal enabled the tsars to sail from the Gulf of Finland up to the Great Palace.

★ The State Rooms
The highlight of the State Rooms is the opulent Throne Room, redesigned by Yuriy Velten in 1770. The relatively restrained stucco ornament-ation, red velvet hangings, and parquet floor provide an exquisite setting for portraits of Russia's imperial family.

Exploring Peterhof Park

THE GROUNDS AT PETERHOF include the Upper, Lower, and Alexandria parks, covering an area of around 1,500 acres. As well as the numerous palaces and fountains, there are tree-lined avenues, wooded paths, and the Baltic shore. Le Blond designed the grounds next to the Great Palace to be laid out in the formal French style with geometrically arranged flower beds, sculptures, summerhouses, and pergolas. The trees and shrubs, including lindens, elms, maples, and roses, were imported from all over Russia and abroad.

Cottage Palace in Alexandria Park

Monplaisir Palace (1714–22), overlooking the Gulf of Finland

Monplaisir

This delightfully unpretentious palace was designed in 1714 by Johann Braunstein. Even after the Great Palace was built, Peter continued to live and entertain at Monplaisir, where his guests were usually subjected to a punishing regime of heavy drinking. At breakfast the coffee cups were filled with brandy, and by nightfall guests were often discovered wandering drunk in the park.

While not as lavish as those of the Great Palace the interiors are still impressive, particularly the wood-paneled Ceremonial Hall. A painting on its vaulted ceiling depicts Apollo surrounded by characters from a masque. Russian icon painters skillfully carried out the decoration of the exquisite Lacquered Study in the Chinese style then in vogue. Peter's collection of canvases by Dutch and Flemish artists hang in the rooms, and there are wonderful views of the gulf from the tsar's Naval Study.

Adjoining Monplaisir is the Catherine Wing, which was built for Tsarina Elizabeth by Rastrelli in 1747–54. Catherine

the Great was staying here in 1762 when her lover, Count Orlov, arrived with news of the coup that was to bring her to the throne *(see p24)*.

Marly Palace

Named after Marly-le-Rois, the king of France's hunting lodge, which Peter the Great visited on a tour of Europe in 1717, this beautifully proportioned country residence was built for the tsar's guests. The rooms open to the public

Elaborate tiled kitchen in the Marly Palace (1720–3)

include the Oak and Plane Tree studies, Peter's bedroom, and the Dining Room. It is set in its own formal garden with sculptures, fountains, a large pond, and Niccolò Michetti's Golden Hill Cascade, which was added in 1731–7.

The Hermitage

Standing in splendid isolation on the shores of the gulf, this elegant pavilion (1721–5), by Braunstein, was conceived as a private dining venue for the tsar and his friends. To highlight the need for solitude, the building was raised on a plinth and surrounded by a moat that was crossed by a small drawbridge. The stuccoed facade is decorated with Corinthian pilasters, elaborate wrought-iron balconies, and enlarged windows. All the servants were confined to the ground floor, and a mechanical device took meals up from the kitchen.

Cottage Palace

The romantic landscaped grounds of Alexandria Park, named after Alexandra, wife of Nicholas I, provide a perfect setting for the Cottage Palace. The Neo-Gothic house is more imposing than the term cottage suggests. The Scottish architect, Adam Menelaws, designed it in 1826–9 for Nicholas I and his wife, who wanted a domestic environment in keeping with their bourgeois tastes.

The Gothic theme is pursued throughout, most effectively in the Great Drawing Room with the rose window motif in the carpet and the lacelike tracery of the stuccoed ceiling. The exquisite 5,200-piece crystal and porcelain dinner service in the Dining Room was made for the royal couple at the Imperial Porcelain factory.

The Fountains at Peterhof

JEAN-BAPTISTE LE BLOND submitted his "water plan" to Peter the Great in 1717, by which time the tsar had begun sketching his own ideas. The centerpiece is the Grand Cascade, fed by the underground springs of the Ropsha Hills about 22 km (14 miles) away. The cascade is a celebration of the triumph of Russia over Sweden *(see p19)*, symbolized by Mikhail Kozlovskiy's glorious sculpture of Samson rending the jaws of a lion. An imaginative variety of fountains, mostly concentrated in the Lower Park, includes triton and lion fountains, dragon fountains with checker-board steps, and smaller fountains with fish-tailed boys blowing sprays of water through conches. Most playful are trick fountains such as the Umbrella, which "rains" on those who come too close.

Detail of the Mezheumnyy Fountain

The Adam Fountain, sculpted by Giovanni Bonazza, was com-missioned by Peter in 1718, along with a similar statue of Eve. The two fountains suggest the earthly paradise the tsar had recreated at Peterhof.

The Roman Fountains were designed by Ivan Blank and Ivan Davydov in 1738–9. The two-tiered marble fountains were inspired by one in St. Peter's Square in Rome.

The Neptune Fountain predates Peterhof by more than 50 years. The Baroque sculpture was erected in 1658 in Nuremberg to mark the end of the Thirty Years War and was sold to Tsar Paul I in 1782 because there was not enough water to make it work.

The Grand Cascade was originally adorned with lead statues that weathered badly and were recast in bronze and gilded after 1799. Shubin, Martos, and other noted sculptors worked to create this stunning cascade.

The Pyramid Fountain (1720s) is one of a number of fountains whose jets create a special shape. Over 500 jets of water rise in seven tiers to create an "obelisk" commemorating the Russian victory over Sweden.

Tsarskoe Selo ❺

Царское Село
Tsarskoe Selo

The lavish imperial palace at Tsarskoe Selo was designed by Rastrelli *(see p93)* in 1752 for Tsarina Elizabeth. She named it the Catherine Palace in honor of her mother, Catherine I, who originally owned the estate. The next ruler to leave her mark on the palace was Catherine the Great, and during her reign she commissioned the Scotsman Charles Cameron to redesign the Baroque interiors according to her more Neo-Classical taste. Cameron also built the ensemble for taking traditional Russian cold and warm baths, containing the Agate Rooms, and the Cameron Gallery. Post-war restoration of the palace continues, and 20 state rooms are now open, as well as the beautiful park.

★ **The Great Hall**
Light streams into Rastrelli's glittering hall illuminating the mirrors, gilded carvings and the vast ceiling painting, The Triumph of Russia *(c.1755), by Giuseppe Valeriani.*

The Great Staircase (1860), by Ippolito Monighetti, ascends to the state rooms on the first floor.

Entrance

Atlantes
The stunning 300-m (980-ft) long Baroque façade is adorned with a profusion of atlantes, columns, pilasters, and ornamented window framings.

0 meters		25
0 yards		25

The Agate Rooms *(see p152)*, part of the imperial *banya* (baths) are faced inside with semi-precious stones from the Urals.

The Cameron Gallery *(see p152)*

The Cavaliers' Dining Room
The table is laid for Tsarina Elizabeth's gentlemen-in-waiting, in the refined gold and white room created by Rastrelli.

The Royal Chapel is richly decorated in dark blue and gold. Built by Chevakinskiy in the 1740s, it contains an elaborate six-tiered iconostasis.

VISITORS' CHECKLIST

Tsarskoe Selo (Pushkin), 25 km (16 miles) S of St. Petersburg. 🚉 *from Vitebsk Station to Detskoe Selo, then bus 371 or 382 (see p220).* **Catherine Palace** 📞 *465 5308.* ⬜ *10am–5pm Wed–Mon.* 🌑 *last Mon of month.* 📷 🎫 🏛 ⬛ **Agate Rooms** ⬜ *10am–4:30pm Thu–Mon.* **Cameron Gallery** ⬛ *temporarily.* **Park** ⬜ *daily.* 📷 *mid-May–Sep.*

★ **Amber Room**
The original amber panels (1709) by Andreas Schlüter were a gift from Friedrich Wilhelm I of Prussia to Peter the Great. The room is slowly being recreated from photos, complete with carved reliefs and panels in Florentine mosaic.

The Blue Drawing Room is characterized by blue floral motifs painted on silk. Among the royal portraits hanging here is a painting of Peter the Great by Ivan Nikitin, dating from around 1720.

To the Lycée and the Church of the Sign *(see p153)*

The Picture Gallery displays canvases by Italian, French, Dutch, and Flemish masters of the 17th and 18th centuries.

★ **Green Dining Room**
Cameron's restrained Neo-Classical style contrasts with the Baroque flamboyance of Rastrelli's work. The exquisite stucco bas-reliefs, sculpted by Ivan Martos, were based on motifs from frescoes discovered in Pompeii.

The French-style formal gardens were laid out in the 1740s. Their formality and symmetry contrasts with the naturalistic English-style landscaping of the park *(see p152)*, created in 1768.

Small Enfilade
A varied selection of furniture and objets d'art *make up the exhibition in these unrestored rooms. Chinese lacquer furniture and Oriental rugs were among the treasures used to furnish the palace in the 19th century.*

STAR FEATURES

★ **The Great Hall**

★ **Amber Room**

★ **Green Dining Room**

Exploring Tsarskoe Selo

THE MAGNIFICENT PARKS and gardens of Tsarskoe Selo (the Tsar's Village) were created out of dense forest by thousands of soldiers and laborers. Work began on the formal gardens in 1744 but later, in 1768, Catherine the Great commissioned one of Russia's first landscaped parks. The 1,400 acres of grounds are dotted with captivating pavilions set around the central lake. The grounds and the town of Tsarskoe Selo, to the northeast of the palace, are also a delight to explore.

Formal gardens in front of Catherine Palace, Catherine Park

Catherine Park

The formal gardens to the southeast of the palace are laid out geometrically with radiating avenues, parterres and terraces, decorous ponds, hedges, elegant pavilions, and Classical statuary. Nearest to the palace are Cameron's sumptuous **Agate Rooms** (1780–87). Their heavily rusticated lower story contrasts with the upper tier, modeled on a Renaissance villa. The building takes its name from the agate, jasper, malachite, and other semiprecious stones covering the interior.

Girl with a Pitcher by Pavel Sokolov (1816)

The impressive **Cameron Gallery**, built in 1783–7, has a rusticated stone ground floor, surmounted by a Neo-Classical peristyle of 44 Ionic columns. Ranged along the colonnade are bronze busts of ancient philosophers, poets, and rulers. In 1792–4 Cameron added a long stone ramp to facilitate access to the gardens for the aging Catherine the Great.

The Neo-Classical **Lower and Upper Baths** were built by Ilya Neyelov in 1777–80. The domed Lower Baths were for the use of courtiers, while the exquisite Upper Baths were reserved for members of the imperial family.

Construction work on Rastrelli's **Grotto** began in 1749, but the original decoration of the interior with more than 250,000 shells continued well into the 1770s.

The gardens' main avenue leads to the **Hermitage** (1756), a Baroque pavilion built by Rastrelli, where Elizabeth would entertain small groups of guests for dinner.

The romantic landscaped area of the lower park was begun in 1768 by master gardeners such as John Bush, who worked under the overall supervision of the architect, Vasiliy Neyelov. A 16-km (10-mile) waterway was built to feed the numerous canals, cascades, and man-made lakes,

including the *pièce de résistance*, the **Great Pond**. From Giacomo Quarenghi's pavilion (1786) on the island, musicians would serenade Catherine and her courtiers as they floated by in gilded gondolas.

A naval theme links Vasiliy Neyelov's Dutch, Neo-Gothic **Admiralty** (1773–7) with the 25-m (82-ft) high **Chesma Column**, which is decorated with ships' prows. The column, designed by Antonio Rinaldi in 1771, commemorates the Russian victory over the Turks in the Aegean.

The reflection of the pink dome and minaret of the **Turkish Bath** shimmers in the placid waters on the far side of the lake. Nearby is Neyelov's colonnaded **Marble Bridge** (1770–76). Perched on a rock overlooking the pond is the **Girl with a Pitcher**, a statue by Pavel Sokolov. The figure inspired Pushkin to write his memorable poem, *Fountain at Tsarskoe Selo*, in which he muses on the girl who has broken her urn and now "sits timelessly sad over the timeless stream."

Evidence of the 18th-century craze for chinoiserie can be found on the border with the wilder Alexander Park where Cameron built his **Chinese Village** in 1782–96. Other examples are Yuriy Velten's **Creaking Pavilion**, so-called because it was designed to creak when visitors entered, and Neyelov's **Great Caprice** (1770s), a hump-backed bridge surmounted by a pagoda-like columned structure.

The Moorish-style Turkish Baths (1852) by Ippolito Monighetti

Creaking Pavilion (1778–86)

The Town of Tsarskoe Selo
This town of some 80,000 inhabitants was developed in the 19th century as a summer resort for the aristocracy. In 1937 it was renamed after the poet Alexander Pushkin *(see p43)*, who was educated at the local **Lycée** in 1811–17, in room No. 14. One of Russia's most prestigious schools, it was founded by Alexander I in 1811 to educate members of the nobility. In 1998 the town took back its original name.

The attractive **Church of the Sign**, dating to 1734, is one of the town's oldest buildings. In a garden next door a statue by Roman Bach depicts Pushkin dressed in the Lycée uniform.

Pushkin and his new bride, Natalya, spent the summer of 1831 in the delightful wooden house, now named **Pushkin's Dacha**. The writer, Nikolai Gogol, was amongst the many friends they entertained here.

On the town's western edge is the **Alexander Palace**, commissioned by Catherine for her grandson, the future Alexander I. Designed in 1792 by Giacomo Quarenghi, the austere, Neo-Classical building has a colonnaded facade and protruding wings. It was the residence of Russia's last tsar, Nicholas II, and his family, who lived here from 1904 until they were placed under house arrest in 1917 *(see p28)*. The exhibition inside includes Nicholas' magnificent Style-Moderne study, designed by Meltzer.

Lycée
◯ 10:30am–4:30pm Wed–Mon.

Pushkin's Dacha
◯ 10:30am–4:30pm Wed–Sun.

Alexander Palace
◯ 10am–4:30pm Wed–Mon.

Alexander Pushkin's statue (1900), by Roman Bach

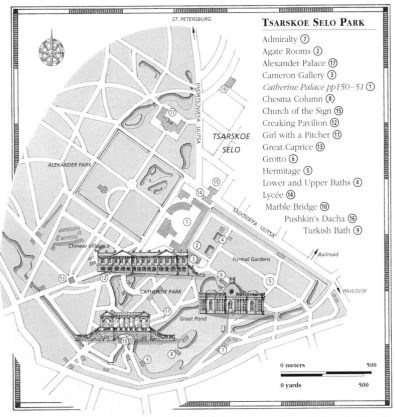

TSARSKOE SELO PARK

Admiralty ⑦
Agate Rooms ②
Alexander Palace ⑰
Cameron Gallery ③
Catherine Palace pp150–51 ①
Chesma Column ⑧
Church of the Sign ⑮
Creaking Pavilion ⑫
Girl with a Pitcher ⑪
Great Caprice ⑬
Grotto ⑥
Hermitage ⑤
Lower and Upper Baths ④
Lycée ⑭
Marble Bridge ⑩
Pushkin's Dacha ⑯
Turkish Bath ⑨

ST. PETERSBURG
DVORTSOVAYA ULITSA
TSARSKOE SELO
ALEXANDER PARK
SADOVAYA ULITSA
Chinese Village
Formal Gardens
Railroad
PAVLOVSK
CATHERINE PARK
Great Pond

0 meters　　　500
0 yards　　　500

Imperial standard of the Romanovs flying at the Catherine Palace ▷

Pavlovsk **6**

Павловск
Pavlovsk

To CELEBRATE THE BIRTH of his heir, Catherine the Great presented her son, the Grand Duke Paul, with these lands in 1777. She also "gave" him her favourite architect, Charles Cameron, to design both palace and park. Work at Pavlovsk (from "Pavel" or Paul) began in 1780 and was continued by Paul's grieving widow, Maria Fyodorovna, long after his death. "English gardens" were at the height of fashion, and inspired Cameron's design of a seemingly natural landscape dotted with pavilions (used for informal parties), romantic ruins, and attractive vistas around the Slavyanka River.

Cold Baths
This austere pavilion was built by Cameron in 1799 as a summer swimming pool, complete with elegant vestibule, paintings, furniture, and rich wall upholstery.

The Apollo Colonnade
Cameron's colonnade (1782–83) encircles a copy of the Apollo Belvedere, above a romantically dilapidated cascade.

Three Graces Pavilion

The Centaur Bridge by Voronikhin (1805) nestles on a bend of the Slavyanka River.

Aviary

Cameron's Dairy (1782) housed both a milking shed and a stylish salon.

★ Pavlovsk Palace
Cameron's elegant Palladian mansion (1782–6) forms the central block of today's palace (see pp158–9), with wings added in 1789 by Paul's favored architect, Vincenzo Brenna.

★ Temple of Friendship
This Doric temple (1780) was the first use of Greek forms in Russia.

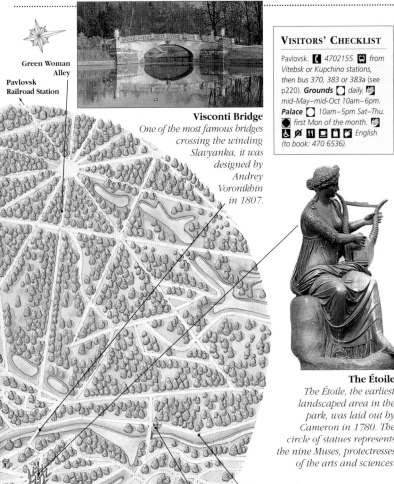

Green Woman Alley

Pavlovsk Railroad Station

VISITORS' CHECKLIST

Pavlovsk. 🎫 4702155. 🚉 from Vitebsk or Kupchino stations, then bus 370, 383 or 383a (see p220). **Grounds** ◯ daily. 📷 mid-May–mid-Oct 10am–6pm. **Palace** ◯ 10am–5pm Sat–Thu. ● first Mon of the month. 📷 ♿ 🚫 🍴 🎁 📷 🛍 🖥 English (to book: 470 6536).

Visconti Bridge
One of the most famous bridges crossing the winding Slavyanka, it was designed by Andrey Voronikhin in 1807.

The Étoile
The Étoile, the earliest landscaped area in the park, was laid out by Cameron in 1780. The circle of statues represents the nine Muses, protectresses of the arts and sciences.

The Beautiful Valley was the favorite spot of Elizabeth, wife of Alexander I.

0 meters	200
0 yards	200

Paul's Mausoleum
(1808–9) bears the inscription "To my beneficent consort."

The Rose Pavilion was the favorite haunt of Maria Fyodorovna from 1812. She held many concerts and literary evenings in this cottage.

STAR FEATURES

★ **Temple of Friendship**

★ **Great Palace**

Pil Tower and Bridge
Brenna's tower (1795–97) contained a spiral staircase, lounge, and library. The bridge was a later addition made in 1808.

Exploring Pavlovsk Palace

Late 18th-century clock, Grecian Hall

CATHERINE COMMISSIONED Charles Cameron to build the Great Palace (1782–86) while Paul and his wife Maria Fyodorovna traveled around Europe incognito as the Comte and Comtesse du Nord. They, meanwhile, bought up everything they saw, including French clocks, Sèvres porcelain, tapestries, and furniture, to fill their new home. Once back in Russia, they brought in Brenna to add taller, more elaborate wings to Cameron's elegant Palladian mansion, turning it into a true palace.

West facade of the Palladian mansion

PLAN OF PAVLOVSK PALACE, FIRST FLOOR

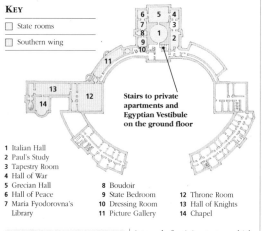

KEY

☐ State rooms

☐ Southern wing

Stairs to private apartments and Egyptian Vestibule on the ground floor

1 Italian Hall
2 Paul's Study
3 Tapestry Room
4 Hall of War
5 Grecian Hall
6 Hall of Peace
7 Maria Fyodorovna's Library
8 Boudoir
9 State Bedroom
10 Dressing Room
11 Picture Gallery
12 Throne Room
13 Hall of Knights
14 Chapel

STATE ROOMS

The Italian Hall, originally by Cameron and Brenna, 1789

NEARLY ALL OF the palace apartments at Pavlovsk, including the official ones, are relatively modest in scale. They reflect Maria Fyodorovna's intensely feminine tastes, which have given Pavlovsk a distinct charm rather than grandeur.

A fire in 1803 necessitated some remodeling of the palace interiors by Andrey Voronikhin. The entrance hall, or Egyptian Vestibule, gained its present appearance after he added the painted bronze figures and zodiac medallions. At the top of the stairs is Brenna's State Vestibule, where the bas-reliefs reflected Paul's passion for all things military. It leads onto the Italian Hall, situated beneath the central cupola, with lantern windows and heavy doors of rosewood and mahogany.

The northern row of rooms on this floor were for Paul, the southern ones for Maria. Paul's Study is dominated by Johann Lampi's fine portrait of Maria (1794), who holds a drawing of six of their children. Beneath it is a model temple of amber, ivory, and gilded bronze, made by Maria herself. Next door, the Tapestry Room is named after the Don Quixote tapestries made by Gobelin and presented to Paul by Louis XVI. The mahogany writing table was made for the new Engineers' Castle *(see p101)* but, after Paul's murder there in 1801 *(see p22)*, Maria moved much of the specially designed furniture to Pavlovsk Palace.

The corner rooms are a Hall of War for Paul and Maria's contrasting Hall of Peace, both richly adorned with bas-reliefs and heavy gilding. Between the two lies the magnificent Grecian Hall, Cameron's Neo-Classical masterpiece.

Maria Fyodorovna's rooms begin with a small, comfortable library. The chair at the desk was designed for her by Voronikhin; note the pots built into the spine for flowers. Her Boudoir has pilasters painted with motifs copied from the Raphael Loggias in the Vatican, and a porphyry fireplace. The State Bedroom was reputedly never slept in but was part of court ceremony. Opposite the

Maria Fyodorovna's Boudoir, designed by Brenna, 1789

Brenna's Picture Gallery (1789), with chandeliers by Johann Zeck

bed is a 64-piece Sèvres toilet set, complete with a coffee cup and an eyecup, which was a gift from Marie Antoinette.

Another present dominates the Dressing Room, a superb set of steel furniture including dressing table, chair, vases, and ink stand made by the renowned gun-makers of Tula (1789). This was presented to Maria by Catherine the Great.

SOUTHERN WING

FROM THE ELEGANTLY curved picture gallery, built in 1798, there are excellent views. Only a few of the paintings, mostly purchased during the young couple's trip to France, are worthy of special notice, as their taste was for applied art.

The largest room in the palace is the Throne Room, designed by Brenna (1797) after Paul became tsar. Despite its name it was generally used for balls and state dinners. The tables are now laid with part of a 606-piece gilded dinner service. Vast blue Sèvres vases

stand on plinths, bought from the factory (Paul and Maria spent huge sums on porcelain there). The ceiling was painted during restoration after World War II (see p26), using an original design.

The Knights of St. John chose Paul as Grand Master when they fled Napoleon's occupation of Malta in 1798. This suited Paul's military taste, and he commissioned vast lamps, thrones, and decorative items (now in the Hermitage) as well as the Hall of Knights for ceremonies of the Order. The pale green room has Classical statues, saved from the Germans in World War II by being buried in the grounds.

The suite of rooms ends with the Imperial Chapel of SS. Peter and Paul, a very un-Orthodox church by Brenna (1797–98), decorated with copies of European paintings.

PRIVATE APARTMENTS

LOCATED ON THE ground floor are the private apartments. The Pilaster Room (1800), with its golden pilasters, is furnished with a dark mahogany suite. The Lantern Study, designed a few years later by Voronikhin, is named after its apsed bay window forming the "lantern."

Maria Fyodorovna's Dressing Room leads into the Bedroom (1805) she actually used (as opposed to the State Bedroom upstairs). Pieces of the original silk were saved in the war and used to edge the new curtains.

The small pink and blue Ballroom was for private parties and has paintings by the most fashionable artist of the day, Hubert Robert. The General Study, used as a family sitting room, is decorated with family portraits The Raspberry Room, Paul's private study, contains paintings with views of Gatchina Palace, made for the Engineers' Castle.

The Lantern Study, one of Voronikhin's most successfully designed interiors, 1804

MARIA FYODOROVNA (1759–1828)

Paul's wife, Maria Fyodorovna, bore 10 children, and Pavlovsk was considered her 11th child. Paul himself preferred Gatchina (see p145) and in 1788 Maria was given Pavlovsk entirely. She devoted all her energy to adorning both palace and park, giving precise directions to designers and architects, who bemoaned their lack of independence. Born Sophia of Württemberg-Stuttgart, Maria had a practical German upbringing which she put to good use. Pieces of her own work, from furniture to family portraits, are throughout the palace.

Inkstand (1795) created from initial design by Maria Fyodorovna

Novgorod 🐧

Detail of bronze
door on Cathedral
of St. Sophia

THE ANCIENT TOWN of Novgorod (New Town) was founded in 859 by the Varangian (Viking) Prince Rurik *(see p17)*. The city's proud tradition of self-government began in the 11th century and lasted until 1478, when Ivan III subjugated the city. Favorably sited on the Volkhov River with convenient connections from Scandinavia to the Aegean, the city of Novgorod became a powerful trading community during this period. In 1570, Ivan the Terrible put Novgorod to the sword, torturing and massacring thousands of its inhabitants when the city plotted against him. It was, however, the rise of St. Petersburg that finally set the seal on Novgorod's decline. Much of the city's splendid cultural heritage, damaged in World War II, is now being restored and can be appreciated in the many medieval churches and picturesque streets of the old town.

Bejeweled metal icon cover on
display in the Chamber of Facets

The Kremlin

Situated on the left bank, or Sofiskaya Storona (Sophia side), of the River Volkhov, the formidable red-brick walls and cone-topped towers of the oval-shaped Detinets, or Kremlin, date from the 11th to the 17th centuries. According to the prevailing practice at the time, the first stone of the original walls was laid on the body of a living child.

Of the many towers, the 17th-century Kukui is the most remarkable, and also the tallest at 32m (105ft). The lower floors once contained a wine cellar and treasury chamber, while the octagonal room beneath the cupola was used, according to chronicles, "for surveying the whole town."

Kremlin walls, with the silver dome of
St. Sophia's Belfry (15th century)

At the heart of the fortress is Novgorod's oldest and largest church, the strongly Byzantine **Cathedral of St. Sophia** (1045–62). It was modeled on the cathedral of the same name in Kiev, but the tendencies of the Novgorod school already appear in the lack of ornament and the scarcity of windows,

necessary because of the cold. On the north wall, a section of whitewash has been removed to reveal the original mosaic effect of the gray-yellow stone and brick facade.

The exquisitely sculpted and extremely rare bronze doors adorning the west side were seized as booty in 1187 from the Swedish town of Sigtuna. In the lower left hand corner there are portraits of the craftsmen, named in the Latin inscription as Riquin and Weissmut. The interior is divided by piers into five aisles, three ending in altar apses. Fragments of early frescoes survive, but the iconostasis is one of the oldest in Russia and contains icons from the 11th–17th centuries.

East of the cathedral is **St. Sophia's Belfry**, much altered since it was first built in 1439. The bells, now displayed below, were cast in the late 16th and early 17th centuries.

The northwest corner of the Kremlin is occupied by the **Archbishops' Court**, in its heyday a powerful body with its own treasury, police force, and military guard. Beneath the 15th-century clock tower an attractive staircase leads to the **Library**, housing magnificent medieval religious manuscripts. Backing onto the cathedral, the **Chamber of Facets** is the most famous part of this ensemble. A superb star-vaulted reception hall dates from 1433 and displays treasures from the cathedral, including goblets, jeweled miters, and icon covers in precious metals.

The 11th-century Cathedral of St. Sophia, the landmark of Novgorod

Within the Kremlin is the **Museum of History, Architecture, and Art**, which houses a magnificent collection of 12th–17th-century icons of the Novgorod school. One of the most remarkable is the 12th-century portable icon of the Virgin of the Sign, whose miraculous image is said to have saved Novgorod from the armies of Prince Andrey Bogolyubskiy of Suzdal in 1169. Scenes from the battle are depicted on a vibrant 15th-century icon *(see p163)*. There are also works by leading 18th- and 19th-century artists, including Dmitriy Levitskiy, Karl Bryullov, and Vasiliy Serov *(see p106)*. The museum has a number of precious public documents and private letters written on birch bark, some of which date from the 11th century. These give details of ordinary, everyday life and are evidence of the unusually widespread literacy among the city's inhabitants.

The carved Royal Gates of an iconostasis in the Museum of History, Architecture, and Art

In the Kremlin's central square, the huge, bell-shaped **Millennium Monument** was sculpted by Mikhail Mikeshin. The monument was unveiled in 1862, a thousand years after Rurik's arrival in Novgorod. The figure kneeling before the Orthodox cross personifies Mother Russia, and, below, the decorative frieze depicts Rurik, Ivan III, Mikhail (the first Romanov tsar), Peter the Great, and many others. The frieze around the base shows over 100 figures: heroes, statesmen, artists, composers, princes and chroniclers from different periods of Russian history.

⊞ Cathedral of St. Sophia
☏ *(81622) 73556.* **◷** *8am–1pm, 2–8pm daily.* **◪**
⛼ Chamber of Facets
☏ *(81622) 73785.* **◷** *10am–6pm Thu–Tue.* **◪ ◪** *English by appt.*
⛼ Museum of History, Architecture and Art
☏ *(81622) 73770.* **◷** *10am–6pm Wed–Mon.* **◪ ◪** *English by appt.*

VISITORS' CHECKLIST

190 km (118 miles) S of St. Petersburg. **⛨** *190,000.* **◪** *from Moscow Station.* **◪** *from Coach Station 2 (see p221).* **ℹ** *Intourist Hotel, ul Dmitrevskaya 16, (81622) 75089.* **◪** *by appt (tel: 73770).*

commercial center, once the site of the medieval market, part of whose wall still stands.

The oldest church on this side of the river, **St. Nicholas' Cathedral** (1113–36), was built by Prince Mstislav. It dominates the area and once symbolized the prince's power.

Novgorod's merchants were eager to show their recognition of God's hand in their prosperity, and so funded many of the city's churches. **St. Paraskeva Pyatnitsa**, erected in 1207 and then rebuilt in 1345, was dedicated to the patron saint of commerce. The more decorative **Church of the Holy Women** and **Church of St. Procopius**, both 16th century, were financed by wealthy Moscow merchants. The fanciful tastes of the Muscovite patrons mark a departure from Novgorod's austere style.

Yaroslav's Court

Across the Volkhov River was the official seat of the princes, known as Yaroslav's Court. The palace of Yaroslav the Wise (1019–54) has since disappeared, but several churches have survived. The area adjacent to the Court is Novgorod's

Millennium Monument, celebrating Novgorod's 1,000 years of history

Yuriev Monastery walls and bell tower with the silvery domes of the Cathedral of St. George in the background

Beyond Yaroslav's Court

In the 12th century, Novgorod boasted over 200 churches, while there are only 30 today. Many of these are hidden away in the quiet hinterland of 19th-century streets to the east of Yaroslav's Court. On Ilina ulitsa, the arrangement of windows, niches, and inset crosses on the **Church of the Savior of the Transfiguration** facade (1374) is almost whimsical. Inside, there are original frescoes by one of Russia's greatest medieval artists, Theophanes the Greek (1335–c.1410), who came from Constantinople and decorated 40 Russian churches. Andrey Rublev (1360–1430), Russia's most famous icon painter, worked under Theophanes at the beginning of his career.

On the same street, the five-domed **Znamenskiy Cathedral**, or Cathedral of the Sign (1682–8), has an attractive gateway and faded frescoes on the outer walls. The beautiful interior was decorated in 1702 by Ivan Bakhmatov.

The **Church of Theodore Stratilates** on Mstinskaya ulitsa to the north was built in 1360–61 by the widow of a wealthy Novgorod merchant. The delicate purple and pink

Fresco inside Znamenskiy Cathedral

frescoes contrast with the harsher colors found in most 14th-century Novgorod frescoes. *The Annunciation,* for example, combines sensitivity and charm with religious intensity.

Farther Afield

A pleasant stroll 3 km (2 miles) south along the river bank leads to the **Yuriev Monastery**. This is the largest and most important monastery in the area, founded in 1030 and built on the orders of Prince Vsevolod. Its imposing Cathedral of St. George was built in 1119–30 by "Master Peter," the first named architect in Russian chronicles. This beautifully proportioned church with its

three asymmetrical cupolas was restored in the 19th century, but unfortunately most of the interior murals were lost. There were once 20 monastic buildings in the complex, dating mainly from the 19th century.

In the woods across the road lies the fascinating open-air **Museum of Wooden Architecture**, which displays churches and peasant huts moved from local villages. Of particular interest are the 17th-century two-tiered Kuritsko Church of the Dormition and the tiny wooden church of St. Nicholas from Tukhel village.

⛪ Yuriev Monastery
Yurevskaya nab. 【 (81622) 73020.
◯ 7am–8pm daily.
🏛 Museum of Wooden Architecture
Yurevo. 【 (81622) 78160.
◯ 10am–6pm (mid-Oct–mid-Apr: 10am–4pm) daily. 📷 🎬

Rebuilt 19th-century peasant hut (*izba*), Museum of Wooden Architecture

Russian Icon Painting

THE RUSSIAN ORTHODOX Church uses icons for both worship and teaching, but never for mere ornament, and there are strict rules for the creation of each image. Icons were believed to be imbued with the force of the saint depicted and were therefore invoked for protection during wars. Because the content was considered more important than the style, old, revered icons were often repainted again and again.

Early stone icon found in Novgorod

The first icons were brought to Russia from Byzantium. Greek masters came too, to train local painters. The northern schools that developed during the 13th–15th centuries were less restricted by Byzantine canons and have an earthy style linked to Russian peasant life. Novgorod, never under the Mongol yoke and with a thriving economy, was the source of many of the finest icons made for the northern monasteries.

Battle of Novgorod and Suzdal
This mid-15th-century work of the Novgorod School is thought to be Russia's earliest historical painting. Icons could have a political purpose – in this case to use Novgorod's great past as a justification for its independence from Moscow. Note the multiple touches of red – a color central to everyday Russian life and typical for icons of the Novgorod School.

Virgin of Vladimir
The most venerated icon in Russia, this 12th-century work was made in Constantinople. Its huge influence on Russian icon painting cannot be overstated.

THE ICONOSTASIS

The iconostasis screens off the sanctuary from the main part of the church, as if it were a boundary between heaven and earth. In Russian practice it is covered with icons strictly arranged in up to six tiers, each with its own dogmatic purpose.

The Festival Tier shows the 12 major church festivals, such as the Entry into Jerusalem and the Crucifixion. Such pictorial representation aided the faith of the illiterate.

The Royal Gates represent the entrance from the temporal world to the spiritual, between which the priests pass during the service.

Christ Enthroned

The Deesis Tier, above the Royal Gates, contains Christ Enthroned, flanked by the Virgin and St. John interceding on behalf of mortal sinners.

The Local Tier is for local saints, to whom the church is dedicated and patron saints of major donors.

Old Testament Trinity by Rublev
Andrey Rublev was one of the greatest artists of the Moscow School. He was strongly influenced by recent developments in Byzantine painting, brought to Russia by Greek masters in the late 14th century. His Trinity icon dates from the early 15th century.

TRAVELERS' NEEDS

WHERE TO STAY 166-173
RESTAURANTS AND CAFÉS 174-185
SHOPS AND MARKETS 186-191
ENTERTAINMENT IN ST. PETERSBURG 192-197

WHERE TO STAY

THERE IS A SERIOUS dearth of good accommodation in St. Petersburg, particularly in the city center and in the lower price bracket. The majority of tourists visiting St. Petersburg arrive with a package tour and are housed in one of the large, modern hotels formerly managed by the State Tourist Agency, Intourist. These are anonymous and rarely central but, on the whole, provide a reasonably good service with many amenities such as restaurants, bars, and sports facilities. The would-be individual tourist is no longer compelled to travel on a package tour,

Doorman at Hotel Europe

as was the case during the Soviet era. Nowadays visas and hotel bookings can be made independently and hotels can be reserved directly or through a booking agency. For the summer months, particularly during the White Nights, it is recommended to make bookings well in advance for the city's most prestigious and centrally located hotels.

Those on a tight budget with no knowledge of Russian are advised to make arrangements in advance. Rooms are limited and visitors with no reservations may be refused. There is a selection of hotels on *pp172–73*.

Pribaltiyskaya, a hotel popular with package tours

WHERE TO LOOK

VERY FEW hotels are located in central St. Petersburg and the hotels listed in this chapter are scattered around the city, often at a distance from the center. Visitors on a package tour usually find they are staying in a former Intourist hotel such as the Pribaltiyskaya or Pulkovskaya situated in modern high-rise areas on the city's outskirts. It is important for the independent traveler to decide at the start what your priorities are going to be: location, price, or service.

HOW TO BOOK

HOTEL RESERVATIONS for the White Nights *(see p51)* should be made up to six months in advance. The best way to book independently is by fax. The larger hotels will require a credit card number, and money will be debited if a cancelation is made less

than 24 hours in advance. Most hotels will confirm your reservation, and this confirmation can be used when applying for a visa *(see p202)*.

The **St. Petersburg International Youth Hostel** can now take bookings by e-mail, which is increasingly being used by other hotels. For a choice of accommodation, the most reliable booking organization in St. Petersburg is **Ost-West Kontaktservice** which also handle guides and transportation *(see p200)*.

FACILITIES

ALL THE HOTELS listed include at least a shower and a television and usually an individual telephone. Most hotels have a luggage room for storing baggage after the midday check-out time.

Ex-Intourist hotels are all very similar, with a vast lobby, several restaurants and cafés, bars, discos, and usually a

sauna. These were built at the height of the Soviet tourist boom with the aim of keeping foreign tourists in restricted areas, generally situated away from the center. As foreigners were bused to and from the sights and were rarely allowed to wander on their own, the hotels tend to be far removed from public transit facilities. While greater freedom is now the norm, limited public transportation from these hotels is often a problem for those seeking independence.

PRICE

LACK OF sufficient competition is the main reason that prices for hotel accommodation in St. Petersburg are still relatively high. Middle range hotels ($70–90 per person) are all located outside the center with encumbent

Fitness center, one of many facilities at the Grand Hotel Europe

public transportation problems. To stay in the city center with all facilities you must opt for top range hotels, such as the Grand Hotel Europe, which can offer anything from an exclusive single room to imperial suites worth several thousand dollars a day.

Prices are rarely on display, and may increase during the tourist season, late May until late September.

Entrance to the luxurious, modern Nevskij Palace Hotel

HIDDEN EXTRAS

MOST HOTELS include local taxes in their prices, with the notable exception of the exclusive Grand Hotel Europe. Breakfast is generally included in the room rate. If it is not, it can be a significant addition to your final bill in the larger hotels. The biggest shock, however, is likely to be the cost of international or even local phone calls from your hotel room. The larger hotels have their own satellite lines that make all calls easy but very expensive. Bear in mind that calls which use the local network are relatively cheap, and phonecards can be purchased to make international calls from street booths *(see p208)*. Even BCL satellite lines in hotel and restaurant lobbies are cheaper than calling through the hotel operator.

The Pribaltiyskaya adds a hefty charge for an individual reservation, which can radically affect the cost of a short stay. Some hotels charge an extra sum for registering your passport, which is in any case required *(see p202)*.

SECURITY

SECURITY IN HOTELS has become stricter in recent years, with the top range establishments using metal-detectors and selective bag searches at entrances. Smaller hotels have a doorman, who may ask to see a visitor's card or identification. Since this is simply a precaution for your protection, there is no reason to object.

Many hotels have safes in the rooms and safety deposit boxes at the front desk. Large sums of money and valuables should always be left in one of these places.

DISABLED TRAVELERS

DUE TO THE thick snow in winter, most buildings in St. Petersburg have steps up to their entrances, making access extremely difficult for disabled visitors. The Grand Hotel Europe and Nevskij Palace, St. Petersburg's two most elite hotels, are the only places that are fully wheelchair accessible and where the staff have been trained to be

Room in the Grand Hotel Europe

of assistance. However, more and more hotels are adding ramps, widening doors and trying to adapt to meet the needs of disabled travelers.

CHILDREN

ST. PETERSBURG has never been vaunted as a great children's destination, and very few of the hotels cater specifically to them. It is possible to arrange babysitters in the Grand Hotel Europe or the Nevskij Palace, if required, but it is best avoided in other hotels.

The elegant Winter Garden Restaurant in the Astoria Hotel

BUDGET HOTELS

Accommodation in St. Petersburg is not cheap by any means, and anyone on a low budget should be prepared for prices corresponding to around $30 or more per person per night for one of the cheaper hotels. The lower-price hotels such as Oktyabrskaya and Rus offer some of the best locations, but also tend to be rather run down. Mir, farther from the center, offers more pleasant surroundings, while Matisov Domik, which is undoubtedly the best of the few hotels in the lower price bracket, combines personal service and attractive location.

Lobby of the small, family-run Matisov Domik

HOSTELS

For the budget traveler seeking comfortable accommodation in a reasonably central location, the functional **St. Petersburg International Youth Hostel** is the cream of the crop. The hostel, which is

Efficient and helpful travel bureau service at the St. Petersburg International Youth Hostel

often booked up well in advance, provides a travel bureau, English-language videos every evening, and excellent advice on St. Petersburg. They also issue invitations for visa applications *(see p202)*.

The slightly larger and less polished **Holiday Hostel**, just behind Finland Station *(see p126)*, tends to be a popular choice with Russian visitors,

making it ideal for those wishing to get into the swing of local life. The most centrally located hostel, right behind the Kazan Cathedral *(see p111)*, is **Hertzen University Hostel**, which is run by the university. While you cannot book with them direct, visa support and bookings are available through **Ost-West Kontaktservice**.

An excellent alternative for those seeking a novel experience is to stay at the quaint **Petrodvorets Sanatorium**, housed in the former stables of Peterhof's magnificent palace *(see pp146–9)*. At very low prices for a double room, and with the hydrofoil *(see p221)* running from the palace

Petrodvorets Sanatorium, occupying the stables at Peterhof

DIRECTORY

ROOM RESERVATIONS

Ost-West Kontaktservice
℃ 279 7045.
FAX 327 3417.

St. Petersburg Bed and Breakfast
Katya Cherkasova.
℃ 219 4116.
FAX 219 4116.

Canongate Books Limited
(*People to People Russia –* introductions to Russians)
14 High Street,
Edinburgh EH1 1TE.
℃ (0131) 557 5111.

HOSTELS

Herzen University Hostel
Общежитие Гос.
Педагогического
Университета имени
Герцена
Obshchezhitie Gos. Pedagogicheskovo Universiteta im. Gertsena
Kazanskaya ulitsa 6.
Map 6 E2.
℃ 314 7472.
FAX 314 7659.

Holiday Hostel
Хостел Холидей
Khostel Kholidey
Ulitsa Mikhaylova 1.
Map 4 C3.
℃ 542 7364.
FAX 325 8559.

Petrodvorets Sanatorium
Санаторий Петродворец
Sanatoriy Petrodvrets
Avrova ulitsa 2,
Peterhof.
℃ 427 5098.
FAX 427 5021.

St. Petersburg International Youth Hostel
3-ya Sovetskaya ulitsa 28.
Map 7 C2.
℃ 325 8018.
FAX 329 8019.
@ ryh@ryh.spb.su

CAMPING

Olgino Motel-Camping
Мотела Ольгино
Motela Olgino
18 km (11 miles) NW of
St. Petersburg,
Primorskoe shosse 18.
℃ 238 3463.

RENTING A DACHA

RIK
РИК
Ulitsa Zelenogorskaya 3,
off Svetlanovskaya
ploshchad
℃ 554 4658.
FAX 554 4942.

Impressive facade of the Oktyabrskaya Hotel, dating from 1847

to the city center during the summer, this offers a marvellous opportunity to stay in a leafy country setting within easy access of St. Petersburg. The food is poor at the sanatorium, but Peterhof has a number of pleasant cafés.

Staying with Families

FOR A REALLY good insight into Russian life, staying with a family can be an interesting and inexpensive option. The system works very much like any bed-and-breakfast in Europe, with prices including breakfast but no other meals, although extra meals can usually be provided at a cost.

Ost-West Kontaktservice has a wide range of families, while **St. Petersburg Bed and Breakfast** offers a more limited selection. All families are checked out personally by the organizations which will then do their best to suit accommodations to your needs.

Canongate Books Limited publishes *Russia* in their *People to People* series, with introductions to over 1,000 Russians willing to offer hospitality and assistance to visitors. You will, of course, be expected to cover your own expenses.

Dacha in pine forest near Repino and the Gulf of Finland *(see p144)*

Camping

ST. PETERSBURG'S weather does not make it ideal for camping. Visitors are restricted to **Olgino Motel-Camping** on the Gulf of Finland, to the northwest of St. Petersburg. The campsite is about 35 minutes' drive from the city with poor public transportation facilities.

Renting a Dacha

FOR THOSE spending some time in and around St. Petersburg, renting a dacha or country house can be an attractive and much more tranquil alternative to staying in the city. One of the most pleasant times of the year to do this is after the snows have thawed and spring has fully set in. For further information contact **Ost-West Kontaktservice** or **RIK**.

Using the Listings

The hotels on pages 172–3 are listed according to area and price category. The symbols summarize the facilities at each hotel.

🛁 all rooms have bath and/or shower unless otherwise indicated

1 single-rate rooms available

🏨 rooms for more than two people available, or an extra bed can be put in a double room

24 24-hour room service

TV television in all rooms

Y minibar in all rooms

▤ air-conditioning in all rooms

🏋 gym/fitness facilities

🏊 swimming pool

🖥 business facilities: message-taking service, fax service, meeting room

🧍 babysitting service

♿ wheelchair access

🛗 lift

P parking available

Y bar

🍴 restaurant

💳 credit and charge cards accepted:

AE American Express
DC Diners Club
MC MasterCard
V VISA
JCB Japanese Credit Bureau

Price categories are based on a standard double room in high season, including breakfast, tax, and service.
⑤ under US$100
⑤⑤ US$100–150
⑤⑤⑤ US$150–200
⑤⑤⑤⑤ US$200–300
⑤⑤⑤⑤⑤ over US$300

Imposing sweep of the 1970s Moskva Hotel facade

Popular Hotels in St. Petersburg

Accommodations in st. petersburg have improved in recent years, but there is still really only a handful of hotels from which to choose. Unfortunately, few of these are conveniently situated for the city center and it is important to decide on your priorities, whether location, price, character, service, or amenities. This selection represents the city's most popular hotels.

Hotelship Peterhof
Staying on board a ship is an appropriately novel way to spend your nights in a city characterized by its waterways and islands.

Pribaltiyskaya
The dark, sedate interiors of this popular package-tour hotel contrast with the stunning views of the Gulf of Finland.

Matisov Domik
The intimate, friendly ambience of this small hotel makes it one of St. Petersburg's most welcoming and pleasant retreats.

Sovietskaya
This 1970s hotel offers wonderful views of the city center from its rotunda bar. At sunset or during White Nights the vista is particularly magical.

Astoria Hotel
One of the city's most luxurious and centrally located hotels, the Astoria is perfect for exploring St. Petersburg on foot. The attractive building overlooks St. Isaac's Square and Cathedral.

St. Petersburg
The package-tour visitors usually housed in the St. Petersburg get one of the city's most beautiful views of the Neva and Palace Embankment from the Bel-Etage café.

Grand Hotel Europe
Situated in the heart of the city, this historic hotel is the finest place to stay in St. Petersburg. Elegant decor and refined service are complemented by many facilities.

Nevskij Palace
This spotless, well-run and efficient hotel is characterized by sparse, bright, modern interiors. It is well located on Nevskiy prospekt and has excellent restaurants and business facilities.

Moskva
Of all St. Petersburg's large tourist hotels, the Moskva enjoys the best location, with good transportation amenities, and bars and cafés both in the hotel and nearby.

Pulkovskaya
Comfortable and clean, this vast, modern hotel has many business facilities, including an auditorium. The hotel's main advantage is its proximity to the airport.

0 kilometers   2

0 miles   2

ST. PETERSBURG

Matisov Domik
Матисов домик

Nab reki Pryazhki 3/1, 190121. **Map** 5 A3. 📞 *219 5445.* FAX *219 7419.* **Rooms:** 23. 🛏 1 ♨ 24 TV 📶 🚹 🚻 📶 P ★ 📶 *MC, V.* ⑤

The foreign diplomatic and business community soon discovered the rare charm of this small family establishment when it opened in 1993, on a small island by the Pryazhka river. With just 23 rooms in a compact modern building overlooking a tree-lined waterway, this is a real getaway location offering very friendly service. For business purposes it has a conference hall and basic fax and photocopier facilities. Transport to the center is by tram only, and it can be difficult to catch a taxi, but from the hotel it is only 15 minutes' walk through attractive streets to the Mariinskiy Theater *(see p119).*

Mir
Мир

Ul Gastello 17, 196135. 📞 *108 5166.* FAX *108 5165.* **Rooms:** 120. 1 ♨ 24 🚹 📶 P 📶 🍴 ⑤

Situated opposite the marvelous 18th-century Chesma Church *(see p130),* this 1970s building is gradually being done up to meet foreign standards. The hotel is becoming more popular and, in the high season, it can be difficult to get a room here. With Moskovskaya metro station and some wonderful examples of Stalinist architecture reasonably close by, Mir enjoys a modest but well-deserved reputation among budget travelers and businesspeople.

Moskva
Москва

Pl Aleksandra Nevskovo 2, 193317. **Map** 8 E3. 📞 *274 0022.* FAX *274 2130.* **Rooms:** 770. 🛏 1 ♨ 24 TV 🚹 🚻 📶 P 📶 🍴 📶 *AE, DC, MC, V.* ⑤

Of all the old Intourist hotels, this is the best situated, right opposite the Alexander Nevsky Monastery *(see pp130–31),* with the metro station nearby as well as many buses, trams, and trolleybuses.

The Moskva once had a bad reputation for attracting second-rate criminals, but now it is just a plain package-tour hotel. The enormous, curving 1970s building is dark inside, and on a scale intended to cater for large groups. It has more personal touches than other Intourist hotels, such as the

traditional Soviet-style key lady sitting by the elevators on each floor, available to help with anything from ironing and emergency clothing repairs to making tea.

Okhtinskaya
Охтинская

Bolsheokhtinskiy pr 4, 195027. 📞 *227 4438.* FAX *227 2618.* **Rooms:** 300. 🛏 1 ♨ 24 TV 📶 🚹 🚻 📶 P 📶 🍴 📶 *AE, DC, MC, V, JCB.* ⑤

With views of the Smolnyy Convent just across the Neva, this 1970s hotel offers clean, bright rooms at reasonable prices. The surrounding area is mainly high-rise, but is pleasant enough. It is a short walk from various bus, tram, and trolleybus routes, which take just under half an hour to reach the center. The Nevsky Melody *(see p196)* entertainment complex just round the corner attracts a noisy crowd in the evenings, but the hotel itself is generally quiet.

Oktyabrskaya
Октябрьская

Ligovskiy pr 10, 193172. **Map** 7 C2. 📞 *277 6330.* FAX *315 7501.* **Rooms:** 672. 🛏 1 ♨ TV 📶 🚹 🚻 📶 🍴 📶 *MC, V.* ⑤

This hotel's fascinating history can be appreciated despite the fact that it is now very run down. Built in 1847, it became a hospital for the starving during World War II, and in 1944 housed the Estonian government forced into exile by the Nazis.

Although room security is poor, the hotel is very conveniently located and is favored by regular visitors to the city, who feel that they are staying in a truly Russian hotel. Its dark, brooding corridors, traditional Russian cakes in the café, and remnants of former glory, such as the bronze statues at the foot of the stairs, add to its character. At peak periods, guests may also be housed in the extension, located opposite Moscow Station, but this should be avoided.

Rus
Русь

Artilleriyskaya ul 1, 191104. **Map** 3 B5. 📞 *273 4683.* FAX *279 3600.* **Rooms:** 163. 🛏 1 ♨ 24 TV 🚹 📶 🍴 📶 *AE, MC, V, JCB.* ⑤

Conveniently located just 15 minutes' walk from Nevskiy prospekt, this modern hotel now lets out many of its rooms as office space. It is the cheapest hotel in the center, but the service and small rooms leave something to be desired. The lack of restaurant is no hardship, with a variety of

good cafés and restaurants only a short walk away. For those with few demands it offers a superb deal. The sauna is to be recommended, but is so popular that it can be difficult to book.

Hotel Deson-Ladoga
Отель Десон-Ладога

Ul Shaumiana 26, 195213. 📞 *528 5628.* FAX *528 5448.* **Rooms:** 96. 🛏 1 ♨ 24 TV 📶 🚹 🚻 📶 P 📶 🍴 📶 *DC, MC, V.* ⑤⑤

This Russo-Hong Kong joint venture hotel is set in an area of 1960s apartment buildings, accessible by direct metro and trolleybus routes from Nevskiy prospekt. Clean and efficient, if somewhat impersonal, it is ideal for those looking for a high standard of service at a moderate price. All staff speak excellent English, while the rooms are bright and spacious and the bathrooms immaculate. The room price includes breakfast and a morning sauna. The restaurant offers both European and Chinese cuisine.

Neptune
Нептун

Nab Obvodnovo kanala 93-a, 191126. **Map** 6 F5. 📞 *315 4965.* FAX *113 3160.* **Rooms:** 70. 🛏 1 ♨ 24 TV 📶 🚹 🚻 📶 🍴 📶 *AE, DC, MC, V.* ⑤⑤

Neptune is one of the few small hotels in town, offering Austrian efficiency and immaculate cleanliness as well as freedom from large package-tour groups. This makes it very popular with business travellers. Just five minutes' walk from Ligovskiy prospekt and plenty of public transportation, or ten minutes from Pushkinskaya metro, this modern building is located in a more industrial part of the center, on the Obvodnyy Canal.

Pulkovskaya
Пулковская

Pl Pobedy 1, 196240. 📞 *123 5122.* FAX *123 5856.* **Rooms:** 840. 🛏 1 ♨ TV 📶 🚹 🚻 📶 P 📶 🍴 📶 *AE, DC, MC, V.* ⑤⑤

The road from the airport emerges into the city at Victory Square, with its vast monument to the Siege of Leningrad *(see p27),* and the Pulkovskaya hotel to your left.

Built by Finnish architects in 1978, this is another large, anonymous tourist hotel. It does have a distinguished ambience, however, that sets it slightly apart from other Intourist hotels. Its restaurants have been revamped (with the addition of Oriental cuisine), and the small cafés are pleasant, but the food is not very exciting.

Sovietskaya
Советская

Lermontovskiy pr 43/1, 198103.
Map 5 B5. **☎** 329 0186. **FAX** 251 8890. **Rooms:** 1000. ⬛ 1 ⬛ 24 📺 ⬛ ⬛ P ⬛ ⬛ AE, MC, V. ⑤⑤

Visitors staying here should be sure to book into the Riga Building (12th and 14th floors reserved for foreigners) or Fontanka Building, which have superb views of the Fontanka river and the city center.

The circular café in the tower offers coffee, wine, and spirits and a vast expanse of glass through which to watch St. Petersburg's famous skyline. During White Nights (*see p51*), the passage from piercing blue to red, orange, and violet can be awe-inspiring. The rooms are modern and sparse, but the service is pleasant, and several trams run from nearby to the center or to the metro.

Hotelship Peterhof
Отель Петергоф

Nab Makarova, near the Tuchkov Bridge, 199053. **Map** 1 A4. **☎** 325 8888. **FAX** 325 8889. **Rooms:** 105. ⬛ 1 ⬛ ⬛ ⬛ P ⬛ ⬛ ★ ⬛ AE, DC, MC, V. ⑤⑤⑤

Since St. Petersburg is a city of islands and waterways, staying on a ship seems very apt. This highly modern boat offers a standard of service that compensates for its inconvenient location – on the north side of Vasilevskiy Island. Transportation is somewhat scarce here, but the hotel runs a fair-priced car service to the center.

There are small cabins on the Main and Upper decks, and more luxurious quarters on the Boat Deck, where the best views are. The Main Deck, where the reception and shops are located, can get busy, so try and get a room higher up. The excellent Svir Restaurant (*see p182*) and Panorama Bar allow you to look out along the Neva as you begin the evening with a cocktail.

Pribaltiyskaya
Прибалтийская

Korablestroiteley ul 14, 199226. **☎** 356 0263. **FAX** 356 0094. **Rooms:** 1200. ⬛ 1 24 📺 ⬛ ⬛ ⬛ ⬛ ⬛ ⬛ P ⬛ AE, DC, MC, V, JCB. ⑤⑤⑤

Situated on the western edge of Vasilevskiy Island, the Pribaltiyskaya offers stunning views over the Gulf of Finland. In summer, families enjoy the beach while the sun dips onto the horizon but never sets, and in winter the bleakness of the iced-over Gulf is breathtaking.

The hotel itself, a vast, 1980s rabbit warren with five restaurants and a small café on every floor is characterized by dark wood furniture and dim lighting. Pribaltiyskaya metro is a bus ride or 20-minute walk away.

St. Petersburg
Санкт-Петербург

Pirogovskaya nab 5/2, 194175. **Map** 3 A2. **☎** 542 8149. **FAX** 248 8002. **Rooms:** 410. ⬛ 1 ⬛ 24 📺 ⬛ ⬛ ⬛ AE, DC, MC, V. ⑤⑤⑤

This hotel changed its name in 1991, when the city of Leningrad became St. Petersburg once more. Still very much a 1960s hotel, it is the first and smallest of the large Intourist structures. The atmosphere is provincial, from the foyer with its potted plants to the little tea rooms on each floor. The rooms are typical tourist hotel fare, but those at the front have magnificent views of the broadest part of the Neva. However, they also face southwest, which means that during White Nights (*see p51*) the sun shines into the rooms for most of the night.

Astoria Hotel
Гостинца Астория

Bolshaya Morskaya ul 39, 190000. **Map** 6 D2. **☎** 210 5757. **FAX** 210 5133. **Rooms:** 436. ⬛ 1 ⬛ 24 📺 ⬛ ⬛ ⬛ ⬛ ⬛ ★ ⬛ AE, DC, MC, V, JCB. ⑤⑤⑤

It's hard to beat the Astoria's front room views, which look out over St. Isaac's Cathedral. This is the perfect place to stay if you want to see St. Petersburg on foot. One of the city's top hotels, the building dates from 1911–12 (*see p79*), although it has undergone renovation. The two parts of the hotel, the Astoria and the former Angleterre, have separate entrances but are connected on upper floors. The Astoria has the most attractive interiors, and the lobby is an elegant place to take afternoon tea, accompanied by harp or piano music. The Angleterre is more modern, with a nightclub and casino (*see p197*). There are two restaurants, the most famous being the Winter Garden (*see p180*).

Grand Hotel Europe
Гранд Отель Европа

Mikhaylovskaya ul 1/7, 191011. **Map** 6 F1. **☎** 329 6000. **FAX** 329 6001. **Rooms:** 301. ⬛ 1 ⬛ 24 📺 ⬛ ⬛ ⬛ ⬛ ⬛ ⬛ ★ ⬛ AE, DC, MC, V. ⑤⑤⑤⑤⑤

The most luxurious and expensive hotel in the city, the Grand Hotel Europe is a superbly restored Style-Moderne monument (*see p101*). The historic interiors offer a range of suites, including the Imperial Suite costing around $2,500 a night.

The Grand Hotel Europe set the standard for all St. Petersburg hotels to strive for when it reopened after renovation in 1991. The impeccable service combines old-fashioned discretion with up-to-date quality, while its restaurants, including the famous Europe (*see p181*), are among the best. The internal yard is now a light and airy atrium where coffee and cakes are served all day. Located just off Arts Square, it is the most central of the city's hotels.

Nevskij Palace Hotel
Невский палас отель

Nevskiy pr 57, 191025. **Map** 7 B2. **☎** 275 2001. **FAX** 301 7323. **Rooms:** 285. ⬛ 1 ⬛ 24 📺 ⬛ ⬛ ⬛ ★ ⬛ AE, DC, MC, V, JCB. ⑤⑤⑤⑤⑤

This top-class modern hotel prides itself on being the base for celebrities and film crews. It may seem a little characterless, but it copes well with both groups and individuals. It has fine restaurants and a great patisserie, the Vienna Café, patronized by expatriates and locals alike.

The hotel's convenient location and good conference and business facilities make it popular with businesspeople. Two of the floors are set aside for non-smokers, and the ground floor has a range of art galleries, banks, and airline offices, plus a good newspaper stand.

BEYOND ST. PETERSBURG

Beresta Palace Hotel
Береста палас отель

Studencheskaya ul 4A, 173014, Novgorod. **☎** (81622) 333 15. **FAX** 317 07. **Rooms:** 226. ⬛ 24 📺 ⬛ ⬛ ⬛ ⬛ P ⬛ ⬛ ★ ⬛ AE, DC, MC, V. ⑤⑤⑤

This is the only truly Western standard hotel in Novgorod, run by the company that manages the Nevskij Palace Hotel. Attractions include great river views from some rooms, good food and efficient service. Novgorod's water has a yellowish tinge, so the hotel's filter makes bathing, not to mention drinking, all the more pleasant. Since the city is much visited by businesspeople during the week, the hotel offers cheap weekend deals, often with transportation from St. Petersburg. Book these by fax or through the Nevskij Palace Hotel in St. Petersburg.

RESTAURANTS AND CAFÉS

THE RESTAURANT SCENE is changing rapidly in St. Petersburg, as specialty eateries, cafés, and bars spring up all over town. Eating out may still not be as exciting as in many European cities, but the options are increasing.

The big hotel restaurants lead the way in the top range, and in recent years the concept of the "business lunch," with an inexpensive fixed price menu, has made its appearance. Since the hotel restaurants are also catering to the local community, they liven things up with regular special events, such as festivals of foreign

Sign for Tbilisi

cuisine or traditional Russian fare. These are advertised in the English-language press *(see p209)*. Ethnic food, from the former Soviet republics as well as from abroad, is a growing trend that provides more variety and a wider selection of vegetarian dishes. Small cafés offer reasonable food and are the most convenient place to eat away from Nevskiy prospekt *(see p108)*. Getting a plain green salad is usually the biggest problem for visitors, but there are a few American and French cafés and bars specially designed to satisfy such cravings for simple fresh food.

Interior of the family-run Staraya Derevnya Restaurant

WHERE TO EAT

RESTAURANTS and cafés are scattered all over town, but it is possible to find good food without straying far from Nevskiy prospekt *(see pp46–9)*. Restaurants in this area cater mainly to foreigners, so they tend to be more expensive and accept credit cards. Cheaper places, such as Pirosmani *(see p181)*, Staraya Derevnya *(see p182)*, and Staroe Kafe *(see p185)*, which are pleasant with reasonable food, are often in inconvenient locations. The moderate outlay on food usually allows for the taxi fare.

TYPES OF RESTAURANT

THE TOP RANGE restaurants largely serve European food with a few select Russian dishes. Smaller, more intimate

venues like 1913 Goda *(see p180)* and Staraya Derevnya pride themselves on serving specifically Russian cuisine. This is generally uncomplicated food such as fried meat or fish with a selection of vegetables and pickles. The increasing

Outdoor café in the arcade of Gostinyy dvor *(see p108)*

number of ethnic and regional restaurants provides a touch of variety. The former Soviet republics, Georgia and Armenia, have both left their mark on Russian cuisine with *lobio* (spicy beans), *shashlyk (see p176)*, and *tolma* (stuffed vine leaves). A full range of these can be found at the Georgian Pirosmani *(see p181)* and Armenian Krunk *(see p183)*.

Indian, Chinese and, more recently, "traditional American" eateries are also popular.

All restaurants require neat dress, although a jacket and tie are rarely required.

READING THE MENU

MOST RESTAURANTS, as well as some cafés, have a summary of their menu in English. The disadvantage of this is that in smaller places the menu may change daily, but only in its Russian version. Thus the English menus are often misleading. Most waiters will make some effort to overcome language difficulties. In restaurants accepting credit cards there is usually at least one English-speaking waiter.

PAYMENT AND TIPPING

MAJOR RESTAURANTS are likely to accept some credit cards, but check beforehand. This guide gives an indication of price range in dollars, but restaurants will not accept foreign currency in payment for a meal, although some may have their own exchange office. Tips are 10–15 percent unless service is already included. To be sure the waiter receives the tip, it is best to give it in cash, rather than including it on a credit card.

OPENING TIMES

ALTHOUGH lunching out is not such an accepted habit among Russians, most restaurants open at midday and stay open until around 11pm or midnight. In rare cases, when for example there is an adjoining casino or nightclub, they may stay open until 1am.

Cafés close early, around 10pm at the latest, while bars, particularly those with live music (see p196), usually stay open until around 2 or 3am.

Last food orders are rarely taken after 11pm, even in bars, and many places stop serving an hour before closing time, so check last order times.

The beautifully decorated interior of the Russian Room in the Ambassador (see p182)

Street sign for Pirosmani

MAKING A RESERVATION

NEARLY ALL restaurants require reservations. Some establishments, notably Pirosmani, refuse to accept casual guests without a reservation, even if they are not fully booked. Some English will be spoken in all major restaurants, but your hotel concierge will be able to make reservations for you.

Apart from in the hotel restaurants, it is usually only possible to reserve a table a few days in advance. The majority of upscale restaurants, however, start taking reservations earlier during the White Nights (see p51). The city's most popular eateries can then be fully booked up to two weeks in advance, so it is wise to plan ahead.

Cafés do not generally require reservations. Since they rely heavily on special events, they may sometimes be unexpectedly closed to the public.

CHILDREN

ALTHOUGH few restaurants or cafés cater directly to children, establishments will rarely refuse entry to them. The only places likely to turn children away are those more geared toward entertainment.

Russians are slowly acquiring the habit of taking their children out to dine with them. The fast food outlets are obviously a good option, and Bistro Sadko's (see p183) can also be accommodating.

On the whole Russians love children, and staff can often be persuaded to adjust a dish to suit a child's special requests.

VEGETARIANS

SINCE RUSSIAN food is very much meat oriented, vegetarian food is limited. The main hotel restaurants all offer several vegetarian dishes while ethnic food, particularly Georgian and Armenian, Indian, and Mexican, may also have a higher proportion of vegetarian cuisine. Those who eat seafood will find the choice considerably broader, but in general finding vegetarian food in Russia may be a somewhat unrewarding task.

SMOKING

NEARLY ALL restaurants will allow smoking, and smoking during meals is considered acceptable. Few places except the hotel restaurants have separate non-smoking areas. In smaller cafés serving food, smoking is often prohibited and desperate smokers may be forced outside.

DISABLED ACCESS

WAITERS and doormen in most restaurants are helpful to those in wheelchairs, but cafés and bars prove more problematic. Not only are there usually stairs either up or down, but the doorways are narrow. The disabled are on the whole limited to the most expensive eateries and bars in the Nevskij Palace Hotel (see p173) and Grand Hotel Europe (see p173).

USING THE LISTINGS

Key to symbols in the listings on pages 180–82.

🍴 fixed price lunch
V vegetarian dishes
👶 suitable for children
♿ wheelchair access
👔 formal dress
▤ air-conditioning
🌳 outdoor eating
♫ live entertainment
🍷 recommended wine list
★ highly recommended
💳 credit cards accepted:
AE American Express
DC Diners Club
MC MasterCard
V VISA
JCB Japanese Credit Bureau

Price categories for a three-course meal for one, including service and tax (excluding wine):
⑤ US$20–30
⑤⑤ US$30–40
⑤⑤⑤ US$40–50
⑤⑤⑤⑤ US$50–60
⑤⑤⑤⑤⑤ over US$60

What to Eat in St. Petersburg

RUSSIA'S VAST RANGE of climates and cultures has produced a diverse culinary repertoire. Traditionally each region has its own cuisine, but dishes such as *shashlyk*, from Georgia, are now popular throughout Russia. Influences from Europe and the Middle East have also added specialties to the Russian table. Despite this diversity, some ingredients, such as sour cream *(smetana)*, curd cheese *(tvorog)*, cucumbers, beets, and dill, are still fundamental to the Russian taste.

Sprig of dill

Khachapuri
Originally from Georgia, these cheese-filled breads come in various shapes and sizes. The traditional filling is sulguni, *a cheese made from sheep milk.*

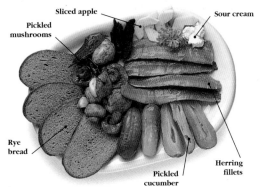

Sliced apple

Pickled mushrooms

Sour cream

Rye bread

Herring fillets

Pickled cucumber

ZAKUSKI
Made up of a variety of hors d'oeuvres, *zakuski* are served as appetizers for lunch or dinner. The spicy and salty flavors stimulate the appetite. Caviar, *kolbasa* (smoked sausages), pickles, and cheese are also typical.

Rassolnik
There are many versions of this classic soup, including recipes using chicken, fish, or kidney. Pickled cucumbers are a vital ingredient in all of them.

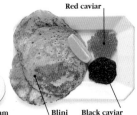

Solyanka
Made from either meat or fish, this soup has a distinctive rich, spicy taste. The meat version has a strong tomato flavor.

Borscht
Borscht gets its color from beets and tastes sour and sweet. It is served hot in winter and chilled in summer.

Shashlyk
This version of a kebab is made from marinated mutton or lamb. The pieces of meat may be interspersed with vegetables such as onions and peppers.

RUSSIAN CAVIAR

Black caviar *(ikra)* is sturgeon roe. It is produced by three species of sturgeon, all found in the Caspian sea. Beluga caviar is the rarest and has a distinctive nutty taste. Osetra has a creamy flavor, often compared to brie, while sevruga tastes of sea salt. Red caviar *(keta)* is salmon roe. Caviar is often served with buckwheat pancakes *(blini)* and sour cream *(smetana)*.

Red caviar

Red caviar jar

Black caviar jar

Sour cream

Blini

Black caviar

Osetrina
The sturgeon is famous for its roe (caviar), but the fish itself is also eaten in a variety of ways, such as salted or smoked.

Savory Pirozhki
Pirozhki can be stuffed with a variety of fillings such as meat and rice, fried cabbage, curd cheese, or mushrooms.

Kotlety po-Kievskiy
Chicken breasts are filled with garlic butter, coated in bread-crumbs, and deep fried. This is called Chicken Kiev in English.

Pelmeny
Originally a Siberian dish, these meat or fish dumplings are typ-ically served in broth or with sour cream, butter, or vinegar.

Kulebiaka
Puff or yeast pastry encloses a filling of salmon, rice, hard-boiled eggs, and mushrooms. The pie is sliced and served cold.

Golubtsy
Ground meat and rice rolled in cabbage leaves, golubtsy are boiled or baked and are often served with a tomato sauce.

DESSERTS

An important part of any Russian meal, most desserts are uncompromisingly rich. Russian cuisine has a wide variety of cakes, pies, tarts, pastries, and ice cream.

Vatrushki are sweet cheese-filled tartlets.

Vareniki are boiled sweet dumplings with various fruit fillings.

Khvorost are deep-fried cookies, with honey and sugar.

Bef Stroganov and Kasha
This dish of sautéed strips of beef in a sour cream, onion, and mushroom sauce is often served with boiled buckwheat (grechnevaya kasha).

Sweet Pirozhki
Made with yeast dough, sweet piroshki can have a variety of fillings, including fruit or jam, and may be served with cream.

Sharlotka
Devised for Tsar Alexander I by French chef Antoine Carême, this sponge cake is filled with custard and fruit purée.

Morozhenoe
Ice cream is traditionally a favorite dessert in Russia. It is often served with fresh fruit.

What to Drink in St. Petersburg

Shot of Starka

R USSIAN VODKA is famous throughout the world, and the Liviz distillery in St. Petersburg is Russia's second largest distillery, the largest being in Moscow. Vodka is thought to have been invented by Muscovite monks in the 14th or 15th century. Peter the Great *(see p18)* was particularly fond of anise- or pepper-flavored vodkas and devised modifications to the distillation process that greatly improved the quality of the finished drink.

Tea is Russia's other national drink. Traditionally made using a samovar and served black, tea has been popular in Russia since the end of the 18th century, when it was first imported from China.

A 19th-century Russian peasant family drinking vodka and tea

CLEAR VODKA

V ODKA IS PRODUCED from grain, usually wheat, although some rye is also used in Russia. St. Petersburg's Liviz distillery produces some excellent vodkas using the famed pure waters from Lake Ladoga. From the cheaper Sankt-Peterburg to the top quality, smooth-tasting Sinopskaya and Diplomat, Liviz dominates the vodka market in northern Russia. They also make Russia's most famous vodka, Stolichnaya (meaning "from the capital city") under license, but mainly for export. A recent and excellent arrival on the market is the Russian Smirnov, made just outside Novgorod *(see pp160–63)* and not to be confused with the Western Smirnoff.

Kubanskaya

Vodka is always served with food in Russia, often with a traditional range of richly flavored accompaniments called *zakuski (see p176)*.

Smirnov   **Sinopskaya**   **Sankt-Peterburg**

FLAVORED VODKA

T HE PRACTICE OF flavoring vodka has entirely practical origins. When vodka was first produced commercially in the Middle Ages, the techniques and equipment were so primitive that it was impossible to remove all the impurities. This left un-pleasant aromas and flavors, which were disguised by adding honey together with aromatic oils and spices. As distillation techniques improved, flavored vodkas became a specialty in their own right. Limonnaya, its taste deriving from lemon zest, is one of the most traditional, as is Pertsovka, flavored with red chili peppers. Okhotnichya (hunter's vodka) has a wider range of flavorings including juniper, ginger, and cloves. Starka (old vodka) is a mixture of vodka, brandy, port, and an infusion of apple and pear leaves, aged in oak barrels.

Pepper vodka

Limonnaya   **Okhotnichya**   **Starka**

MAJOR WINE REGIONS

- ■ Wine growing region
- ▨ Moldova
- ▨ Ukraine
- ▨ Russia
- ▨ Georgia
- ▨ Armenia
- ▨ Azerbaijan
- — International borders

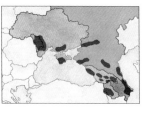

WINE

THE SOVIET UNION was one of the world's largest producers of wine (*vino*), but many of the major wine regions are now republics in their own right. Several indigenous types of grape are cultivated in the different regions, along with many of the more familiar international varieties.

Georgia is considered the best wine-making area. Its wines include those made from the Rkatsiteli grape, characterized by a floral aroma and subtle, fruity flavor, and the Gurdzhaani, which gives a unique, slightly bitter touch. Among its best red wines is the smooth Mukuzani. Moldova produces white, sparkling wines in the south and central regions, and the south is also known for its red wines. Since 1799, Moldova also produces a sweet, champagne-like wine called Shampanskoe.

White and red Georgian wine   **Shampanskoe**

OTHER ALCOHOLIC DRINKS

BRANDY (KONYAK) WAS ORIGINALLY a by-product of wine-making, and commercial production only began in Russia in the 19th century. Armenian brandy is one of the finest with a distinctive vanilla fragrance, resulting from its ageing in 70–100-year-old oak barrels. Georgia and Daghestan also produce good brandies. St. Petersburg beer (*pivo*) is among the best in Russia. Baltika, Vena, and Stepan Razin make a full range of beers in bottles and on draft. Since few preservatives are used, the true taste is preserved. Various imported beers are also available.

Baltika Beer   **Armenian brandy**

OTHER DRINKS

KVAS IS A MILDLY ALCOHOLIC DRINK made from rye and barley, consumed by adults and children alike. Russia's vast range of mineral waters (*mineralnaya voda*) includes many with unusually high mineral contents. Mineral waters from the Caucasus, Siberia, and Georgia are particularly prized. Also widely available are fruit juices (*sok, mors,* or *kompot*), including apple, tomato, and cranberry (*klyukva*), a traditional Russian favorite.

Mineral water   **Kvas**   **Cranberry juice**

TEA

RUSSIAN TEA IS SERVED BLACK with a slice of lemon and is usually drunk from tall glasses rather than cups. Sweetened with jam instead of sugar, tea (*chay*) is an ideal accompaniment to rich cakes and pastries. The boiling water for tea traditionally comes from a samovar. The water is used to brew a pot of tea, from which a little is poured into the glasses. This is then diluted with more hot water.

A glass of tea, with jam (*varenye*) to sweeten it

THE SAMOVAR

Made from brass or copper, samovars traditionally provided boiling water for a whole variety of domestic purposes and used to be an obligatory wedding gift. Modern ones are made of stainless steel and used mainly for boiling water to make tea. Sometimes eggs are put in the top to cook in the boiling water. The word samovar comes from *samo* meaning "itself" and *varit* meaning "to boil."

CENTRAL
ST. PETERSBURG

Demyanova Ukha
Демьянова уха

Kronverkskiy prospekt 53. **Map** 1 C3.
312 8090. noon–11pm daily.

Demyanova ukha literally means Demyan's fish soup, but in Russian folklore it stands for hospitality and over-eating home-cooked dishes. Everything is done to make this homey restaurant live up to its name. Only fish dishes are served, from the famous ukha (clear soup with fish dumplings) to sturgeon, salmon, pike, and trout, plus local delicacies such as voblya, which is caught locally in May and smells like fresh cucumbers. The interior is decorated like the inside of an izba, or peasant's hut, and booking is advised as this is one of the few good restaurants near the Peter and Paul Fortress (see pp66–7).

Literary Café
Литературное кафе

Nevskiy prospekt 18. **Map** 6 E1.
312 6057. noon–11pm daily.

Located in the former Wolf and Beranger coffee house, from which Pushkin departed for his fatal duel in 1837 (see p83), the Literary Café (Literaturnoye cafe) seeks to echo the best of early 19th-century culture. String quartets and poetry readings set in the vaulted rooms have made the restaurant very popular, albeit largely with tourists. Its mainly Russian menu offers reasonably good food, but dining here is really more of an historical than a gourmet experience.

Nikolay
Николай

Bolshaya Morskaya ul 52. **Map** 5 C2.
311 1402. noon–midnight (bar: 7pm–last customer) daily.

Housed in the elegant mid-19th-century Polovtsov Mansion on leafy Bolshaya Morskaya ulitsa (see p122), this restaurant, which also comprises the "Matador" bar, was, in Soviet days, the formal dining room of the Union of Architects. The walls have retained the original walnut paneling, embossed leather, and painted scenes of chivalry, making this one of the most truly historic restaurant interiors. Booking is advised, although the quality of food and service does not match the impressive ambience. The menu consists of standard Russian dishes, and the clientele is mostly foreign.

Tandoor
Тандор

Voznesenskiy prospekt 2. **Map** 6 D1.
312 3886. noon–11pm daily . ★ AE, DC, MC, V, JCB.

The best Indian restaurant in town, Tandoor is a popular choice with Indian businessmen. The menu offers no Russian or European food at all. Most dishes are moderately spiced, but the more adventurous may like to try the hotter varieties. There are home made breads, three kinds of lassi and a variety of vegetarian dishes. With its cool, pleasant interior, oil paintings of the Raj and a carved wooden elephant, plus its central location opposite the Admiralty (see p78), Tandoor gets very overbooked throughout the year, so reservations are advised.

1913 God
1913 год

Voznesenskiy prospekt 13. **Map** 5 C3.
315 5148. noon–1am daily. DC, MC, V. ★

Conveniently placed for visits to the Mariinskiy Theater (see p119), this small restaurant provides the best of Russian food and service at a modest price. The name recalls Russia's so-called "best year," when the country celebrated three centuries of Romanov rule. Portions are generous and the restaurant takes pride in rural Russian dishes such as draniki, or potato pancakes, with bacon and sour cream, as well as more international dishes such as lobster fricassee. The restaurant is popular with the city's artists and critics. Booking ahead is advised.

Bistro le Français
Бистро ле Франсез

Galernaya ulitsa 20. **Map** 5 B2.
315 2465. 11am–3am (bar: 9pm–3am) daily.

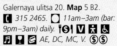

AE, DC, MC, V.

The local French community flocks to this delightful, bustling bistro situated just behind the Senate and Synod by St. Isaac's Square (see p79). With its checked tablecloths, home made bread, and regularly changing menu, this is one of St. Petersburg's few "national" restaurants to successfully recreate the atmosphere of a traditional French bistro. It has no token Russian dishes; instead it serves specialties such as foie gras, pavé de boeuf in a red wine sauce, and the chef's own mouth-watering crème brûlée. English and French are spoken and it is advisable to book ahead.

Milano
Милано

Karavannaya ulitsa 8. **Map** 7 A1.
314 7348. noon–midnight daily. AE, DC, MC, V, JCB.

Clean-cut lines and simplicity give the Milano a very north-Italian feel. In summer, it is a delight to leave the heat and bustle of Nevskiy prospekt for this cool trattoria, while in winter the restaurant is warm and inviting. Mediterranean seafood is the house specialty, the unusual scampi with cognac being the most expensive dish on the menu. Little is available for the true vegetarian. Three-course business lunches are served before 5pm, children are not allowed in after 6pm, and there is live music on Fridays and Saturdays.

Staraya Tamozhnya
Старая таможня

Tamozhennyy pereulok 1. **Map** 1 C5.
327 8980. 9pm–3am daily. MC, V.

Specializing in Russian food and hospitality, Staraya Tamozhnya (The Old Customs House) is almost the only restaurant on the Strelka (see pp58–9) of Vasilevskiy Island. It is a perfect place for snacks or lunch, and offers an appetizing dinner menu including steaks in a variety of marinades and sauces, and tender rabbit cooked in sour cream. The extensive wine list caters to all price ranges. Live jazz and Russian folk music in the evenings inspire dancing on the small dance floor.

Vienna
Вена

Malaya Morskaya ul 13/8. **Map** 6 D1.
311 3227. noon–midnight daily. AE, MC.

Very popular with wealthy locals, Vienna is situated close to the Hermitage (see pp84–93). White and pink decor, with trelliswork and mirrors, makes the interior very light and airy. The menu is written in English, as the restaurant is often used by tourist groups. The otherwise European selection of dishes also includes a wide range of different blini and caviar. Reservations and formal dress are recommended.

Winter Garden
Зимний сад

Hotel Astoria, Bolshaya Morskaya ul 39. **Map** 6 D2. 210 5815. noon–11:30pm daily. AE, MC, V.

With its string quartet, conservatory feel, and echoes of 1950s seaside resorts, the Winter Garden (*Zimniy sad*) of the Astoria Hotel (*see p173*), retains its old world charm.

During World War II, Hitler planned to hold his victory party here once he had taken Leningrad (*see p27*), but he never succeeded in entering the city. The Winter Garden may have relied too heavily on that kind of fame in the past, but the food is improving. The blini, caviar and sturgeon *shashlyk* (kebab) are excellent. Booking is recommended for evening meals.

Adamant
Адамант

Nab reki Moyki 72. **Map** 5 C2.
📞 *311 5575.* ⭘ *noon–midnight daily.* 🍽 V 🍴 ♿ T 🍷 🥂
📷 V. $$$

Situated just off St. Isaac's Square (*see p79*) on the Moyka canal, the elegant Adamant is a top-quality restaurant and booking is advised. Like many of the city's restaurants catering mostly to rich Russians, there is a great emphasis on seafood, but one of Adamant's real delights is the rarely found mature *shchi* (traditional cabbage soup), which is left to bake for a whole day. The menu's poor translation, however, may prevent you from choosing the best dishes.

Bella Leone
Белла Леоне

Vladimirskiy prospekt 9. **Map** 7 A2.
📞 *113 16/0.* ⭘ *noon–midnight daily.* V 🍴 ♿ T 🍷 🥂 🎵 🎶
📷 AE, MC, V. $$$

In keeping with the fashions of its wealthy clientele, Bella Leone has noticeably altered its character in recent years. Once specializing in Italian dishes, the restaurant has since introduced seafood delicacies and Russian dishes to its menu.

With an autographed wall bearing signatures of famous visitors such as Liza Minelli and Michael Caine, the restaurant puts an emphasis on fashion and fame, as well as cuisine. Lobster fricassee or crab-stuffed chicken are highly recommended, and the service and atmosphere add to the pleasure of eating here. Booking is advised after 7pm. The check includes a service charge.

Chopsticks
Чопстикс

Grand Hotel Europe, Mikhaylovskaya ulitsa 1/7. **Map** 6 F1. 📞 *329 6000.*
⭘ *noon–11pm daily.* V 🍴 ♿
🍷 🥂 ★ 📷 AE, DC, MC, V, JCB.
$$$

In some respects, this is an ordinary Chinese restaurant, with an average range of Chinese dishes in a rather typical interior. In the context of St. Petersburg, however, Chopsticks offers a welcome alternative to the standard Russo-European fare.

You are advised to book, especially for dining in the evening, to savour this oasis of calm in the heart of St. Petersburg. With its superb service and serene ambience, it offers a reasonably priced, hassle-free evening out.

Rossi's
Росси

Grand Hotel Europe, Mikhaylovskaya ulitsa 1/7. **Map** 6 F1. 📞 *329 6000.*
⭘ *noon–11pm daily.* V 🍴 ♿
🍷 🥂 ★ 📷 AE, DC, MC, V.
$$$

Excellent freshly prepared antipasti and home made pasta are served at this elegant, modern Italian restaurant, which maintains a great reputation. If you are willing to pay the price, and don't want the pomp and display of the Europe, Rossi's is unbeatable. Small, stylish touches, such as the balance and contrast of color when serving a yellow buttery sauce and black tagliatelle, set this place apart.

Senat-Bar
Сенат Бар

Galernaya ulitsa 1. **Map** 5 C1.
📞 *314 9253.* ⭘ *11am–5am daily.*
🍽 V 🍴 🍷 🥂 📷 AE, DC, MC, V, JCB. $$$

The vast selection of wines and beers available at this Dutch-owned bar and restaurant give, it an edge over other establishments in town. Well used to serving foreigners of all nationalities, the staff speaks good English and offers sound advice on the menu. Vegetarian dishes are few, but can be specially prepared. Otherwise, pork chops with plums, banana, and bacon, or carpaccio made from tender veal in a basil dressing with Parmesan cheese and spices are a carnivore's delight. Desserts are varied and delicious. The Senat Bar gets very full during the summer months, and late diners are advised to book, since it gets busier after 9pm.

Dvoryanskoe Gnezdo
Дворянское гнездо

Ulitsa Dekabristov 21. **Map** 5 C3.
📞 *312 3205.* ⭘ *noon–1am daily.*
🍽 V 🍴 T 🍷 🥂 🎵 🎶
★ 📷 AE, DC, MC, V, JCB.
$$$$$

The city's most distinguished restaurant, Dvoryanskoe Gnezdo (The Noble Nest) is small, intimate, and

wholly luxurious, with unintrusive service. Housed in the former summer house of the Yusupov Palace (*see p120*), just around the corner from the Mariinsky Theater (*see p119*), it is one of the few places to do pre- and post-theater suppers.

Pre-dinner drinks are served in the small bar upstairs, before you are brought down to the candle-lit dining room, where the menu is a gourmet's delight. Dishes such as lamb fillets with poppy seed and sage crust or poached monkfish on a bed of green olives are made with care and attention and invariably fresh ingredients. Serious (if not officially formal) dress and booking are recommended.

Europe
Европа

Grand Hotel Europe, Mikhaylovskaya ulitsa 1/7. **Map** 6 F1. 📞 *329 6000.*
⭘ *7–10.30am (breakfast), 7–11pm daily;* noon–3pm Sun (brunch). 🍽
V 🍴 ♿ T 🍷 🥂 ★ 📷 AE, DC, MC, V. $$$$$

The exclusive and lavish Europe, with its magnificent Style-Moderne interior, has been one of the city's top restaurants since it opened at the beginning of the 20th century. With excellent restoration, superb food, silver service and inventive menu, this elegant restaurant is hard to fault. The cost, however, is high, with wine list prices ranging from $50 to $1,500. Sunday brunch is an alternative way of enjoying the Europe for those not wishing to be quite so extravagant. Reservations are recommended at any time.

FARTHER AFIELD

Pirosmani
Пиросмани

Bolshoy prospekt 14, Petrogradskaya.
Map 1 B3. 📞 *235 6456.* ⭘ *noon–11pm daily.* V 🍴 ♿ 🎵 🎶 ★ $

Booking is absolutely imperative at this restaurant, where wholesome Georgian food is served in a marvelously kitsch recreation of a Georgian hill village, complete with a stream, and with two of the tables on "rafts." The restaurant takes its name from Georgia's most famous painter, a self-taught artist who influenced the Russian avant-garde. Try not to sit too close to the singer, as it can become difficult to talk.

Vegetarians and carnivores alike will enjoy eggplant stuffed with walnuts or *lobio* (spicy beans), fried *sulguni* (salty cheese) is a rich delicacy. There are hearty meat soups and main courses such as *shashlyk* of pork, chicken, or fish served in spicy and garlic sauces.

Staraya Derevnya
Старая деревня

Savushkina ul 72. *431 0000.* *1–10pm daily.* ★ $

In this family-run restaurant the owners seek to create an early 20th-century feel with Viennese chairs, intimate tables with fresh flowers, antique sideboards and exhibitions of work by local artists. The menu is mainly traditional Russian, with some European dishes. In the evenings there is live music, such as traditional gypsy music and Russian ballads. Prince Charles ate here during a visit to the city, and the restaurant continues to enjoy a good reputation with the foreign community and visitors. Located in a leafy suburb of St. Petersburg, out toward the Gulf of Finland, it is best reached by taxi.

Ambassador
Амбассадор

Nab reki Fontanki 14. **Map** 3 A5. *272 9181.* *1pm–midnight daily.* *AE, DC, MC, V, JCB.* $$

Take your pick of the European Room, decorated in early 19th-century Neo-Classical style, or the Russian Room, with traditional low vaults and a painted ceiling. A pleasure to walk to, particularly during the White Nights *(see p51)*, this intimate restaurant is opposite the Engineers' Castle *(see p101)*, just across the Fontanka river. The fare is a mixture of Russian and European, including all the old favorites such as caviar, *borshch*, and steak, accompanied by balalaika music, or jazz on Mondays.

Le Café Bahlsen

Nevskiy pr 142. **Map** 7 C2. *271 2811.* *1pm–1am (Oct–Apr: noon–midnight) daily.* *AE, DC, MC, V.* $$

The only German restaurant and café in St. Petersburg that is not a *bierstube*, Le Café Bahlsen is small and modern with views onto Nevskiy prospekt. It is very popular with those who like to eat out somewhere good but with no pretensions. For the truly hungry, they do a massive grill platter, cooked on a hot stone at your table, with spices you add yourself, and a double vodka to chase it.

Admiralty
Адмиралтейство

Nevskij Palace Hotel, Nevskiy pr 57. **Map** 7 B2. *275 2001.* *5–11pm daily.* *AE, DC, MC, V, JCB.* $$$

A nautical theme prevails in this restaurant. Model ships and copies of the angels on the facade of the Admiralty building *(see p78)* are scattered around. The Russian menu includes many Georgian dishes such as *lobio* (spiced beans) and *satsivi* (chicken in a spicy walnut sauce), as well as *khachapuri* (cheese breads). Those who want good, reasonably priced food in the comfort of a hotel will find it here, albeit without too much excitement.

Afrodite
Афродита

Nevskiy pr 86. **Map** 7 B2. *275 7620.* *noon–1am daily.* ★ *AE, DC, MC, V, JCB.* $$$

Afrodite started a fashion that quickly spread to other upscale places – it was the the city's first Western-style seafood restaurant. It also serves the widest selection of delicacies, including alligator with red paprika sauce or barracuda steak. Traditional Russian dishes, such as homemade *pelmeny* (beef dumplings), and delicious salads are also on the menu. However, with its unobtrusive service and pastel-colored walls, the Afrodite may seem lacking in atmosphere.

Imperial
Империал

Nevskij Palace Hotel, Nevskiy pr 57. **Map** 7 B2. *275 2001.* *7–10:30am (breakfast), 7–11pm daily; noon–4pm Sun (brunch).* *AE, DC, MC, V.* $$$

Situated on the first floor of the Nevskij Palace Hotel, the Imperial has a glazed facade offering excellent views over Nevskiy prospekt. This is actually the hotel's breakfast room, but for dinner they offer a straightforward international haute cuisine menu, well cooked and well presented. The main drawback is the rather too hotel-like neutrality of the interior, but the desserts are heavenly, the wine is good and, if you like watching the world go by, no other restaurant matches it.

Svir
Свирь

Hotelship Peterhof, nr Tuchkov Bridge. **Map** 1 A4. *325 8888.* *noon–11pm daily.* ★ *AE, DC, MC, V.* $$$

The Svir has made a name for itself with its monthly food festivals, which compensate for the relative lack of variety in the city's other restaurants. Whether the food is Mexican, Italian, or Turkish, they fly in skilled chefs to bring a bit of sunshine to the winter months. In the summer cooling fruit and cocktails are added to the menu. It can be fun dining on the river, but getting to the hotelship is a chore. A taxi (10 minutes from Nevskiy prospekt) is more or less obligatory.

Landskrona
Ландскрона

Nevskij Palace Hotel, Nevskiy pr 57. **Map** 7 B2. *275 2001 ext 201.* *12:30pm–1am daily.* ★ *AE, DC, MC, V, JCB.* $$$$$

The best of European cuisine and a high standard of service are offered here in a modern interior. A jazz duo, rather than the classical music heard in other leading restaurants around the city, adds an unusual touch. The food, however, is as classical as the silver service, with complimentary hors d'oeuvres, obligatory white wine sorbet between courses and dishes such as the divine beef fillet in a blue cheese sauce, or terrine of rabbit in a cider jelly, which come in vast portions.

Novgorod

Detinets
Детинец

Intercession Tower, Detinets (the Kremlin). *(81622) 746 24.* *11am–6pm, 7–11pm daily.* $

In a useful position for visitors, the Detinets is located right inside the Kremlin, and offers good traditional Russian cuisine. The attractive medieval interior of the 16th-century Intercession Tower, with its vaulted ceiling, makes an excellent setting for hearty Russian potato salads and meat-based dishes. The stews are tasty and filling; the *pelmeny* are homemade. The Detinets is a perfect lunch stop on a visit to this wholeheartedly medieval city. There is live music in the restaurant every evening except Monday.

Beresta
Береста

Studencheskaya ul 3. *(81622) 304 01.* *6:30–11am, noon–5pm, 6–11pm daily.* *AE, DC, MC, V.* $$$

For those wanting a little more than Russian simplicity, the Beresta is a good choice, found in the Beresta Palace Hotel *(see p173)*. It has a changing, international menu and a range of Russian dishes. Just 15 minutes' walk from the Kremlin, it is a convenient dinner spot before the return to St. Petersburg.

Light Meals and Snacks

THE EXTERIOR, and sometimes even the interior, of a café usually gives little indication of what is available, making it difficult to differentiate between a good and a bad establishment at first glance. Many of the newer places have Western-style names and decor and offer foreign cuisine, but are often quite expensive. Russian and ethnic cafés, however, can serve tasty food ranging from a simple sandwich to a reasonably priced three-course meal. These cafés are scattered all over the city, and some are worth making a special trip to, and you can generally rely on most of them for a good, unpretentious meal or snack. In most places, meat dominates the menu, so vegetarians might have a difficult time.

The distinction between bars, such as the "pubs" and German cafés, and other establishments is often blurred. Even small cafés and pastry shops offer beer and spirits at any time of the day, and many are open past midnight.

RUSSIAN

THE LOCAL foreign community often sticks to familiar fast food and steaks, but traditional Russian dishes such as *borshch, pelmeny* (dumplings filled with meat), beef wrapped in cheese, and *draniki* (potato pancakes, a traditional rural dish) are widely offered.

Priboy is well located just behind the Hermitage *(see pp84–93)*, while **Diana**, **Nik**, and **Aprel-Palmira** are also close to Nevskiy prospekt *(see p108)*. The cellarlike **Krokodil** is popular with the bohemian crowd and tends to host special events as well as offering a sound traditional menu. **Kafe Ambassador** has the advantage of late opening hours – until 5am – as well as excellent views across the Fontanka to the Engineers' Castle *(see p101)*. Also on the Fontanka is **Staroe kafe**. Just off St. Isaac's Square *(see p79)* is the **Idiot**, named after the Dostoevsky novel, which has both literary and culinary pretensions, offering books for sale and poetry readings as well as local beer and food. Although it ostensibly stays open until 11pm, it actually closes when the last customer leaves, often around 4am.

For those wanting to try the famous Russian *blini* (pancakes), a number of places serve them in both savory and sweet varieties, stuffed with caviar, cottage cheese, salty *brinza* cheese, or apricots.

Russkiye bliny and **Skazka** have a wide selection of inexpensive pancakes and *blinchiki* (folded pancakes), while **La Chandeleur** offers a broader, more Gallic menu, which includes alcohol.

GEORGIAN AND ARMENIAN

GEORGIAN AND Armenian food is much loved by locals, despite the independence of these former states. **Metekhi** and **Tbilisi** offer a selection of *lobio* (spicy beans), *satsivi* (chicken in a spicy walnut sauce), *kharcho* (heavy meat soup), and the ubiquitous *shashlyk* (kebab). **Baghdad**'s specialty is *manty*, an Uzbek version of *pelmeny*, and noodle soups, while they also do a delicious *koreyskiy salat* (spicy Oriental carrot salad). The decoration in this tiny basement café is also impressive. **Shakherezade** makes excellent, if rather oily, hummus and falafel. **Krunk** describes itself as an Armenian café. Despite this, the menu is largely made up of international dishes, except for *dolma* (their Armenian version of stuffed vine leaves).

PIZZA AND PASTA

PIZZA AND PASTA houses are highly popular with locals, particularly wealthy couples. For visitors, especially non-Russian-speaking visitors, these places pose fewer language problems and provide familiar, easy meals. Pizza is common, and there are well-known Western names such as **Pizza Hut**. **Pizza House** is the oldest take-out spot in St. Petersburg and serves some of the thinnest pizzas ever seen. **La Strada** is a model example of how to convert a gloomy yard into a flashy, two-story interior. At the lower end of the scale, **Pizza Pronto** is a cheap and cheerful alternative.

GERMAN

THE FIRST GERMAN (and non-state-owned) bar to open in St. Petersburg was **Chayka**, which is still a noisy and busy bar offering generous portions of wurst and fries or Baltic herring. While similar establishments such as **Antwerpen** and **Nevskiy 40** are more important for their location than the quality of their food (which is not bad), places like **Le Café Bahlsen** and **Schwabskiy domik** offer a more traditional menu and are popular with the many German businesspeople and tourists who flood the city. Nevskij Palace's **Bierstube** probably has the greatest variety of both German and Austrian dishes, but at a higher price. As in the majority of Russian restaurants, most meals are meat-based.

NORTH AMERICAN

FOR THOSE craving big juicy steaks, salvation lies in **Daddy's Steak Room** and **Montreal Steak**. Despite its more distant location, Daddy's is popular all year round and, with the opening of Montreal Steak in the center of town, carnivores are assured of a good, reliable meal. **California Grill** is slightly less expensive and oriented toward a student clientèle, while **Bistro Sadko** is a St. Petersburg institution – an American bar offering hamburgers, fries, and tempting desserts, as well as salads, vegetarian options and a Russian menu. It also provides one of the best places to stop and people-watch on busy Nevskiy prospekt.

For key to symbols *see p291*

MEXICAN AND SPANISH

ST. PETERSBURG WAS overcome when **La Cucaracha** opened its doors in 1995 and tequila mania hit the city. Cocktails, tortilla chips and dips, or delicious full meals served mostly by Mexican waiters and with live Mexican music, mean continued popularity for this comfortable bar. Just a few hundred yards up the Fontanka, **Snack Bar Casa de Don Quixote** has good music, and the café is open all night. It is never particularly lively but is highly recommended for a snack, drink or cup of coffee in the early hours of the morning.

FAST FOOD

THE LAST FEW YEARS have seen an increase in the number of fast food outlets, led by **Grill Master**, **Carrol's**, and **McDonalds**. In addition to the standard international chains, however, St. Petersburg has three excellent local options right in the center. **Green Crest** offers salads, rarely found elsewhere, with plenty of mayonnaise, and **Minutka** has a selection of both salads and sandwiches. Popular with ravers and clubgoers, as well as those who have been out watching the bridges go up during White Nights *(see p51)*, is **Layma**, which is open 24 hours. It serves steak and chops with fries, plus soups, *pirozhki*, salads, beer, and genuine fresh-squeezed orange juice.

Hamburger stands are making an appearance on the streets of St. Petersburg, but the Russian idea of fast food is a small open sandwich with fish, cheese, or salami, or *pirozhki* (pirogi), small, doughy patties filled with cabbage, rice, and egg, or with something sweet like apple. It is best to avoid the fried *pirozhki* with meat and sausages that are sold up and down Nevskiy prospekt.

Arab food stands all over town have made *shawerma* and kebabs an alternative to hamburgers. If tempted, you are advised to buy from an Arab seller, rather than Russian, as the difference between *shawerma* and hamburger can become blurred.

PASTRIES AND SWEETS

RUSSIANS ARE notoriously sweet-toothed and tea is never offered without cookies or cakes in private homes. Cakes and pastries are sold in most of the city's cafés, and ice cream is eaten on the street in both winter and summer. The Oriental delights of **Shakherezade**, offering a variety of honey and almond sweets such as *paklava* (baklava), are popular with locals and, as with most Russian cafés, they offer mounds of whipped cream piled with fresh and dried fruits and nuts. **Sladkoezhka** (literally sweet-eater) has almost entirely fresh cream desserts. Sweet pastries galore can be taken out at the bakery **Nevskiy 27**, or eaten in at the canalside **Kafe Sankt-Peterburg**, which has tables on an outdoor terrace in summer. More luxurious cheesecakes and pastries are the fare at **Nik**, or can be tried at a higher price in the **Vienna Café** of the Nevskij Palace Hotel *(see p173)*. Traditional English tea are offered on the mezzanine of the **Grand Hotel Europe** *(see p173)* and in the lounge of the **Astoria Hotel** *(see p173)*, usually accompanied by live classical music.

PUBS

A COMBINATION OF English and Irish pubs and German bars, the city's "pubs" are often run by foreigners. Although the interiors and the food tend to be a little unadventurous, the beer is generally good. Draft Guinness is available at two Irish bars, **Mollie's Irish Bar** and **Shamrock**, the latter conveniently located opposite the Mariinskiy Theater *(see p119)*. **Korsar** and **Rose Pub** both provide a varied and highly energetic program of live music and themed entertainment, but probably the liveliest place of all is **Tribunal**. A total contrast is the strangely named **Wooden**

Pub, which looks more like a small barn than anything else and is very quiet. Here they serve huge portions of filling and wholesome food at moderate prices. The **Maltiyskiy orden**, also known as The Mermaid, has a summer terrace on the Moyka.

EATING OUT ON DAY TRIPS

FINDING A PLACE to have lunch outside the city can seem difficult. Pavlovsk *(see pp156–9)* and Peterhof *(see pp146–9)* now have reasonable restaurants in the palaces themselves, although space is limited at Peterhof during the summer. Pavlovsk also has the kitsch **Podvorye** just beside the station, a fun experience with folk songs and traditional Russian meals in a pseudo-traditional mansion. In Peterhof there is also the tiny and inexpensive **Trapeza** café just along from the east entrance to the park.

Tsarskoe Selo does not have a decent café in the palace itself *(see pp150–55)*, but the town is well supplied with small cafés along the central Oranzhereynaya ulitsa in addition to the adequate **Tsarskoe Selo** restaurant at the station.

Oranienbaum *(see p144)* and Gatchina *(see p145)*, further removed from the tourist trail, are a gastronomic desert, and it is best to take a picnic with you. For those travelling to Ilya Repin's house at Repino *(see p144)*, the only alternative to a picnic is barbecued *shashlyk* at the roadside, or the restaurant at the Repino sanatorium, which should be avoided. Most hotels and a few cafés in the centre of St. Petersburg, such as **La Chandeleur**, can provide packed meals.

Novgorod *(see pp160–63)* has more to offer in terms of luncheon venues. Try the **Detinets** café in the Kremlin, or the **Beresta**, which offers excellent European cuisine. The **Aziya** restaurant serves good Korean food in an intimate setting, and a quick pizza can be snatched at **Kafe Charodeyka**, situated just opposite the entrance to Novgorod's historic Kremlin.

DIRECTORY

RUSSIAN

Aprel-Palmira
Апрель-Пальмира
Pushkinskaya ul 16.
Map 7 B3. 164 6303.

Diana
Диана
Sadovaya ul 56.
Map 6 D3. 310 9355.

Idiot
Идиот
Nab reki Moyki 82.
Map 5 C2. 315 1675.

Kafe Ambassador
Кафе Амбассадор
Nab reki Fontanki 14.
Map 3 A5. 275 9522.

Krokodil
Крокодил
Galernaya ul 18.
Map 5 C1. 314 9437.

La Chandeleur
Bolshaya Konyushennaya
ulitsa 1. **Map** 2 E5.
314 8380.

Nik
Ник
Vladimirskiy pr 1.
Map 7 A2. 311 7693.

Priboy
Прибой
Nab reki Moyki 19.
Map 2 E5. 311 8285.

Russkiye bliny
Русские блины
Ul Furmanova 13.
Map 3 A4. 279 0559.

Skazka
Сказка
Nevskiy pr 27.
Map 6 E1. 315 9490.

Staroe kafe
Старое кафе
Nab reki Fontanki 108.
Map 6 E4. 316 5111.

GEORGIAN AND ARMENIAN

Baghdad
Багдад
Furshtatskaya ul 35.
Map 3 C4. 272 2355.

Krunk
Крунк
Solyanoy per 14.
Map 3 A5. 273 4523.

Metekhi
Метехи
Ul Belinskovo 3.
Map 7 A1. 272 3361.

Shakherezade
Шахерезада
Razyezhaya ul 3.
Map 7 A3. 112 4271.

Tbilisi
Тбилиси
Sytnynskaya ul 10.
Map 2 D2. 232 9391.

PIZZA AND PASTA

La Strada
Страда
Bolshaya Konyushennaya
ulitsa 27. **Map** 6 E1.
312 4700.

Pizza House
Пицца-Хаус
Podolskaya ul 23.
Map 6 E5. 316 2666.

Pizza Hut
Пицца-хат
Nab reki Moyki 71/16.
Map 5 C2. 315 7705.

Pizza Pronto
Пицца-пронто
Zagorodnyy pr 8.
Map 7 A3. 315 8948.

GERMAN

Antwerpen
Антверпен
Kronverkskiy pr 13/2.
Map 2 E2. 233 9746.

Bierstube
Бирштубе
Nevskij Palace Hotel,
Nevskiy pr 57. **Map** 7 B2.
275 2001.

Chayka
Чайка
Nab kanala Griboedova 14.
Map 6 E1. 312 4631.

Le Café Bahlsen
Nevskiy pr 142. **Map** 7 C2.
271 2811.

Nevskiy 40
Невский 40
Nevskiy pr 40. **Map** 6 F1.
312 2457.

Schwabskiy domik
Швабский домик
Novocherkasskiy pr 28/19.
528 2211.

NORTH AMERICAN

Bistro Sadko
Бистро Садко
Mikhaylovskaya ulitsa 1/7.
Map 6 F1. 329 6000.

California Grill
Nevskiy pr 176.
Map 8 E3. 274 2422.

Daddy's Steak Room
Moskovskiy pr 73.
252 7744.

Montreal Steak
Apraksin per 22.
Map 6 E3. 310 9256.

MEXICAN AND SPANISH

La Cucaracha
See p197.

**Snack Bar Casa de
Don Quixote**
В гостях у Дон-Кихота
House of Friendship,
Nab reki Fontanki 21.
Map 7 A1. 210 4517.

FAST FOOD

Carrol's
Кэрролс
Kamennoostrovskiy pr 31.
Map 2 D1.

Green Crest
Грин крест
Vladimirskiy pr 7.
Map 7 A2. 113 1380.

Grill Master
Гриль Мастер
Nevskiy pr 46. **Map** 6 F1.
Sadovaya ul 22. **Map** 6 F2.

Layma
Лайма
Nab kanala Griboedova 16.
Map 6 E1. 315 5545.

McDonalds
Kamennoostrovskiy pr 39.
Sennaya pl 4. **Map** 6 E3.

Minutka
Минутка
Nevskiy pr 20. **Map** 6 E1.
325 8224.

PASTRIES AND SWEETS

Kafe Sankt-Peterburg
Кафе Санкт-Петербург
Nab kanala Griboedova 5.
Map 6 E1. 210 7673.

Nevskiy 27
Невский 27
Nevskiy pr 27. **Map** 6 E1.
312 1080.

Sladkoezhka
Сладоежка
Marata ul 11. **Map** 7 B2.
315 4880.

Vienna Café
Кафе Вена
Nevskiy pr 57. **Map** 7 B2.
275 2001.

PUBS

Korsar
See p197.

Maltiyskiy orden
Мальтийский орден
Nab reki Moyki 6.
Map 2 E5. 314 8989.

Mollie's Irish Bar
See p197.

Rose Pub
See p197.

Shamrock
See p197.

Tribunal
See p197.

Wooden Pub
Chaikovskovo ul 36.
Map 3 B4. 275 7147.

DAY TRIPS

Aziya
Азия
Shteikova ul 22, Novgorod.
(81622) 722 27.

Beresta
See p182.

Detinets
See p182.

Kafe Charodeyka
Кафе Чародейка
Volosova ul 1/1, Novgorod.
(81622) 751 54.

Podvorye
Подворье
Filtrovskoye shosse 16,
Pavlovsk. 465 1399.

Trapeza
Трапеза
Kalininskaya ul 9, Peterhof.
427 9393.

Tsarskoe Selo
Царское Село
Detskoe Selo Train Station,
Tsarskoe Selo.
470 1349.

SHOPS AND MARKETS

ATRIP ROUND St. Petersburg's shops, markets, and large department stores provides an intriguing insight into local life. In addition to the many traditional stores, the city is dotted with street-sellers trading in an eclectic miscellany of goods.

Shopping in Russia requires a certain amount of spontaneity, flexibility, and even a sense of adventure, since you never quite know when and where you will find what is

Matryoshka **doll**

needed. As a rule, shop windows reveal surprisingly little about what might be found inside. In recent years, imported goods (sold at inflated prices) have sadly pushed out many local products. Vodka, caviar, and time-honored Russian crafts and toys, however, make wonderful gifts.

Most shops tend to be concentrated around the city's main streets such as Nevskiy, Kamennoostrovskiy, and Bolshoy (Petrogradskaya) prospekts.

Clothes in showroom of local designer Tatyana Parfyonova

OPENING HOURS

OPENING HOURS vary, but stores are usually open from around 10am until 7pm or later. Most close for an hour at lunch, food stores generally between 1–2pm, and consumer goods stores between 2–3pm. On Sunday, the large department stores are open between 11am–6pm, and each area has food stores and a pharmacy open all day.

HOW TO PAY

CASH PAYMENTS can be made only in roubles and nowadays prices are rarely quoted in foreign currency. Paying in non-Russian currency is a criminal offense. The only place where you might be able to pay in foreign currency is at a tourist market. Between 10am and 6pm, there is no shortage of exchange offices *(see p206)*,

some in the shops themselves, where you can get roubles for cash or on a credit card. There are relatively few stores, even those selling imported goods, that will accept credit card payments. The larger antique shops are the exception to this rule, and nearly all now accept VISA and MasterCard.

In most shops, customers are forced to peer at goods stacked behind the counter. If you would like a closer look, just point to what you want and say "*mozhno*" ("may I?"). To purchase something, pay for it at the cash desk and then return to collect the item from the counter. Shop assistants will usually realise if you do not speak Russian and will write down the prices for you to hand to the cashier. In theory, defective goods can be taken back if you keep the receipt.

Russian box camera (1920s)

BARGAINING ETIQUETTE

IF A SET PRICE is displayed at markets, this indicates no bargaining. In all other cases you can usually get some reduction if you haggle, especially since visitors are often likely to be quoted a higher price than locals. Haggling in Russia, however, is not to be treated as a pleasant pastime. It is a serious matter, so do not bother unless you genuinely intend to buy.

BUYING ART AND ANTIQUES

BY LAW, all objects pre-1956, and all precious objects such as gold, silver, jewelry, and furs, are subject to strict export controls. Works of art, including contemporary water-colors, also fall under this ruling, aas do books published before 1946. All suitcases are x-rayed at the airport check-in, so

Second-hand bookstore sign

it is pointless to try to hide, for instance, an icon with a metal cover. In practice, prints and watercolors without frames are generally ignored, and unless a book is extremely rare you are likely to be able to export it. Permission to export books is processed fairly quickly by the **Russian National Library**. Permission for art objects can be received from a department of the **Ministry of Culture**, but it

EXPORT PERMISSIONS

Russian National Library
Российскаяа национальная
библиотека
*Rossiyskaya natsionalnaya
biblioteka*
Sadovaya ulitsa 18.
Map 6 F2. 219 9007.

Ministry of Culture
Министерство культуры
Ministerstvo kultury
Naberezhnaya Kanala
Griboedova 107.
Map 5 C3. 314 8234.

DLT department store

is so complicated that the art gallery or artist from whom you are purchasing should undertake this for you. They generally have their own contacts that should make the complicated process faster.

If you have not obviously tried to cheat customs, any objects not allowed through customs can simply be handed over to someone staying in St. Petersburg. Otherwise, the item will be placed in storage at the airport, for which, if you wish to reclaim it later, there will be a charge. Objects unclaimed for a year are confiscated, as are objects that have obviously been hidden to avoid detection. Valuable pieces will be donated to a museum.

DEPARTMENT STORES

KNOWN AS "univermag" or universal store, Russian department stores generally evolved from the old trading rows, which were literally rows of kiosks owned by different traders. Present-day department stores have in fact altered very little from their original kiosk style and still operate as a complex of sections or boutiques. Every visitor to St. Petersburg should explore **Gostinyy dvor** (see p108) and **Passazh** (see p48) as well. Although they now have a large proportion of imported goods, and prices for local goods are relatively high, it is worthwhile observing what the locals are buying. **DLT**, also in the city center, is more Western in layout and is

in itself an interesting piece of Style-Moderne architecture. To empty your pockets of any surplus roubles after a visit to St. Petersburg, a good place to stop off en route to the airport is **Moskovskiy univermag**.

MARKETS AND BAZAARS

MANY LOCALS shop for food in one of the numerous markets dotted around the city. The most centrally located market is **Kuznechnyy**, just off Nevskiy prospekt, which sells flowers, fruit, vegetables, delicious homemade cream cheese, and wonderful natural honey that you can sample. In front of the main entrance old ladies sell mushrooms in autumn, wool socks in winter, flowers in summer, and a hundred other odds and ends from pickled cucumbers and dried fish to old shoes and the family crystal.

These days the yard inside **Apraksin market** (see p95) is best known for wholesale and retail sales of liquor, cigarettes, and clothes, especially Turkish leather jackets.

Flea markets, thought by the local administration to reflect badly on the city's image, are perpetually being moved on. Yet sellers continue to pop up relentlessly at the city's main fruit and vegetable markets.

Slightly different are the metal kiosks that could once be found everywhere but now tend to be concentrated on **Sennaya ploshchad** (see p122). Petersburgers come here from all over the city to buy a variety of cheap food. Souvenir watercolors and prints are sold throughout the

year at **Vernisazh**, an open-air market that takes place outside St. Catherine's Church (see p48). **Rynok suvenirov**, a small tourist market near the Church on Spilled Blood (see p100), sells both the best and cheapest selection of matryoshka dolls (see p189). You are also likely to find handmade chess sets, watches, fur hats, old cameras, t-shirts, and military paraphernalia.

Women selling a variety of goods outside Kuznechnyy market

MUSEUM SHOPS

SOME OF THE best quality souvenirs, whether jewelry, matryoshka dolls, prints, or books, are usually found in the museums. The **Hermitage** (see pp84–93) has an excellent second-hand bookstall, while its main shop offers reproduction prints and objects, and books on the city and its art. A superb selection of souvenirs and jewelry is sold in the **Menshikov Palace** (see p62), and the **Russian Museum** (see pp104–107) produces a good range of souvenirs such as scarves, jewelry, textiles, and reproduction posters and cards, to accompany special exhibitions. Their shops also have a large stock of beautiful art books. Other large museum shops are found in the **Peter and Paul Fortress** (see pp66–7) and the palaces at **Pavlovsk**, **Peterhof**, and **Tsarskoe Selo** (see pp146–59).

Souvenirs sold at the tourist market opposite the Church on Spilled Blood

What to Buy in St. Petersburg

Decorative box

IT IS EASY to find interesting and beautiful
souvenirs in St. Petersburg. They range
in price from small, enameled badges,
which sell for very little, to hand-painted
Palekh boxes and samovars, which can be very
expensive. Traditional crafts were encouraged
by the state in the old Soviet Union, and many
items, such as lacquered boxes and bowls, matryoshka dolls,
wooden toys, and chess sets, are still made by craftsmen and
women using age-old methods. Memorabilia from the Soviet
era also make good souvenirs, and Russia is definitely the
best place to buy the national specialties, vodka and caviar.

Vodka and Caviar

*An enormous variety of both clear and
flavored vodkas (such as lemon and
pepper) is available (see p178). They
make excellent accompaniments to
black caviar (ikra) and red caviar
(keta), which are often served with
blini (see p176).*

Clear
vodka

Flavored
vodka

Red
caviar

Black caviar

Samovar

*Used to boil water to make tea,
samovars come in all shapes and
sizes (see p179). A permit is needed
to export a pre-1945 samovar.*

Malachite
egg

Amber
ring

Semiprecious Stones

*Malachite, amber, jasper, and
a variety of marbles from the
Ural mountains are used to
make a wide range of items –
everything from jewelry and
chess sets to inlaid table tops.*

Wooden Toy

*These crudely carved
wooden toys often
have moving parts.
They are known
as Bogorodskiye
toys and make
charming gifts.*

Matryoshka Dolls

*These dolls fit one inside the other and
come in a huge variety of styles. The
traditional dolls are the prettiest, but
the models painted to represent Soviet
political leaders are also very popular.*

Chess Sets

*Chess is an extremely popular
pastime in Russia. Chess sets
made from all kinds of material, including malachite, are
widely available. This wooden
chess set is painted in the same
style as the matryoshka dolls.*

LACQUERED ARTIFACTS

Painted wooden or papier-mâché artifacts make popular souvenirs and are sold all over the city. The exquisite hand-painted, lacquered Palekh boxes can be very costly, but the eggs decorated with icons and the typical red, black, and gold bowls are more affordable.

Palekh Box

The art of miniature painting on papier-mâché items originated in the late 18th century. Artists in the four villages of Palekh, Fedoskino, Mstera, and Kholui still produce these hand-painted marvels. The images are based on Russian fairytales and legends.

Painted wooden egg

Bowl with Spoon

The brightly painted papier-mâché bowls and spoons made in Khokhloma are coated with a hard lacquer. They are not, however, resistant to boiling liquid.

Russian hand-painted tray

Tuners

Strings

Musical Instruments

Russian folk music uses a wide range of musical instruments. This gusli is similar to the Western psaltery and is played by plucking the strings with both hands. Also available are the brightly painted balalaika and the bayan (accordion).

Russian Scarf

These brilliantly colored traditional woolen shawls are good for keeping out the cold of a Russian winter. Mass-produced polyester versions are also available, mostly in big department stores, but these are not as warm.

Soviet Memorabilia

An eclectic array of memorabilia from the Soviet era is for sale. Old banknotes, coins, pocket watches, and Red Army kits, including belt buckles, badges, and other military items, can be found alongside watches with cartoons of KGB agents on their faces.

Gzhel Vase

Ceramics with a distinctive blue and white pattern are produced in Gzhel, an area near Moscow. Ranging from figurines to household dishes, they are popular with Russians and visitors alike.

Pocket watch

Badge with Soviet symbols

Red Army leather belt

Where to Shop in St. Petersburg

THE MAIN DEPARTMENT stores in the city center stock everything from souvenirs to vodka and furs, all of a high quality. Some of the smaller shops on and around Nevskiy prospekt, however, give you more chance to avoid the crowds; they also tend to be cheaper. In a city that prides itself on its native intellectuals, books and art are appropriately St. Petersburg's other main exports. Soviet memorabilia have also become very popular.

VODKA AND CAVIAR

BUYING VODKA from anywhere other than a reputable shop is not advisable. Cheaper brands can be fairly potent, and a certain amount of illegal vodka still makes its way into the smaller outlets. **Gostinyy dvor** department store and **Yeliseev's** are the most central and reliable places for vodka. Alternatively, the **Liviz** outlets normally stock a good range. The better local brands of clear vodka are the Russian Smirnov and Sinopskaya *(see p178)*.

For good quality caviar, Yeliseev's fish department and **Ryba** are the best places to go, and on occasions they have fresh caviar, for which you bring your own jar. Other reputable supermarkets in the center are **Bestrun** and **Prima** which is open 24 hours.

Sennaya ploshchad and **Apraksin dvor** markets have the cheapest food products in the city, but check the date on caviar tins. In the summer it is best to buy only from shops with refrigerators.

SOUVENIRS AND CRAFTS

DURING THE summer months when traders set up stalls by all the major tourist spots, St. Petersburg is flooded with *matryoshka* dolls, shawls, and painted lacquerware. In the winter, by contrast, it often seems as if everything has gone into hibernation. **Rynok suvenirov** and **Vernisazh** markets, however, operate all year round. The museum shops also stock souvenirs and crafts, and some (such as in the Hermitage) also sell art books.

Probably the smallest souvenir shop, **Matryoshka** is also one of the best, but places like **Nasledie** and **Khudozhest-vennyye promysly** have a

larger variety. The city's porcelain factory makes some fine china, particularly coffee cups, and has its own outlet, **Farfor**. Locally made porcelain, glass, and crystal is also sold at **Farfor, Khrustal, Steklo**.

SOVIET MEMORABILIA

ARTIFACTS from the Soviet era are often now produced specially for the tourist market. For original blatant propaganda material, **Sekunda** has one of the best stocks. The **Rynok suvenirov** market also has military paraphernalia. Soviet badges are compact and easily transportable. A small selection at moderate prices can be found in antique shops such as **Antikvariat**. Busts of Lenin abound, and the little shop on the first floor of the military bookshop **Dom voyennoy knigi** usually has a cheap selection. They also sell old cameras of all designs, from the 1920s to the 1970s.

ANTIQUES AND ART

BEARING IN MIND all the restrictions on antiques and art, it is still worth seeing what might fall outside the export rules, whether it be a small watercolor, a modern print, or a quaint 1960s tea service from stalls at **Apraksin dvor**. Shops such as **Antik tsentr**, **Tertsiya**, and **Rapsodiya** are mainly for the tourist trade, while **Peterburg Antikvariat** caters to all, but is at the top of the price range. Only buy an expensive object subject to customs regulations if you are sure the relevant paperwork and export applications can be obtained *(see p202)*.

Paintings all require export licences, but galleries generally do this themselves, so drop in to **Palitra** or the

Soyuz khudozhnikov and see what they have. The most original and exciting gallery is **Borey**, which has rapidly changing exhibitions and performance art to watch.

BOOKS

ST. PETERSBURGERS perceive their city as an intellectual focal point, with a great literary and artistic past. The center has many new and second-hand bookshops, which also tend to sell prints and often antiques. The best, and most famous, are the magnificent **Dom knigi** *(see p47)* and **Knizhnaya lavka pisateley**. Art books, both new and old, can be found at **Iskusstvo**, **The Art Shop** and **Mir**, while if you are looking for English-language literature, **Planeta** sells new classics and second-hand thrillers. Rummaging around antiquarian shops, such as **Bukinist**, **Staraya kniga**, and **Na Liteynom** can turn up interesting old prints, literature, and travel guides, but foreign language publications tend to be heavily overpriced. **Severnaya lira** sells sheet music, ranging from classical to folk songs, as well as instruments, CDs, and books.

FASHION AND ACCESSORIES

CLOTHES, SHOES, and other accessories are generally imported nowadays, and the big names in fashion shopping are all foreign. Only one local designer has opened her own showroom, **Tatyana Parfyonova modnyy dom**, and her garments have been purchased by the Russian Museum *(see pp104–7)*.

Locally made jewelry of semiprecious stones from the Urals and amber from the Baltic is sold in outlets such as **Kristall** and souvenir shops such as **Samotsvety** and **Nasledie**. One north-Russian speciality is niello silver jewelry, with its distinctive patterns and pictures etched in black.

For furs, the city offers a wide variety and a range of prices. Traditional Russian hats can be bought all year round in the department stores.

DIRECTORY

DEPARTMENT STORES

DLT
ДЛТ
Bolshaya Konyushennaya
ulitsa 21/23.
Map 6 E1.

Gostinyy dvor
Гостиный двор
Nevskiy prospekt 35.
Map 6 F2.

Moskovskiy univermag
Московский универмаг
Moskovskiy prospekt 205.

Passazh
Пассаж
Nevskiy prospekt 48.
Map 6 F1.

MARKETS AND BAZAARS

Andreevskiy rynok
Андреевский рынок
Bolshoy prospekt,
Vasilevskiy Island.
Map 5 A1.

Apraksin dvor
Апраксин двор
Sadovaya ulitsa.
Map 6 E2.

Kuznechnyy rynok
Кузнечный рынок
Kuznechnyy pereulok 3.
Map 7 A3.

Rynok suvenirov
Рынок сувениров
Kanal Griboedova, by
Church on Spilled Blood.
Map 2 E5.

Sennaya ploshchad
Сенная площадь
Sennaya ploshchad.
Map 6 D3.

Vernisazh
Вернисаж
Nevskiy prospekt 32–34.
Map 6 E1.

SHOPS

Antik tsentr
Антик-центр
(Antiques)
Nalichnaya ulitsa 21.

Antikvariat
Антиквариат
(Antiques)
Ulitsa Marata 10.
Map 7 B3.

The Art Shop
(Art Books)
Nevskiy prospekt 52.
Map 6 F1.

Bestrun
Бестран
(Food)
Bolshaya Morskaya ul 11.
Map 6 D1.

Borey
Борей
(Art)
Liteynyy prospekt 58.
Map 7 A1.

Bukinist
Букинист
(Old Books)
Liteynyy prospekt 59.
Map 7 A1.

Dom knigi
Дом книги
(Books)
Nevskiy prospekt 28.
Map 6 E1.

Dom voyennoy knigi
Дом военной книги
(Military books, cameras
and memorabilia)
Nevskiy prospekt 20.
Map 6 E1.

Farfor
Фарфор
(Porcelain)
Nevskiy prospekt 111.
Map 7 C2.

Farfor, Khrustal, Steklo
Фарфор, Хрусталь,
Стекло
(Porcelain, crystal & glass)
Nevskiy prospekt 64.
Map 7 A2.

Iskusstvo
Искусство
(Art shop)
Nevskiy prospekt 16.
Map 6 D1.

Khudozhestvennyye promysly
Художественные
промыслы
(Souvenirs)
Nevskiy prospekt 51.
Map 7 B2.

Knizhnaya lavka pisateley
Книжная лавка
писателей
(Books)
Nevskiy prospekt 66.
Map 7 A2.

Kristall
Кристалл
(Jewelry)
Nevskiy prospekt 34.
Map 6 E1.

Liviz (vodka outlets)
Ulitsa Plekhanova 2.
Map 6 E2.
Ulitsa Zhukovskovo 27.
Map 7 B1.
Ulitsa Belinskovo 6.
Map 7 A1.

Matryoshka
Матрешка
(Souvenirs)
Nevskiy prospekt 27.
Map 6 E1.

Mir
Мир
(Art books)
Nevskiy prospekt 13.
Map 6 D1.

Na Liteynom
На Литейном
(Antiques)
Liteynyy prospekt 61 (in
the yard).
Map 7 A2.

Nasledie
Наследие
(Souvenirs)
Nevskiy prospekt 116.
Map 7 B2.

Palitra
Палитра
(Art)
Nevskiy prospekt 166.
Map 8 D3.

Peterburg Antikvariat
Петербург Антиквариат
(Antiques)
Nevskiy prospekt 54.
Map 6 F1.

Planeta
Планета
(Books)
Liteynyy prospekt 30.
Map 3 A5.

Prima
Прима
(Food)
Bolshaya Morskaya ul 26.
Map 6 D1.

Rapsodiya
Рапсодия
(Antiques)
Bolshaya Konyushennaya
ulitsa 13.
Map 2 E5.

Ryba
Рыба
(Food)
Nevskiy prospekt 21.
Map 6 E1.

Samotsvety
Самоцветы
(Souvenirs & jewelry)
Mikhaylovskaya ulitsa 4.
Map 6 F1.

Sekunda
Секунда
(Soviet memorabilia)
Liteynyy prospekt 61 (in
the yard).
Map 7 A2.

Severnaya lira
Северная лира
(Sheet music, instruments,
and books)
Nevskiy prospekt 26.
Map 6 E1.

Soyuz khudozhnikov
Союз художников
(Art)
Bolshaya Morskaya
ulitsa 38.
Map 6 D2.

Staraya kniga
Старая книга
(Second-hand books,
antiques & prints)
Nevskiy prospekt 18.
Map 6 D1.

Tatyana Parfyonova modnyy dom
Татьяна Парфенова
модный дом
(Clothes)
Nevskiy prospekt 51.
Map 7 B2.

Tertsiya
Терция
(Antiques)
Italyanskaya ulitsa 5.
Map 6 E1.

Yeliseev's
Елисеевский гастроном
(Food)
Nevskiy prospekt 56.
Map 6 F1.

ENTERTAINMENT IN ST. PETERSBURG

S T. PETERSBURG has an impressive and varied choice of entertainment. Its ballet, opera, classical music, and theater are among the best in the world. In addition to this, a thriving and vibrant nightlife is made up of numerous rock and jazz clubs, bars, discos, nightclubs, and casinos.

Increasingly, international artists are adding St. Petersburg to their tours, and mainstream now exists harmoniously alongside underground in music, theater, and cinema. The

Folk dancer

St. Petersburg Philharmonia and the Mariinskiy (Kirov) Ballet dancers *(see p119)* deserve their impressive reputation, though this means they are often away on tour. Along the Nevskiy prospekt, street musicians are usually found, from local accordionists to Peruvian musicians. The White Nights in June have given birth to many festivals *(see p51)* that take over all the city venues. At this time of year St. Petersburg moves to the sounds of classical music, rock, pop, and jazz.

The magnificent, gilded interior of the Yusupov Theater

ENTERTAINMENT INFORMATION

S T. PETERSBURG can be quite a difficult city to keep up with, as both official and unofficial events are organized at short notice. Even the programs of major venues, such as the Mariinskiy Theater, can change.

The best regular listings in English can be found in the Friday edition of *The St. Petersburg Times*, a twice-weekly newspaper, and in the monthly magazine *Pulse (see p209)*, both free in hotels, foreign bars, and shops. These listings are selective and tend toward youth culture. A much broader range of information, including details about exhibitions, performances, and other special events, is provided in a complete program produced each month, in Russian, by

Mariinskiy poster pillar

the **Institute of Cultural Program**. Classical concerts and theater are also advertised at ticket offices and kiosks *(teatralnaya kassa)*.

Most of the theaters and concert halls close down for July, August, and part of September because their companies go on tour. This may deprive visitors of local performers, so some theaters bring in guest companies from Moscow and abroad. Smaller venues, such as the Yusupov Theater *(see p120)* and the Hermitage Theater *(see p84)*, depend on foreign visitors and maintain their program all summer. Matinees start at midday and evening performances at 7pm (6:30pm at the Mariinskiy Theater).

BUYING TICKETS

T O DO THINGS the Russian way, tickets must be purchased with cash and in person. Theater ticket offices and kiosks can be found all over town, offering tickets up to a week in advance. They display a full program (in Russian) of all theater and classical music performances for the next ten days and are usually open daily from 10am–1pm and 4–7pm. Offices within theaters tend to work from 11am–3pm and 4–8pm and sell tickets up to a month in advance. The Philharmonia *(see p194)* sells season tickets for a series of concerts.

For non-Russian speakers, the best service for booking tickets is provided either by a hotel concierge or **Ost-West Kontaktservice**, where staff speak English and German.

A few venues, notably the Mariinskiy Theater *(see p119)* and the Mussorgsky Theatre of Opera and Ballet *(see p98)*, have separate ticket prices for foreigners and Russian citizens. Russian-speaking visitors who try to buy the cheaper, Russian-only tickets may be refused entry if discovered.

Tourists may find they can still obtain tickets for sold-out performances at the Mariinskiy Theater if they go on the day. As in most cities, scalpers sell tickets for major events but beware of possible fakes or high prices.

Ticket for a theater performance

Spectacular performance of the famous *Sleeping Beauty* ballet

LATE NIGHT TRANSPORTATION

THE METRO CLOSES at midnight, and buses run until 12:15 (infrequently after 11pm). There is no all-night public transit, so take a taxi late at night. Avoid private taxis that wait outside hotels and bars, they are far more costly than official yellow cabs *(see p219)*.

CHILDREN'S ENTERTAINMENT

THERE ARE relatively few public facilities for children in St. Petersburg. Many theaters, notably **TYuZ** and **Zazerkalye**, stage plays in Russian for children, but few give English-language performances. At New Year, however, some theaters stage English shows.
The **Circus** is an obvious choice for children, with a permanent site on the Fontanka, while in the summer a circus tent also goes up at Avtovo metro. Look out for posters and announcements in listings.
Classical concerts for children are held at the **Children's Philharmonia**, and the two puppet theaters offer a wide variety of fairytales and short

plays. Alternatively, the **Interior Theater** displays costumes and special effects.

WHITE NIGHTS FESTIVALS

THERE ARE AT LEAST four or five festivals bearing the name White Nights *(see p51)*. The original and most internationally respected is the classical music festival, now known as Stars of the White Nights. This incorporates special performances in the Mariinskiy *(see p119)* and other theaters. Ticket prices for concerts and ballet during the White Nights sometimes double.
Jazz and art festivals are also now associated with the White Nights name, leading to an explosion of events in June.

A group of street musicians entertaining the crowds

THE RUSSIAN CIRCUS

Circuses first appeared in Russia in the early 19th century, but it was not until 1876–7 that Russia's first permanent circus building was erected for Giuseppe Ciniselli's Italian circus. St. Petersburg's circus is still based at this historic site, modernized in 1963, and continues to practise the traditional training, skills, and animal acts (some animal-lovers may find these distressing) which have made the Russian circus justifiably famous.

Acrobatic performers, St. Petersburg's circus

The Arts

FOR A CITY RENOWNED WORLDWIDE for its rich tradition in ballet and classical music, it is not surprising that St. Petersburg has a wide range of cultural events. An evening at the Mariinskiy is an essential part of any visit to the city, but it is also worth venturing into the many other theaters, music halls, and churches to absorb more of the city's cultural diversity. Classical music is vastly popular, and local orchestras are much in demand the world over. In addition, there are the evocative sounds of church choirs, the lively ambience of folk cabarets, and numerous festivals *(see pp50–53)* held to encourage young musicians, composers, filmmakers, and dancers.

BALLET

SOME OF THE BEST dancers in the world have come from the **Mariinskiy Theater** *(see p119)*. Its main company tours for much of the year, but usually gives performances in St. Petersburg during the winter months. The greatest highlight of the year is the Christmas performances of *The Nutcracker*, danced largely by children from the Vaganova Ballet School *(see p110)*.

Dancers from the Mariinskiy also perform in the **Hermitage Theater** and the **Mussorgsky Theater of Opera and Ballet**. At the **Rimsky-Korsakov Conservatory** *(see p120)* ballet is of varied quality, but often includes dancers from abroad.

Outside the more traditional spheres, Boris Eifmann's modern ballet company is very popular, but the success of recent years has been Valery Mikhaylovskiy's entirely male Mushchkoy Ballet, performing classics such as *Swan Lake*, complete with tutus. They perform at venues like the **Great October Concert Hall**.

OPERA

TCHAIKOVSKY'S OPERA *Eugene Onegin*, Mussorgsky's *Boris Godunov*, and Prokofiev's *Love of Three Oranges* remain stalwarts in any repertory. Operas are performed (usually in their original language) at the **Mussorgsky Theater of Opera and Ballet** and the **Mariinskiy Theater**. Valery Gergiev's brilliant artistic direction and sensitive conducting at the Mariinskiy have made a huge difference to standards in recent years. The more intimate 18th-century **Hermitage Theater** and the tiny **Yusupov Theater** stage lighter operas.

CLASSICAL MUSIC

THE COMPOSERS Tchaikovsky, Shostakovich, Mussorgsky, and Rimsky-Korsakov lived in St. Petersburg, and their music is performed frequently.

The **Great Philharmonia** *(see p98)*, the **Small Philharmonia** *(see p48)* and **Glinka Capella** *(see p112)*, are all historic venues for classical concerts. The former is where the renowned St. Petersburg Philharmonic Orchestra plays when it is not on tour. Russian emigrés such as the violinist Gidon Kremer are frequent visitors, and foreign conductors such as Claudio Abbado and the late Sir Georg Solti have also performed here.

The Hermitage has its own orchestra, which has a highly active independent life, with concerts in the **Hermitage Theater** *(see p84)* and international tours. The **Menshikov Palace** *(see p62)* has some excellent original restored keyboard instruments, including an 18th-century English organ, on which concerts are given.

CHURCH MUSIC

THE MUSIC OF an Orthodox choir resounding over the priest's intoning is perhaps one of the most evocative sounds in Russia. Professional singers from the Capella and elsewhere often sing in church choirs. The best can be heard on Saturday evening and Sunday morning services at the Holy Trinity Cathedral in Alexander Nevskiy Monastery *(see p130)* and at the **Cathedral of the Transfiguration** *(see p127)*. The services in the **Kazan Cathedral** *(see p111)* are also of a high standard. More formal religious music can be heard in the **Smolnyy Cathedral** *(see p128)*.

FOLK MUSIC

THE LOCAL tourist industry encourages visits to concerts of Russian folk music and dancing. The ensembles can be very good, with balalaikas and *bayans* or accordions, girls with red kerchiefs and whirling Cossack dancers. Some of the best performances are found at the **Beloselskiy-Belozerskiy Palace** and the **Nikolaevskiy Palace**.

Many restaurants include a folk cabaret, though these tend to be kitsch and fairly raucous. For authentic Russian village folk songs, Podvorye Restaurant *(see p184)* in Pavlovsk has an excellent small ensemble.

STREET MUSIC

DEMOCRACY had the unexpected effect of allowing many informal activities such as busking, which brought some highly talented musicians onto the streets. As skilled players stake their ground, the sounds of music fill the city's streets. The two underpasses beneath Nevskiy prospekt by Gostinyy Dvor are busy busking spots, while other metro stations are popular sites for old ladies singing Russian romances, rather like ballads.

THEATER

FOR MANY YEARS, the Soviet Union's leading light in the drama world was the **Bolshoy Dramatic Theater** (BDT), which remains the city's main traditional theater. The **Alexandriinskiy Theater** *(see p110)*, whose company is the oldest in Russia, offers a wider repertoire than the BDT.

In recent years, Lev Dodin's direction of the **Malyy Drama Theater** has brought it international fame, even though all performances are in Russian.

Productions of such plays as the *Cherry Orchard*, may be interesting to experience, but other theaters, staging modern plays, are likely to be less accessible to non-Russian speakers. The **Kommissar-zhevskaya, Liteynyy**, and **Akimov** theaters also have good reputations.

MOVIE THEATERS

MOST THEATERS now show Hollywood blockbusters, but the majority of foreign films are dubbed rather than subtitled. The **Spartak Cinema** shows dubbed European classics, while the **Leningrad Cinema** has popular films in

English twice weekly. The hi-tech **Crystal Palace** also has regular showings in English.

A large number of film festivals are held every year, often including films in the original language. *The St. Petersburg Times* gives full coverage of all festivals including the main Festival of Festivals (*see p51*).

DIRECTORY

TICKETS

Tickets are sold in city kiosks and individual theaters unless otherwise stated.

BALLET AND OPERA

Hermitage Theater
Эрмитажный театр
Ermitazhnyy teatr
Dvortsovaya nab 34.
Map 2 E5. **(** 311 9025.
(Tickets from city kiosks and hotels only.)

Mussorgsky Theater of Opera and Ballet
Театр оперы и балета имени Мусоргского
Teatr opery i baleta imeni Musorgskovo
Pl Iskusstv 1. **Map** 6 E1.
(219 1949.
● *late Jul–Aug.*
(Tickets for foreigners from the theater and hotels only.)

Mariinskiy Theater
Мариинский театр
Mariinskiy teatr
Teatralnaya pl 1. **Map** 5 B3.
(114 5264.
● *late Jul–Aug.*
(Tickets for foreigners from the theater and hotels only.)

Great October Concert Hall
Большой концертный зал Октябрьский
Bolshoy kontsertnyy zal Oktyabrskiy
Ligovskiy pr 6. **Map** 7 C1.
(277 6960.

Rimsky-Korsakov Conservatory
Консерватория имени Римского-Корсакова
Konservatoriya imeni Rimskovo-Korsakova
Teatralnaya pl 3. **Map** 5 C3.
(312 2519.

Yusupov Theater
Юсуповский театр
Yusupovskiy teatr
Yusupovskiy dvorets, nab reki Moyki 94. **Map** 5 B3.
(314 9883.

CLASSICAL MUSIC

Glinka Capella
Капелла имени Глинки
Kapella imeni Glinki
Nab reki Moyki 20.
Map 2 E5. **(** 314 1058.

Menshikov Palace
Меньшиковский дворец
Menshikovskiy dvorets
Universitetskaya nab 15.
Map 1 B5. **(** 213 1112.

Great Philharmonia (Shostakovich Hall)
Большой зал филармонии имени Шостаковича
Bolshoy zal Filarmonii imeni Shostakovicha
Mikhaylovskaya ulitsa 2.
Map 6 F1 **(** 110 4257.

Small Philharmonia (Glinka Hall)
Малый зал филармонии имени Глинки
Malyy zal Filarmonii imeni Glinki
Nevskiy pr 30. **Map** 6 F1.
(311 8333.

CHURCH MUSIC

Church of the Transfiguration
Спасо-Преображенский собор
Spaso-Preobrazhenskiy sobor
Preobrazhenskaya pl 1.
Map 3 B5. **(** 272 3662.
✚ *10am & 6pm daily.*

Holy Trinity Cathedral
Свято-Троицкий собор

Svyato-Troitskiy sobor
Alexander Nevsky Monastery, pl Aleksandra-Nevskovo. **Map** 8 E4.
(274 3606.
✚ *10am & 6pm daily.*

Kazan Cathedral
Казанский собор
Kazanskiy sobor
Kazanskaya ploshchad 2.
Map 6 E1. **(** 311 4826.
✚ *9am & 6pm daily.*

Smolnyy Cathedral
Смольный собор
Smolnyy sobor
Ploshchad Rastrelli 3.
Map 4 F4.
(311 3560.

FOLK MUSIC

Beloselskiy-Belozerskiy Palace
Дворец Белосельских-Белозерских
Dvorets Beloselskikh-Belozerskikh
Nevskiy pr 41. **Map** 7 A2.
(315 5236.

Nikolaevskiy Palace
Николаевский дворец
Nikolaevskiy dvorets
Pl Truda 4. **Map** 5 B2.
(311 9304.

THEATER

Akimov Comedy Theater
Театр комедии имени Акимова
Teatr komedii imeni Akimova
Nevskiy pr 56. **Map** 6 F1.
(312 4555.

Alexandriinskiy Theater
Александринский театр
Aleksandriinskiy teatr
Ploshchad Ostrovskovo 2.
Map 6 F2.
(312 1545.

Bolshoy Drama Theater (BDT)
Большой драматический театр
Bolshoy dramaticheskiy teatr
Nab reki Fontanki 65.
Map 6 F2. **(** 310 0401.

Komissarzhevskaya Drama Theater
Театр им. Комиссаржевской
Teatr im Komissarzhevskoy.
Italyanskaya ulitsa 19.
Map 6 F1. **(** 311 3102.

Liteyniy Theater
Театр на Литейном
Teatr na Liteynom
Liteynyy pr 51. **Map** 7 A1.
(273 44 58.

Malyy Drama Theater
Малый драматический театр
Malyy dramaticheskly teatr
Ulitsa Rubinshteyna 18.
Map 7 A2. **(** 113 2078.

Molodyozhnyy Theater
Молодёжный театр
Molodyozhnyy teatr
Nab reki Fontanki 114.
Map 3 A5. **(** 316 6564.

MOVIE THEATERS

Crystal Palace
Кристалл–Палас
Kristal-Palace
Nevskiy pr 72. **Map** 7 A2.
(272 2382.

Leningrad Cinema
Кинотеатр Ленинград
Kinoteatr Leningrad
Potemkinskaya ulitsa 4.
Map 3 C4. **(** 273 3116.

Spartak Cinema
Кинотеатр Спартак
Kinoteatr Spartak
Ul Saltykova-Shchedrina 8.
Map 3 C5.
(272 7897.

Live Music and Nightlife

ST. PETERSBURG was at the heart of the underground Soviet rock scene and some of the best new Russian sounds still originate here. Rock, rockabilly, and jazz clubs have sprung up in abandoned bomb shelters and theaters all over the city, and most feature an eclectic mix, with live music one night and alternative fashion shows or avant-garde films the next. The nightclub scene, offering mostly rave and techno music, is moving out of the bunkers and into vast halls with strobe lights that attract the nouveaux riches. The newly moneyed classes are also the main clients at the city's casinos.

ROCK VENUES

UNDER THE Soviet regime, Leningrad rock was rebellious without being overtly political. Though there is now less emphasis on the lyrics, Russian rock still owes much to the past, while also managing to incorporate the latest in Western music trends.

There is a wide variety of styles, from pop to hard rock. **Moloko** is a cheap venue offering live rock and a good atmosphere. **Polygon** is popular with fans of hard rock.

Rockabilly gave birth to **Money Honey Saloon**, which in turn led to an explosion of rockabilly groups in the city. **Cosmonaut** and **Vatrushka** only hold special events but maintain a high standard with the latest in St. Petersburg rock.

Mass rock and pop concerts are held in the **Oktyabrskiy kontsertnyy zal**, **Yubileynyy dvorets sporta**, and **SKK**.

JAZZ VENUES

FOR MANY YEARS the jazz scene was dominated by David Goloshchokin, who set up the **Jazz Philharmonic Hall** where, as its name suggests, dancing or talking are often prohibited. As young musicians emerged, the resulting competition on the jazz scene led Goloshchokin to open the **Ellington Hall**, which is more like a relaxed Western jazz club. For improvisation and innovative jazz, **JFC Jazz Club** leads the way, with a variety of acid-jazz and blues. The musicians who make the club such a success also perform on a guest basis elsewhere. **Kvadrat Jazz Club** is where

many young musicians meet for jam sessions. In summer, the city's best swing band can be seen free of charge on the corner of Nevskiy prospekt and Mikhaylovskaya ulitsa.

BARS

A NUMBER OF BARS, such as **Shamrock**, the Mexican **La Cucaracha**, **Mollie's Irish Bar**, or the **Rose Pub**, have live music. **Bistro Sadko**, in the Grand Hotel Europe, was one of the few official bars where new bands used to play. It has recently been left behind by the appearance of numerous rock clubs, but maintains the tradition by putting on occasional live music.

Liverpool is an all-round Beatles experience, hosting live bands playing nothing but Beatles cover versions.

Two venues occupy a special place on the city's entertainment scene, neither of them exactly bars or art clubs. **Fish Fabrique**, hidden away in the depths of the artists' colony dubbed "Pushkinskaya desyat," is a drinking club, occasional concert venue, film club, and favourite hang-out for punks, rock 'n' rollers, and youth in general. The **Idiot**, named after Dostoevsky's novel (*see p123*), has rapidly become one of the city's most popular bars for young intellectuals and artistic foreigners. The scatter cushions and stacks of books make it an ideal place to relax in the daytime, or to attend a poetry reading in the evening. **Korsar** and **Chayka** both have regular jazz evenings, while the noisy **Tribunal**, always filled with a young crowd, has occasional discos.

NIGHTCLUBS AND DISCOS

SMALLER, MORE DIVERSE clubs, such as the underground **Griboedov**, are still very much of the alternative culture trend, playing a variety of the latest hits from Europe, and hosting fashion shows and other cultural events. **Port Club** goes one step farther, providing video halls and an art gallery.

Nevsky Melody is a vast entertainment complex, with casinos, restaurants, and nightclubs. **Candyman**, the place for the pop and TV elite, is a huge disco and dance hall located on the outskirts of town in the high-rise heartland. **Domenico's** introduces a touch of humor with its occasional live Russian pop and erotica. One of the most respectable clubs, **Hollywood Nites**, invites more serious acts and has one of the city's best casinos. **Metro**, mainly for the young and upwardly mobile, plays house, techno, and Russian dance music. **Piramid**, with its Egyptian theme, is always fun. **Harley Davidson Club** is another example of a good theme club. The "erotic" **Monroe Club** has video screens and peepshows, as well as Russian and European pop music and dancing.

On the gay scene, **69 Club** is where things are happening, while other gay clubs tend to come and go. Since gay culture in St. Petersburg is very much involved in the art world, events are often advertised at Saturday exhibitions in the New Academy of Fine Arts at Pushkinskaya ulitsa 10.

CASINOS

FREQUENT CHANGES to local legislation have had a negative effect on the city's handful of casinos. Since they are visited mainly by the wealthiest band, casinos tend to attract many members from the semicriminal classes. **Premier**, in the Titan Cinema, has roulette and cards and is a trouble-free option along with **Venice**, **Astoria Club**, and **Hollywood Nites**. All are top of the list for quality and style. **Nevsky Melody** is more lively but a little impersonal.

DIRECTORY

ROCK VENUES

Cosmonaut
Космонавт
Kosmonavt
Bronnitskaya ulitsa 24.
Map 6 E5.
📞 316 2040.
🕐 7–11pm Fri & Sat.

Moloko
Молоко
Perekupnoy pereulok 12.
Map 8 D3.
📞 274 9467.
🕐 7–11:30pm Thu–Sat.

Money Honey Saloon
Apraksin dvor 14.
Map 6 E2.
📞 310 0147.
🕐 7:30pm–midnight daily.

Oktyabrskiy kontsertnyy zal
Октябрьский
концертный зал
Ligovskiy prospekt 6.
Map 7 C1.
📞 275 1273.

Polygon
Полигон
Poligon
Lesnoy prospekt 65.
(Check listings for events.)

SKK
СКК
Prospekt Yuriya Gagarina 8.
📞 298 1211.

Vatrushka
Ватрушка
Ul Pravdy 10. **Map** 7 A3.
📞 164 3236.
(Check listings for special
events only.)

Yubileynyy dvorets sporta
Юбилейный дворец
спорта
Prospekt Dobrolyubova 18.
Map 1 B3.
📞 119 5601/5604.

JAZZ VENUES

Ellington Hall
Эллингтоновский зал
Ellingtonovskiy zal
Zagorodnyy prospekt 27.
Map 6 F3.
📞 164 8565.
🕐 7–11pm Wed–Sun.

Jazz Philharmonic Hall
Джаз-Филармоник холл
Dzhaz-filarmonik kholl
Zagorodnyy prospekt 27.
Map 6 F3.
📞 164 8565.
🕐 7–11pm Wed–Sun.

JFC Jazz Club
Shpalernaya ulitsa 33.
Map 3 C4.
📞 272 9850.
🕐 7–11pm daily.

Kvadrat Jazz Club
Джаз клуб квадрат
Dzhaz klub kvadrat
Ul Pravdy 10. **Map** 7 A3.
📞 315 9046.
🕐 8–11pm Tue.

BARS

Bistro Sadko
Grand Hotel Europe,
Mikhaylovskaya ulitsa 1/7.
Map 6 F1. 📞 329 6000.
🕐 noon–1am daily.

Chayka
Чайка
Naberezhnaya kanala
Griboedova 14. **Map** 6 E1.
📞 312 4631.
🕐 11am–3am daily.

La Cucaracha
Nab reki Fontanki 39.
Map 7 A2.
📞 110 4006.
🕐 noon–1am Sun–Thu,
noon–5am Fri & Sat.

Fish Fabrique
Pushkinskaya ulitsa 10,
5th floor. **Map** 7 B2.
🕐 7pm–midnight Wed,
9pm–5:30am Fri & Sat.

Idiot
Nab reki Moyki 82.
Map 5 C2. 📞 315 1675.
🕐 noon–11pm daily.

Korsar
Корсар
Bolshaya Morskaya
ulitsa 14. **Map** 6 D1.
📞 219 4184.
🕐 1pm–1am Mon–Fri,
1pm–4am Sat & Sun.

Liverpool
Ливерпуль
Liverpul
Ulitsa Mayakovskovo 16.
Map 7 B1.
📞 279 2054.
🕐 11am–2am daily.

Mollie's Irish Bar
Ulitsa Rubinshteyna 30.
Map 7 A3.
📞 319 9768.
🕐 11am–2am daily.
(Live music Tue–Thu & Sun.)

Rose Pub
Роуз паб
Furshtadtskaya ulitsa 1/14.
Map 3 A4.
📞 275 3554.
🕐 noon–2am daily.

Shamrock
Ulitsa Dekabristov 27.
Map 5 B3.
📞 219 4625.
🕐 noon–2am daily.
(Live music Mon, Thu, Sat.)

Tribunal
Corner of Angliyskaya nab
& proezd Dekabristov.
Map 5 C1.
📞 311 1690.
🕐 11am–4am daily.

NIGHTCLUBS AND DISCOS

69 Club
Клуб 69
Klub 69
2-ya Krasnoarmeyskaya
ulitsa 6.
Map 6 D5.
📞 259 5163.
🕐 1pm–6am Tue–Sun.

Candyman
Кэндимен
Kendimen
Prospekt Kosygina 17.
📞 521 1410.
🕐 10pm–7am Wed–Sun.

Domenico's
Доменикос
Nevskiy prospekt 70.
Map 7 A2.
📞 272 5717.
🕐 noon–6am daily.

Griboedov
Грибоедов
Voronezhskaya ulitsa 2A.
Map 7 B4.
📞 164 4355.
🕐 11pm–5:30am
Thu–Sat.

Harley Davidson Club
Ulitsa Kurchatova 1/39.
📞 247 6500.
🕐 noon–late daily.

Hollywood Nites
Nevskiy prospekt 46.
Map 6 F1.
📞 311 6077.
🕐 8pm–6am daily.

Metro
Метро
Ligovskiy prospekt 174.
📞 166 0204.
🕐 10pm–6am daily.

Monroe Club
Клуб Монро
Klub Monro
Nab kanala Griboedova 8.
Map 6 E1.
📞 312 1331.
🕐 noon–11pm Tue–Sun,
5–11pm Mon.

Nevsky Melody
Невские Мелодии
Nevskie Melodii
Sverdlovskaya nab 62.
📞 227 1596.
🕐 10pm–6am daily.

Piramid
Пирамид
Ulitsa Lomonosova 1.
Map 6 F2.
📞 312 3600.
🕐 10pm–6am Thu–Sun.

Port Club
Клуб Порт
Klub Port
Pereulok Antonenko 2
(in yard).
Map 6 D2.
📞 314 2609.
🕐 3pm–6am daily.

CASINOS

Astoria Club
Клуб Астория
Klub Astoriya
Malaya Morskaya ul 20.
Map 6 D1.
📞 210 5020.
🕐 6pm–6am daily.

Premier
Премьер
Nevskiy prospekt 47.
Map 7 A2.
📞 315 7893.
🕐 noon–9am.

Venice
Венеция
Venetsiya
Ulitsa Korablestroiteley 21.
📞 356 4661.
🕐 7pm–6am daily.

Survival
Guide

Practical Information 200-209
Getting to St. Petersburg 210-212
Getting Around St. Petersburg 213-221

PRACTICAL INFORMATION

Sign advertising Ost-West Kontaktservice

THE STREET SIGNS and maps of St. Petersburg are not as difficult to negotiate as it may first appear when confronted with daunting Cyrillic letters. Not only do hotels, restaurants, and all service sectors attempt to compensate by being helpful to foreigners, but in recent times the city has started putting up English signs pointing out major sights and shops.

Conventional tourist offices do not exist in the city, and information centers, along with other services such as foreign exchange offices, are often concentrated in hotels and other areas frequented by foreigners. Once out on the street, things will seem unfamiliar, but with a modicum of patience and determination everything is eventually possible, from making international telephone calls and changing money to finding emergency medical treatment.

Telecommunications are rapidly gaining ground, but, as quality improves, prices come closer to, and occasionally outstrip, Western equivalents.

Grand Hotel Europe concierge

TOURIST INFORMATION

THE CITY'S HOTELS provide the main source of guidance for tourists in St. Petersburg. In the Europe, Nevskij Palace, and Hotelship Peterhof the concierge will provide travel and booking services and general assistance. Other, Russian-run, hotels have a Service Bureau offering similar services, although advice is often indifferent. **Ost-West Kontaktservice** runs a reliable, free tourist information service as well as selling maps and booking accommodations and entertainment.

English-language newspapers (see p209) give details on events and up-to-the-minute opening hours for museums.

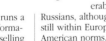

Ticket office sign

EXCURSIONS

HOTELS CAN BOOK guided group tours and day trips in several languages. In addition to city tours and canal cruises, there are day trips to the suburban palaces and Novgorod (see pp144–63).

Ost-West Kontaktservice offers several excellent tours, in English and German. City-run excursions, which gather tourists on Palace Square by the Admiralty (see p83) and the Portik Rusca on Nevskiy prospekt (see p48), tend to be in Russian only, as do ordinary river cruises (see p218).

On summer weekends there are helicopter tours operating on a turn-up basis from the Peter and Paul Fortress (see pp66–7). Groups of 20 can book through **Baltic Airlines**.

ADMISSION CHARGES

MANY MUSEUMS and theaters, notably the Hermitage (see pp84–93), the Russian Museum (see pp104–107) and the Mariinskiy (see p119) charge foreigners considerably more than Russians, although prices are still within European and American norms. Students and schoolchildren are entitled to discounts. Credit cards are not accepted at any sights.

The ticket office or *kassa* is often far from the entrance, so look for the KACCA sign.

Tour helicopter picking up tourists by the Peter and Paul Fortress

OPENING HOURS

MOST SIGHTS open standard hours, 10 or 10:30am to 6pm, with no break for lunch, and close one day a week. They also close one day at the end of each month for major cleaning; this date varies so phone to check. Parks, including those around the palaces, are usually open from 8am to 8pm, later during White Nights.

Sign for open (otkryto)

Sign for closed (zakryto)

VISITING CHURCHES

ATTENDING an Orthodox service is a fascinating experience. Since services tend to run for several hours, it is generally fine simply to drop in. It is polite to make a donation and certain dress codes must be observed: no shorts; men should remove hats; ladies should cover their shoulders and chest and preferably wear a hat or headscarf. Women in pants are accepted in town churches, but all monasteries will strictly enforce the no pants rule. The most

important services are
on Saturday evening,
Sunday morning, and
on church holidays.

Most major faiths are
represented in the city.
Churches tend to be
open all day from
early morning till late.
Church service times
are published in
Friday's *St. Petersburg
Times (see p209).*

Friends greeting with a handshake

Language

CYRILLIC, the alphabet used
in the Russian language,
is named after the 9th-century
monk Cyril who invented it.
The apparent similarity between Cyrillic and Roman letters
can be misleading. Some
letters are common to both
alphabets; others look similar
but represent totally different
sounds. Various systems of
transliteration are in usage,
but they do not differ enough
to cause serious confusion.

Most people who come into
contact with tourists speak
some English, and passers-by
on the street will do their best
if asked directions. Knowledge
of a few Russian words *(see
pp252–6)* will be appreciated
and taken as a sign of respect.

Etiquette

DESPITE AN ever increasing
Westernization of manners
and language, the use is still
strictly in force of the formal
you (*vy*) and the informal (*ty*).

On public transportation, it
is accepted that young men
should relinquish their seats
to children or the elderly.

Smoking is prohibited in movie
theaters, museums, theaters,
and on public transportation.
Areas are usually allocated for
smoking in these places.

Drinking and
smoking are two
activities in which
the Russians take
great pleasure and
frequent toasts are
required to justify
the filling and
draining of glasses.
At a private home
you should always
offer a toast to the hostess (*za
khozyayku*) or to the host (*za
khozyayina*). Introductions,
and greetings among friends
take place with a handshake.

Paying and Tipping

ROUBLES ARE the sole valid
currency in Russia *(see
p207)*. Some large shops and
hotels give prices in American
dollars or Deutschmarks, but
all cash payments must be in
roubles only. Credit cards are
accepted in some restaurants
and most hotels, but rarely in
shops, other than those selling
imported goods at a much
higher price than abroad.

Tipping is a matter of choice,
but baggage handlers at the
airport and the train station
may ask or expect exorbitant
sums. Simply pay as you think
fit; a few roubles are sufficient.

Addresses

RUSSIAN ADDRESSES are given
in reverse order: index/zip
code, city, street name, house
number, apartment number,
and finally name of person.

After 1917, many streets and
sights were renamed to avoid
imperial connotations or in
order to commemorate new
Soviet heroes. Since the city
itself resumed its
original name after
a referendum in
1991, most streets
in the center have
officially reverted
to their pre-1917
names, while
others are still
being discussed.
The area surroun-
ding the city, however, is still
the Leningrad Region. Many
people happily use both the
original and Soviet names; no
offense is caused when one is
used in preference to another.

**House number and
Cyrillic street name**

Index/zip code	City	Street name

193015 Санкт-Петербург
улица Восстания
д. 34, кв. 52
Милане Прекрасной

House number	Apartment number	Name of recipient

Bridge Opening Times

**Dvortsovyy most (leading to Vasilevskiy Island),
raised to allow ships access along the Neva**

From early April until mid-November, when navi-
gation is possible on the Neva River, all its bridges
are raised between approximately 2am and 5am
except for one short break. Make sure you are on
the right side of the river before the bridges go up.
Dvortsovyy most: 1:55–3:05am & 3:15–4:45am.
Troitskiy most: 2–4:40am.
Most Leytenanta Shmidta: 1:55–4:50am.
Liteynyy most: 2:10–4:40am.
Birzhevoy most: 2:25–3:20am & 3:40–4:40am.
Tuchkov most: 2:20–3:10am & 3:40–4:40am.
Most Petra Velikovo: 2:45–4:55am.
Most Aleksandra Nevskovo: 2:35–4:50am.
Volodarskiy most: 2–3:45am & 4:25–5:45am.

Ost-West Kontaktservice, offering free advice and literature to visitors

VISAS

VISAS ARE REQUIRED for all visitors to Russia. Package tour companies will organize visas for you, but independent travelers need to arrange their own. This can be a complex, time-consuming process, and by far the easiest option is to pay a small fee for your travel agency to obtain a visa for you. The alternative is to go in person to the Russian Embassy where visas are issued. Document requirements change regularly, and it is essential to check these in advance. You will need to show proof of either pre-booked accommodations or an invitation (visa support) from a tour company, business, or private individual in Russia. **Ost-West Kontaktservice** can fax express invitations directly. Private invitations cannot be faxed and the process of issuing them takes at least one month through **OVIR** (Visa Registration Department).

The cost of a visa ranges from around $16 for a short-term, single entry visa to about $150 for multiple entry business visas. A visa usually takes ten days, but for an extra fee can be arranged in one day.

Inside Russia, visa extensions can be granted only by the organization that issued the initial invitation. If you over-

Official Russian visa

stay, expect to be stopped at the airport and turned back until you have either obtained the necessary extension visa or paid a considerable fine.

CUSTOMS AND IMMIGRATION

PASSPORTS AND VISAS are checked thoroughly at immigration. All visitors must fill out a customs declaration form, available in several languages. These completed forms are returned to customs, together with a new form on departure. Essentially there are no limitations on the amount of money allowed into Russia, but visitors should have less hard currency on departure and Russian money cannot be exported. Items of considerable value, such as diamond jewelry and computers, should be noted on the customs form on entry. All such valuables must be re-exported, or import duty will be charged. On arrival and departure, all items of luggage go through X-ray machines.

Departure customs are strict, particularly with works of art and antiques *(see p186)*, but there should be no problem at all with modest quantities of consumer goods.

REGISTRATION

ALL FOREIGNERS must register with **OVIR** within three days of arrival and obtain a stamp of registration on their visa. Hotels automatically do this for their guests, but those staying in private accommodations must register at the branch of **OVIR** where their invitation was issued. For an extended visa an application must be made at the same local branch. Visitors who forget to register become liable for a fine and can be prevented from leaving Russia until all the necessary paperwork is in order.

EMBASSIES AND CONSULATES

ANYONE INTENDING to reside in Russia for longer than three months is advised to register with their consulate or embassy. If visitors are hospitalized, robbed, imprisoned, or otherwise rendered helpless, consular officials will help make arrangements, find an interpreter, or at least offer advice. They can re-issue passports and in some emergency cases provide money to get visitors home.

Great Britain, US, Canada, and South Africa have consulates in St. Petersburg. Visitors from New Zealand, Australia or Ireland, however, have to contact their embassies in Moscow.

DISABLED TRAVELERS

ST. PETERSBURG has almost no facilities for the disabled. Transit is inaccessible; entrances have steps and narrow doors, and there are rarely public elevators, so it is hard for disabled travelers to get around.

STUDENT TRAVELERS

INTERNATIONAL student cards of all kinds are accepted for discounts in museums and on rail and air travel booked through the **International Youth Hostel** *(see p168)* or its affiliated agent, **Sindbad Travel**.

Sign for St. Petersburg's International Youth Hostel

TRAVELING WITH CHILDREN

RUSSIANS adore children, and travelers in the company of under-tens are likely to attract a good deal of attention and many compliments. Russian *babushki* (grannies) also think nothing of telling parents of their failings.

Men's toilet sign

Women's toilet sign

The city has many play parks and during school vacations temporary playgrounds are sometimes set up around town.

Museums and public trans-portation are free for under-fives. Schoolchildren pay the full price on transit but pay a reduced price at museums.

Children playing on temporary bouncy castle in Palace Square

PUBLIC TOILETS

MANY CAFÉS and bars have no toilet facilities, and in general the rather unhygienic public toilets are best avoided. It is much better to go to the nearest hotel or, if lacking an alterna-tive, to use the pay toilets in department stores, for example. The person who takes the money hands out toilet paper rations.

PHOTOGRAPHY

PHOTOGRAPHIC restrictions have more or less disap-peared. In museums expect to purchase a ticket for the right to photograph or use a video camera – tripods and flashes are prohibited.

ELECTRICAL APPLIANCES

THE ELECTRICAL CURRENT IS 220 V. Two-pin plugs are required, but some of the old Soviet two-pin sockets do not take modern European plugs that have slightly thicker pins. American appliances require a 220:110 current adaptor. Adaptors are widely available in St. Petersburg.

TIME DIFFERENCE

ST. PETERSBURG, throughout the year, follows Moscow time, which is eight hours ahead of Eastern Standard Time. Russia has recently come into line with the rest of Europe and now puts its clocks forward one hour at the end of March and back at the end of October.

CONVERSION TABLE

US Standard to Metric
1 inch = 2.54 centimeters
1 foot = 30 centimeters
1 mile = 1.6 kilometers
1 ounce = 28 grams
1 pound = 454 grams
1 US quart = 0.946 litre
1 US gallon = 3.785 liters

Metric to US Standard
1 millimeter = 0.04 inches
1 meter = 3 feet, 3 inches
1 kilometer = 0.6 miles
1 gram = 0.04 ounces
1 kilogram = 2.2 pounds
1 liter = 1.1 US quarts

Standard Russian two-pin plug

DIRECTORY

TOURIST INFORMATION AND GUIDED TOURS

Ost-West Kontaktservice
Ul Mayakovskovo 7.
Map 4 B1. (279 7045.
FAX 327 3417.

Baltic Airlines
Baltiyskie avialinii
Nevskiy pr. 7/9, Office 12.
Map 5 D1.
(FAX 311 0084.

VISA FORMALITIES IN US

Panorama Travel, Ltd.
156 Fifth Ave., Suite 1019,
New York, NY 10010.
((212) 741-0033.
FAX (212) 645-6276.

Russian Travel Bureau, Inc.
255 East 44th St.,
New York, NY 10017
((212) 986-1500.
FAX (800) 847-1800.

VISA FORMALITIES IN RUSSIA

OVIR
Овир
(Tsentralnyy district)
Foreign department,
Pereulok Krylova 5.
Map 6 F2. (310 4117.
◯ 10am–6pm Mon–Fri.

EMBASSIES AND CONSULATES

Australia
Moscow, Kropotkinskiy
pereulok 13.
((095) 956 6070.
FAX (095) 956 6170.

Canada
Malodetskoselskiy pr 32.
Map 5 E3. (325 8448.
FAX 325 8393.

Ireland
Moscow, Grokholskiy per 5.
((095) 742 0901;
(095) 2806500.
FAX (095) 742 0920.

New Zealand
Moscow, Povorskaya ul 7.
((095) 956 3579.
FAX (095) 956 3589.

South Africa
Nab reki Moyki 11.
Map 1 E5. (325 6363.

UK
Pl Proletarskoy Diktatury 5.
Map 4 E4. (325 6036.
FAX 325 6073.

US
Furstadskaya ulitsa 15.
Map 3 B4. (275 1701.
FAX 110 7022.

DISABLED TRAVEL

Society for the Advancement of Travel for the Handicapped
347 Fifth Ave., Suite 610,
New York, NY 10016.
((212) 447-7284.

STUDENT TRAVEL

International Youth Hostel
3-ya Sovetskaya ul 28.
Map 7 C2.
(329 8018.
FAX 329 8019.
@ ryh@ryh.spb.su

Sindbad Travel
3-ya Sovetskaya ul 28.
Map 7 C2.
(327 8384.
FAX 329 8019.
@ sindbad@ryh.spb.su

Personal Security and Health

D ESPITE LURID media reports worldwide about the mafia, St. Petersburg is still a relatively safe city. Petty crime should be the only concern for tourists, and even this is generally avoided if the usual precautions are taken. Make copies of your passport and visa, note traveler's check and credit card numbers, and, for language reasons, keep a card with your Russian address on it.

Medical insurance is essential, as local healthcare compares poorly with Western standards, and English-speaking services or medical evacuation via Finland are very expensive. Many medicines are readily available, but it is best to bring specific medicines needed.

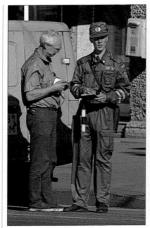

GAI policemen checking documents

PROTECTING YOUR PROPERTY

E VERY VISITOR to Russia is seriously advised to take out travel insurance. Once in St. Petersburg, simple rules should be observed, such as not displaying large sums of money; carrying cash in a concealed money belt, and keeping passports, tickets and all valuables in the hotel safe whenever possible. Security in Western-run hotels is very high, but in all hotels it is advisable to place valuables in the safe. Traveler's checks (see p206) may have an insurance policy but are expensive to use and are easily laundered in Russia.

Avoid the gypsies who occasionally group on Nevskiy prospekt, apparently begging. If they do approach, do not stop for them and keep a firm hold of your possessions.

If you have property stolen, report it to the local police station for insurance purposes. They are unlikely to have an interpreter, so you should ask your hotel for assistance.

Beat-cops or *gorodovoy*, identifiable by their red caps

PERSONAL SAFETY

T HE GREATEST danger faced by foreigners is that posed by pickpockets and petty thieves who might use violence if they meet with resistance. As in any country, it is advisable to hand over belongings that are demanded with menace.

The mafia, an organization largely overrated by the media nowadays, has almost no contact with tourists, who are generally much less wealthy than Russian businessmen.

Women on their own are unlikely to encounter sexual harrassment, though they should ignore lowlifes and avoid taking a cab alone at night. The main threats to people on the

streets come from local drivers, who see all pedestrians as a nuisance, and from manhole covers, which tend to rock or even collapse under your feet.

POLICE

S EVERAL KINDS of police operate on St. Petersburg's streets. Their uniforms change according to the weather, with the addition of fur hats and big coats in the winter.

Nevskiy prospekt now has the *gorodovoy* or beat-cop, an institution revived in 1997 to

Free, state-run ambulance service

New-look police fleet as Volvos (top) replace Ladas (below)

Fire engine in central St. Petersburg

create the reassuring presence of educated, young policemen who should be capable of giving directions in a foreign language. The red uniform caps they wear in the summer months inspired the nickname "Red Riding Hood."

The other street officers or militia *(militsya)* wear dark blue-gray combat-style uniforms, and many carry guns. The uniform is similar to the riot police or OMON, the only difference being their badges.

Militsya **policeman**

Totally separate are the GAI (ГАИ) or traffic police, whose uniforms have a badge on the chest and shoulder. They can stop any vehicle to check documents.

The militia and traffic police supplement their low incomes by fining people for minor infringements, notably for crossing Nevskiy between signals. It is best to pay the moderate "fine" imposed – no more than 50 roubles.

PHARMACIES

THE BEST PHARMACIES *(apteka)*, are located along Nevskiy prospekt. These sell many imported medicines, some with Russian instructions, others in their original language. Strong medications can be bought over the counter, so prescriptions are not necessary. Every assistant is a trained pharmacist and can advise alternative drugs. If you have very specific requirements, particularly insulin, you should bring a sufficient supply for your stay.

MEDICAL TREATMENT

IF YOU GET SICK, seek advice at your hotel, which should have its own doctor. Several companies, notably **Emergency Medical Consulting** and

American Medical Center, specialize in dealing with foreigners. They cover everything from dental care, X-rays, and pre-natal care to medical evacuation. Their charges are fairly high, but they are used to dealing with foreign insurance policies. Slightly cheaper is the **Clinic Complex**, which has English-speaking Russian doctors and can deal competently with minor emergencies.

For those in need of immediate attention, the emergency department of the **Trauma Clinic of the Central District** is just off Nevskiy prospekt. English is not spoken here, but basic care involving stitches or injections can be administered.

If you are taken to a local hospital and require further treatment, it is advisable to contact either your consulate or one of the above medical centers. They can arrange to have you moved or alternatively they can oversee your treatment in the hospital.

Pharmacy in a Nevskiy underpass

HEALTH PRECAUTIONS

VISITORS AND residents should not drink tap water, which contains heavy metals and *giardia*, a parasite causing stomach problems. To be safe drink bottled water only.

Foreign food often unsettles the stomach, but Russian food is unlikely to do any serious harm. Avoid fruit and raw vegetables that may have been washed in tap water, and the meat pies sold on the streets.

In past years diphtheria has become more prevalent, and inoculation is advisable. Of growing concern is the rise in syphilis, HIV, and other sexually transmitted diseases.

Sign for pharmacy or *apteka*

MOSQUITOES

MOSQUITOES *(komari)* are rife between June and late September. Repellents are available locally, but not all are very effective and it is best to come well equipped. Burning oils, sprays, or plugs that heat chemical tablets are recommended at night, particularly out on the Gulf of Finland or in the woods.

DIRECTORY

EMERGENCY SERVICES

Fire *(pozhar)*
01.

Police *(militsiya)*
02.

Ambulance *(skoraya pomoshch)*
03.

MEDICAL SERVICES

American Medical Center
Serpukhovskaya ul 10. **Map** 6 E5.
326 1730. 24 hours.

Clinic Complex
Ao Poliklinicheskiy kompleks
Moskovskiy pr 22. **Map** 6 D5.
316 6272. 24 hours.

Dental Palace
Millionnaya ul 10. **Map** 2 E5.
314 1459.

Emergency Medical Consulting
Izmailovskiy pr 14, entrance fr Sovetskiy per.
112 6510 (24-hour call service).

Trauma Clinic of the Central District
Travmpunkt pripoliklinike n. 35
Malaya Konyushennaya ul 2.
Map 6 E1.
311 4396. 24 hours.

PHARMACIES

Nevskiy pr 5.
312 7078.

Nevskiy pr 66.
315 5881.

Nevskiy pr 83.
277 6065.

24-Hour Pharmacy
Nevskiy pr 22.
314 0859.

Banking and Local Currency

S T. PETERSBURG IS MOVING into the credit card age, and major European debit and credit cards can now be used in hotels and some restaurants and shops. Everywhere else, however, cash is the norm, and roubles are the only legal currency. The city is well provided with exchange points where you can turn your currency (US dollars still being the most popular), traveler's checks, or credit cards into roubles, at varying rates of commission. Since bank rates are so good, money should never be changed on the streets. What appear to be higher offers from individuals will lead to visitors being cheated.

CHANGING MONEY

Sign for Russian exchange office
(*obmen valuty*)

R OUBLES CANNOT be obtained outside Russia, but there are numerous exchange offices throughout St. Petersburg, including at the airport. Some offices open 24 hours a day. A passport has to be shown when changing money. Any visible defect on foreign bank notes, especially vertical tears or ink or water stains, makes them invalid in Russia and they will be refused at the exchange. Make sure that all bills brought into Russia are in good condition, and that any US dollars were issued after 1990.

Official currency exchange slip

On completion of an exchange transaction, a receipt slip is issued. Keep these slips safe as they will need to be attached to the customs declaration form filled in on arrival in Russia (*see p202*), and returned to customs on departure.

Automatic cash dispenser

BANKS AND EXCHANGE OFFICES

N ONE OF THE foreign banks in Russia offers over-the-counter services, and the most reliable Russian banks are **Inkombank** and **Promstroybank**. Exchange offices are plentiful in St. Petersburg. They are often branches of banks, offering both cash currency exchange and cash advances on credit or debit cards. Larger branches also cash traveler's checks. Exchange offices often work long hours: the branches of Inkombank at the Europe and Nevskij Palace hotels are open 24 hours, with short breaks in the wee hours. Inkombank and **Most-bank** offer the best rates.

A fast and safe way of transferring cash to Russia is by Western Union, available at Promstroybank, Inkombank, Most-bank, and the **American Express** office.

CREDIT CARDS

I T IS NOW POSSIBLE to obtain cash, both roubles and US dollars, with a credit card through the larger banks and from automatic cash dispensers, which are springing up all over town. The local commission is between 2 and 5 percent, plus whatever the

card company charges. The most commonly accepted card is VISA, with MasterCard, Eurocard, Diners Club, and American Express much less widely recognized. The cash dispensers at **Most-bank** take MasterCard, VISA, and Eurocard. It is best to take out cash in roubles; less commission is charged this way.

Lost or stolen credit cards should be reported immediately to the credit card company back home.

DIRECTORY

BANKS

American Express
Grand Hotel Europe,
Ground Floor Concourse,
Mikhaylovskaya ulitsa 1/7.
Map 6 F1. 〖 *329 6060*.
○ *9am–5pm daily.*

Inkombank
Инкомбанк
Grand Hotel Europe,
Ground Floor Concourse,
Mikhaylovskaya ulitsa 1/7.
Map 6 F1. ○ *24 hours daily.*

Inkombank
Инкомбанк
Nevskij Palace Hotel Concourse,
Nevskiy prospekt 57. **Map** 7 B2.
○ *24 hours daily.*

Most-bank
Мост-банк
Nevskiy prospekt 27. **Map** 6 E1.
○ *9:30am–1pm & 2pm–7:30pm daily.*

Promstroybank
Промстройбанк
Mikhaylovskaya ulitsa 4.
Map 6 F1. ○ *9:30am–1pm & 3pm–7pm daily (Sun until 6pm).*

CASH DISPENSERS

Hotel Astoria
Гостиница Астория
Bolshaya Morskaya ulitsa 39.
Map 6 D2. 〖 *VISA, Eurocard.*

Grand Hotel Europe
Гранд Отель Европа
Ground Floor Concourse,
Mikhaylovskaya ulitsa 1/7.
Map 6 F1. 〖 *VISA.*

Most-bank
Мост-банк
Nevskiy prospekt 27. **Map** 6 E1.
〖 *VISA, Eurocard, MasterCard.*

TRAVELER'S CHECKS

BANKS CHARGE at least 3 percent to cash traveler's checks. Only the large banks, such as **Promstroybank**, **Most-bank**, and **Inkombank**, offer this service. The cheapest alternative is American Express checks. The commission on these is only 2 percent if they are cashed at the **American Express** office. Traveler's checks can only be used as payment for goods or services in the largest hotels, and are acceptable only in US dollars, Deutschmarks, British pounds, and French francs. In all cases dollar checks are preferred.

LOCAL CURRENCY

THE RUSSIAN currency is the rouble (or ruble), written рубль or abbreviated to p. or руб. The higher denominations of roubles are available in bills, which all bear images of Russian cities; the lower denominations in coins. The kopek, of which there are 100 in a rouble, is coin only.

The designs of bills changed several times in the 1990s. In 1998 the rouble was revalued because of its stronger value and lower inflation, and new bills were issued. Values were divided by 1,000 (1,000 roubles became 1 rouble). Visitors exchanging money will be given new bills, but the old ones are valid until 1999, and prices may be shown in both.

Banknotes

New notes come in denominations of 10, 50, 100 and 500 roubles. Pre-1998 notes have the same designs as their new equivalents. Divide the old face value by 1,000 to get their new worth. From December 31, 1998, only major banks will exchange them.

10 roubles

50 roubles

100 roubles

500 roubles

Coins

The revaluation of the Russian rouble in 1998 led to the revival of the long-uncirculated but much-loved kopek. Traditionally, the rouble had always consisted of 100 kopeks. As well as coins for 1, 2, and 5 roubles, there are now coins for 1, 5, 10, and 50 kopeks. Any coins which were issued before 1997, prior to revaluation, are essentially valueless and you are perfectly within your rights to refuse to accept them.

1 rouble   **2 roubles**   **5 roubles**

1 kopek   **10 kopeks**   **50 kopeks**

Communications

International telephone sign

Telecommunications is one of the biggest growth areas in northwest Russia. A once-antiquated phone system has rapidly been brought up to date, with satellite and digital lines, and direct dialing worldwide. The same period has seen an explosion of magazines, newspapers, and TV channels. Unfortunately, ordinary home phone lines and everyday mail are not improving at the same rate, but St. Petersburg offers many inexpensive and efficient alternatives.

TELEPHONE SERVICES

Blue BCL satellite phone booths are installed at the airport, business centers, hotel lobbies, and some restaurants. They operate on credit cards and BCL phonecards are widely available.

The local system, Petersburg Telephone Network (PTS) or *cnm*, is perfectly adequate and much cheaper. PTS phone booths are green and located on the streets and in some metro stations. The **Central Telegraph Office** also has dozens of international and

BCL satellite phone

local PTS phones. Calls abroad can be made directly from a card-operated PTS phone. PTS phonecards come in units and are available from kiosks and post offices. International calls require at least 100 units. Intercity and international calls are cheaper between 10pm and 8am and on weekends.

Non-card PTS phones can only be used for local calls. These operate on metro tokens, which can be bought in metro stations *(see p215)*. All phone booths, both PTS and BCL, display instructions in English. Local calls are free of charge.

USING A PTS CARD-OPERATED PHONE

2 Wait until the display tells you to insert your card.

3 Insert your card in the slot, where it should remain for the duration of the call.

1 When using a PTS card phone, begin by lifting the receiver.

4 When your card has been cleared, dial the number. PTS phones require you to press the star button when there is an answer.

5 When you have finished your call, hang up, and remove your card only when instructed to by the display.

A PTS phonecard

Using a PTS Token Phone
Lift the receiver and check that you have a dial tone before you dial the number. When you are connected, drop the metro token into the slot at the top of the phone.

Metro token

Post office sign

POSTAL SERVICES

The state-run, international postal system is generally slow and unreliable, and it is best to avoid it, except when sending postcards. Efficient and cheap services are run by **Westpost** and **Post International** who offer ordinary, express, courier, and poste restante services. American Express *(see p206)* also operates a poste restante service for cardmembers. The Europe and Nevskij Palace hotels *(see p173)* run cheap and remarkably quick postal services, taking about five days to the US, which costs about $2 per letter.

Distinctive pale blue mailbox

Ordinary post offices, such as the **Main Post Office** *(see p122)* and those in hotels, sell normal and commemorative Russian stamps, postcards, envelopes, and local phonecards. Russian mailboxes are marked Почта *(Pochta)* and are most plentiful in the city center. Tourists should use the small pale blue boxes. The yellow ones are used for special local services only.

Commemorative Russian stamps

Westpost on Nevskiy prospekt

FAX, TELEX, TELEGRAM, AND E-MAIL SERVICES

MOST OF THE CITY hotels and the **Main Post Office** offer fax, telex, and telegram services. Telegrams in foreign languages can also be sent from the **Central Telegraph Office**. **Post International** offers fax and e-mail services.

COURIER SERVICES

ST. PETERSBURG is well supplied with courier services. **DHL**, **Federal Express**, and **TNT** take about two days to Europe and three to Australasia and the US. A slower but cheaper service is provided by local companies **Westpost** and **Post International**. Anything other than papers, especially computer discs, must go through customs, which can add an extra day.

TELEVISION AND RADIO

RUSSIAN-LANGUAGE television is dominated by imported soap operas, which are dubbed rather than subtitled. Channel 6 shows NBC News in English every morning at 8:30am, while the best news in Russian is on NTV, or on Channel 5 for local news.

Most hotels have satellite television offering Eurosport, CNN, BBC World Service TV, NBC, and many other Western programs.

The best English-language radio broadcasts on shortwave are still BBC World Service and Voice of America. A few local radio stations, such as Radio Modern (104 FM) and Radio Maximum (102.8 FM), do English music programs.

NEWSPAPERS AND MAGAZINES

THERE ARE THREE English-language newspapers and magazines available in the city, which are distributed free to all hotels, major restaurants, and most fast-food chains. *The St. Petersburg Times* appears twice weekly with international and sports news and coverage of local events. The Friday edition provides detailed listings and reviews. The monthly *Pulse* is leisure oriented, and its listings section is worth checking. *Neva News* runs occasional local history articles, which are of interest, and each edition has a useful pull-out map of the city and its major sights.

Foreign papers can be picked up at highly inflated prices from the major hotels.

St. Petersburg local newspapers

GETTING TO ST. PETERSBURG

ST. PETERSBURG IS SLOWLY regaining its popularity as a tourist destination, after the drop in numbers during the early 1990s. Now, as the number of businessmen regularly traveling in and out is also rising, the number of flights and alternative means of travel is increasing. Flying remains the most popular way of traveling to St. Petersburg, for both individuals and groups, with the train from Moscow or Helsinki a close second.

Aeroflot plane landing
in St. Petersburg

Independent travel in Russia is difficult and costly, and it is worth considering a package tour. American companies run a variety of tours with specialty guides, which often include St. Petersburg and Moscow. Since overall tourist numbers are still limited, package tours are not among the cheapest. Shopping around can uncover some good deals, particularly on flights with stop-overs in Europe or off-season packages.

Stalinist architecture at Pulkovo 2, St. Petersburg's international airport

ARRIVING BY AIR

DIRECT FLIGHTS to St. Petersburg from Ireland, US, Canada, South Africa, and Australasia are either extremely limited or simply do not exist. The usual route from these destinations is to fly via a European city or via Moscow, where you can transfer to another flight or continue by road or rail. Most flights from the US leave from New York, then to Helsinki and on to your Russian destination.

Direct flights from the UK to St. Petersburg run five days a week on British Airways and three days on Aeroflot. There are connecting flights on other airlines every day, and these are often much cheaper. A plane trip from London takes around three-and-a-half hours, or about six hours with a stopover in a European city.

The only direct flight to St. Petersburg from Ireland is a weekly Aeroflot service from Shannon on the west coast.

From the US, Aeroflot operates a direct flight from New York to St. Petersburg three times a week. From Canada and South Africa, direct flights, also on Aeroflot, go only to Moscow. Traveling from Australasia can be fairly complicated. The most usual route is to pick up a European carrier in Singapore, with a stopover in Europe.

Passengers are sometimes required to confirm onward flights through the airline you are traveling with or the **Central Air Communication Agency** on Nevskiy prospekt.

ST. PETERSBURG AIRPORTS

INTERNATIONAL FLIGHTS arrive at **Pulkovo 2** which, although recently modernized, is still small and relatively primitive. Its separate arrival and departure buildings each have a small duty-free shop. Arrivals also has a

foreign exchange office. On arrival, the longest wait is likely to be for baggage, while departures on the weekend can be hectic and it is best to arrive at least 90 minutes before a flight in tourist season.

Pulkovo 1 is for domestic flights only. The 1970s building is cramped and dark, but foreigners and those using commercial flights to and from Moscow have a separate arrival and departure lounge. Located on the first floor, this has its own entrance, which cannot be reached from inside the main terminal building.

GETTING INTO THE CITY

BOTH AIRPORTS are located 17 km (11 miles) south of the city center. The major hotels operate cars to pick up individual tourists for a cost of around $45. The service, which can be charged to

Limousine transfer service from the
Grand Hotel Europe (see p181)

Ordinary yellow taxi waiting outside
the domestic airport, Pulkovo 1

**No. 13 bus from Pulkovo 2 to
Moskovskaya metro station**

Minibus or *marshrutnoye taksi*

the hotel bill, should always
be requested when making a
hotel booking. The luxury
taxis waiting at the airport tend
to undercut hotel cars by only
about $5, while ordinary yellow
cabs, rarely found at the international airport, are a great
deal cheaper, charging around
$10–15 in roubles. Official
yellow cabs are usually plentiful at the domestic airport.

Anyone on a more limited
budget, and who has already
changed money at the airport,
can take the No. 13 bus (from
Pulkovo 2) and No. 39 (from
Pulkovo 1) to Moskovskaya

metro station. Minibuses,
known as *marshrutnoye taksi*
or route taxi, travel the same
route and charge a minimally
higher fare *(see p219)*.

TRAVELING BY TRAIN

Rᴀɪʟ ɪs a relatively cheap
way to travel from Finland,
Moscow, and within Russia in
general, although European
student discount
passes provide
little or no reduc-
tion in fares.

Ten trains a
day run in each
direction be-
tween Moscow
and **Moscow
Station**, and two
between Helsinki and **Finland
Station** *(see p126)*. For those
with time and some sense of
adventure, it is possible to

**Ticket office or *kassa* at
Central Train Ticket Office**

**Exterior of Finland Station, the point of arrival
for daily trains from Helsinki in Finland**

travel by train from London to
St. Petersburg via Central
Europe (Warsaw, Prague,
Berlin). It takes about three
days and is generally more
costly than flying. The trains
are comfortable and usually
run on time, but carriages can
be overcrowded and thefts are
common. Transit visas may
also be necessary for countries
such as Ukraine. The simplest
and most reliable
route is via Belarus
(Belorussia) which
accepts a Russian
visa for transit
passengers. (All
visitors to Russia
need a visa and
obtaining one can
be a complicated
procedure. For information on
visa acquisition see page 202.)

Trains traveling from Eastern
Europe arrive and depart from
Vitebsk or **Warsaw
Station**. Tickets for
train journeys from
St. Petersburg
should be bought
from the upstairs
booking hall at the
**Central Train
Ticket Office**.

Taxis from stations
can be overpriced,
but all train stations
have efficient transit
connections.

TRAVELING BETWEEN MOSCOW AND ST. PETERSBURG

Many visitors fly in to Moscow and out of St. Petersburg, or vice versa. The most popular form
of transportation between the two cities is the train, of which there are ten a day. Daytime trains
take about ten hours, while faster night-time trains take eight and a half hours. Prices vary according to the class of the train – the Red Arrow being most
expensive – and the choice of seat. All trains have a choice of *SV*
(two-person compartment), *coupé* (four-person), *platzkarte* (open
seating), or *sidyashchyy* (open seating). All except *sidyashchyy* are
sleepers. For daytime traveling
sidyashchyy is more comfortable
and cheaper than *platzkarte*.
One-way prices range from the
equivalent in roubles of around
$80 for *SV* to $12 for *sidyashchyy*. There is an additional
charge for bed linen when you purchase your ticket. On
budget trains, the *provodnik*, or car attendant, will issue and
charge for bed linen. Food may be available, but it is best to
travel with your own supplies.

Regular commercial flights connecting the two cities take
about 50 minutes. These are run by Aeroflot and independent
companies such as Pulkovo and Transaero. A one-way
ticket costs $180 in roubles on Pulkovo Airlines, and a
round-trip around $240. Tickets are sold at the airport, or at
the **Central Air Communication Agency**. Traveling by
boat to and from Moscow is also possible *(see p212)*.

**SV compartment on the luxurious
Red Arrow train from Moscow**

**St. Petersburg – Moscow
sign in train carriage**

One of Finnord's buses

TRAVELING BY BUS

COMFORTABLE buses run to and from Helsinki in Finland, offering a cheaper alternative to the train. **Finnord** runs one daytime bus and one overnight in each direction; the trip takes around seven hours. Bus companies do not always use the city's inconvenient bus stations but will drop off instead at various locations in St. Petersburg. Finnord's final stop is at their office on Italyanskaya ulitsa. Advance booking is advised with this company as many Russians take advantage of these buses to go shopping in Lappeenranta, just over the border, or in Helsinki itself.

TRAVELING BY BOAT

ARRIVING by boat can be one of the most exciting and novel ways to approach St. Petersburg. However, ferries and cruises operate irregularly and it is best to check with a travel agent for details.

Ferries from Scandinavia usually dock at the **Maritime Passenger Terminal**, on the west side of Vasilevskiy Island. Trolleybus No. 10 and bus No. 7 run from here to the center or, heading in the other direction, to Primorskaya metro station.

In summer, river cruises between Moscow and St. Petersburg are run along the Volga and across Lake Ladoga. The trips, lasting about two weeks, take in many sights en route, making this a very pleasurable way to see more of Russia. The cruises can be booked through **Panorama Travel Ltd** in the US. The ships dock at St. Petersburg's **River Terminal**, ten minutes' walk from Proletarskaya metro station. Cruise companies run buses to and from the city center.

Luxury cruise ships from the US and elsewhere arrive at the city's cargo port, 5 km (3 miles) southwest of the center. Access to the port is restricted, so the ships have their own buses to carry tourists into town and back.

Ferry moored at Maritime Passenger Terminal on western edge of Vasilevskiy Island

DIRECTORY

TOUR COMPANIES IN THE US

Panorama Travel, Ltd
156 Fifth Ave., Suite 1019,
New York, NY 10010.
📞 *(212) 741-0033.*
FAX *(212) 645-6276.*

Russian Travel Bureau, Inc.,
255 East 44th St.,
New York, NY 10017.
📞 *(212) 986-1500.*
FAX *(212) 847-1800.*

AIRPORT INFORMATION

Pulkovo 1
Пулково 1
📞 *104 3822.*
Pulkovo 2
Пулково 2
📞 *104 3444.*

AIRLINE OFFICES

Austrian Airlines
Nevskiy pr 57. **Map** 7 B2.
📞 *325 3260.*
📞 *104 3443 (Pulkovo 2).*

British Airways
Malaya konyushennaya ulitsa 1/3. **Map** 6 E1.
📞 *325 2565.*
📞 *104 3749 (Pulkovo 2).*

Central Air Communication Agency
Nevskiy pr 7/9. **Map** 6 D1.
📞 *315 0072 (inter).*
📞 *311 8093 (dom & CIS).*

Delta Airlines
📞 *331 5819.*

Finnair
Malaya Morskaya ulitsa 19.
Map 6 D1.
📞 *315 9736.*
📞 *104 3739 (Pulkovo 2).*

KLM
Zagorodnyy prospekt 5.
Map 7 A3.
📞 *325 8989.*

Lufthansa
📞 *314 4979.*
📞 *104 3432 (Pulkovo 2).*

Malev Hungarian Airlines
📞 *315 5455.*
📞 *104 3435 (Pulkovo 2).*

SAS
📞 *325 3255.*
📞 *104 3443 (Pulkovo 2).*

Transaero
Liteynyy pr 48.
Map 7 A1.
📞 *279 6463/1974.*

TRAINS

All Train Inquiries
📞 *168 0111.*

Central Train Ticket Office
Центральные железно
Tsentralniye zhelezno
Nab kanala Griboedova 24
(upstairs for foreigners).
Map 6 E2.
📞 *162 3344.*

Finland Station
Финляндский вокзал
Finlyandskiy vokzal
Pl Lenina 6.
Map 3 B3.

Moscow Station
Московский вокзал
Moskovskiy vokzal
Pl Vosstaniya.
Map 7 C2.

Vitebsk Station
Витебский вокзал
Vitebskiy vokzal
Zagorodnyy prospekt 52.
Map 6 E4.

Warsaw Station
Варшавский вокзал
Varshavskiy vokzal
Nab Obvodnovo
kanala 118.

BUSES

Finnord
Italyanskaya ulitsa 37.
Map 6 F1.
📞 *314 8951.*

BOATS

Maritime Passenger Terminal
Морской пассажирский вокзал
Morskoy passazhirskiy vokzal
Pl Morskoy Slavy.
📞 *355 1310.*

River Terminal
Речной вокзал
Rechnoy vokzal
Prospekt Obukhovskoy
Oborony 195.
📞 *262 0239/8994.*

GETTING AROUND ST. PETERSBURG

Sign indicating pedestrian crossing

LTHOUGH PUBLIC transit in the city is abundant, efficient, and very cheap, the most enjoyable way to get around and fully appreciate St. Petersburg is on foot. A glance at a map reveals that some attempt was made to bestow the city with a rational, organized layout, which makes it considerably easier to negotiate. When exhaustion sets in, however, a boat cruise along the waterways can be a wonderful way to become acquainted with the city.

Nevskiy prospekt is where many of the city's transit routes and main roads meet. Metro lines, tram, bus, and trolleybus routes radiate out from here, criss-crossing the city with a network of tracks and overhead wires. It is possible to travel without too much difficulty to almost anywhere in town from this main avenue.

Driving is not recommended due to the combination of poor road conditions, aggressive Russian driving, and over-eager traffic police.

WALKING

IN SOME AREAS, particularly around Palace Embankment, sights are situated so close together that using public transportation from place to place is pointless. A few of the more scattered sights are at some distance (20 mins on foot) from the nearest transit and walking the last stretch is often the most practical option. Apart from the ease, getting around on foot can be a most rewarding way to explore the city, allowing you to soak up the atmosphere and appreciate the fascinating architectural and sculptural detail on many of St. Petersburg's buildings.

As soon as the sun appears, in winter as well as in summer, people of all ages emerge onto the streets and into the

Street sign for Nevskiy prospekt

parks. Locals are very fond of walking, whether it be promenading up and down Nevskiy prospekt, or ambling around the Neva at 2am during the White Nights *(see p51)*. The Summer Gardens *(see p95)* and Mikhaylovskiy Gardens have long been popular with Petersburgers. For longer walks mixed with some architectural interest, two good areas to try are Kamenniy and Yelagin islands *(see pp136–7)*, with their official residences and dachas, many dating from the early years of the 20th century.

For a romantic stroll around the city away from the traffic, walk along the Moyka or Griboedov canals *(see pp134–5)*. To the south of Nevskiy prospekt, majestic buildings gradually give way to smaller, 19th-century residential buildings, with rows of trees by the waterside and leafy squares and courtyards.

Drivers have little respect for pedestrians, and traffic is the main hindrance to walking. Cars drive on the right-hand side, so look left first when crossing the road. If there is a pedestrian underpass, use it and, if not, look for a light-controlled red-and-green pedestrian crossing. Crossings without lights are marked by a blue sign showing a pedestrian, but these are simply

Street signs indicating street directions and major shops

recommended crossing sites and drivers are not obliged to stop. Be warned that if you are caught crossing a road where there are no marked crossings, you are liable to be fined by a traffic officer *(see p205)*.

There are few bicycles on the roads, but those cyclists tend to ignore traffic lights and signs of all descriptions, causing an additional hazard for the unwary pedestrian.

Sign showing a pedestrian underpass

On the main city streets, sponsored dark blue nameplates give the street names in both Russian and English. Elsewhere, black-on-white street names are in Russian (i.e., Cyrillic) only. Many maps, like the free pull-out in *Neva News* *(see p209)*, give the main street names in Cyrillic and in transliteration. If you get lost, a dual-language map can be helpful when asking Russian passersby for assistance.

Excellent walking tours in English, both general and on specialized topics, can be booked through **Ost-West Kontaktservice** *(see p200)*.

Mikhaylovskiy Gardens, behind the Russian Museum *(see pp104–107)*

Traveling by Metro

Blue neon metro sign

Since above-ground transit is the most efficient means of getting around the city center, the metro is used mainly to get to and from the outskirts of the city. As a tourist attraction, the metro's stunning stations, intended by Stalin to be "palaces for the people," should be high on your itinerary. The metro is safe and runs until just after midnight. Traveling in the late evening will avoid most of the two million people estimated to use the metro each day. The main setback is that signs are only in Cyrillic but, with just four lines, negotiating the network is fairly straightforward.

Steep escalators to platforms

Exterior of Ploshchad Vosstaniya metro station

glass columns. The metro now has 58 stations, ranging in ambience from the dim lighting and memorial atmosphere of Ploshchad Muzhestva (Courage Square, 1975) near Piskarovskoe Memorial Cemetery *(see p126)*, to the 1980s vulgarity of Udelnaya and the clean coldness of Sadovaya (1992).

The Metro as a Tourist Attraction

The soviet union's best architects were employed to design St. Petersburg's metro stations. Thousands of tons of marble, granite, and limestone were used to face the walls, and sculptures, mosaics, and chandeliers were commissioned from leading artists. The first line opened in 1955, its eight stations connecting ploshchad Vosstaniya with the new Stalinist apartment buildings in the southwest and the city's largest factory, the Kirov Factory. This line is one of the most fascinating, being the supreme embodiment of Stalinist style and ideals. The station at Kirovskiy Zavod is a fine example, a vast basilica, a temple to the factory workers. The line's crowning glory has to be Avtovo, incorporating a wealth of style and detail, even down to the molded

The Network

The metro is vital for getting to and from the farther afield hotels and the airport. The four lines run from the outskirts through the center, where they intersect at one of six main stations. Trains run every few minutes during the day and every five minutes late at night and, although doors into stations close at midnight, the last trains leave the center ten minutes after this. There

Mosaics and unusual glass columns at richly decorated Avtovo metro station

is no rush hour as such, but the metro tends to be full at most times of the day, which makes it very safe. Platforms are not staffed, but there is an attendant in a booth at the bottom of each escalator who can call for assistance.

Because of the many waterways in the city, stations are buried deep underground, and long escalators lead down to the platforms. Stand on the right, leaving the left side free for those walking.

New stations are still being added; the latest ones being Krestovskiy Ostrov and Staraya Derevnya on the yellow line. Structural problems on the red line have resulted in its closure between Lesnaya and Ploshchad Muzhestva. A courtesy bus service runs between these stations.

Directional sign listing all stops on this line in Cyrillic

Interchange sign listing all stations on the other line

Finding Your Way

Before setting foot in St. Petersburg's metro, make sure you have a network map with the Cyrillic and transliterated names to hand. All signs inside the metro are in Cyrillic only and wall maps have become rare in station ticket halls and on the trains. Inside a station, the name is written only on the far wall of the platform which means that, if the train is in the station, or if you are on the train itself, it is not possible to see the sign.

Metro platform sign showing stations and interchanges

Busy stations in the city center have a central concourse with safety doors between the concourse and the trains. When the train stops, these doors open, and only then do the train doors open. At these stations, a map of the line you are on can be found on the concourse. Other stations have platforms, and the map of the line is on the wall on the far side of the tracks.

Before the train doors close, the driver will announce *"Ostorozhno. Dveri zakryva-yutsya"* (Be careful. The doors are closing). As the train approaches a stop, the driver will say the name of that and the next station, and mention if you need to change here for another line. It is always best to count your stops, in case you miss the announcements.

To change to another line, follow the interchange signs for перехoд (*perekhod* – crossing). The exception is at Tekhnologicheskiy Institut, where the two southbound lines are on parallel platforms, as are the two northbound lines, so to continue in the same direction on another line you simply cross the central concourse.

Exits are marked выход (*vykhod*). Some stations, such as of the Moskovskaya (for the airport) and Gostinyy Dvor, have two or more exits, sometimes far apart from each other.

TICKETS AND TRAVEL CARDS

THE MOST COMMON means of paying for the metro is the token (*zheton*), purchasable only from metro stations, but also usable on public phones (*see p208*). Magnetic cards, valid for ten trips, are also available. When traveling on the red line, due to the line closure between Les-naya and Ploshchad Muzhestva, you will have to take the courtesy bus part of the way so, for con-venience, purchase a single-trip magnetic transit (*tranzitnyy*) card. This ticket can be reused when returning to the metro to continue your journey.

Machines are installed at the top of the escalators; the larger ones are clearly marked for the use of magnetic cards only, while the others are for tokens. Cards must be inserted with the magnetic strip facing up. If you try to go through a machine without paying, an automatic barrier closes in front of you. At the right of the barrier, an attendant checks passes and then lets in a barrierless gate. Travelers with magnetic cards cannot pass through this machine.

Monthly magnetic passes for the metro or for all forms of public transportation are valid for an infinite number of trips during a calendar month. They can be pur-chased only at the beginning of the month (or on the 16th for half-monthly passes). There are no ticket checks once you are past the barriers inside the station.

Metro token

ST. PETERSBURG'S METRO

KEY

--- Line closed

Пр Просвещения / *Pr Prosveshcheniya*
Девяткино / *Devyatkino*
Озерки / *Ozerki*
Гражданский пр / *Grazhdanskiy Pr*
Старая деревня / *Staraya derevnya*
Удельная / *Udelnaya*
Академическая / *Akademicheskaya*
Крестовский остров / *Krestovskiy ostrov*
Пионерская / *Pionerskaya*
Политехническая / *Politekhnicheskaya*
Чкаловская / *Chkalovskaya*
Черная речка / *Chernaya Rechka*
Пл Мужества / *Pl Muzhestva*
Приморская / *Primorskaya*
Спортивная / *Sportivnaya*
Петроградская / *Petrogradskaya*
Лесная / *Lesnaya*
Василеостровская / *Vasileostrovskaya*
Горьковская / *Gorkovskaya*
Выборгская / *Vyborgskaya*
Гостиный двор / *Gostinyy Dvor*
Пл Ленина / *Pl Lenina*
Пл Восстания / *Pl Vosstaniya*
Чернышевская / *Chernyshevskaya*
Невский пр / *Nevskiy Pr*
Маяковская / *Mayakovskaya*
Сенная пл / *Sennaya Pl*
Садовая / *Sadovaya*
Владимирская / *Vladimirskaya*
Пушкинская / *Pushkinskaya*
Достоевская / *Dostoevskaya*
Технологический инст / *Tekhnologicheskiy Inst*
Лиговский пр / *Ligovskiy Pr*
Технологический инст / *Tekhnologicheskiy Inst*
Балтийская / *Baltiyskaya*
Пл Александра Невского / *Pl Aleksandra Nevskovo*
Нарвская / *Narvskaya*
Фрунзенская / *Frunzenskaya*
Пл Александра Невского / *Pl Aleksandra Nevskovo*
Кировский завод / *Kirovskiy Zavod*
Моск ворота / *Mosk vorota*
Елизаровская / *Elizarovskaya*
Новочеркасская / *Novocherkasskaya*
Автово / *Avtovo*
Электросила / *Elektrosila*
Ломоносовская / *Lomonosovskaya*
Ладожская / *Ladozhskaya*
Ленинский пр / *Leninskiy Pr*
Парк Победы / *Park Pobedy*
Пролетарская / *Proletarskaya*
Пр болшевиков / *Pr Bolshevikov*
Пр Ветеранов / *Pr Veteranov*
Московская / *Moskovskaya*
Обухово / *Obukhovo*
Ул Дыбенко / *Ul Dybenko*
Звездная / *Zvezdnaya*
Рыбацкое / *Rybatskoe*
Купчино / *Kupchino*

Monthly travel cards, valid on all forms of city transportation

Traveling by Tram, Bus, and Trolleybus

Tram-stop sign, seen hanging over the rails

OVERGROUND TRANSIT is crowded during the day, particularly at rush hour, but it is still the best way to make short trips around the city or simply to sightsee. In the center of town, an array of tramline tracks and overhead tram and trolleybus cables crisscross many roads. Each form of transport has its advantages and disadvantages. Trolleybuses are frequent and conveniently routed but overcrowded; trams run on a less main-line route across town and are less busy but noisy; buses are usually sporadic. The newer outlying areas, however, are often accessible only by bus. On all forms of public transitt you are unlikely to get a seat during the day; more frequent and comfortable, but more expensive, are the commercial bus and minibus routes.

People getting on a tram

TRAMS

TRAMS OFFER a marvelous way to see St. Petersburg and discover some of the lesser known areas. Trams are less crowded than trolleybuses, so there is more chance of finding a seat. Tram stops are marked by red and white signs suspended on wires above the tram rails. Separate islands for people to board are found only on wide roads outside the center; elsewhere passengers wait on the sidewalk. When the tram doors open, the oncoming traffic must wait and let passengers cross to and from the sidewalk. In practice, there is always one car that cannot wait, so take care before crossing.

At various crossroads along the route, the driver may need to change switches on the rails. He will open his door or the front passenger door to do this. Do not attempt to board or exit a tram when it has stopped for this purpose.

Tram at a stop in front of the Mariinskiy Theater

GENERAL INFORMATION

TRAMS, BUSES, and trolleybuses start at around 5:30am, and a little later along the middle of the routes. The services operate with rather arbitrary frequency during the day and very infrequently after 11pm, grinding more or less to a halt around midnight. Only a few of the city bus routes display timetables. Each form of aboveground transit has its own separate stops, and distances between them can be great.

Lining up is not standard practice, so be prepared for an unruly rush to get on first. Trams, buses, and trolleybuses can be boarded at the front, middle, or back. The front eight seats are reserved for the disabled, the elderly, and people with children, all of whom have precedence getting on and off at the front. On board, a conductor collects the fares.

As a stop approaches, people near an exit may be asked *Vy vykhodite?* ("are you getting out?"), which really means "could you move aside?." At busy times, head for the exit well before your stop, or prepare to do some pushing.

Good for sightseeing is the No. 10 trolleybus, which runs from ploshchad Aleksandra Nevskovo through the center and across Vasilevskiy Island *(see pp56–63)* to Primorskaya metro station. Other scenic routes are the No. 12 tram from the Field of Mars *(see p94)* to the east of the city, the No. 22 bus from the Smolnyy Institute *(see p128)* via St. Isaac's Square *(see p79)* and the Mariinskiy Theater *(see p119)* toward the Stalinist architecture in the southwest, and the No. 46 bus from the Field of Mars up Kamennoostrovskiy prospekt *(see p70)* and onto Kamenniy Island *(see pp136–7).*

Sign for a bus stop, showing name of stop and bus numbers

BUSES AND MINIBUSES

BUSES OPERATE mostly on the outskirts of the city. All services run about every 20 minutes, sometimes less often. Bus stops in the city center are marked by white signs with a red letter "A" for *avtobus*, placed by the side of the road or attached to building walls. These are slowly replacing the old-style yellow signs.

Side view of a single section tram

City trolleybus on Nevskiy prospekt

A commercial bus on Vasilevskiy Island

TICKETS AND TRAVEL CARDS

A FLAT FARE is payable on all forms of transportation, whatever the length of the ride. Tickets are purchased from the conductor (who wears a red armband saying "Кондуктор" but is not in uniform) or, on commercial transit, from the driver. The ticket must be bought before the next stop after you got on, and large items of baggage must be paid for separately. Fines for non-payment can be imposed on the spot by plain-clothes inspectors. If you are accused of evasion, check that the inspect-or has an identity document. Fines are payable in roubles only, and should not come to more than a few dollars' worth.

The cheapest way to travel in St. Petersburg, if you are staying a few weeks or more, is to buy a monthly or half-monthly card for all forms of transport, including the metro (*see pp214–15*). The magnetic monthly card, or *yedinyy bilet*, is valid from the first to the last day of a calendar month and cannot be bought any time in between. Half-monthly *yedinyy bilety* run from the 16th to the end of the month (they are not available for the first half of the month). Separate monthly cards are also sold for each form of transit. Travel cards are valid for trips to Tsarskoe Selo and Pavlovsk, but not Peterhof, Gatchina, or Oranienbaum (*see pp220–21*).

Many routes are now dupli-cated by commercial buses or minibuses, marked with a "T" before the route number or with an "Э" for express. Fares on these buses are two to three times those on noncommercial equivalents, and are paid to the driver when getting on or off – just follow what other passengers do. These buses can be hailed or requested to stop anywhere along the route.

TROLLEYBUSES

TROLLEYBUSES ARE the most frequent form of transport along the city's main artery, Nevskiy prospekt. They offer convenient routes and stops around the city but are nearly always overcrowded. Ticket inspectors are most often on patrol on trolleybuses.

Trolleybus stops are marked by small blue and white signs suspended from wires, indicat-ing the trolleybus numbers. On main roads, stops are also marked by other signs on building walls. These show what seems to be a flat-topped blue "M," but is in fact an italic "T" for *trolley-bus*, placed on a white background.

The power rods on the roofs of the trolleybuses are known famil-iarly as "horns" *(roga)* or "little whiskers" *(usiki)*. Occasionally these become detached from the overhead cables and the trolleybus lurches to a halt. It is the driver's responsibility to reattach them, causing a slight but generally negligible delay.

Trolleybus-stop sign on building wall

Waiting at a trolleybus stop on Nevskiy prospekt, near ploshchad Vosstaniya

Canal and River Cruises

Sign for water taxi

S T. PETERSBURG'S MANY natural waterways were adapted and added to, so they resembled Peter the Great's beloved Amsterdam *(see pp20–21)*. Indeed, it would be true to say the city vies for the title "Venice of the North."

A selection of cruises, for small and large groups, and in open and closed boats, depart from bridges along Nevskiy prospekt. They offer opportunities to see more of the city, especially for those unable to walk long distances. Forming part of any cruise are the broad Fontanka River with its Neo-Classical palaces, the leafy Moyka River with its ironwork bridges, and the Griboedov canal that twists and turns its way through southwest St. Petersburg. Bring a bottle of champagne, a picnic lunch, and a warm sweater, and just relax.

Canal cruise on the Moyka

GENERAL INFORMATION

T HE WEATHER plays a vital role in determining the exact time of year canal cruises are available. Most boats operate daily from mid-May to late September. Their routes also vary because regular construction work, reinforcing the granite embankments, sometimes prevents movement along small parts of the canals.

The Gulf of Finland is tidal, and this affects the Neva and inland waterways. Stong winds can cause the water level to rise significantly, and all boat trips may then be canceled.

GUIDED CANAL TRIPS

L ARGE, COVERED cruise boats depart every 30 minutes, between 11:30am and 8pm, from the Anichkov Bridge on Nevskiy prospekt *(see p49).*

Tickets for the next available boat can be bought from the kiosk on the embankment, although tickets may be sold in advance for later cruises on the same day. The trip lasts 70 minutes and takes in the Moyka, Griboedov, and Fontanka. Weather permitting, the boats usually go out onto the Neva, where you can see superb views of the whole city.

Ticket kiosk for canal trip, Anichkov Bridge

Foreigners pay around $5 in roubles for these trips, slightly more than the Russians. The guided tour is in Russian only. Large groups are advised to reserve in advance, through the kiosk or by phone, especially during school vacations. Boat trips providing guided tours in English can be booked at any of the major hotels.

During hot weather, it can get very stuffy inside the boats. The visibility through the scratched perspex windows can also be less than perfect at times. If you wish to stand outside to see better, there is a platform at the back of the boat, but there may be an extra charge. Take your own soft drinks and sandwiches, as these are rarely available on board these cruises.

NEVA CRUISES

A VARIETY OF BOATS cruise up and down the Neva between the Gulf of Finland and the River Station *(Rechnoy vokzal)* to the southeast. The trips, operating hourly between 10am and 10pm, last an hour. Foreigners pay more than the locals, but the tickets are not expensive and can be bought on the landing stage or on the boat. The boats leave from the landing stage opposite the Bronze Horseman on Decembrists' Square, and from the one near the main entrance of the Hermitage *(see p75).*

These boat trips are a pleasant way of passing the time rather than a serious sightseeing opportunity. Food and drink are usually served, and in the evenings, alcohol is available on some of the boats.

Luxury catered cruises for up to ten people can be booked in advance for trips along the Neva. These cost about $50 per hour, with an extra $15 or more per person for catering.

Cruise boat on the Neva with the Hermitage and Palace Embankment in the background

Water taxis moored on Griboedov canal near Kazanskiy most by Nevskiy prospekt

WATER TAXIS

WATER TAXIS are similar to private motorboats, carrying anything from 4 to 20 people. During White Nights, boats run late into the night.

For a small boat, wait at the landing stage on the north side of Politseyskiy most where Nevskiy prospekt (*see pp46–9*) crosses the Moyka, or alongside the Gostinyy Dvor metro station on the Griboedov canal close to Kazanskiy most. Larger boats may need to be reserved at least a couple of hours in advance to ensure their availability.

Prices are negotiable but generally range from about $30 to $50 an hour, depending on the size of the boat and the route you decide to follow. One hour takes you along the inland waterways, but an extra half hour includes the Neva, crossing over to go around the Peter and Paul Fortress (*see pp66–7*) and giving a good view of all the waterfronts. Most drivers can at least point out major sights in English; others can give you a basic guided tour. If you ask in advance, it may be possible to find an English-speaking guide. Boats can be booked in advance with a small deposit, but they are generally plentiful and are best picked up spontaneously.

Since the boats are open and it can be cold on the waterways, particularly at night, warm clothing is necessary, even during the summer months. There is usually at least one blanket on board for anyone who needs extra warmth. Pilots allow you to do more or less as you like on board the boat as long as it is safe. The pilots are undisturbed by the noise of popping corks or other sounds of merrymaking.

Water taxis on the Moyka by Politseyskiy most

Taxis

ST. PETERSBURG's official yellow taxis are gradually being replaced by unmetered private cabs. Most locals, however, use the cheaper alternative of catching a *chastnik*, effectively hitching a ride in any passing vehicle.

St. Petersburg's bright yellow taxi

OFFICIAL TAXIS

THE CITY'S DISTINCTIVE yellow official taxi fleet has, in recent years, faced tough competition from expensive private taxi firms, which run imported modern cars. The private taxis, which usually charge a flat fare agreed in advance, tend to monopolize certain areas near many major hotels, restaurants, bars, and the airport. In order to save money, try hailing a yellow cab a short distance away from these places.

Whatever type of taxi you choose to take, always name your destination before getting in. Taxis are not obliged to take you, and they may refuse or simply drive away if they do not wish to take you. Taxi fares are relatively inexpensive.

Newer cabs are fitted with modern meters, which indicate the sum to be paid, but meters in the older taxis are unreliable or even switched off. For this reason it is wise to agree on a price before starting out on a journey to avoid unnecessary confusion. If you feel you have been over-charged it is worth disputing the matter.

In some areas, official taxis are not readily available, and you must either book one by phone or hope for a *chastnik*.

CHASTNIKI

FOR MANY YEARS Russians have been used to flagging down private drivers, who are easier to locate and often cheaper to use than official taxis. A 1997 local ruling seeks to ban *chastniki* or at least make them purchase a taxi license. Unless this takes serious effect (and Russians are notorious for ignoring such rulings) you may find that an ordinary car stops when you stick out your hand to hail a taxi. Do not get into any car with anyone other than the driver already in it. Neither private cars or taxis are particularly recommended if traveling alone at night.

As with ordinary taxis, name your destination and settle a price before setting off. Private cars are cheaper than taxis, and the drivers are also more likely to help with baggage.

St. Petersburgers flagging down a *chastnik*, or private car

Traveling out of St. Petersburg

EVERY WEEKEND DURING THE SUMMER, and even in winter, many locals leave the city. They head for their dacha or for the woods, to gather seasonal fruits and vegetables, go cross-country skiing or visit one of the former imperial summer residences. Buses and suburban trains operate frequently throughout the year and are the usual means of transportation to sites out of town. Peterhof is an exception as it is accessible by hydrofoil across the Gulf of Finland. Foreigners tend to take arranged bus excursions out of town but, with a bit of planning, traveling independently can be part of the fun.

Passengers boarding suburban train at Vitebsk Station

Interior view of one of St. Petersburg's suburban trains

SUBURBAN TRAINS

THESE ARE THE most convenient ways to visit most of the outlying sights. Tickets can be bought from the local cash desks *(prigorodnyye kassy)* at each station. Round-trip are no cheaper than two one-way tickets. Note that smoking is prohibited and that, between the hours of 10am and midday, there is often a break in the timetable.

Style-Moderne architecture in Vitebsk Station restaurant

GETTING TO TSARSKOE SELO AND PAVLOVSK

TRAINS for Tsarskoe Selo *(see pp150–53)* and Pavlovsk *(see pp156–9)* depart every 20 minutes from **Vitebsk Station**. The line was originally built for the royal family to reach their summer residences, and the station is a marvelous example of Style-Moderne architecture. The ticket office is on the right of the main building. All local trains take about 25 minutes, stopping first at Tsarskoe Selo (Detskoe Selo), then Pavlovsk.

At Detskoe Selo station, the 382 and 371 buses go to Tsarskoe Selo, stopping near the palace. At Pavlovsk, the train station is opposite the entrance to the park, through which it is a pleasant half-hour walk to the palace, or catch bus No. 370, 370a, 383, or 383a.

The 370 and 383 buses also run between Pavlovsk palace and Detskoe Selo Station. City bus tickets and monthly passes continue to be valid.

The No. 287 bus is a convenient way to get to Tsarskoe Selo from ploshchad Pobedy, south of Moskovskaya metro.

GETTING TO PETERHOF AND ORANIENBAUM

THERE ARE SUBURBAN trains for Peterhof *(see pp146–9)* and Oranienbaum *(see pp144–5)* departing every 20 minutes from **Baltic Station**. The trains that reach Oranienbaum are those destined for Kalishche, or Oranienbaum itself.

For Peterhof, get off the train at Novyy Petergof (40 minutes from town), from where it is ten minutes to the palace on bus No. 351, 352, 354 or 355.

By far the easiest and most pleasant way to get to Peterhof during the summer months is by hydrofoil, which costs about $5 in roubles each way.

Oranienbaum is the first stop after the Gulf of Finland comes into view an hour into the journey. Turn right out of the station and walk about 200 m (650 ft) to the main road. Almost directly opposite is the entrance to the park, and from here it is only a five minute walk to the Great Palace or into the heart of the park.

GETTING TO GATCHINA

TRAINS RUN approximately every half hour from **Baltic Station** to Gatchina *(see p145)* and the trip takes an hour. Opposite Gatchina train station is a short road leading directly to the square in front of the palace. Trains also run from **Warsaw Station**, arriving at a different station in the town, farther from the palace.

Alternatively, there is a bus No. 431, which departs from ploshchad Pobedy, south of Moskovskaya metro station. On this particular suburban route, city bus tickets and monthly passes are not valid.

GETTING TO REPINO AND THE GULF OF FINLAND

For Repino (see p144) and the Gulf of Finland, trains depart every 20 minutes or so from **Finland Station**. Tickets should be bought at cash desks within the main building. Avoid any train marked Beloostrov or Krugovoy.

At Repino, cross the main road, head down the hill toward the Gulf of Finland and turn left onto the asphalt road until you reach Penaty.

Bus No. 411 also runs to Repino and stops right outside Penaty. The bus leaves from Chernaya Rechka metro.

Bus No. 948 to Novgorod

GETTING TO NOVGOROD

Bus no. 948 leaves for Novgorod (see pp160–63) every two hours from **Bus Station 2**. A quicker alternative to the four-hour bus trip is to travel on the weekend by train. The weekend train sets off from **Moscow Station** just before 7am and takes two-and-a-half hours. It returns to St. Petersburg around 6pm.

DRIVING IN ST. PETERSBURG

Car rental is still not widely available in Russia, and, at present, cars and minibuses in St. Petersburg can only be rented with company drivers. This can be organized through hotels and firms like **Hertz** who have a pickup point at the airport.

For the few who do find themselves at the wheel, there are a number of things to bear in mind. An international licence and insurance are required, as are documents proving you have the right to drive the car. A registration or rental agreement with your name, or a witnessed power of attorney *in Russian* from the registered owner, will usually suffice. Traffic police (see p205) have the right to stop you and check your documents. They can also fine you on the spot for minor infringements, such as having a dirty number plate, not having a first-aid kit, or more serious offenses such as drunk driving. Drivers are not allowed to drink any alcohol whatsoever. The traffic police are highly active since they regard fining drivers as a means to increasing their income.

Local drivers tend to ignore rules of the road and do more or less as they like, so be on your guard. Drive on the right and make no left turns on any main roads unless a road sign indicates that it is permitted.

In winter conditions, driving requires studded tires as chains can be damaged on tram lines and vice versa. It is also advisable not to use your handbrake in cold weather as it has a tendency to freeze.

Unleaded gas is rarely available, and you should use nothing lower than octane 98. There is a charge for parking in most parts of the city center. The Nevskij Palace and Europe hotels (see p173) have 24-hour security parking, which is recommended since car theft is a fairly popular business in St. Petersburg.

Road sign in Russian indicating driver must stop

DIRECTORY

TRAIN AND BUS STATIONS

All train information
📞 168 0111.

Baltic Station
Балтийский вокзал
Baltiyskiy vokzal
Nab Obvodnovo kanala 120.

Bus Station 2
Автобусный вокзал 2
Avtobusnyy vokzal 2
Nab Obvodnovo kanala 36.
Map 7 C5. 📞 166 5777.

Finland Station
Финляндский вокзал
Finlyandskiy vokzal
Pl Lenina 6. **Map** 3 B3.

Moscow Station
Московский вокзал
Moskovskiy vokzal
Pl Vosstaniya. **Map** 7 C2.

Vitebsk Station
Витебский вокзал
Vitebskiy vokzal
Zagorodnyy pr 52. **Map** 6 E4.

Warsaw Station
Варшавский вокзал
Varshavskiy vokzal
Nab Obvodnovo kanala 118.

CAR RENTAL

Hertz
Ulitsa Nekrasova 40. **Map** 7 B1.
📞 272 5045. 📠 275 3800.

THE HYDROFOIL TO PETERHOF

Hydrofoil arriving at the Hermitage landing stage

The most enjoyable and by far the most scenic way to reach the imperial summer palace of Peterhof is the 45-minute trip across the Gulf of Finland by hydrofoil. The service runs from early June until early October and sets off from the second landing stage outside the Hermitage (see p75), where a weekly timetable is posted. Generally hydrofoils operate every hour from 9:30am with the last boat returning at 6pm. Buy your return ticket on arrival at Peterhof. A fee is charged to enter the lower park and this ticket is needed to get back into the park to return by hydrofoil.

St. Petersburg Street Finder

Pausing on the steps of Kazan Cathedral

THE KEY MAP below shows the areas of St. Petersburg covered by the *Street Finder*. The map references given throughout the guide for sights, restaurants, hotels, shops, or entertainment venues refer to the maps in this section. All the major sights have been clearly marked so they are easy to locate. The key below shows other features marked on the maps, such as post offices, metro stations, ferry stops, and churches. The *Street Finder* index lists street names in transliteration, followed by Cyrillics (on the maps, Cyrillics are given only for major roads). This guide uses the now reinstated old Russian street names, rather than the Soviet versions *(see p201)*. Places of interest are listed by their English name.

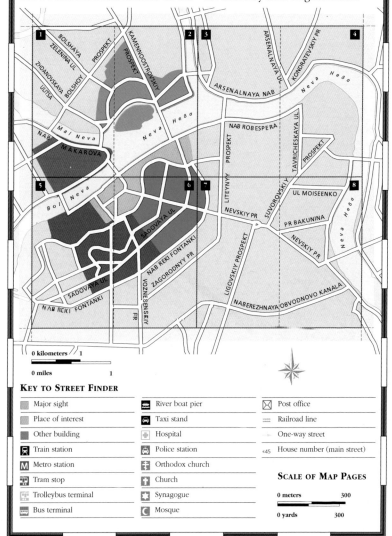

0 kilometers 1

0 miles 1

Key to Street Finder

Major sight	River boat pier	Post office
Place of interest	Taxi stand	Railroad line
Other building	Hospital	One-way street
Train station	Police station	«45 House number (main street)
Metro station	Orthodox church	
Tram stop	Church	**Scale of Map Pages**
Trolleybus terminal	Synagogue	0 meters 300
Bus terminal	Mosque	0 yards 300

Street Finder Index

1-ya Krasnoarmeyskaya ulitsa
1-Я КРАСНОАРМЕЙСКАЯ УЛИЦА   **6 D5**

1-ya Sovetskaya ulitsa
1-Я СОВЕТСКАЯ УЛИЦА   **7 C2**

2-y Luch, ulitsa   2-Й ЛУЧ, УЛИЦА   **8 F5**

2-ya Krasnoarmeyskaya ulitsa
2-Я КРАСНОАРМЕЙСКАЯ УЛИЦА   **6 D5**

2-ya i 3-ya linii   2-Я И 3-Я ЛИНИИ   **1 A4**

2-ya Sovetskaya ulitsa
2-Я СОВЕТСКАЯ УЛИЦА   **7 C2**

3-ya Krasnoarmeyskaya ulitsa
3-Я КРАСНОАРМЕЙСКАЯ УЛИЦА   **6 D5**

3-ya Sovetskaya ulitsa
3-Я СОВЕТСКАЯ УЛИЦА   **7 C2**

4-ya Krasnoarmeyskaya ulitsa
4-Я КРАСНОАРМЕЙСКАЯ УЛИЦА   **6 D5**

4-ya i 5-ya linii   4-Я И 5-Я ЛИНИИ **1 A4, 5 A1**

4-ya Sovetskaya ulitsa
4-Я СОВЕТСКАЯ УЛИЦА   **7 C1**

5-ya Krasnoarmeyskaya ulitsa
5-Я КРАСНОАРМЕЙСКАЯ УЛИЦА   **6 D5**

5-ya Sovetskaya ulitsa
5-Я СОВЕТСКАЯ УЛИЦА   **7 C1**

6-ya i 7-ya linii   6-Я И 7-Я ЛИНИИ **1 A5, 5 A1**

6-ya Sovetskaya ulitsa
6-Я СОВЕТСКАЯ УЛИЦА   **7 C1**

7-ya Sovetskaya ulitsa
7-Я СОВЕТСКАЯ УЛИЦА   **7 C1**

8-ya Krasnoarmeyskaya ulitsa
8-Я КРАСНОАРМЕЙСКАЯ УЛИЦА   **5 C5**

8-ya Sovetskaya ulitsa
8-Я СОВЕТСКАЯ УЛИЦА   **8 D1**

9-ya Krasnoarmeyskaya ulitsa
9-Я КРАСНОАРМЕЙСКАЯ УЛИЦА   **5 C5**

9-ya liniya   9-Я ЛИНИЯ   **5 A1**

9-ya Sovetskaya ulitsa
9-Я СОВЕТСКАЯ УЛИЦА   **8 D1**

10-ya Krasnoarmeyskaya ulitsa
10-Я КРАСНОАРМЕЙСКАЯ УЛИЦА   **5 B5**

10-ya Sovetskaya ulitsa
10-Я СОВЕТСКАЯ УЛИЦА   **8 D1**

11-ya liniya   11-Я ЛИНИЯ   **5 A1**

13-ya Krasnoarmeyskaya ulitsa
13-Я КРАСНОАРМЕЙСКАЯ УЛИЦА   **5 C5**

A

Academy of Arts   **5 B1**

Admirala Lazareva, naberezhnaya
АДМИРАЛА ЛАЗАРЕВА, НАБЕРЕЖНАЯ   **1 A1**

Admiralteyskaya naberezhnaya
АДМИРАЛТЕЙСКАЯ НАБЕРЕЖНАЯ   **5 C1**

Admiralteyskiy proezd
АДМИРАЛТЕЙСКИЙ ПРОЕЗД   **6 D1**

Admiralteyskovo Kanala, naberezhnaya
АДМИРАЛТЕЙСКОВО КАНАЛА, НАБЕРЕЖНАЯ   **5 B2**

Admiralteyskiy prospekt
АДМИРАЛТЕЙСКИЙ ПРОСПЕКТ   **5 C1**

Admiralty   **5 C1**

Akademika Lebedeva, ulitsa
АКАДЕМИКА ЛЕБЕДЕВА, УЛИЦА   **3 B2**

Akademika Sakharova, ploshchad
АКАДЕМИКА САХАРОВА, ПЛОЩАДЬ   **1 B5**

Aleksandra Nevskovo, most
АЛЕКСАНДРА НЕВСКОГО, МОСТ   **8 F3**

ABBREVIATIONS & USEFUL WORDS

ul	ulitsa	street
pl	ploshchad	square
pr	prospekt	avenue
per	pereulok	lane
	most	bridge
	sad	garden
	shosse	road

Aleksandra Nevskovo, ploshchad
АЛЕКСАНДРА НЕВСКОГО, ПЛОЩАДЬ   **8 E3**

Aleksandra Nevskovo, ulitsa
АЛЕКСАНДРА НЕВСКОГО, УЛИЦА   **8 E3**

Aleksandrovskiy park
АЛЕКСАНДРОВСКИЙ САД   **2 D3**

Alexander Nevsky Monastery   **8 E4**

Angliyskaya naberezhnaya
АНГЛИЙСКАЯ НАБЕРЕЖНАЯ   **5 B2**

Angliyskiy most   АНГЛИЙСКИЙ МОСТ   **5 B5**

Anichkov most   АНИЧКОВ МОСТ   **7 A2**

Anichkov Palace   **7 A2**

Antonenko, pereulok
АНТОНЕНКО, ПЕРЕУЛОК   **6 D2**

Apraksin Market   **6 E2**

Apraksin pereulok
АПРАКСИН ПЕРЕУЛОК   **6 E3**

Aptekarskiy pereulok
АПТЕКАРСКИЙ ПЕРЕУЛОК   **2 E5**

Armenian Church   **6 F1**

Arsenalnaya naberezhnaya
АРСЕНАЛЬНАЯ НАБЕРЕЖНАЯ   **3 B3**

Arsenalnaya ulitsa
АРСЕНАЛЬНАЯ УЛИЦА   **3 C1**

Artilleriyskaya ulitsa
АРТИЛЛЕРИЙСКИЙ УЛИЦА   **3 B5**

Artillery Musuem   **2 D3**

Arts Square   **6 F1**

Astoria Hotel   **6 D2**

Atamanskaya ulitsa
АТАМАНСКАЯ УЛИЦА   **8 D5**

Atamanskiy most   АТАМАНСКИЙ МОСТ **8 D5**

B

Bakunina, prospekt
БАКУНИНА, ПРОСПЕКТ   **8 D2**

Bankovskiy most   БАНКОВСКИЙ МОСТ **6 E2**

Bankovskiy pereulok
БАНКОВСКИЙ ПЕРЕУЛОК   **6 E2**

Barmaleeva, ulitsa   БАРМАЛЕЕВА, УЛИЦА **1 C1**

Barochnaya ulitsa   БАРОЧНАЯ УЛИЦА **1 A1**

Baskov pereulok
БАСКОВ ПЕРЕУЛОК   **3 B5, 7 C1**

Batayskiy pereulok
БАТАЙСКИЙ ПЕРЕУЛОК   **6 E5**

Belinskovo, ulitsa
БЕЛИНСКОГО, УЛИЦА   **7 A1**

Belinskovo, most   БЕЛИНСКОГО, МОСТ **7 A1**

Birzhevaya liniya   БИРЖЕВАЯ ЛИННЯ **1 B5**

Birzhevaya ploshchad
БИРЖЕВАЯ ПЛОЩАДЬ   **1 C5**

Birzhevoy most   БИРЖЕВОЙ МОСТ   **1 C4**

Birzhevoy pereulok
БИРЖЕВОЙ ПЕРЕУЛОК   **1 B4**

Birzhevoy proezd   БИРЖЕВОЙ ПРОЕЗД   **1 C5**

Blagoeva, ulitsa   БЛАГОЕВА, УЛИЦА   **1 C3**

Blokhina, ulitsa   БЛОХИНА, УЛИЦА   **1 B3**

Bobruyskaya ulitsa   БОБРУИСКАЯ УЛИЦА   **3 B1**

Bolshaya Konyushennaya ulitsa
БОЛЬШАЯ КОНЮШЕННАЯ УЛИЦА   **6 E1**

Bolshaya Monetnaya ulitsa
БОЛЬШАЯ МОНЕТНАЯ УЛИЦА   **2 D2**

Bolshaya Morskaya ulitsa
БОЛЬШАЯ МОРСКАЯ УЛИЦА   **5 B2**

Bolshaya Moskovskaya ulitsa
БОЛЬШАЯ МОСКОВСКАЯ УЛИЦА   **7 A3**

Bolshaya Podyacheskaya ulitsa
БОЛЬШАЯ ПОДЬЯЧЕСКАЯ УЛИЦА   **5 C4**

Bolshaya Posadskaya ulitsa
БОЛЬШАЯ ПОСАДСКАЯ УЛИЦА   **2 E2**

Bolshaya Pushkarskaya ulitsa
БОЛЬШАЯ ПУШКАРСКАЯ УЛИЦА   **1 C2**

Bolshaya Raznochinnaya ulitsa
БОЛЬШАЯ РАЗНОЧИННАЯ УЛИЦА   **1 A1**

Bolshaya Zelenina ulitsa
БОЛЬШАЯ ЗЕЛЕНИНА УЛИЦА   **1 A1**

Bolshoy prospekt (Vasilievskiy Island)
БОЛЬШОЙ ПРОСПЕКТ   **1 A5, 5 A1**

Bolshoy prospekt (Petrogradskaya)
БОЛЬШОЙ ПРОСПЕКТ   **1 B3, 1 C1**

Bolshoy Sampsonievskiy prospekt
БОЛЬШОЙ САМПСОНИЕВСКИЙ ПРОСПЕКТ   **3 A1**

Bonch-Bruevicha, ulitsa
БОНЧ-БРУЕВИЧА, УЛИЦА   **4 F5**

Borodinskaya ulitsa
БОРОДИНСКАЯ УЛИЦА   **6 F3**

Borovaya ulitsa   БОРОВАЯ УЛИЦА   **7 A4**

Botkinskaya ulitsa
БОТКИНСКАЯ УЛИЦА   **3 A2**

Boytsova, pereulok
БОЙЦОВА, ПЕРЕУЛОК   **6 D4**

Bronnitskaya ulitsa   БРОННИЦКАЯ УЛИЦА **6 E5**

Bronze Horseman, The   **5 C1**

C

Cabin of Peter the Great   **2 F3**

Cathedral of SS. Peter and Paul   **2 D4**

Cathedral of the Transfiguration   **3 B5**

Chapaeva, ulitsa   ЧАПАЕВА, УЛИЦА   **2 F1**

Chekhova, ulitsa   ЧЕХОВА, УЛИЦА   **7 B1**

Chernomorskiy pereulok
ЧЕРНОМОРСКИЙ ПЕРЕУЛОК   **5 C1**

Chernyakhovskovo, ulitsa
ЧЕРНЯХОВСКОГО, УЛИЦА   **7 B5**

Chernyshevskovo, prospekt
ЧЕРНЫШЕВСКОГО, ПРОСПЕКТ   **3 B4**

Chernyshevskovo, sad im
ЧЕРНЫШЕВСКОГО, САД ИМ   **8 D2**

Chaykovskovo, ulitsa
ЧАЙКОВСКОГО, УЛИЦА   **3 A4**

Chkalovskiy prospekt
ЧКАЛОВСКИЙ ПРОСПЕКТ   **1 A2**

Circus   **7 A1**

Commandant's House   **2 D4**

Cruiser Aurora   **2 F3**

D

Decembrists' Square   **5 C1**

Degtyarnaya ulitsa   ДЕГТЯРНАЯ УЛИЦА **8 D2**

Degtyarnyy pereulok
ДЕГТЯРНЫЙ ПЕРЕУЛОК   **4 E5, 8 D1**

Dekabristov, ulitsa
ДЕКАБРИСТОВ, УЛИЦА   **5 A3**

Dekabristov, Proezd
ДЕКАБРИСТОВ, ПРОЕЗД   **5 C1**

Derptskiy pereulok
ДЕРПТСКИЙ ПЕРЕУЛОК   **5 B5**

Divenskaya ulitsa   ДИВЕНСКАЯ УЛИЦА   **2 E2**

Dmitrovskiy pereulok
ДМИТРОВСКИЙ ПЕРЕУЛОК   **7 B2**

Dnepropetrovskaya ulitsa
ДНЕПРОПЕТРОВСКАЯ УЛИЦА   **7 C5**

Dobrolyubova, prospekt
ДОБРОЛЮБОВА, ПРОСПЕКТ   **1 B3**

Dostoevskovo, ulitsa
ДОСТОЕВСКОГО, УЛИЦА   **7 A4**

Dostoevsky House-Museum   **7 B3**

Drovyanaya ulitsa   ДРОВЯНАЯ УЛИЦА   **5 B5**

Drovyanoy pereulok
ДРОВЯНОЙ ПЕРЕУЛОК   **5 A4**

Dumskaya ulitsa   ДУМСКАЯ УЛИЦА   **6 E2**

Dvortsovaya naberezhnaya
ДВОРЦОВАЯ НАБЕРЕЖНАЯ   **2 D5**

Dvortsovaya ploshchad
ДВОРЦОВАЯ ПЛОЩАДЬ   **6 D1**

Dvortsovyy most   ДВОРЦОВЫЙ МОСТ   **1 C5**

Dzhambula, pereulok
ДЖАМБУЛА, ПЕРЕУЛОК   **6 F3**

E

Egipetskiy most   ЕГИПЕТСКИЙ МОСТ   **5 B5**

Egorova, ulitsa   ЕГОРОВА, УЛИЦА   **6 D5**

Engineers' Castle   **2 F5**

Engineer's House   **2 D3**

The English Quay   **5 B2**

Evgenevskaya ulitsa
ЕВГЕНЬЕСКАЯ УЛИЦА   **8 D2**

F

Feodosiyskaya ulitsa
ФЕОДОСИЙСКАЯ УЛИЦА   **4 F1**

Field of Mars   **2 F5**

Finland Station   **3 B3**

Finskiy pereulok
ФИНСКИЙ ПЕРЕУЛОК   **3 B2**

Fonarnyy most   ФОНАРНЫЙ МОСТ   **5 C2**

Fonarnyy pereulok
ФОНАРНЫЙ ПЕРЕУЛОК   **5 C2**

Furmanova, ulitsa
ФУРМАНОВА УЛИЦА   **3 A4**

Furshtatskaya ulitsa
ФУРШТАТСКАЯ УЛИЦА   **3 B4**

G

Galernaya ulitsa   ГАЛЕРНАЯ УЛИЦА   **5 A2**

Gatchinskaya ulitsa
ГАТЧИНСКАЯ УЛИЦА   **1 B1**

Gazovaya ulitsa   ГАЗОВАЯ УЛИЦА   **1 B1**

Gimnazicheskiy pereulok
ГИМНАЗИЧЕСКИЙ ПЕРЕУЛОК   **1 A2**

Glinka Capella   **2 E5**

Glinki, ulitsa   ГЛИНКИ, УЛИЦА   **5 B3**

Glinyanaya ulitsa   ГЛИРЯНАЯ УЛИЦА   **8 D5**

Glukhaya Zelenina ulitsa
ГЛУХАЯ ЗЕЛЕНИНА УЛИЦА   **1 A1**

Glukhoozerskoe shosse
ГЛУХООЗЕРСКОЕ ШОССЕ   8 D5

Goncharnaya ulitsa   ГОНЧАРНАЯ УЛИЦА 7 C2

Gorokhovaya ulitsa   ГОРОХОВАЯ УЛИЦА 6 D1

Gorstkin most   ГОРСТКИН МОСТ   6 E3

Gostinyy Dvor   6 F2

Grafskiy pereulok
ГРАФСКИЙ ПЕРЕУЛОК   7 A2

Grand Hotel Europe   6 F1

Grazhdanskaya ulitsa
ГРАЖДАНСКАЯ УЛИЦА   6 D3

Grecheskaya ploshchad
ГРЕЧЕСКАЯ ПЛОЩАДЬ   7 C1

Grecheskiy prospekt
ГРЕЧЕСКИЙ ПРОСПЕКТ 7 C1

Griboedova, naberezhnaya Kanala
ГРИБОЕДОВА, НАБЕРЕЖПАЯ КАНАЛА   5 A4

Grivtsova, pereulok
ГРИВЦОВА, ПЕРЕУЛОК   6 D2

Grodnenskiy pereulok
ГРОДНЕНСКИЙ ПЕРЕУЛОК   3C5

H

Hermitage, The   2 D5

Horseguards' Manège   5 C2

House of Fabergé   6 D1

I

Ilicha, pereulok   ИЛЬИЧА, ПЕРЕУЛОК   6 E4

Imperial Stables   2 E5

Inzhenernaya ulitsa
ИНЖЕНЕРНАЯ УЛИЦА   6 F1

Inzhenernity most
ИНЖЕРНЕРНАЯ МОСТ   2 F5

Ioannovskiy most
ИОАННОВСКИЙ МОСТ   2 E3

Isaakievskaya ploshchad
ИСААКИЕВСКАЯ ПЛОЩАДЬ   5 C2

Ispolkomskaya ulitsa
ИСПОЛКОМСКАЯ УЛИЦА   8 D3

Italyanskaya ulitsa
ИТАЛЬЯНСКАЯ УЛИЦА   6 F1

Izhorskaya ulitsa   ИЖОРСКАЯ УЛИЦА   1 B2

Izmaylovskiy most
ИЗМАЙЛОВСКИЙ МОСТ   5 C4

Izmaylovskiy prospekt
ИЗМАЙЛОВСКИЙ ПРОСПЕКТ   5 C5

K

Kaluzhskiy pereulok
КАЛУЖСКИЙ ПЕРЕУЛОК   4 E4

Kamennoostrovskiy prospekt
КАМЕННООСТРОВСКИЙ ПРОСПЕКТ   2 D1

Kanonerskaya ulitsa
КАНОНЕРСКАЯ УЛИЦА   5 B4

Karavannaya ulitsa   КАРАВАННАЯ УЛИЦА 7 A1

Kavalergardskaya ulitsa
КАВАЛЕРГАРДСКАЯ УЛИЦА   4 E4

Kazan Cathedral   6 E1

Kazanskaya ploshchad
КАЗАНСКАЯ ПЛОЩАДЬ   6 E2

Kazanskaya ulitsa
КАЗАНСКАЯ УЛИЦА   6 D2

Kazanskiy most   КАЗАНСКИЙ МОСТ   6 E1

Kazarmennyy pereulok
КАЗАРМЕННЫЙ ПЕРЕУЛОК   2 F1

Kharkovskaya ulitsa
ХАРЬКОВСКАЯ УЛИЦА   8 D3

Khersonskaya ulitsa   ХЕРСОНСКАЯ УЛИЦА 8 D2

Khersonskiy proezd
ХЕРСОНСКАЯ ПРОЕЗД   8 E3

Khrustalnaya ulitsa
ХРУСТАЛЬНАЯ УЛИЦА   8 F5

Kirillovskaya ulitsa
КИРИЛЛОВСКАЯ УЛИЦА   8 E1

Kirov Museum   2 D1

Kirpichnyy pereulok
КИРПИЧНЫЙ ПЕРЕУЛОК   6 D1

Klimov pereulok   КЛИМОВ ПЕРЕУЛОК   5 B5

Klinicheskaya ulitsa
КЛИНИЧЕСКАЯ УЛИЦА   3 A2

Klinskiy prospekt
КЛИНСКИЙ ПРОСПЕКТ   6 E5

Kolokolnaya ulitsa
КОЛОКОЛЬНАЯ УЛИЦА   7 A2

Kolomenskaya ulitsa
КОЛОМЕНСКАЯ УЛИЦА   7 B3

Kolpinskaya ulitsa   КОЛПИНСКАЯ УЛИЦА 1 B2

Komissara Smirnova, ulitsa
КОМИССАРА СМИРНОВА, УЛИЦА   3 A1

Komsomola, ulitsa   КОМСОМОЛА, УЛИЦА 3 C3

Kondratevskiy prospekt
КОНДРАТЬЕВСКИЙ ПРОСПЕКТ   4 D2

Konnaya ulitsa   КОННАЯ УЛИЦА   8 D2

Konnogvardeyskiy bulvar
КОННОГВАРДЕЙСКИЙ БУЛЬВАР   5 B2

Konnyy pereulok   КОННЫЙ ПЕРЕУЛОК   2 E2

Konstantina Zaslonova, ulitsa
КОНСТАНТИНА ЗАСЛОНОВА, УЛИЦА   7 A4

Konstantinogradskaya ulitsa
КОНСТАНТИНОГРАДСКАЯ УЛИЦА   8 D4

Konyushennaya ploshchad
КОНЮШЕННАЯ ПЛОЩАДЬ   2 E5

Korolenko, ulitsa   КОРОЛЕНКО, УЛИЦА   3 B5

Korpusnaya ulitsa   КОРПУСНАЯ УЛИЦА   1 A1

Kotovskovo, ulitsa
КОТОВСКОГО, УЛИЦА   2 E1

Kovenskiy pereulok
КОВЕНСКИЙ ПЕРЕУЛОК   7 B1

Krasnoselskaya ulitsa
КРАСНОСЕЛЬСКАЯ УЛИЦА   1 B2

Krasnovo Kursanta, ulitsa
КРАСНОГО КУРСАНТА, УЛИЦА   1 A2

Krasnovo Tekstilshchika, ulitsa
КРАСНОГО ТЕКСТИЛЬЩИКА, УЛИЦА   4 F5

Krasnoy Svyazi, ulitsa
КРАСНОЙ СВЯЗИ, УЛИЦА   3 C5

Krasnyy most   КРАСНЫЙ МОСТ   6 D2

Krasnoarmeyskiy most
КРАСНОАРМЕЙСКИЙ МОСТ   5 C4

Kremenchugskaya ulitsa
КРЕМЕНЧУГСКАЯ УЛИЦА   8 D4

Kronverkskaya naberezhnaya
КРОНВЕРКСКАЯ НАБЕРЕЖНАЯ   2 D3

Kronverkskaya, ulitsa
КРОНВЕРКСКАЯ, УЛИЦА   2 D2

Kronverkskiy prospekt
КРОНВЕРКСКИЙ ПРОСПЕКТ   1 C3

Kronverkskiy most
КРОНВЕРКСКИЙ МОСТ   2 D4

Kropotkina, ulitsa
КРОПОТКИНА, УЛИЦА   1 C2

Krylova, pereulok
КРЫЛОВА, ПЕРЕУЛОК   6 F2

Kryukova Kanala, naberezhnaya
КРЮКОВА КАНАЛА, НАБЕРЕЖПАЯ **5 B2**

Kshesinskaya Mansion **2 E3**

Kulibina, ploshchad
КУЛИБИНА, ПЛОЩАДЬ **5 A4**

Kunstkammer **1 C5**

Kurskaya ulitsa КУРСКАЯ УЛИЦА **7 A5**

Kutuzova, naberezhnaya
КУТУЗОВА, НАБЕРЕЖНАЯ **2 F4, 3 A4**

Kuybysheva, ulitsa КУЙБЫШЕВА, УЛИЦА **2 E3**

Kuznechnyy pereulok
КУЗНЕЧНЫЙ ПЕРЕУЛОК **7 A3**

Kvarengi, pereulok
КВАРЕНГИ, ПЕРЕУЛОК **4 F4**

L

Labutina, ulitsa ЛАБУТИНА, УЛИЦА **5 B4**

Ladygina, pereulok
ЛАДЫГИНА, ПЕРЕУЛОК **5 B5**

Lakhtinskaya ulitsa ЛАХТИНСКАЯ УЛИЦА **1 B1**

Lazaretnyy pereulok
ЛАЗАРЕТНЫЙ ПЕРЕУЛОК **6 E4**

Lebyazhevo Kanala, naberezhnaya
ЛЕБЯЖЬЕВО КАНАЛА, НАБЕРЕЖПАЯ **2 F5**

Lenina, ploshchad ЛЕНИНА, ПЛОЩАДЬ **3 B3**

Lenina, ulitsa ЛЕНИНА, УЛИЦА **1 B1**

Lermontovskiy prospekt
ЛЕРМОНТОВСКИЙ ПРОСПЕКТ **5 B3**

Leshtukov most ЛЕШТУКОВ МОСТ **6 F3**

Lesnoy prospekt ЛЕСНОЙ ПРОСПЕКТ **3 B1**

Letniy sad ЛЕТНИЙ САД **2 F5**

Levashovskiy prospekt
ЛЕВАШОВКИЙ ПРОСПЕКТ **1 A1**

Leytenanta Shmidta, most
ЛЕЙТЕНАНТА ШМИДТА, МОСТ **5 B1**

Leytenanta Shmidta, naberezhnaya
ЛЕЙТЕНАНТА ШМИДТА, НАБЕРЕЖПАЯ **5 A1**

Lieutenant Shmidt Bridge **5 B1**

Ligovskiy prospekt
ЛИГОВСКИЙ ПРОСПЕКТ **7 B4**

Literary Café **6 E1**

Liteynyy most ЛИТЕЙНЫЙ МОСТ **3 A3**

Liteynyy prospekt
ЛИТЕЙНЫЙ ПРОСПЕКТ **3 A5, 7 A1**

Lizy Chaykinoy, ulitsa
ЛИЗЫ ЧАЙКИНОЙ, УЛИЦА **1 C3**

Lodeynopolskaya ulitsa
ЛОДЕЙНОПОЛЬСКАЯ УЛИЦА **1 B1**

Lomonosova, most ЛОМОНОСОВА, МОСТ **6 F3**

Lomonosova, ploshchad
ЛОМОНОСОВА, ПЛОЩАДЬ **6 F2**

Lomonosova, ulitsa
ЛОМОНОСОВА, УЛИЦА **6 F2**

Lutheran Church **6 E1**

Lva Tolstovo, ulitsa
ЛЬВА ТОЛСТОГО, УЛИЦА **2 D1**

Lviniy most ЛЬВИНЫЙ МОСТ **5 C3**

M

Main Post Office **5 C2**

Makarenko, pereulok
МАКАРЕНКО, ПЕРЕУЛОК **5 C4**

Makarova, naberezhnaya
МАКАРОВА, НАБЕРЕЖНАЯ **1 A4**

Maklina, prospekt
МАКЛИНА, ПРОСПЕКТ **5 A3**

Malaya Grebetskaya ulitsa
МАЛАЯ ГРЕБЕЦКАЯ УЛИЦА **1 B2**

Malaya Konyushennaya ulitsa
МАЛАЯ КОНЮШЕННАЯ УЛИЦА **6 E1**

Malaya Monetnaya ulitsa
МАЛАЯ МОНЕТНАЯ УЛИЦА **2 E1**

Malaya Morskaya ulitsa
МАЛАЯ МОРСКАЯ УЛИЦА **6 D1**

Malaya Posadskaya ulitsa
МАЛАЯ ПОСАДСКАЯ УЛИЦА **2 E2**

Malaya Pushkarskaya ulitsa
МАЛАЯ ПУШКАРСКАЯ УЛИЦА **1 C2**

Malaya Raznochinnaya ulitsa
МАЛАЯ РДЗНОЧИННАЯ УЛИЦА **1 B2**

Malaya sadovaya ulitsa
МАЛАЯ САДОВАЯ УЛИЦА **6 F1**

Malaya Zelenina ulitsa
МАЛАЯ ЗЕЛЕНИНА УЛИЦА **1 A1**

Malodetskoselskiy prospekt
МАЛОДЕТСКОСЕЛЬСКИЙ ПРОСПЕКТ **6 E5**

Malookhtinskiy prospekt
МАЛООХТИНСКИЙ ПРОСПЕКТ **8 F2**

Malyy prospekt МАЛЫЙ ПРОСПЕКТ **1 B2**

Manezhnyy pereulok
МАНЕЖНЫЙ ПЕРЕУЛОК **3 B5**

Marata, ulitsa МАРАТА, УЛИЦА **6 F4, 7 A4**

Marble Palace **2 E4**

Mariinskiy proezd
МАРИИНСКАЯ ПРОЕЗД **4 D5**

Mariinskiy Theater **5 B3**

Markina, ulitsa МАРКИНА УЛИЦА **1 C2**

Marsovo pole МАРСОВО ПОЛЕ **2 F5**

Masterskaya ulitsa МАСТЕРСКАЯ УЛИЦА **5 A3**

Matveev pereulok
МАТВЕЕВА ПЕРЕУЛОК **5 B3**

Mayakovskovo, ulitsa
МАЯКОВСКОГО УЛИЦА **3 B5, 7 B1**

Melnichnaya ulitsa
МЕЛЬНИЧНАЯ УЛИЦА **8 F5**

Mendeleevskaya liniya
МЕНДЕЛЕЕВСКАЯ УЛИЦА **1 C5**

Menshikov Palace **1 B5, 5 B1**

Michurinskaya ulitsa
МИХАЙЛОВСКАЯ УЛИЦА **2 E2**

Mikhaylovskaya ulitsa
МИХАЙЛОВСКАЯ УЛИЦА **6 F1**

Mikhaylova, ulitsa
МИХАЙЛОВА УЛИЦА **3 C2**

Mikhaylovskiy sad
МИХАЙЛОВСКИЙ САД **2 F5, 6 F1**

Millionnaya ulitsa
МИНЕРАЛЬНАЯ УЛИЦА **2 E5**

Mineralnaya ulitsa
МИНЕРАЛЬНАЯ УЛИЦА **3 C1**

Minskiy pereulok
МИНСКИЙ ПЕРЕУЛОК **5 B3**

Mira, ulitsa МИРА, УЛИЦА **2 D2**

Mirgorodskaya ulitsa
МИРГОРОДСКАЯ УЛИЦА **8 D3**

Moiseenko, ulitsa
МОИСЕЕНКО, УЛИЦА **8 D1**

Mokhovaya ulitsa
МОХОВАЯ УЛИЦА **3 A4, 7 A1**

Monastyrki, naberezhnaya Reki
МОНАСТЫРКИ, НАБЕРЕЖПАЯ РЕКИ **8 E5**

Monchegorskaya ulitsa
МОНЧЕГОРСКАЯ УЛИЦА **1 B2**

Moskatelnyy pereulok
МОСКАТЕЛЬНЫЙ ПЕРЕУЛОК **6 E2**

Moskovskiy prospekt
МОСКОВСКИЙ ПРОСПЕКТ   6 D3

Moskvinoy, prospekt
МОСКВИНОЙ ПРОСПЕКТ   5 C5

Mozhayskaya ulitsa   МОЖАЙСКАЯ УЛИЦА 6 E5

Muchnoy pereulok   МУЧНОЙ ПЕРЕУЛОК 6 E2

Myasnaya ulitsa   МЯСНАЯ УЛИЦА   5 A4

Myasnikova, ulitsa   МЯСНИКОВА УЛИЦА 5 C4

Mytninskaya naberezhnaya
МЫТНИНСКАЯ НАБЕРЕЖНАЯ   1 C4

Mytninskaya ulitsa
МЫТНИНСКАЯ УЛИЦА   8 D2

Mytninskiy pereulok
МЫТНИНСКИЙ ПЕРЕУЛОК   1 C3

N

Naval Museum   1 C5

Neftyanaya doroga   НЕФТЯНАЯ ДОРОГА 7 C5

Nekrasova, ulitsa   НЕКРАСОВА, УЛИЦА 7 B1

Nesterova, pereulok
НЕСТЕРОВА, ПЕРЕУЛОК   1 B3

Neva Gate   2 E4

Nevskiy prospekt
НЕВСКИЙ ПРОСПЕКТ   6 D1, 7 A2

New Holland   5 B2

Nikolskaya ploshchad
НИКОЛЬСКАЯ ПЛОЩАДЬ   5 C4

Novgorodskaya ulitsa
НОВГОРОДСКАЯ УЛИЦА   4 E5, 8 E1

Novoadmiralteyskovo Kanala, naberezhnaya
НОВОАДМИРАЛТЕЙСКОГО КАНАЛА,
НАБЕРЕЖНАЯ   5 A2

Novokamennyy most
НОВОКАМЕННЫЙ МОСТ   7 B5

O

Obukhovskaya ploshchad
ОБУХОВСКАЯ ПЛОЩАДЬ   6 D4

Obukhovskiy most   ОБУХОВСКИЙ МОСТ 6 D4

Obukhovskoy Oborony, prospekt
ОБУХОВСКОЙ ОБОРОНЫ ПРОСПЕКТ   8 F4

Obvodnovo Kanala, naberezhnaya
ОБВОДНОГО КАНАЛА, НАБЕРЕЖНАЯ   6 F5, 7 A5

Ochakovskaya ulitsa   ОЧАКОВСКАЯ УЛИЦА 4 E4

Odesskaya ulitsa   ОДЕССКАЯ УЛИЦА   4 E4

Ofitserskiy pereulok
ОФИЦЕРСКИЙ ПЕРЕУЛОК   1 A3

Oranienbaumskaya ulitsa
ОРАНИЕНБАУМСКАЯ УЛИЦА   1 B1

Ordinarnaya ulitsa   ОРДИНАРНАЯ УЛИЦА 1 C1

Orenburgskaya ulitsa
ОРЕНБУРГСКАЯ УЛИЦА   3 A2

Orlovskaya ulitsa   ОРЛОВСКАЯ УЛИЦА 4 D3

Orlovskiy pereulok
ОРЛОВСКИЙ ПЕРЕУЛОК   7 C2

Ostrovskovo, ploshchad
ОСТРОВСКОГО, ПЛОЩАДЬ   6 F2

Ozernyy pereulok   ОЗЕРНЫЙ ПЕРЕУЛОК 7 C1

P

Palace Square   6 D1

Panteleymonovskiy most
ПАНТЕЛЕЙМОНОВСКИЙ МОСТ   2 F5

Paradnaya ulitsa   ПАРАДНАЯ УЛИЦА   4 D5

Pavlogradskiy pereulok
ПАВЛОГРАДСКИЙ ПЕРЕУЛОК   7 B5

Pechatnika Grigoreva, ulitsa
ПЕЧАТНИКА ГРИГОРЬЕВА, УЛИЦА   7 A4

Penkovaya ulitsa   ПЕНЬКОВАЯ УЛИЦА 2 F3

Perekupnoy pereulok
ПЕРЕКУПНОЙ ПЕРЕУЛОК   8 D3

Pestelya, ulitsa   ПЕСТЕЛЯ, УЛИЦА   3 A5

Peter Gate   2 E3

Petra Alekseeva, ulitsa
ПЕТРА АЛЕКСЕЕВА, УЛИЦА   6 D2

Petra Velikovo, most
ПЕТРА ВЕЛИКОГО, МОСТ   4 F5

Petrogradskaya naberezhnaya
ПЕТРОГРАДСКАЯ НАБЕРЕЖНАЯ   2 F1

Petrovskaya naberezhnaya
ПЕТРОВСКАЯ НАБЕРЕЖНАЯ   2 E3

Petrozavodskaya ulitsa
ПЕТРОЗАВОДСКАЯ УЛИЦА   1 B1

Pevcheskiy most   ПЕВЧЕСКИЙ МОСТ   2 E5

Pevcheskiy pereulok
ПЕВЧЕСКИЙ ПЕРЕУЛОК   2 E2

Pinskiy pereulok   ПИНСКИЙ ПЕРЕУЛОК 2 F2

Pionerskaya ploshchad
ПИОНЕРСКАЯ ПЛОЩАДЬ   6 F4

Pionerskaya ulitsa   ПИОНЕРСКАЯ УЛИЦА 1 A2

Pirogova, pereulok
ПИРОГОВА, ПЕРЕУЛОК   5 C2

Pirogovskaya naberezhnaya
ПИРОГОВСКАЯ НАБЕРЕЖНАЯ   2 F1, 3 A2

Pisareva, ulitsa   ПИСАРЕВА, УЛИЦА 5 A3

Plutalova, ulitsa   ПЛУТАЛОВА, УЛИЦА 1 C1

Pochtamtskaya ulitsa
ПОЧТАМТСКАЯ УЛИЦА   5 C2

Pochtamtskiy most
ПОЧТАМТСКИЙ МОСТ   5 C2

Pochtamtskiy pereulok
ПОЧТАМТСКИЙ ПЕРЕУЛОК   5 C2

Podezdnoy pereulok
ПОДЪЕЗДНОЙ ПЕРЕУЛОК   6 F4

Podkovyrova, ulitsa
ПОДКОВЫРОВА, УЛИЦА   1 C1

Podolskaya ulitsa   ПОДОЛЬСКАЯ УЛИЦА 6 E5

Podrezova, ulitsa   ПОДРЕЗОВА, УЛИЦА 1 C1

Politseyskiy most
ПОЛИЦЕЙСКИЙ МОСТ   6 E1

Polozova, ulitsa   ПОЛОЗОВА, УЛИЦА 1 C1

Polskiy sad   ПОЛЬСКИЙ САД   6 D4

Poltavskaya ulitsa
ПОЛТАВСКАЯ УЛИЦА   7 C3

Polyustrovskiy prospekt
ПОЛЮСТРОВСКИЙ ПРОСПЕКТ   4 F1

Potseluev most   ПОЦЕЛУЕВ МОСТ   5 B3

Potemkinskaya ulitsa
ПОТЕМКИНСКАЯ УЛИЦА   3 C4

Povarskoy pereulok
ПОВАРСКОЙ ПЕРЕУЛОК   7 B2

Prachechnyy pereulok
ПРАЧЕЧНЫЙ ПЕРЕУЛОК   5 C2

Pravdy, ulitsa   ПРАВДЫ, УЛИЦА   7 A3

Preobrazhenskaya ploshchad
ПРЕОБРАЖЕНСКАЯ ПЛОЩАДЬ   3 B5

Predtechenskiy most
ПРЕДТЕЧЕНСКИЙ МОСТ   7 B5

Professora Ivashentseva, ulitsa
ПРОФЕССОРА ИВАШЕНЦЕВА, УЛИЦА   8 D3

Professora Kachalova, ulitsa
ПРОФЕССОРА КАЧАЛОВА, УЛИЦА   8 F5

Proletarskoy Diktatury, ulitsa
ПРОЛЕТАРСКОЙ ДИКТАТУРЫ, УЛИЦА   **4 E4**

Proletarskoy Diktatury, ploshchad
ПРОЛЕТАРСКОЙ ДИКТАТУРЫ, ПЛОЩАДЬ   **4 E4**

Pryadilnyy pereulok
ПРЯДИЛЬНЫЙ ПЕРЕУЛОК   **5 B5**

Przhevalskovo, ulitsa
ПРЖЕВАЛСКОГО УЛИЦА   **6 D3**

Pskovskaya ulitsa   ПСКОВСКАЯ УЛИЦА   **5 A4**

Pudozhskaya ulitsa   ПУДОЖСКАЯ УЛИЦА   **1 B1**

Pushkinskaya ulitsa
ПУШКАРСКАЯ УЛИЦА   **7 B3**

Pushkarskiy pereulok
ПУШКАРСКИЙ ПЕРЕУЛОК   **2 D2**

Pushkin House-Museum   **2 E5**

R

Radishcheva, ulitsa
РАДИЩЕВА, УЛИЦА   **3 C5, 7 C1**

Railway Museum   **6 D4**

Rastrelli, ploshchad
РАСТЕЛЛИ ПЛОЩАДЬ   **4 E4**

Razezzhaya ulitsa   РАЗЪЕЗЖАЯ УЛИЦА   **7 A3**

Reki Fontanki, naberezhnaya
РЕКИ ФОНТАНКИ, НАБЕРЕЖНАЯ   **2 F4, 5 A5, 7 A1**

Reki Moyki, naberezhnaya
РЕКИ МОЙКИ, НАБЕРЕЖНАЯ   **2 E5, 5 A3**

Reki Pryazhki, naberezhnaya
РЕКИ ПРЯЖКИ, НАБЕРЕЖНАЯ   **5 A3**

Rentgena, ulitsa   РЕНТГЕНА, УЛИЦА   **2 D1**

Repina, ploshchad   РЕПИНА, ПЛОЩАДЬ   **5 A4**

Repina, ulitsa   РЕПИНА, УЛИЦА   **1 B5**

Revelskiy pereulok
РЕВЕЛСКИЙ ПЕРЕУЛОК   **5 B5**

Reznaya ulitsa   РЕЗНАЯ УЛИЦА   **1 A1**

Rimskovo-Korsakova, prospekt
РИМСКОГО-КОРСАКОВА, ПРОСПЕКТ   **5 A4**

Rimsky-Korsakov Conservatory   **5 B3**

Rizhskiy prospekt
РИЖСКИЙ ПРОСПЕКТ   **5 A5**

Robespera, naberezhnaya
РОБЕСПЬЕРА, НАБЕРЕЖНАЯ   **3 B4**

Romenskaya ulitsa   РОМЕНСКАЯ УЛИЦА   **7 B4**

Ropshinskaya ulitsa
РОПШИНСКАЯ УЛИЦА   **1 B2**

Rostral Columns   **1 C5**

Rubinshteyna, ulitsa
РУБИНШТЕЙНА, УЛИЦА   **7 A2**

Russian Museum   **6 F1**

Ruzovskaya ulitsa   РУЗОВСКАЯ УЛИЦА   **6 E5**

Rybatskaya ulitsa   РЫБАЦКАЯ УЛИЦА   **1 B2**

Ryleeva, ulitsa   РЫЛЕЕВА, УЛИЦА   **3 B5**

S

Sablinskaya ulitsa
САБЛИНСКАЯ УЛИЦА   **1 C2**

Sadovaya ulitsa   САДОВАЯ УЛИЦА **2 F5, 5 A5**

Sakharnyy pereulok
САХАРНЫЙ ПЕРЕУЛОК   **3 A1**

Saltykova-Shchedrina, ulitsa
САЛТЫКОВА-ЩЕДРИНА, УЛИЦА   **3 B5**

Sampsonievskiy most
САМПСОНИЕВСКИЙ МОСТ   **2 F2**

Sapernyy pereulok
САПЕРНЫЙ ПЛОЩАДЬ   **3 B5**

Saratovskaya ulitsa
САРАТОВСКАЯ УЛИЦА   **3 A2**

Semenovskiy most   СЕМЕНОВСКАЯ МОСТ **6 E3**

Sennaya ploshchad   СЕННАЯ ПЛОЩАДЬ   **6 D3**

Serpukhovskaya ulitsa
СЕРПУХОВСКАЯ УЛИЦА   **6 E5**

Sezdovskaya i 1-ya linii
СЪЕЗДОВСКАЯ И 1-Я ЛИНИИ   **1 A4**

Sezzhinskaya ulitsa
СЪЕЗЖИНСКАЯ УЛИЦА   **1 B3**

Shamsheva, ulitsa   ШАМШЕВА УЛИЦА   **1 C2**

Shchepyanoy pereulok
ЩЕПЯНОЙ ПЕРЕУЛОК   **5 C4**

Shcherbakov pereulok
ЩЕРБАКОВ ПЕРЕУЛОК   **7 A2**

Sheremetev Palace   **7 A1**

Shevchenko, ploshchad
ШЕВЧЕНКО, ПЛОЩАДЬ   **5 B1**

Shpalernaya ulitsa   ШПАЛЕРНАЯ УЛИЦА   **3 A4**

Shvedskiy pereulok
ШВЕДСКИЙ ПЕРЕУЛОК   **6 E1**

Siniy most   СИНИИ МОСТ   **6 D2**

Sinopskaya naberezhnaya
СИНОПСКАЯ НАБЕРЕЖНАЯ   **4 F5, 8 E2**

Smolnaya naberezhnaya
СМОЛЬНАЯ НАБЕРЕЖНАЯ   **4 E2**

Smolnovo, alleya   СМОЛЬНОГО, АЛЛЕЯ   **4 F4**

Smolnovo, sad   СМОЛЬНОГО САД   **4 F4**

Smolnovo, ulitsa   СМОЛЬНОГО, УЛИЦА   **4 F3**

Smolnyy Convent   **4 F4**

Smolnyy Institute   **4 F4**

Smolnyy proezd   СМОЛЬНЫЙ ПРОЕЗД   **4 F4**

Smolnyy prospekt
СМОЛЬНЫЙ ПРОСПЕКТ   **4 F5**

Solyanoy pereulok
СОЛЯНОЙ ПЕРЕУЛОК   **3 A4**

Sotsialisticheskaya ulitsa
СОЦИАЛИСТИЧЕСКАЯ УЛИЦА   **7 A4**

Sovetskiy pereulok
СОВЕТСКИЙ ПЕРЕУЛОК   **6 D5**

Soyuza Pechatnikov, ulitsa
СОЮЗА ПЕЧАТНИКОВ, УЛИЦА   **5 A4**

Sredniy prospekt   СРЕДНИЙ ПРОСПЕКТ **1 A5**

Srednyaya Koltovskaya ulitsa
СРЕДНЯЯ КОЛТОВСКАЯ УЛИЦА   **1 A1**

Srednyaya Podyacheskaya ulitsa
СРЕДНЯЯ ПОДЬЯЧЕСКАЯ УЛИЦА   **5 C3**

SS. Peter and Paul Cathedral   **2 D4**

St. Andrew's Cathedral   **1 A5**

St. Isaac's Cathedral   **5 C2**

St. Isaac's Square   **5 C2**

St. Nicholas' Cathedral   **5 C4**

Starorusskaya ulitsa
СТАРОРУССКАЯ УЛИЦА   **8 D2**

Stavropolskaya ulitsa
СТАВРОПОЛЬСКАЯ УЛИЦА   **4 E4**

Stieglitz Museum   **3 A5**

Strelninskaya ulitsa
СТРЕЛЬНИНСКАЯ УЛИЦА   **1 C2**

Stremyannaya ulitsa   СТРЕМЯННАЯ УЛИЦА **7 A2**

Stroganov Palace   **6 E1**

Summer Gardens   **2 F4**

Summer Palace   **2 F4**

Suvorovskaya ploshchad
СУВОРОВСКАЯ ПЛОЩАДЬ   **2 F4**

Suvorovskiy prospekt
СУВОРОВСКИЙ ПРОСПЕКТ   **4 D5, 7 C2**

Svechnoy pereulok   СВЕЧНОЙ ПЕРЕУЛОК   **7 A3**

Sverdlovskaya naberezhnaya
СВЕРДЛОВСКАЯ НАБЕРЕЖПАЯ   **4 D2**

Sytninskaya ulitsa
СЫТНИНСКАЯ УЛИЦА   **2 D2**

T

Tambovskaya ulitsa   ТАМБОВСКАЯ УЛИЦА   **7 B5**

Tatarskiy pereulok
ТАТАРСКИЙ ПЕРЕУЛОК   **1 C3**

Tauride Palace   **4 D4**

Tavricheskaya ulitsa
ТАВРИЧЕСКАЯ УЛИЦА   **4 D5**

Tavricheskiy pereulok
ТАВРИЧЕСКИЙ ПЕРЕУЛОК   **4 D4**

Tavricheskiy sad   ТАВРИЧЕСКИЙ САД   **4 D4**

Teatralnaya ploshchad
ТЕАТРАЛЬНАЯ ПЛОЩАДЬ   **5 B3**

Teatralnyy most
ТЕАТРАЛЬНЫЙ МОСТ   **2 F5**

Telezhnaya ulitsa   ТЕЛЕЖНАЯ УЛИЦА   **8 D3**

Tiflisskaya ulitsa
ТИФЛИССКАЯ УЛИЦА   **1 C5**

Torgovyy pereulok
ТОРГОВЫЙ ПЕРЕУЛОК   **6 F3**

Transportnyy pereulok
ТРАНСПОРТНЫЙ ПЕРЕУЛОК   **7 B4**

Trinity Bridge   **2 E4**

Trinity Square
ТРОИЦКАЯ ПЛОЩАДЬ   **2 E3**

Troitskiy most   ТРОИЦКИЙ МОСТ   **2 E4**

Trubetskoy Bastion   **2 D4**

Truda, ploshchad   ТРУДА, ПЛОЩАДЬ   **5 B2**

Truda, ulitsa   ТРУДА, УЛИЦА   **5 B2**

Tsiolkovskovo, ulitsa
ЦИОЛКОВСКОГО, УЛИЦА   **5 A5**

Tuchkov most   ТУЧКОВ МОСТ   **1 A4**

Tuchkov pereulok   ТУЧКОВ ПЕРЕУЛОК   **1 A4**

Tulskaya ulitsa   ТУЛЬСКАЯ УЛИЦА   **4 E5**

Turgeneva, ploshchad
ТУРГЕНЕВА ПЛОЩАДЬ   **5 B4**

Tverskaya ulitsa   ТВЕРСКАЯ УЛИЦА   **4 D4**

Twelve Colleges   **1 C5**

Tyushina, ulitsa   ТЮШИНА УЛИЦА   **7 A5**

U

Ulyany Gromovoy, pereulok
УЛЬЯНЫ ГРОМОВОЙ, ПЕРЕУЛОК   **7 C1**

Universitetskaya naberezhnaya
УНИВЕРСИТЕТСКАЯ НАБЕРЕЖПАЯ   **1 C5, 5 B1**

V

Vatutina, ulitsa   ВАТУТИНА, УЛИЦА   **4 D1**

Vereyskaya ulitsa   ВЕРЕЙСКАЯ УЛИЦА   **6 E5**

Vinokurtsevskiy proezd
ВИНОКУРЦЕВСКИЙ ПРОЕЗД   **6 F5**

Vitebskaya ulitsa   ВИТЕБСКАЯ УЛИЦА   **5 A4**

Vladimirskaya ploshchad
ВЛАДИМИРСКАЯ ПЛОЩАДЬ   **7 A3**

Vladimirskiy prospekt
ВЛАДИМИРСКИЙ ПРОСПЕКТ   **7 A2**

Vodoprovodnyy pereulok
ВОДОПРОВОДНЫЙ ПЕРЕУЛОК   **4 D4**

Volkhovskiy pereulok
ВОЛХОВСКИЙ ПЕРЕУЛОК   **1 B4**

Volodi Yermaka, ulitsa
ВОЛОДИ ЕРМАКА, УЛИЦА   **5 A4**

Volokolamskiy pereulok
ВОЛОКОЛАМСКИЙ ПЕРЕУЛОК   **7 A4**

Volynskiy pereulok
ВОЛЫНСКИЙ ПЕРЕУЛОК   **6 E1**

Voronezhskaya ulitsa
ВОРОНЕЖСККЯ УЛИЦА   **7 A5**

Vorontsov Palace   **6 F2**

Voskova, ulitsa   ВОСКОВА, УЛИЦА   **1 C2**

Vosstaniya, ploshchad
ВОССТАНИЯ, ПЛОЩАД   **7 C2**

Vosstaniya, ulitsa
ВОССТАНИЯ, УЛИЦА   **3 C5, 7 C1**

Voznesenskiy prospekt
ВОЗНЕСЕНСКИЙ ПРОСПЕКТ   **5 C4**

Vvedenskaya ulitsa
ВВЕДЕНСКАЯ УЛИЦА   **1 C2**

Vvedenskovo kanala, naberezhnaya
ВВЕДЕНСКОГО КАНАЛА, НАБЕРЕЖПАЯ   **6 E4**

Vyborgskaya ulitsa
ВЫБОРГСКАЯ УЛИЦА   **3 A1**

W

Winter Palace   **2 D5**

Y

Yablochkova, ulitsa   ЯБЛОЧКОВА, УЛИЦА   **1 C3**

Yakobshtadtskiy pereulok
ЯКОБШТАДТСКИЙ ПЕРЕУЛОК   **5 C5**

Yakubovicha, ulitsa
ЯКУБОВИЧА, УЛИЦА   **5 B2**

Yaroslavskaya ulitsa
ЯРОСЛАВСКАЯ УЛИЦА   **4 E5**

Yefimova, ulitsa   ЕФИМОВА, УЛИЦА   **6 E3**

Yeliseev's   **6 F1**

Yusupov Palace   **5 B3**

Yusupovskiy sad   ЮСУПОВСКИЙ САД   **6 D3**

Z

Zagorodnyy prospekt
ЗАГОРОДНЫЙ ПРОСПЕКТ   **6 E4, 7 A3**

Zakharevskaya ulitsa
ЗАХАРЬЕВСКАЯ УЛИЦА   **3 B4**

Zamkovaya ulitsa   ЗАМКОВАЯ УЛИЦА   **2 F5**

Zerkalnyy pereulok
ЗЕРКАЛЬНЫЙ ПЕРЕУЛОК   **8 F5**

Zhdanovskaya naberezhnaya
ЖДАНОВСКАЯ НАБЕРЕЖПАЯ   **1 A2**

Zhdanovskaya ulitsa
ЖДАНОВСКАЯ УЛИЦА   **1 A2**

Zhukova, ulitsa   ЖУКОВА УЛИЦА   **4 F1**

Zhukovskovo, ulitsa
ЖУКОВСКОГО, УЛИЦА   **7 B1**

Zodchevo Rossi, ulitsa
ЗОДЧЕГО РОССИ, УЛИЦА   **6 F2**

Zoological Museum   **1 C5**

Zoologicheskiy sad
ЗООЛОГИЧЕСКИЙ САД   **2 D3**

Zvenigorodskaya ulitsa
ЗВЕНИГОРОДСКАЯ УЛИЦА   **6 F4, 7 A4**

Zverinskaya ulitsa
ЗВЕРИНСКАЯ УЛИЦА   **1 B3**

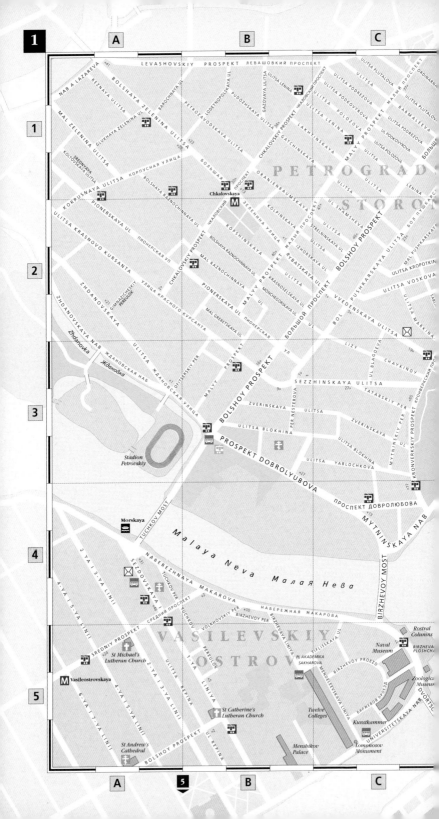

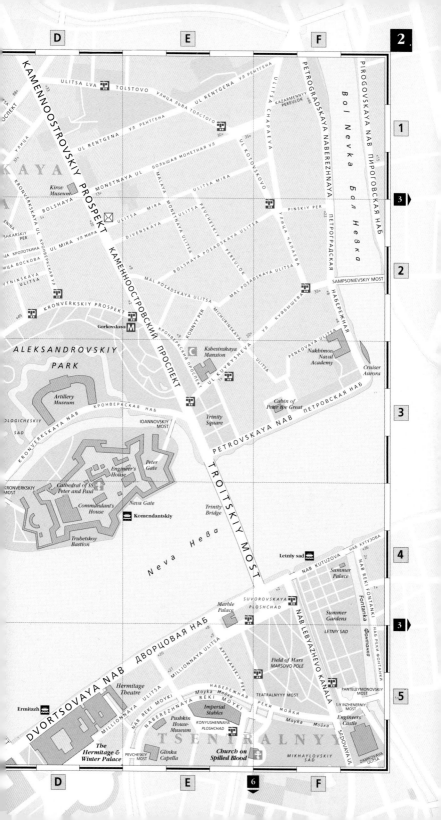

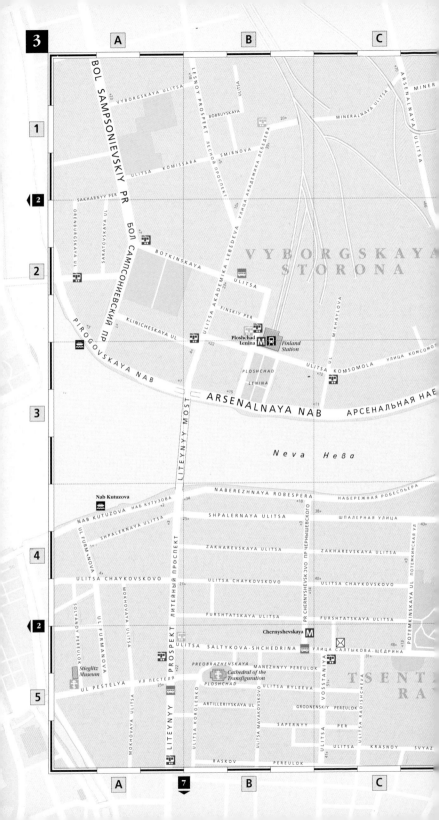

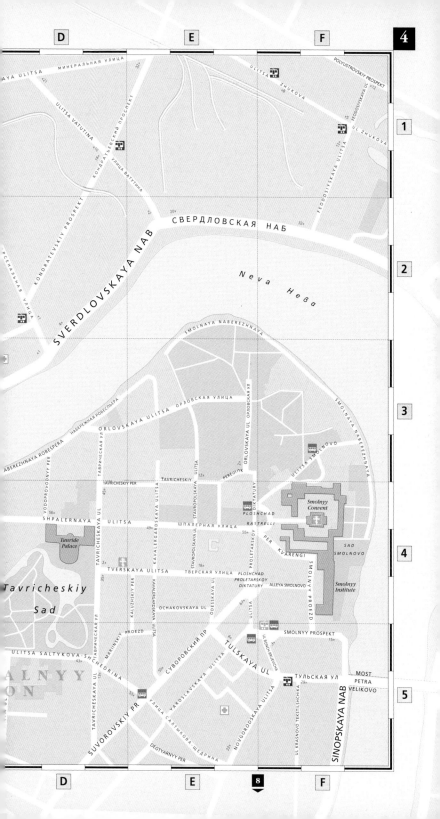

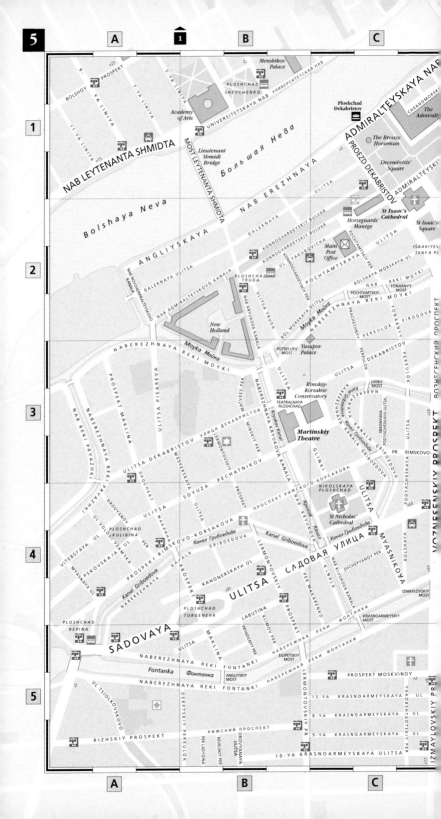

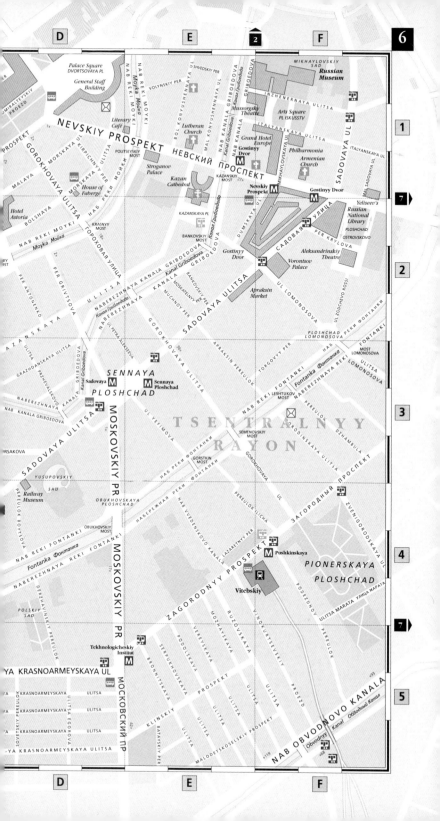

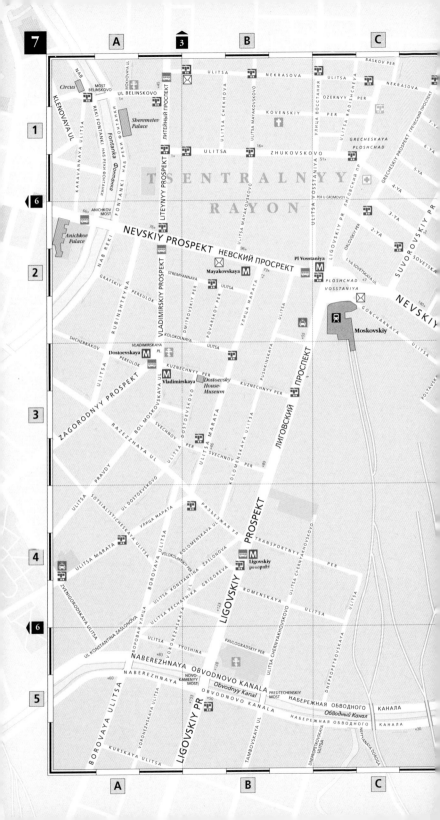

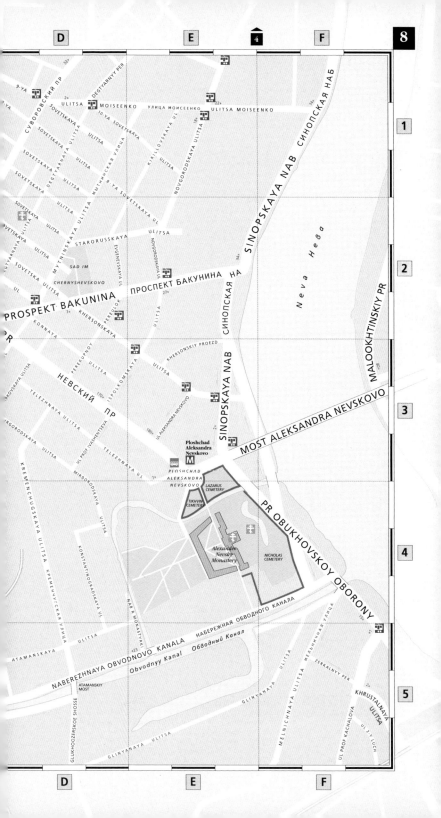

General Index

Page numbers in **bold** type refer to main entries.

1913 Goda 180
69 Club 197

A

Abamelek-Lazarev, Prince 134
Abbado, Claudio 194
Abraham's Sacrifice (Rembrandt) 86
Academy of Arts 40, **63**
Academy of Sciences 25
  Street-by-Street map 58
Academy of Sciences Library
  Street-by-Street map 59
Adam, Yegor
  Bridge Passage 35
  Great Stables Bridge 134
  Singers' Bridge 37, 112
Adamant 181
Adamini, Domenico 134
Adamini House 134
Addresses, writing 201
Admiralty 78
  Street-by-Street map 77
Admiralty (restaurant) 182
Admiralty (Tsarskoe Selo) 152
Admiralty Gardens 46
Admission charges 200
Aeroflot Building 46
Afrodite 182
Agate Rooms (Tsarskoe Selo) 152
Air travel **210–211**, 212
  traveling between Moscow and
  St. Petersburg 211
Airports 210, 212
Aivazovskiy, Ivan 106
Akhmatova, Anna 44, **129**
  Anna Akhmatova Museum 41, 129
  "The Bivouac of the
  Comedians" 134
  portrait by Nathan Altman 43
Akimov Comedy Theater 195
Alcohol 178–9
Aleksandrinskiy Theater 110
Aleksandrovskiy Park 70
Alexander I, Tsar
  Alexander Column 83
  Alexander Palace (Tsarskoe
  Selo) 153
  and Carlo Rossi 110
  Gonzaga Cameo 88
  Kamennoostrovskiy Palace 136
  Lycée (Tsarskoe Selo) 153
  Napoleonic Wars 22
  Yelagin Island 126
Alexander II, Tsar
  assassination 26, 92, 100, 134
  assassination attempt 135
  Church on Spilled Blood 100, 132
  Edict of Emancipation 23
  tomb of 68–9
  Winter Palace 93
Alexander III, Tsar 26
  Anichkov Palace 109
  Church on Spilled Blood 100
  Fabergé Easter eggs 82
  Gatchina 145
  Russian Museum 104
  statue of 94
Alexander Column 83
Alexander Nevsky Bridge 37
Alexander Nevsky Monastery
  130–31, 195

Alexander Palace (Tsarskoe Selo) 153
Alexandra, Tsarina (wife of
  Nicholas I) 148
Alexandria Park (Peterhof) 148
Alexandriinsky Theater 195
Alexis, Tsar 17
Alexis, Tsarevich
  Peter and Paul Fortress 66
  Trubetskoy Bastion 69
Altman, Nathan 43
Ambassador (restaurant) 182
Ambulances 204, 205
Amenemhet III, Pharaoh 89
Amenhotep III, Pharaoh 63
American Express 206
American food **183**, 185
American Medical Center 205
Andreevskiy Rynok 191
Andrey Vladimirovich, Grand Duke
  72, 121
Andropov, Yuri 30, 31
The Angel with the Golden Hair
  (icon) 106
Angelico, Fra 90
Anichkov, Lieutenant Colonel
  Mikhail 109
Anichkov Bridge 37
  St. Petersburg's Best: Bridges and
  Waterways 35
  statues 49
Anichkov Palace 49, **109**, 110
Anikushin, Mikhail 101, 131
Anna Akhmatova Museum 41
Anna Ivanovna 19
d'Anthès, Georges 83, 113
Antik Tsentr 191
Antikvariat 191
Antiques
  export permissions 186–7
  shops 190
Antwerpen 185
Apothecary's Island 136
Apraksin Dvor 191
Apraksin family 111
Apraksin Market **111**
Aprel-Palmira 185
Apyshkov, Vladimir 136
Arakcheev, Count Aleksey 135
Archbishop's Court (Novgorod) 160
Architecture
  Style Moderne 65, **71**
Archives of the War Ministry
  Street-by-Street map 66
Area codes 208
Argunov, Fyodor 129
Aristov, Leonid 82
Armenian Church 48, **108**
Armenian food **183**, 185
Art
  artists **45**
  export permissions 186–7
  Russian icon painting **163**
  shops 190
  see also Museums and galleries
Art Nouveau *see* Style Moderne
Art Shop 191
Artillery Museum 41, **70**
Artists 45
Arts Square **101**
  Street-by-Street map 98–9
Assignment Bank 135
Association of Travelling Art
  Exhibitions 106
Astoria Club 197
Astoria Hotel **79**, 170

Street-by-Street map 77
ATMs 206
Aurora see Cruiser *Aurora*
Austerlitz, Battle of (1805) 22
Australian Embassy 203
Austrian Airlines 212
Autumn in St. Petersburg 52
Autumn in Tsarskoe Selo 52
Avant-garde 29, 107
Aziya 185

B

Bach, Robert 120
Baghdad (café) 185
Bakhmatov, Ivan 162
Bakst, Léon 45, 107
  Ballets Russes 119
  Portrait of Sergey Diaghilev 104
Ballet **194**, 195
  Ballet in St. Petersburg 118
  Ballets Russes 107, 118, **119**
  dancers and choreographers 45
  Imperial School of Ballet 110
  and "World of Art" movement 26
Baltic Airlines 203
Baltic Station 221
Balzac, Honoré de 94
Bank Bridge 37
  St. Petersburg's Best: Bridges
  and Waterways 35
Banking 206
Banknotes 207
Baranovskiy, Gavriil
  Buddhist Temple 137
  Yeliseev's 71, 109
Barbizon school 91
Barclay de Tolly, Mikhail
  statue of 111
Bargaining 186
Barge-Haulers on the Volga
  (Repin) 105
Barrikada Cinema 46
Bars 183, **196**, 197
  opening times 175
Basquiat, Jean-Michel 94
Bazaars 187, 191
Bazhenov, Vasiliy 101
Beauharnais, Josephine 88
Bed and breakfast 169
Beethoven, Ludwig van 101
Behrens, Peter 76, 79
Della Leone 181
Beloselskiy-Belozerskiy Palace 49, 195
Bely, Andrei 44
Benois, Alexandre 117
  Ballets Russes 119
  "World of Art" movement 45, 107
Benois, Leontiy 104, 112
Benois House
  Street-by-Street map 117
Beresta 182
Beresta Palace Hotel 173
Bergholts, Olga 126
Bernini, Gian Lorenzo 47
Bessel and Co 49
Bestran 191
Bierstube 185
Bird statue (Gabriadze) 99
Bistro Le Français 180
Bistro Sadko 197
"The Bivouac of the Comedians" 134
Blank, Ivan 149
Blaue Reiter 107
Blok, Aleksandr 44, 134
"Bloody Sunday" (1905) 26, 73, 83

Blue Crest (Kandinsky) 39
Boat House
　Street-by-Street map 67
Boats
　boat trips 36
　canal and river cruises 218–19
　Cruiser *Aurora* 41, 73
　ferries and cruises 212
　hydrofoils 221
　Naval Museum 59, 60
　water taxis 219
Bogolyubov, Veniamin 116
Bogolyubskiy, Prince Andrey 161
Bolshaya Morskaya ulitsa 122
Bolshaya Zelinina ulitsa, No. 28 71
Bolsheviks
　Finland Station 126
　Kshesinskaya Mansion 72
　Russian Revolution 27
　Smolnyy Institute 128
Bolshoy Drama Theater (BDT) 195
Bolshoy Prospekt (Vasilevskiy
　Island) 62
Bonazza, Giovanni 149
Bookstores 190
Borey 191
Boris Godunov, Tsar 17
Borodin, Aleksandr 44
Borodino, Battle of (1812) 23
Botanical Gardens 136
Boucher, Franáois 91
The Brasserie 181
Braunstein, Johann 148
Brenna, Vincenzo
　Engineer's Castle 101
　Gatchina 145
　Pavlovsk 156, 157, 158, 159
Brest-Litovsk, Treaty of (1917) 29
Brezhnev, Leonid 30, 53
　death of 31
Bridge Passage
　St. Petersburg's Best: Bridges and
　Waterways 35
Bridges 34–7
　Lieutenant Shmidt Bridge 63
　opening times 201
　Panteleymon Bridge 99
　St. Petersburg's Best: Bridges and
　Waterways 34–5
　Singers' Bridge 37, 112, 135
　Trinity Bridge 65
British Airways 212
Brodsky, Joseph 44
Bronze Horseman (Falconet) 75,
　78–9
　Street-by-Street map 76
Bronze Horseman (Pushkin) 37,
　69, 78
Brullo, Nikolay 122
Bryullov, Aleksandr
　Guards Headquarters 83
　Lieutenant Shmidt Bridge 34, 63
　Lutheran Church 112
　Marble Palace 94
　St. Isaac's Cathedral 80
　Winter Palace 93
Bryullov, Karl 161
　The Last Day of Pompeii **105**, 106
　Virgin in Majesty 81
Buddhist Temple 137
Budget hotels 168
Bukinist 191
Bus Station 2 221
Bus travel 212
Buses 216–17

Bush, George 30
Bush, John 152
Byron, Lord 113

C

Cabin of Peter the Great 41, 73
Café Bahlsen 182, 185
Cafés **174**
　light meals and snacks 183–5
　opening times 175
California Grill 185
Cameron, Charles
　Chinese Village (Tsarskoe
　Selo) 152
　Pavlovsk 25, 156–7, 158
　Tsarskoe Selo 150, 151, 152
Cameron Gallery (Tsarskoe Selo) 152
Camping 168, **169**
Canadian Embassy 203
Canadian food 183, 185
Canals **34–7**
　cruises 218–19
　St. Petersburg's Best: Bridges and
　Waterways 34–5
　A Walk along St. Petersburg's
　Waterways 134–5
Candyman 197
Canova, Antonio 90
Caravaggio
　A Young Man Playing a Lute 90
Carrol's 185
Cars
　chastniki 219
　driving in St. Petersburg 221
　renting 221
Casinos **196**, 197
Castles
　Engineers' Castle 40, 99, 101
Cathedrals
　Cathedral of St. Sophia (Novgorod)
　141, **160**, 161
　Cathedral of SS. Peter and Paul
　19, 41, 67, **68–9**
　Cathedral of the Transfiguration
　127
　Kazan Cathedral 33, 47, **111**,
　135, 195
　St. Andrew's Cathedral 63
　St. Isaac's Cathedral 23, 75, 76,
　80–81
　St. Nicholas' Cathedral 115,
　117, **120**
　St. Nicholas' Cathedral
　(Novgorod) 161
　Smolnyy Cathedral 195
　Smolnyy Convent 128
　Trinity Cathedral 130
　Znamenskiy Cathedral
　(Novgorod) 162
　see also Churches
Catherine I, Tsarina 19, **21**
　and Prince Menshikov 62
　St. Andrew's Cathedral 63
　Summer Garden 95
　Tsarskoe Selo 150
Catherine II (the Great) 19, **22**,
　24–5, 93, 108
　Alexander Palace (Tsarskoe
　Selo) 153
　Anichkov Palace 109
　Bronze Horseman (Falconet) 78–9
　Cabin of Peter the Great 73
　Chesma Palace 130
　The Enlightened Empress 24–5
　Gatchina 145

Catherine II (the Great), (cont.)
　Griboedev Canal 36
　Hermitage 84–7, 88, 90–91
　Marble Palace 94
　Monplaisir (Peterhof) 148
　monument to 110
　Oranienbaum 144
　Pavlovsk 156, 158, 159
　Peterhof 147
　Smolnyy Convent 128
　statue of 49
　Summer Gardens 95
　Tauride Palace 128
　Tsarskoe Selo 141, 150, 152
　Voltaire's library 110
Catherine Palace *see* Tsarskoe Selo
Catherine Park (Tsarskoe Selo) 152
Caviar
　shops 190
　What to Eat in St. Petersburg 176
Cavos, Albert
　Bolshaya Morskaya ulitsa
　mansion 122
　Main Post Office 122
Celebrated St. Petersburgers 42–5
Cemeteries
　Lazarus Cemetery 131
　Piskarevskoe Memorial
　Cemetery 126
　Tikhvin Cemetery 131
Central Air Communication
　Agency 212
Central District Tax Office 49
Central Park of Culture and Rest 126
Central Telegraph Office 209
Central Theater Ticket Office 193
Central Train Ticket Office 212
Cézanne, Paul 91, 107
Chabrol, Vincent 35
Chaev, Sergey 136
Chagall, Marc 45
　The Circus 45
　Russian Museum 104, 107
Chagin, Vladimir 137
Chamber of Facets (Novgorod) 160
La Chandeleur 185
Chardin, Jean-Baptiste
　*Still Life with the Attributes of the
　Arts* 91
Charles XII, King of Sweden
　Battle of Poltava 18, 21, 68
Chastniki 219
Chayka 197
CHEKA 29
Chekhov, Anton 110
Chemiakin, Mikhail
　statue of Peter the Great 67
Cherepanov family 123
Chernenko, Konstantin 30, 31
Chernobyl nuclear power station 31
Chesma Church 130
Chesma Column (Tsarskoe Selo)
　152
Chesma Palace 130
Chevakinskiy, Savva
　New Holland 121
　St. Nicholas' Cathedral 120
　Sheremetev Palace 129
　Tsarskoe Selo 151
Chicherin, Nikolay 46
Children 203
　entertainment 193
　in hotels 167
　in restaurants 175
Children's Philharmonia 193

Chinese Palace (Oranienbaum) 141, **144**
Chinese Village (Tsarskoe Selo) 152
Chopsticks 181
Choreographers **45**, 118
Christ in Majesty (Klodt) 80
Christmas 53
Churches (general)
  music **194**, 195
  visiting 200–201
Churches (individual)
  Armenian Church 48, **108**
  Chesma Church 130
  Church of the Annunciation 130
  Church of the Holy Women (Novgorod) 161
  Church of Saint Catherine 48
  Church of St. John the Baptist 136
  Church of St. Procopius (Novgorod) 161
  Church of the Savior of the Transfiguration (Novgorod) 162
  Church of the Sign (Tsarskoe Selo) 153
  Church on Spilled Blood 98, **100**, 134
  Church of Theodore Stratilates (Novgorod) 162
  Church of the Three Saints 63
  Church of the Transfiguration 195
  Dutch Church 47, 135
  Lutheran Church 47, **112**
  St. Paraskeva Pyatnitsa (Novgorod) 161
  see also Cathedrals
Ciniselli, Giuseppe 193
Circus 193
  Street-by-Street map 99
The Circus (Chagall) 45
City Day 50
Civil War (1918–20) 27, 29
Classical music **194**, 195
Claude Lorrain 90
Climate 50–53
Clinic Complex 205
Clothes
  shops 190
  visiting churches 200
Cocteau, Jean 43
Coins 207
Cold War 27, 30
Commandant's House 41, **69**
  Street-by-Street map 66
Communications 208–9
Communism
  Russian Revolution 28
Concerts **194**, 195
Constantine, Grand Duke 23
Constitution Day 53
Consulates **202**, 203
Convents
  Smolnyy Convent 128
Conversion table 203
Corot, Camille 91
Corps des Pages 111
Corsair 185
Cosmonaut 197
Cosmonaut's Day 50
Cossacks
  Russian Revolution 28
Cottage Palace (Peterhof) 148
Country estates
  Gatchina 145
  Oranienbaum 144–5

Country estates (cont.)
  Pavlovsk 156–9
  Peterhof 146–9
  Tsarskoe Selo 150–53
Courier services 209
Cox, James 85
Craft shops 190
Cranach, Lucas the Elder
  Venus and Cupid 90
Creaking Pavilion (Tsarskoe Selo) 152
Credit cards 201, **206**
  in hotels 166
  in restaurants 174
  in shops 186
Crime 204
Cruiser *Aurora* **73**
  Russian Revolution 29, 41
Cruises 212, **218–19**
Crystal Palace 195
Cuban missile crisis (1962) 30
La Cucaracha 197
Currency 207
Currency exchange 206
Customs and immigration 202
The Cyclist (Goncharova) 40, 107
Cyril, St. 17, 201
Cyrillic language 201

D

Dacha 50, 51
  renting 169
Daddy's Steak Room 185
Dance *see* Ballet
La Danse (Matisse) 87
Dante Alighieri 113
Danzas, Konstantin 83
Dashkova, Princess Yekaterina 110
Davydov, Ivan 149
Dawe, George 92
"Death Gate" 69
Decembrist Rebellion (1825) **23**, 111
  Commandants' House 69
Decembrists' Square 78
  Street-by-Street map 76
Defenders of the Motherland Day 53
Degas, Edgar 91
Delacroix, Eugène 91
Demertsov, Fyodor 135
Demidov, Pyotr 122
Demut-Malinovskiy, Vasiliy 83, 105
Demyanova Ukha 180
Dental Palace 205
Department stores **187**, 191
Derviz, Barons von 121
Detinets 182, 185
DHL Express Center 209
DHL Worldwide Express 209
Diaghilev, Sergey 43, 45
  Bakst's portrait of 104
  Ballets Russes 118, **119**
  Tauride Palace 128
  "World of Art" movement 107
Diana (café) 185
Diderot, Denis
  and Catherine the Great 24, 91
  Myatlev House 79
Disabled travelers **202**, 203
  in hotels 167
  in restaurants 175
Discos **196**, 197
DLT 191
Doctors 205
Dolgorukov family 136
Dolgorukov Mansion 136
Dom Knigi 191

Dom Plus 168
Dom Voyennoy Knigi 191
Domenico's 197
Donskoy, Prince Dmitriy 17
Dostoevsky, Fyodor **123**
  Crime and Punishment 43, 44
  Dostoevsky House-Museum **130**
  Engineers' Castle 101
  imprisonment 69
  Kaznachevskaya ulitsa apartment 135
  Literary Café 83
  Malaya Morskaya ulitsa 82
  tomb of 131
Drinks
  What to Drink in St. Petersburg 178–9
Duma Tower 48
Duncan, Isadora 79
Dutch Church 47, 135
Dvorianskoe Gnezdo 181

E

E-mail services 209
Ea Haere Ia Oe (Gauguin) **87**, 91
Easter Sunday 50, 53
Edict of Emancipation (1861) 23
Egyptian Bridge 37
  St. Petersburg's Best: Bridges and Waterways 34
Eifmann, Boris 194
Electrical appliances 203
Elizabeth, Tsarina **19**
  Anichkov Palace 49, 109
  Cathedral of the Transfiguration 127
  death 22
  Monplaisir (Peterhof) 148
  Peterhof 146
  Smolnyy Convent 128
  Tsarskoe Selo 141, 150, 152
  Winter Palace 92
Elizabeth, Tsarina (wife of Alexander I) 157
Ellington Hall 197
Embassies **202**, 203
Emergency Medical Consulting 205
Emergency services 205
Engineers' Castle 40, **101**
  Street-by-Street map 99
Engineer's House 41, **68**
  Street-by-Street map 67
English Quay 121
Enlightenment 24–5
Entertainment **192–7**
  ballet **194**, 195
  buying tickets 192
  children's entertainment 193
  church music **194**, 195
  classical music **194**, 195
  festivals 50–53
  folk music **194**, 195
  information 192
  late night travel 193
  live music and nightlife 196–7
  movies 195
  opera **194**, 195
  Russian circus 193
  street music **194**, 195
  theater 194–5
  White Nights festivals 193
Eternal Flame 94
Etiquette 201
Europe (restaurant) 181
Excursions 200

Export permissions
    art and antiques 186–7

F

Fabergé 82
    House of Fabergé 82
Fabergé, Agathon 82
Fabergé, Carl 82
Fabergé, Gustav 82
Falconet, Etienne-Maurice 91
    Bronze Horseman 22, 75, 76, **78–9**
Farfor 191
Farfor, Khrustal, Steklo 191
Fashion House 47, 135
Fashion shops 190
Faskhoutdinov, Emil 45
Fast food **184**, 185
Faxes 209
Federal Express 209
Ferries 212
Festival of Festivals 51
Festivals **50–53**
    White Nights festivals 193
Field of Mars 94
Film see Movies
Filonov, Pavel 45
Finland, Gulf of 141
    cruises 218
    hydrofoils 221
    traveling to 221
Finland Station **126**, 212, 221
Finnair 212
Finnord 212
Fire services 205
Fish Fabrique 197
Floods 37, 69
    The Bronze Horseman (Pushkin) 78
Fokine, Michel 45
    Ballet in St. Petersburg 118
    Ballets Russes 119
    house on Theater Square 117
Folk music 194, 195
Follenveider's mansion 137
Fomin, Ivan 134, 137
Fontana, Giovanni-Maria
    Menshikov Palace 62
    Oranienbaum 144
Fontana, Ludwig
    Grand Hotel Europe 98, 101
Fontanka River 36, 125
    cruises 218
Food and drink
    health precautions 205
    light meals and snacks 183–5
    What to Drink in St. Petersburg
        178–9
    What to Eat in St. Petersburg 176–7
    see also Restaurants
Fountains
    Peterhof 149
Fragonard, Jean Honoré 91
Franchioli, Enrico 119
Friedrich, Caspar David 91
Friedrich Wilhelm I, King of
    Prussia 151
From the Avant-garde to the Present 50
Futurism 107

G

Gabriadze, Rezo
    Bird statue 99
Gagarin, Yuriy 30
Gagarina, Princess 122
Galleries see Museums and galleries
Gardens see Parks and gardens

Gasoline 221
Gatchina 141, **145**
    eating out on day trips 184
    traveling to 220
Gaudí, Antonio 71
Gauguin, Paul 91
    Ea Haere Ia Oe **87**, 91
Gausvald, Yevgeniya 137
Gaveman, Adolph 62
Ge, Nikolay 107
Geisler, Mikhail 122
General Staff Building 135
Georgian food 183, 185
Gergiev, Valery 194
German food **183**, 185
Giorgione 90
Girl with a Pitcher (Sokolov) 152
Glasnost (openness) 30
Glinka, Mikhail 44
    Glinka Capella 112
    portrait by Repin 44
    statue of 120
    tomb of 131
Glinka Capella **112**, 195
Gogen, Aleksandr von 71
    Kshesinskaya Mansion 71, 72
Gogol, Nikolai 42, 44
    Alexandrinskiy Theater 110
    Malaya Morskaya ulitsa 82
    Nevskiy Prospekt 108
    Pushkin's Dacha (Tsarskoe
        Selo) 153
    Zverkov House 135
Golovin, Aleksandr 119
Goncharova, Natalya (painter) 107
    The Cyclist 40, 107
Goncharova, Natalya (Pushkin's
    wife) 83
    Pushkin House-Museum 113
    Pushkin's Dacha (Tsarskoe Selo) 153
Gorbachev, Mikhail 30, 31
Gorky, Maxim
    Repin's portrait of 144
Gostinyy Dvor 15, 48, **97–113**
    area map 97
    Arts Square 98–9
    Church on Spilled Blood 100
    map 97
    Russian Museum 104–7
Gostinyy dvor (department store) 191
Grand Ducal Mausoleum 69
    Street-by-Street map 67
Grand Hotel Europe **101**, 171, 173
    cash dispenser 206
    Street-by-Street map 98
Great Caprice (Tsarskoe Selo) 152
Great Northern War 18, 21, 65
Great Palace (Peterhof) 146–7
Great Philharmonia see Philharmonia,
    Great
Great Pond (Tsarskoe Selo) 152
Great Purges 72
Great Stables Bridge 134
El Greco 90
Green Crest 185
Greuze, Jean-Baptiste 91
Griboedov, Aleksandr 47
Griboedov (nightclub) 197
Griboedov Canal 36, 47
    cruises 218
    A Walk along St. Petersburg's
        Waterways 134–5
Grigoriev, Boris
    Portrait of the Director Vsevolod
        Meyerhold 107

Grill Master 185
Guided tours 203
Guslistiy, Boris 122
Gypsies 204

H

Handball on the Square 51
Hannibal, Abram 113
Hanska, Countess Eveline 94
Harley Davidson Club 197
Health care 204, 205
Heine, Heinrich 113
Hermann, Josef 80
Hermitage 40, **84–93**
    Classical art 88
    Flemish, Dutch and German art 90
    floor plan 86–7
    French and English art 90–91
    Italian and Spanish art 90
    19th and 20th century art 91
    Oriental art 88–9
    prehistoric art 88
    Russian art 89
    St. Petersburg's Best: Palaces and
        Museums 38
    Visitors' Checklist 85
    Winter Palace 92–3
Hermitage (Peterhof) 148
Hermitage (Tsarskoe Selo) 152
Hermitage Theater 34, 195
Hertz 221
Herzen University Hostel 168
History 17–31
Hitler, Adolf 79
Holiday Hostel 168
Holidays, public 53
Hollywood Nites 197
L'Homme aux Bras Croisés
    (Picasso) 91
Horseguards' Manège 79
    Street-by-Street map 76
Hospitals 205
Hostels 168–9
Hotel Astoria 173
    ATM 206
Hotel Deson Ladoga 172
Hotels **166–73**
    budget hotels 168
    children in 167
    disabled travelers 167
    facilities 166
    hidden extras 167
    hostels 168–9
    how to book **166**, 168
    Popular hotels in St. Petersburg
        170–71
    price 166–7
    security 167
    where to look 166
Hotelship Peterhof 170, 173
Houdon, Jean-Antoine 91
    statue of Voltaire 87
House of Books 47, 71
House of Fabergé 82
Hydrofoils 221

I

Iconostasis 163
Icons
    Russian Museum 106
    Russian icon painting 163
Idiot 197
Ilyin, Lev 99
Imperial (restaurant) 182
Imperial Ballet School 45, 118

Imperial Porcelain Factory 25
Imperial School of Ballet 110
Imperial Stables **113**, 134
Independence Day 51
Ingal, Vladimir 116
Inkombank 206
Inoculations 205
Insect repellents 205
Institute of Cultural Initiatives 193
Institute of Russian Literature
    Street-by-Street map 59
Insurance
    medical 204
    travel 204
Interior Theater 193
International Women's Day 50, 53
International Youth Hostel 203
Irish Embassy 203
Isaac of Dalmatia, St. 76
Isayeva, Vera 126
Iskusstvo 191
Ivan I, Tsar 17
Ivan III, Tsar 17, 161
    Novgorod 160
Ivan IV the Terrible, Tsar 17, 19
    Novgorod 160
Ivan V, Tsar 18
    Streltsy Rebellion 20
Ivan VI, Tsar 68
Ivan Gate 68
    Street-by-Street map 67
Ivanov, Victor
    portrait of Lenin 28

J

Jacot, Paul 101, 135
Jazz 196, 197
    White Nights Swing Jazz Festival 51
Jazz Philharmonic Hall 197
JFC Jazz Club 197

K

Kabakov, Ilya 94
Kafe Ambassador 185
Kafe Charodeyka 185
Kafe Sankt-Peterburg 185
Kamenniy Island
    A Walk around Kamenniy and
    Yelagin Islands 136–7
Kamennoostrovskiy Palace 136
Kamennoostrovskiy prospekt 70
    Style-Moderne architecture 71
Kamennoostrovskiy Theater 136
Kamenskiy, Valentin 131
Kandinsky, Vasily 104, 107
    Blue Crest 39
Karsavina, Tamara 119
Kavos, Albert
    Kamennoostrovskiy Theater 136
    Mariinskiy Theater 119
    Mussorgsky Theater of Opera and
    Ballet 101
Kazan Cathedral 33, 47, 111
    church music 195
    A Walk along St. Petersburg's
    Waterways 135
Kelch 82
Kerensky, Aleksandr 29, 145
Khrushchev, Nikita 30
Khudozhestvennyye Promysly 191
Kiev 17
Kiprenskiy, Orest 45
Kirov, Sergey 70
    assassination 27, 41, 72, 129
    Kirov Museum 72

Kirov Ballet *see* Mariinskiy Ballet
Kirov Museum 41, 72
Kirov Theater *see* Mariinskiy Theater
Klenze, Leo von 84
KLM 212
Klodt, Pyotr
    Anchikov Bridge statues 35, 49
    Christ in Majesty 80
    monument to Nicholas I 77, 79
    statue of Ivan Krylov 95
    tomb of 131
Kneller, Sir Godfrey 91
Knight at the Crossroads (Vasnetsov)
    106, 107
Knights of St. John 159
Knizhnaya Lavka Pisateley 191
Kokorinov, Aleksandr 63
Kolokolnikov, Fedot 120
Kolokolnikov, Menas 120
Komissarzhevskaya Drama
    Theater 195
Korean War (1950–4) 30
Korsar 197
Kozintsev, Grigoriy 42, 45, 70
Kozlovskiy, Mikhail 149
Kramskoy, Ivan 106, 131
Kremer, Gidon 194
Kremlin (Novgorod) 141, **160–61**
Krestovka River 136
Krestovskiy Island 136, 137
Kristall 191
Krokodil 185
Kronstadt mutiny (1921) 27
Kropotkin, Prince Pyotr 69
Krunk 185
Krylov, Ivan
    statue of 95
    tomb of 131
Kryukov Canal 36
Kshesinskaya, Matilda 45, 72
    ballet shoes 118
    Kshesinskaya Mansion 72
Kshesinskaya Mansion 71, 72
    St. Petersburg's Best: Palaces and
    Museums 39
Kunstkammer 41, **60–61**
    Street-by-Street map 58
Kutuzov, Field Marshal Mikhail
    defeats Napoleon 23, 111
    statue of 111
    tomb of 111
Kuznechnyy Rynok 191
Kvadrat Jazz Club 197

L

Labor Day 53
Lacquered artifacts 189
Ladoga, Lake 141
Laika 30
La Mothe, Vallin de
    Academy of Arts 63
    Church of St. Catherine 48
    Gostinyy Dvor 109
    New Holland 121
    Small Hermitage 85
    Yusupov Palace 120
Lampi, Johann 158
Landé, Jean-Baptiste 110, 118
Landskrona 182
Language 201
Lantern Bridge 37
Large Large Puppet Theater 193
Larionov, Mikhail 107
The Last Day of Pompeii (Bryullov)
    105, 106

Layma 185
Lazarev, Ioakim 108
Lazarus Cemetery 131
Le Blond, Jean Baptiste
    Fountains at Peterhof 149
    Great Palace (Peterhof) 146, 147
    Peterhof Park 148
Le Nain, Louis 90
Lemaire, François 80
Lenin, Vladimir 61, 94
    armored car 70
    Finland Station 126
    Kshesinskaya Mansion 72
    New Economic Policy 27
    1917 Revolution 83
    portrait of 28
    Russian Revolution 28
    Smolnyy Institute 128, 129
    statue of 126, 129
    What is to be Done? 26
Leningrad Cinema 195
Leningrad Film Studios (Lenfilm) 70
Leonardo da Vinci
    The Litta Madonna 86, 90
Lermontov, Mikhail 83
Levinson, Yevgeniy 126
Levitan, Isaak 107
Levitskiy, Dmitriy 45, 161
    Portrait of E I Nelidova 106
Libraries
    Academy of Sciences Library 59
    Pushkin House-Museum 113
    Russian National Library 48
Lichtenstein, Roy 94
Lidval, Fyodor
    Astoria Hotel 79
    Grand Hotel Europe 101
    Kamennoostrovskiy prospekt
    house 70, 71
Lieutenant Shmidt Bridge 37, **63**
    St. Petersburg's Best: Bridges and
    Waterways 34
Life Guards' Mounted Regiment 79
Lion Bridge 37
    St. Petersburg's Best: Bridges and
    Waterways 34
    Street-by-Street map 117
El Lissitskiy 107
Liszt, Franz 129
Literary Café 46, **83**, 180
    A Walk along St. Petersburg's
    Waterways 135
Liteynyy Bridge 37
Liteynyy Theater 195
The Litta Madonna (Leonardo
    da Vinci) 86, 90
Little Stable Bridge 37
Liverpool 197
Locke, John 91
Lomonosov *see* Oranienbaum
Lomonosov, Mikhail 45
    grave of 131
    Lomonosov Monument 58
    Oranienbaum 145
    statues of 25, 61
Lomonosov Bridge 37
    St. Petersburg's Best: Bridges and
    Waterways 35
Lomonosov Monument 58, 61
Louis XVI, King of France 158
Lower and Upper Baths (Tsarskoe
    Selo) 152
Lucchini, Giovanni 60
Ludwig, Irene 94
Ludwig, Peter 94

Lufthansa 212
Lumière brothers 70
Lutheran church 47, **112**
Lvov, Nikolay 122
Lvov, Prince 29
Lyalevich, Marian 47
Lycée (Tsarskoe Selo) 41, 153

M

McDonalds 185
Magazines 209
  entertainments listings 192
Main Post Office 122, 209
Malaya Morskaya ulitsa 82
Malev Hungarian Airlines 212
Malevich, Kazimir 45
  Russian Museum 104, 107
  State Institute of Artistic Culture 79
  Supremus No. 56 29
Maltiyskiy Orden 185
Malyshev, Ignatiy 100
Malyy Drama Theater 195
Mamontov, Savva 107
Maps
  Arts Square 98–9
  Celebrated St. Petersburgers 42–3
  Farther afield 125
  Greater St. Petersburg 12–13
  metro 215
  Nevskiy Prospekt 46–9
  Palace Embankment 75
  Peter and Paul Fortress 66–7
  Peter the Great's new city 20–21
  Petrogradskaya 65
  Popular hotels in St. Petersburg 170–71
  Russian Federation 10–11
  St. Isaac's Square 76–7
  St. Petersburg 14–15
  St. Petersburg and environs 11
  St. Petersburg's Best: Bridges and Waterways 34–5
  St. Petersburg's Best: Palaces and Museums 38–9
  St. Petersburg's surroundings 142–3
  Sennaya Ploshchad 115
  Street Finder 222–37
  Strelka 58–9
  Theater Square 116–17
  Tikhvin Cemetery 131
  Tsarskoe Selo park 153
  Vasilevskiy Island 57
  A Walk along St. Petersburg's Waterways 134–5
  A Walk around Kamenniy and Yelagin Islands 136–7
  Walks in St. Petersburg 133
Marble Bridge (Tsarskoe Selo) 152
Marble Palace 40, **94**
Maria, Grand Duchess (daughter of Nicholas I) 77
Maria Alexandrovna, Tsarina 119
Maria Fyodorovna, Tsarina **159**
  Anichkov Palace 109
  Fabergé eggs 82
  Pavlovsk 141, 156, 157, 158, 159
  Yelagin Island 126
Maria Pavlovna, Grand Duchess 94
Marie Antoinette, Queen of France 159
Mariinskiy (Kirov) Ballet Company 45, 118, 184
Mariinskiy Palace 79
  Street-by-Street map 77

Mariinskiy Theater **119**, 195
  Street-by-Street map 116
Marionette Puppet Theater 193
Maritime Passenger Terminal 212
Maritime Victory Park 137
Markets **187**, 191
  Apraksin Market 111
  Nicholas market 117
  Round Market 134
Marly Palace (Peterhof) 148
The Marriage of Emperor Constantine (Rubens) 93
Martini, Simone 90
Martos, Ivan
  Grand Cascade (Peterhof) 149
  Tsarskoe Selo 151
Master of Flemalle 90
Master Peter 162
Matisov Domik 170, 172
Matisse, Henri 91, 107
  La Danse 87
Matryoshka 191
Mattarnovyy, Georg 60
Matveev, Andrey 106
Matveev, Fyodor 106
A Meal in the Monastery (Perov) 105
Medical treatment 204, 205
Meltzer, Roman
  Alexander Palace (Tsarskoe Selo) 153
  Follenveider's mansion 137
  Winter Palace 93
Mendeleev, Dmitriy 45, 61
Menelaws, Adam 148
Menshikov, Prince Aleksandr 21, **62**
  Bolshoy Prospekt 62
  Menshikov Palace 38, 40, 62
  Oranienbaum 144, 145
  Twelve Colleges 61
Menshikov Palace 40, **62**
  concerts 195
  St. Petersburg's Best: Palaces and Museums 38
Menus 174
Messmacher, Maximilian
  Bolshaya Morskaya ulitsa mansion 122
  Stieglitz Museum 39, 127
Metekhi 185
Methodius, St. 17
Metro 214–15
Metro (disco) 197
Mexican food **184**, 185
Meyerhold, Vsevolod 134
  portrait of 107
  Theater Museum 110
Mezentseva, Galina 45
Michelangelo 90
Michetti, Niccoló 148
Mikeshin, Mikhail 110, 161
Mikhail I, Tsar 17, 161
Mikhail Aleksandrovich, Grand Duke 94
Mikhail Pavlovich, Grand Duke 104
Mikhailovskiy Palace
  Russian Museum 104
  St. Petersburg's Best: Palaces and Museums 39
  Street-by-Street map 98
Mikhaylov, Andrey 120
Mikhaylovskiy, Valery 194
Milano 180
Millenium Monument (Novgorod) 161
Millionaires' Street 94

Miloslavskiy family 18
Minibuses 216–17
Ministry of Culture 186
Ministry of State Property
  Street-by-Street map 77
Mint
  Street-by-Street map 66
Minutka 185
Mir (hotel) 172
Mir (shop) 191
Mollie's Irish Bar 197
Molodyozhnyy Theater 195
Moloko 197
Monasteries
  Alexander Nevsky Monastery **130–31**, 195
  Yuriev Monastery 162
Monet, Claude 91
Money 206–7
Money Honey Saloon 197
Mongols 17
Monighetti, Ippolito
  Tsarskoe Selo 150, 152
  Yusupov Palace 120
Monplaisir (Peterhof) 148
Monroe Club 197
Montferrand, Auguste de
  Alexander Column 83
  Bolshaya Morskaya ulitsa mansions 122
  St. Isaac's Cathedral 79, 80, 81
  St. Isaac's Square 79
Montreal Steak 185
Monuments
  Monument to Rimsky-Korsakov 116
  Monument to the Heroic Defenders of Leningrad 41
  Victory Monument 131
Morozov, Ivan 91
Moscow
  traveling between Moscow and St. Petersburg 211
Moscow Station 212, 221
Moskovskiy univermag 191
Moskva 171, 172
Mosque
  Kamennoostrovskiy Prospekt 70
Mosquitoes 205
Most-bank 206
  ATM 206
Mother (Petrov-Vodkin) 104
Movies 195
  Festival of Festivals 51
  film directors 45
  Leningrad Film Studios 70
Moyka River 36
  cruises 218
  A Walk along St. Petersburg's Waterways 134–5
Mstislav, Prince 161
Murillo, Bartolomé Esteban 90
Museums and galleries (general) **38–41**
  admission charges 200
  photography in 203
  St. Petersburg's Best: Palaces and Museums 38–9
  shops in 187
Museums and galleries (individual)
  Academy of Arts 40, **63**
  Anna Akhmatova Museum 41, **129**
  Artillery Museum 41, **70**
  Cabin of Peter the Great 41, **73**
  Cathedral of SS. Peter and Paul 41

Museums and galleries (individual), (cont.)
  Commandant's House 41, 66, **69**
  Cruiser *Aurora* 41, **73**
  Dostoevsky House-Museum 41, **130**
  Engineers' Castle 40, **99**
  Engineer's House 41, 67, **68**
  Hermitage 40, **84–93**
  Institute of Russian Literature 59
  Kirov Museum 41, 72
  Kshesinskaya Mansion 71, 72
  Kunstkammer 41, 58, **60–61**
  Lycée (Tsarskoe Selo) 41
  Marble Palace 40, **94**
  Menshikov Palace 38, 40, **62**
  Museum of Anthropology and Ethnography 41, 61
  Museum of History, Architecture, and Art (Novgorod) 161
  Museum of Hygiene 99
  Museum of Musical Life 41, 129
  Museum of Russian Political History 39, 41, **72**
  Museum of Wooden Architecture (Novgorod) 162
  Naval Museum 41, 59, **60**
  Pushkin House-Museum 41, **113**, 134
  Railroad Museum 41, **123**
  Repino 41, 144
  Russian Museum 40, 94, 98, **104–7**
  Stieglitz Museum 40, **127**
  Stroganov Palace 40, **112**
  Summer Palace 95
  Theater Museum 41, 110
  Trubetskoy Bastion 41, 66, **69**
  Tsarskoe Selo 151
  Winter Palace 92–3
  Zoological Museum 41, 58, **60**
Mushroom gathering 52
Music
  ballet **118**, **194**, 195
  church music **194**, 195
  classical music **194**, 195
  folk music **194**, 195
  Glinka Kapella 112
  live music and nightlife 196–7
  Museum of Musical Life 41, 129
  Musical Encounters in the Northern Palmyra 53
  Musical Spring in St. Petersburg 50
  opera **194**, 195
  Rimsky-Korsakov Conservatory 116, **120**
  Sound Ways Modern Music Festival 53
  Stars of the White Nights Classical Music Festival 51
  street music **194**, 195
  Virtuosi 2000 50
  White Nights Rock Music Festival 51
  White Nights Swing Jazz Festival 51
Musicians 44
Mussorgsky, Modest 44
  concerts 194
  Mariinskiy Theater 119
  opera 194
  tomb of 131
Mussorgsky Theater of Opera and Ballet 101, 195
  Street-by-Street map 98
Myatlev House 79

N

Na Liteynom 191
Nabokov, Vladimir 122
Napoleon I, Emperor 111, 159
  Alexander Column 83
  invasion of Russia 22, 23
  Kamennoostrovskiy Palace 136
Napoleonic Wars 22
Narodniki 23
Naryshkin Bastion
  Street-by-Street map 66
Naryshkin family 18
Nasledie 191
Naval Museum 41, **60**
  Street-by-Street map 59
Navy Day 51
Neff 80
Nelidova, E I
  portrait of 106
Neptune 172
Nesterov, Mikhail 100
Neva, River 36
  bridges 36–7
  cruises 218
Neva Gate 69
  Street-by-Street map 66
Nevskij Palace Hotel 171, 173
Nevskiy 40 185
Nevskiy Prospekt **46–9**, 97, **108**
Nevsky, Alexander
  Alexander Nevsky Monastery 130
  defeats Teutonic Knights 17
  St. Isaac's Cathedral 80, 81
  sarcophagus and memorial 89
  tomb of 130–31
Nevsky Melody 197
New Exchange Bazaar
  Street-by-Street map 59
New Hermitage 84, 135
New Holland 121
New Year's Eve 53
New Zealand Embassy 203
Newspapers 209
Neyelov, Ilya 152
Neyelov, Vasilii 152
Nicholas I, Tsar
  Cottage Palace (Peterhof) 148
  Decembrist Rebellion 23, 78
  Hermitage 84
  St. Isaac's Square 79
  Smolnyy Convent 128
  statue of 77, 79
  Summer Gardens 95
Nicholas II, Tsar 68, 85
  Alexander Palace (Tsarskoe Selo) 153
  Fabergé Easter eggs 82
  and Matilda Kshesinskaya 72
  murder of 29
  Russian Museum 104
  Russian Revolution 26, 28
  Winter Palace 93
Nicholas market
  Street-by-Street map 117
"Nicholas Railroad" 23
Nicolas, Vladimir 120
Nightclubs **196**, 197
Nijinsky, Vaslaw 45
  Ballet in St. Petersburg 118
  Ballets Russes 119
Nik 185
Nikitin, Ivan 106, 151
Nikolaev, Leonid 72
Nikolaevskiy Palace 195

Nikolai Nikolaevich, Grand Duke 121
Nikolay 180
Novgorod 141, **160–62**
  eating out on day trips 184
  restaurants 182
  traveling to 221
Novgorod School 160, 161
  Russian icon painting 163
  Russian Museum 106
Nureyev, Rudolf 45, 110
  Ballet in St. Petersburg 118
Nystad, Peace of (1721) 19

O

Obvodnyy 36
October Concert Hall 195
Okhtinskaya 172
Oktyabrskaya 172
Oktyabrskiy kontsertnyy zal 197
Old Testament Trinity (Rublev) 163
Olgino Motel-Camping 168
Opening hours 200
  bridges 201
  restaurants 175
  shops 186
Opera **194**, 195
Oranienbaum 40, 141, **144–5**
  eating out on day trips 184
  traveling to 220
Orlov, Count Alexey 24
Orlov, Count Grigoriy 108
  Gatchina 145
  Marble Palace 94
  Monplaisir (Peterhof) 148
Orthodox Church *see* Russian Orthodox Church
Osner, Karl 68
Ost-West Kontaktservice
  buying tickets 192
  hotel bookings 166, 168
  tourist information 200, 203
Ostrovsky, Aleksandr 110
Ostrovskiy Square 110
OVIR 202, 203

P

Palace Bridge 36
Palace Embankment 15, 75–95
  area map 75
  Hermitage 84–93
  St. Isaac's Cathedral 80–81
  St. Isaac's Square 76–7
Palace Square 83
Palaces **38–40**
  Alexander Palace (Tsarskoe Selo) 153
  Anichkov Palace 49, **109**, 110
  Beloselskiy-Belozerskiy Palace 49
  Chesma Palace 130
  Cottage Palace (Peterhof) 148
  Kamennoostrovskiy Palace 136
  Marble Palace 94
  Marly Palace (Peterhof) 148
  Menshikov Palace 62
  Mikhailovskiy Palace 98, 104
  Monplaisir (Peterhof) 148
  Oranienbaum 144–5
  Peterhof 146–9
  St. Petersburg's Best: Palaces and Museums 38–9
  Sheremetev Palace 129
  Stroganov Palace 47, **112**, 135
  Summer Palace 95
  Tauride Palace 128
  Tsarskoe Selo 150–53

Palaces (cont.)
  Vorontsov Palace 111
  Winter Palace 92–3
  Yelagin Palace 126, 137
  Yusupov Palace 116, 120
Palitra 191
Parks and gardens (general)
  opening hours 200
Parks and gardens (individual)
  Admiralty Gardens 46
  Aleksandrovskiy Park 70
  Botanical Gardens 136
  Catherine Park (Tsarskoe Selo) 152
  Central Park of Culture and
  Rest 126
  Gatchina 145
  Maritime Victory Park 137
  Oranienbaum 145
  Pavlovsk 156
  Peterhof 146, 148–9
  Summer Gardens 95
  Tauride Palace 128
  Tsarskoe Selo 151, 152
Parland, Alfred 100
Passazh 191
Passazh Arcade 48
Passports 202
Pasta houses 183
Pastries and sweets 177, 184, 185
Patouillard, René 35
Paul I, Tsar
  assassination 22
  and Carlo Rossi 110
  Engineers' Castle 99, 101
  Gatchina 141, 145
  Kazan Cathedral 111
  Mausoleum (Pavlovsk) 157
  Neptune Fountain (Peterhof) 149
  Pavlovsk 156, 158, 159
  Pavlovskiy Guards 94
  Tauride Palace 128
Pavlov, Ivan 45, 61
Pavlova, Anna 42, 45
  Ballet in St Petersburg 118
  Ballets Russes 119
  Imperial School of Ballet 110
Pavlovsk 40, 141, 156–9
  eating out on day trips 184
  floor plan 158
  private apartments 159
  St. Petersburg's Best: Palaces and
  Museums 38
  southern wing 159
  state rooms 158–9
  traveling to 220
  Visitors' Checklist 157
  World War II 27
Pel, Aleksandr 122
"People's Will" group 26, 135
Peredvizhniki see Wanderers
Perestroika (restructuring) 30
Peretyatkovich, Marian 46
Perov, Vasiliy 107
  A Meal in the Monastery 105
Personal safety 204
Peter II, Tsar 19, 68
Peter III, Tsar 19
  assassination 22
  Oranienbaum 144
  Pugachev Pretender 24
Peter and Paul Fortress
  history 18
  Street-by-Street map 66–7
Peter Gate 68
  Street-by-Street map 67

Peter the Great, Tsar 18–19, 20–21,
106, 107, 161
  Academy of Sciences Library 59
  Admiralty 78
  Alexander Nevsky Monastery
  130–31
  Apothecary's Island 136
  Bronze Horseman (Falconet) 75,
  76, 78–9
  Cabin of Peter the Great 41, 73
  canals 36
  Cathedral of SS. Peter and Paul 68
  City Day 50
  Hermitage 88, 89
  Kunstkammer 58, 60–61
  Marly Palace (Peterhof) 148
  Menshikov Palace 62
  Monplaisir (Peterhof) 148
  navy 60
  New Holland 121
  oak tree 136
  Peter Gate 68
  Peterhof 146–9
  portrait by Nikitin 151
  portrait by Weenix 62
  Preobrazhenskiy Life-Guards 134
  statues of 67, 99
  Streltsy Rebellion 20
  Summer Gardens 95
  Summer Palace 39, 40, 95
  tomb of 69
  Tsarskoe Selo 151
  Twelve Colleges 61
  Vasilevskiy Island 57
  vodka 178
  Winter Palace 92
Peter the Great Bridge 37
Peterburg Antikvariat 191
Peterhof 40, 141, 146–9
  Cottage Palace 148
  eating out on day trips 184
  fountains 149
  The Hermitage 148
  Marly Palace 148
  Monplaisir 148
  St. Petersburg's Best: Palaces and
  Museums 38
  traveling to 220
  Visitors' Checklist 147
Petipa, Marius 45
  Ballet in St. Petersburg 118
  tomb of 131
Petrashevtsy Circle 123
Petrodvorets Sanatorium 168
Petrogradskaya 15, 65–73
  area map 65
  Peter and Paul Fortress 66–7
  Style Moderne in St. Petersburg 71
Petrov-Vodkin, Kuzma
  Mother 104
Petrovskiy Stadium 137
Pharmacies 205
Philharmonia, Great (Shostakovich
Hall) 43, 99, 194, 195
Philharmonia, Small (Glinka Hall) 48,
194, 195
Photography 203
Picasso, Pablo
  Hermitage 91
  L'Homme aux Bras Croisés 91
  Marble Palace 94
  Russian Museum 107
Pimenov, Nikolay 80
Pimenov, Stepan 83, 110
Pineau, Nicholas 146

Piramid 197
Pirosmani 181
Piskarevskoe Memorial
Cemetery 126
Pissarro, Camille 91
Pizza House 185
Pizza houses 183
Pizza Hut 185
Pizza Pronto 185
Planeta 191
Podvorye 185
Polenov, Vasiliy 107
Police 204–5
Police Bridge 135
Political prisoners 69
Polovtsov, Aleksandr
  Bolshaya Morskaya ulitsa
  mansion 122
  Kameniy Island mansion 137
  Stieglitz Museum 127
Poltava, Battle of (1709) 19, 21
Polygon 197
Popov, Aleksandr 45
Port Club 197
Portik Ruska 48
Portrait of E I Nelidova
  (Levitskiy) 106
Portrait of Sergey Diaghilev
  (Bakst) 104
Portrait of the Director Vsevolod
  Meyerhold (Grigoriev) 107
Post International 209
Post Office No. 11 209
Postal services 208–9
  Main Post Office 122
Postels, Fyodor von 71
Potemkin, Prince Grigoriy 25
  Anichkov Palace 109
  Peacock Clock 85
  Tauride Palace 128
Potemkin, Pyotr 91
Poussin, Nicolas 90
"Prague Spring" 30
Premier 197
Preobrazhenskiy Life-Guards 134
Pribaltiyskaya 170, 173
Priboy 185
Prima 191
Prince Lobanov-Rostovskiy Mansion
  Street-by-Street map 77
Prisoners, political 69
Progal 168
Progressive Tours 203, 212
Prokofiev, Sergey
  opera 194
  Rimsky-Korsakov Conservatory
  116, 120
Promstroybank 206
PTS card-operated phones 208
Public holidays 53
Public toilets 203
Pubs 184, 185
Pugachev Rebellion (1773–5) 22, 24
Pulkovo 212
Pulkovskaya 171, 172
Puppet theaters 193
Pushkin (town) see Tsarskoe Selo
Pushkin, Alexander 43, 44
  The Bronze Horseman 23, 37,
  69, 78
  death 83
  Fountain at Tsarskoe Selo 152
  funeral 113
  Literary Café 46, 83
  Lycée (Tsarskoe Selo) 41

Pushkin, Alexander (cont.)
Pushkin House-Museum 39,
   113, 134
Repin's portrait of 144
statues of 101, 153
Tsarskoe Selo 153
Pushkin, Natalya *see* Goncharova,
   Natalya
Pushkin House-Museum 41, **113**, 134
St. Petersburg's Best: Palaces and
   Museums 39
Pushkin's Dacha (Tsarskoe Selo) 153

Q

Quarenghi, Giacomo
Academy of Sciences 25, 58
Alexander Palace (Tsarskoe
   Selo) 153
Anichkov Palace 109
English Quay buildings 121
grave of 131
Hermitage 84
Horseguards' Manège 76, 79
New Exchange Bazaar 59
Round Market 134
Smolnyy Institute 128
Tsarskoe Selo 152
Quarenghi's Stalls 49

R

RADAR 203
Radio 209
Railway Museum 41, **123**
Railroads *see* Trains
Rainfall 52
Raphael 63, 84, 90, 130
Rapsodiya 191
Rasputin, Grigoriy 26
Chesma Palace 130
death 40, 72, **121**
Yusupov Palace 116, 120
Rastrelli, Bartolomeo 19, **93**
Anichkov Palace 109
Catherine Palace (Tsarskoe
   Selo) 38
Smolnyy Convent 128
Monplaisir (Peterhof) 148
Peterhof 146, 147
Stroganov Palace 112
Tsarskoe Selo 150, 152
Vorontsov Palace 111
Winter Palace 85, 92
Rastrelli, Bartolomeo Carlo
bust of Peter the Great 89
Gostinyy Dvor 108–9
statue of Peter the Great 101
Razumovskiy, Aleksey 49, 109
Red Bridge 37
Red Guard 28
Reed, John 79
Registration of foreigners 202
Rembrandt 90
   Abraham's Sacrifice 86
Renoir, Pierre Auguste 91
Renting cars 221
Repin, Ilya 42, 45, 106–7
Academy of Arts 63
   Barge-Haulers on the Volga 105
   dacha 141
grave of 144
   Portrait of Mikhail Glinka 44
Repino 41, **144**
Repino 41, 144
eating out on day trips 184
traveling to 221

Restaurants **174–85**
children in 175
disabled travelers 175
Novgorod 182
opening times 175
payment and tipping 174–5
reading the menu 174
reservations 175
smoking in 175
types of restaurant 174
vegetarian food 175
What to Eat in St. Petersburg 176–7
where to eat 174
Revolution (1905) 26
Palace Square 83
Trinity Square 73
Revolution (1917) 26, **28–9**
Cruiser *Aurora* 73
Finland Station 126
Kshesinskaya Mansion 72
Smolnyy Institute 128
Trinity Bridge 37
Reynolds, Sir Joshua 91
Rezanov, Aleksandr 94
Ribera, José de 90
Rimsky-Korsakov, Nikolai 44
concerts 194
Glinka Kapella 112
Monument to Rimsky-Korsakov 116
Rimsky-Korsakov Conservatory 120
tomb of 131
Rimsky-Korsakov Conservatory **120**
ballet and opera 195
Street-by-Street map 116
Rinaldi, Antonio
Chesma Column (Tsarskoe
   Selo) 152
Marble Palace 94
Oranienbaum 144
River Terminal 212
Rivers 36
cruises 218–19
A Walk along St. Petersburg's
   Waterways 134–5
Robert, Hubert 159
Rock music **196**, 197
White Nights Rock Music
   Festival 51
Rodchenko, Alexander 107
Romanov dynasty 94
beginning of 17
end of 27, 28
Rose Pub 185, 197
Rossi, Carlo **110**
Anichkov Palace 109
Arts Square 98, 101
Decembrists' Square 78
General Staff Building 83, 135
grave of 131
Mikhailovsky Palace 39, 98, 104, 105
Ostrovskiy Square 110
Palace Square 83
Russian Library 110
Senate building 76, 78
Synod building 76, 78
ulitsa Zodchevo Rossi 110
Yelagin Palace 126, 136–7
Rostral Columns **60**
City day 50
Street-by-Street map 59
Round Market 134
Rowley, Master John 89
Rubens, Peter Paul 90, 130
   *The Marriage of Emperor
   Constantine* 93

Rubinstein, Anton 44
Rimsky-Korsakov Conservatory
   116, 120
Rublev, Andrey 162
   Old Testament Trinity 163
Russian Museum 106
Rudnev, Lev 94
Rumyantsev, Nikolai 121
Rurik, Prince 17
Novgorod 160, 161
Rus 172
Rusca, Luigi 48
Russian Federation
map 10–11
Russian Museum 40, **104–7**
floor plan 104–5
folk art 107
icons 106
Marble Palace 94
St. Petersburg's Best: Palaces and
   Museums 39
1700–1860 (art dating from) 106
Street-by-Street map 98
20th-century art 107
Visitors' Checklist 105
The Wanderers and Fin de
   Siècle 106–7
Russian National Library 48, 186
Russian Orthodox Church
Christmas 53
Easter Sunday 50, 53
history 17
Iconostasis 163
music 194
Russian icon painting 163
visiting churches 200–201
Russian Revolution *see* Revolution
   (1917)
Russkiye Bliny 185
Russo-Japanese War (1904–5) 26
Russo-Turkish Wars 22
Ruysch, Frederik 60–61
Ryba 191

S

Saburov, Pyotr 88
Safety 204–5
St. Andrew's Cathedral 63
St. Isaac's Cathedral 23, 75, **80–81**
Street-by-Street map 76
St. Isaac's Square 79
Street-by-Street map 76–7
St. Nicholas' Cathedral 115, **120**
Belfry 117, 120
Street-by-Street map 117
St. Nicholas Cathedral (Novgorod) 161
St. Panteleymon's Bridge 37
Street-by-Street map 99
St. Paraskeva Pyatnitsa (Novgorod) 161
St. Petersburg (hotel) 171, 173
St. Petersburg Academy of Arts 19
St. Petersburg Bed and Breakfast 168
St. Petersburg International Hostel 168
St. Petersburg University
Twelve Colleges 58, **61**
St. Sophia's Belfry (Novgorod) 160
Sakharov, Andrei 30, 31
SALT talks 30
Samotsvety 191
Samovars 179
SAS 212
Schädel, Gottfried 62, 144
Schlüsselburg Fortress 69
Schlüter, Andreas 95, 151
Schmidt, Karl 82

Schöne, Vasiliy 137
School No. 210 46
Schröter, Viktor 119
Scientists 45
Scott's Tours 203, 212
"Secret House" 66, 69
Security 204–5
    in hotels 167
Sekunda 191
Senat Bar 181
Sennaya Ploshchad 15, **115–23**
    area map 115
    Ballet in St. Petersburg 118
    market 191
    Theater Square 116–17
Serov, Vasiliy 161
Severnaya Lira 191
Shakespeare, William 42, 113
Shakherezade 185
Shalyapin, Fyodor 41
    Opera House 70
    Repin's portrait of 144
    Theater Museum 110
Shamrock 197
Shchedrin, Silvestr 45, 106
Shchukin, Sergey 91
Shebuev, Vasiliy 63
Sheremetev, Field Marshal Boris 129
Sheremetev family
    Museum of Musical Life 41
    Sheremetev Palace 129
Sheremetev Palace 125, 129
Shmidt, Lieutenant Pyotr
    Lieutenant Shmidt Bridge 37, 63
Shopping **186–91**
    art and antiques 186–7, 190
    bargaining etiquette 186
    books 190
    department stores **187**, 191
    fashion and accessories 190
    how to pay 186
    markets and bazaars 187, 191
    museum shops 187
    opening hours 186
    souvenirs and crafts 190
    Soviet memorabilia 190
    vodka and caviar 190
    What to Buy in St. Petersburg 188–9
Shostakovich, Dmitriy 43, 44
    concerts 194
    film music 45
    Mariinskiy Theater 119
    Rimsky-Korsakov Conservatory
        116, 120
    Seventh Symphony 27
    Victory Monument 131
Shubin, Fedot 130, 149
Shustov, Smaragd 136
Shwabski Domik 185
Siege of Leningrad (1941–4) 27
    Hermitage 85
    Monument to the Heroic Defenders
        of Leningrad 41
    Piskarevskoe Memorial
        Cemetery 126
    Victory Monument 131
"Silver Age," poetry 44, 129
Sindbad Travel 203
Singers' Bridge 37, 112, 135
Sisley, Alfred 91
The Six-Winged Seraph (Vrubel) 107
Skating 53
Skazka 185
Skiing 53
SKK 197

Sladoyezhka 185
Slavs 17
Sledges 53
Small Hall of the Philharmonia see
    Philharmonia, Small
Small Stables Bridge 134
Smoking 201
    in restaurants 175
Smolnyy Cathedral 195
Smolnyy Convent 128
Smolnyy district 125
Smolnyy Institute 128–9
Snack Bar Casa de Don Quixote 185
Snow 52
Sobchak, Anatoly 31
Social-Democratic Workers party 26
Socialist Realism 27
Sokolov, Pavel 34
    Girl with a Pitcher 152
Solti, Sir Georg 194
Solzhenitsyn, Alexander 30
Sophia, Regent 18
Sound Ways Modern Music
    Festival 52
Souvenir shops 190
Souvenirs (market) 191
Soviet memorabilia 190
Sovietskaya 170, 173
Soyuz Khudozhnikov 191
Space race 30
Spanish food **184**, 185
Spartak Cinema 195
Speranskiy, Sergey 131
Sphinx 57
Spring in St. Petersburg 50
Sputnik 30
SS. Peter and Paul Cathedral see
    Cathedral of SS. Peter and Paul
Stakenschneider, Andrey
    Beloselskiy-Belozerskiy Palace 49
    English Quay 121
    Millionaires' Street 94
    Pavilion Hall (Hermitage) 85
Stalin, Joseph 119, 125
    assassination of Kirov 41, 72
    dictatorship 27
    Khrushchev denounces 30
    metro stations 214
    purges 27, 72, 129
Staraya Derevnya 182
Staraya Kniga 191
Staraya Tamozhnya 180
Staroe Kafe 185
Starov, Ivan
    Tauride Palace 128
    Trinity Cathedral 130
Stars of the White Nights Classical
    Music Festival 51
Stasov, Vasiliy
    Cathedral of the Transfiguration 127
    Imperial Stables 113
    Literary Café 83
    Pavlovskiy Guards barracks 94
    Smolnyy Convent 128
Stieglitz, Baron Aleksandr 127
Stieglitz Museum 40, **127**
    St. Petersburg's Best: Palaces and
        Museums 39
Still Life with the Attributes of the
    Arts (Chardin) 91
Stone Bridge 135
La Strada 185
Stravinsky, Igor 44
    Ballets Russes 119
Street music **194**, 195

Strelka
    Street-by-Street map 58–9
Streltsy Guards 18, 20
Streltsy Rebellion (1682) 18, **20**
Stroganov, Count Sergey 112
Stroganov Palace 40, 47, 112
    A Walk along St. Petersburg's
        Waterways 135
Student travelers 202, 203
Style Moderne 65, **71**
    Kamennoostrovskiy prospekt 70
    Kshesinskaya Mansion 72
    Yeliseev's 109
Suburban trains 220–21
Summer Gardens 95
Summer in St. Petersburg 51
Summer Palace 40, **95**
    St. Petersburg's Best: Palaces and
        Museums 39
Sunshine 51
Suprematism 107
Supremus No. 56 (Malevich) 29
Surikov, Vasiliy 107
Svir 182
Swan Canal 36
    St. Petersburg's Best: Bridges and
        Waterways 35
Swimming 53
Symbolists 107
Syuzor, Pavel 47, 71

T

Tamanskiy, Pyotr 70
Tandoor 180
Tatlin, Vladimir 79
Tatyana Parfyonova Modnyy Dom 191
Tauride Palace 128
Taurit, Robert 126
Taxis 193, **219**
    airport 211
Tbilisi (café) 185
Tchaikovsky, Pyotr 42, 44, 49
    concerts 194
    death 82
    Mariinskiy Theater 119
    opera 194
    Pathétique symphony 101
    Rimsky-Korsakov Conservatory
        116, 120
    tomb of 131
Tea 178, **179**
Teachers' Day 52
Telegraph 209
Telephones **208**, 209
    in hotels 167
Television 209
Telex 209
Temperatures 53
Terborch, Gerard 90
Tertsiya 191
Teutonic Knights 17
Theater **194–5**
    Kamennoostrovskiy Theater 136
    Theater Festival of the Baltic
        Countries 52
    Theater Museum 41, 110
Theater Bridge 37, 134
Theater Square
    Street-by-Street map 116–17
Theophanes the Greek 162
Thirty Years War 149
Thomon, Thomas de
    grave of 131
    Naval Museum 60
    Rostral Columns 60

Tickets
  entertainments 192
  kiosks 193
  metro 215
  travel 217
Tikhvin Cemetery 131
Tilsit, Peace of (1807) 22
Time of Troubles (1605–13) 17
Time zones 203
Tipping 201
  in restaurants 175
Titian 63, 90
TNT Express Worldwide 209
Toasts 201
Toilets 203
Tolstoy, Leo
  War and Peace 23, 111, 121
Torelli, Stefano 94
Tourist information 200, 203
Trains 212
  Railroad Museum 41, **123**
  suburban trains 220–21
  traveling between Moscow and
    St. Petersburg 211
  traveling to St. Petersburg 211
Traitteur, Georg von
  Bank Bridge 37, 135
  Lion Bridge 37
  Small Stable Bridge 35
  Theater Bridge 35
Trams 216
Transaero 212
Trapeza 185
Trauberg, Leonid 45, 70
Trauma Clinic of the Central
  District 205
Travel **210–19**
  air 210–11, 212
  buses and minibuses 212, 216–17
  canal and river cruises 218–19
  cars 221
  ferries and cruises 212
  hydrofoils 221
  insurance 204
  late night travel 193
  Metro 214–15
  St. Petersburg's surroundings 142
  taxis 193, 219
  trains 211, 212
  trams 216
  traveling out of St. Petersburg
    220–21
  trolleybuses 217
  walking 213
  water taxis 219
Travel cards 217
Traveler's checks 204, 207
Trezzini, Domenico
  Cathedral of SS. Peter and
    Paul 68
  Church of the Annunciation 130
  Peter and Paul Fortress 66
  Peter Gate 67, 68
  Summer Palace 95
  Twelve Colleges 61
Trezzini, Giuseppe
  Church of the Three Saints 63
Tribunal 197
Trinity Bridge 37, 65
  St. Petersburg's Best: Bridges and
    Waterways 35
Trinity Cathedral 130
Trinity Square 73
Trinity Sunday 51
Triscomi, Paolo 77

The Triumph of Russia (Valeriani) 150
Trolleybuses 217
Trotsky, Leon 27
  Civil War 123
  imprisonment 69
  murder 29
  Russian Revolution 28, 29
Trubetskoy, Prince Pavel 94
Trubetskoy Basin 69
Trubetskoy Bastion 41
  Street-by-Street map 66
Tsarskoe Selo 40, 141, 150–53
  Autumn in Tsarskoe Selo 52
  Catherine Park 152
  eating out on day trips 184
  map 153
  St. Petersburg's Best: Palaces and
    Museums 38
  Town of Tsarskoe Selo 153
  traveling to 220
  Tsarskoe Selo Park 153
  Visitors' Checklist 151
Tsarskoe Selo (café) 185
Turkish Bath (Tsarskoe Selo) 152
Twelve Colleges 61
  Street-by-Street map 58
TYuZ 193

U

UK Embassy 203
Ulitsa Zodchevo Rossi 110
US Embassy 203

V

Vaccinations 205
Vaganova, Agrippina 45
  Ballet in St. Petersburg 118
  Vaganova Ballet School 110
Valeriani, Giuseppe
  The Triumph of Russia 150
Van Dyck, Anthony 90, 130
Van Gogh, Vincent 91
Vasilevsky Island 14, **57–63**
  area map 57
  Strelka 58–9
Vasiliev, Aleksandr 126
Vasnetsov, Viktor 107
  Church on Spilled Blood
    mosaics 100
  Knight at the Crossroads 106, 107
Vegetarian food 175
Velázquez, Diego de Silva y 90
Velten, Yuriy
  Armenian Church 48, 108
  Chesma Church 130
  Chesma Palace 130
  Church of St. John the Baptist
    136
  Creaking Pavilion (Tsarskoe
    Selo) 152
  Hermitage Theater 34
  Large Hermitage 84
  Peterhof 147
  Small Hermitage 85
  Summer Gardens 95
Venice (casino) 197
Venus and Cupid (Cranach) 90
Vereshchagin, Nikolay 89
Vernisazh 191
Victory Day 50, 53
Victory Monument 131
Vienna (restaurant) 180
Vienna Café 185
Virgin in Majesty (Bryullov) 81
Virtuosi 2000 50

Visas 202, 203
  rail travel 211
Vist, Aleksandr 63
Vitali, Ivan 80, 81
Vitebsk Station 212, 221
Vladimir, Grand Prince 17
Vladimir Aleksandrovich, Grand
  Duke 94
Vladimir Kirilovich, Grand Duke
  tomb of 67, 69
Vodka **178**
  buying 190
Volkhov, River 160
Volleyball by the Fortress 51
Voltaire 22, 113
  correspondence with Catherine
    the Great 24
  library of 110
  statue of 87
Voronikhin, Andrey
  Academy of Arts 63
  Centaur Bridge (Pavlovsk) 156
  grave of 131
  Kazan Cathedral 47, 111
  Pavlovsk 158, 159
  Visconti Bridge (Pavlovsk) 157
Vorontsov, Prince Mikhail 111
Vorontsov Palace 111
Voyages Jules Verne 212
Vrubel, Mikhail 107
  The Six-Winged Seraph 107
Vsevolod, Prince 162

W

Walks in St. Petersburg **133–7**, 213
  A Walk along St. Petersburg's
    Waterways 134–5
  A Walk around Kamenniy and
    Yelagin Islands 136–7
Wanderers *(Peredvizhniki)* 45, 63,
  106–7
Warhol, Andy 94
Warsaw Pact 30
Warsaw Station 212, 221
Water
  health precautions 205
Water taxis 219
Waterways 34–7
  St. Petersburg's Best: Bridges and
    Waterways 34–5
  A Walk along St. Petersburg's
    Waterways 134–5
Watteau, Antoine 90–91
Weather 50–53
Wedgwood, Josiah
  Green Frog Service 91, 130
Weenix, Jan 62
Westpost 209
Weyden, Rogier van der 90
Wheelchair access *see* Disabled
  travelers
White Nights festivals **51**, 193
White Nights Rock Music Festival 51
White Nights Swing Jazz Festival 51
White Russians 27
Wine 179
Winter Canal 36
  St. Petersburg's Best: Bridges and
    Waterways 34
  A Walk along St. Petersburg's
    Waterways 134
Winter Garden 180–81
Winter in St. Petersburg 53
Winter Palace 40, 85, 87, **92–3**
  storming of 28–9

Witte, Count Sergey 70
Women, safety 204
Wooden Pub 185
"World of Art" movement **26**, 45, 107
World War I 26–7
World War II 27
　　Monument to the Heroic Defenders of Leningrad 41
　　Victory Day 50
　　Victory Monument 131
　　see also Siege of Leningrad
Wright of Derby, Joseph 91
Writers 44

Y

Yaroslav the Wise 161
Yaroslav's Court (Novgorod) 161
Yefimov, Nikolay 77

Yegorov, Pyotr 95
Yelagin Island
　　A Walk around Kamenniy and Yelagin Islands 136–7
Yelagin Palace 40, **126**
　　A Walk around Kamenniy and Yelagin Islands 137
Yeliseev, Pyotr 109
Yeliseev's 49, **109**, 191
　　Style Moderne in St. Petersburg 71
Yeltsin, Boris 30, 31
　　Constitution Day 53
Yesenin, Sergey 79
A Young Man Playing a Lute (Caravaggio) 90
Yubileynyy dvorets sporta 197
Yuriev Monastery 162
Yusupov, Prince Felix 111, 121
Yusupov family 116, 120

Yusupov Palace 40, **120**
　　Street-by-Street map 116
Yusupov Theater 195

Z

Zakharov, Andrey
　　Academy of Arts 63
　　Admiralty 78
　　grave of 131
Zarudnyy, Ivan 67, 68
Zazerkalye 193
Zeck, Johann 159
Zhivago 80
Znamenskiy Cathedral (Novgorod) 162
Zoological Museum 41, 60
　　Street-by-Street map 58
Zurbarán, Francisco 90
Zverkov House 135

Acknowledgments

DORLING KINDERSLEY would like to thank the following people whose contributions and assistance have made the preparation of this book possible.

MAIN CONTRIBUTORS

CHRISTOPHER RICE holds a PhD in Russian history from the University of Birmingham. He and his wife, Melanie, also a writer, first visited Russia in 1978 and have been returning regularly ever since. Together they have written numerous travel guides to the city and to a variety of other destinations, including Prague, Berlin, and Istanbul, as well as the *Eyewitness Travel Guide to Moscow.*

CATHERINE PHILLIPS is an art historian who arrived in Russia in 1985 and has lived there ever since, moving to St. Petersburg in 1989. She covered major events for British and American TV and radio during the early years of *perestroika* and authored and contributed to some of the first guides to the new Russia. Today she concentrates on translating and editing scholarly texts and writing for works of reference.

ADDITIONAL CONTRIBUTOR

ROSE BARING began to study Russian at the age of 12. She has an MA in Modern History and divided her time between London, Moscow, and St. Petersburg for much of the early 1990s. She has written guides to St. Petersburg, Moscow, and other destinations, including the *Eyewitness Travel Guide to Istanbul.*

SPECIAL ASSISTANCE

DORLING KINDERSLEY would like to thank Ian Wizniewski (food and drink consultant), Valera Katsuba (photo permissions), Marina Maydanyuk (researcher), Oleksiy Nesnov (language consultant), Victoria Rachevskaya (language consultant), Yuliya Motovilova of the St. Petersburg Tourist Company and the staff of Peter TIPS, and Sylvain Borsi at Nikita's restaurant, London, for preparing the food for *What to Eat in St. Peterburg.*

PROOFREADER

Stewart J Wild.

INDEXER

Hilary Bird.

DESIGN AND EDITORIAL ASSISTANCE

Liz Atherton, Laurence Broers, Dawn Davies-Cook, Claire Folkard, Freddy Hamilton, Paul Hines, Leanne Hogbin, Adam Moore, Fiona Morgan, Jane Oliver, Marianne Petrou, Luke Rozkowski, Alison Stace, P. Todd-Naylor, Ingrid Vienings, Veronica Wood.

ADDITIONAL ILLUSTRATIONS

Claire Littlejohn, John Woodcock.

ADDITIONAL PHOTOGRAPHY

Victoria Buyvid, Andy Crawford, Erich Crichton, Neil Fletcher, Steve Gorton, Paul Miller, Ian O'Leary, Clive Streeter.

PHOTOGRAPHY PERMISSIONS

THE PUBLISHER would like to thank all those who gave permission to photograph at their establishments, including museums, palaces, cathedrals, churches, restaurants, hotels, shops and other sights, too numerous to thank individually.

PICTURE CREDITS

t = top; tl = top left; tlc = top left center; tc = top center; trc = top right center; tr = top right; cla = center left above; ca = center above; cra = center right above; cl = center left; c = center; cr = center right; clb = center right below; cb = center below; crb = center right below; bl = bottom left; b = bottom; bc = bottom center; bcl = bottom center left; br = bottom right; d = detail.

The publisher would like to thank the following individuals, companies and picture libraries for their kind permission to reproduce their photographs:

AISA, Barcelona: 18t, 44t, 55 (insert), 106tr; AKG, London: 16, 17t, 20bl/cl, 20–21cl, 25tl, 26cl, 27c, 28br, Erich Lessing 28bl, 29c, 37b, 42cl/bl/br, 43br; ANCIENT ART & ARCHITECTURE COLLECTION: 45cr; APA: Jim Holmes 93tl; AXIOM: Jim Holmes 151b.

VALENTIN BARANOVSKY: 84bl, 85tl, 193t; IAN BAVINGTON-JONES: 130t; YURI BELINSKY: 31t; BRIDGEMAN ART LIBRARY, London/New York: 151c; Forbes Magazine Collection 28–9c; State Hermitage, St. Petersburg 21cb, 24–5c, 25cl, 86t/b, 87t/b, 88b, 89tr/b, 90t/b, 91t/c, *La Danse,* Henri Matisse (1910) @ Succession Henri Matisse/DACS 1998 87c; Private Collection *20th Century Propaganda Poster 1920,* D Moor @ DACS 1998 29tr; State Russian Museum, St. Petersburg *The Cyclist,* Natalya Goncharova (1913) @ ADAGP, Paris and DACS, London 1998 40b; Tretyakov Gallery, Moscow 19t, *The Circus,* Marc Chagall, 1919 @ ADAGP, Paris and DACS, London 1998 45tl.

CAMERA PRESS: Roxana Artacho 85bl; DEMETRIO CARRASCO: 2–3, 6b, 15b, 36t, 53bl, 76ca, 80bl, 93cr/br, 102–103; CENTRAL STATE ARCHIVE OF PHOTOGRAPHS AND FILM DOCUMENTS, ST. PETERSBURG: 42t, 72c, 110c, 118bl; JEAN-LOUP CHARMET: 23t; CHRISTIE'S IMAGES: 82b; CORBIS: Dean Conger 52tr; E. O Hoppe/Bettmann 118cr; Bob Krist 193b; Library of Congress 28tl; Michael Nicholson 150t; Gianni Dagli Orti 8–9, 119bl; Steve Raymer 31crb, 118br; State Hermitage, St. Petersburg 24bl; State Russian Museum 25bl.

E T ARCHIVE: Bibliotheque Nationale, Paris 17cl; Hermitage, St. Petersburg 88t, 89tl; MARY EVANS PICTURE LIBRARY: 9 (insert), 19b, 21br, 22c, 23c, 24cl/br, 25br, 26t, 29br, 62b, 139 (insert), 159bl, 199 (insert).

GIRAUDON: State Russian Museum 43cr, 105cr; Tretyakov Gallery, Moscow 163cr. ROBERT HARDING PICTURE LIBRARY: 84br;

MICHAEL HOLFORD: 18c, 19c, 21bl; HULTON GETTY: 43tr, 118cl, 121c, 178tr;

INTERIOR ARCHIVE: Fritz von der Schulenburg 159c.

KATZ PICTURES: 165 (insert); KEA PUBLISHING SERVICES: Francesco Venturi 92 (all three); DAVID KING COLLECTION: 29tl, 30t, 45b, 69b, 129c.

PAUL MILLER: 51cr.

NOVOSTI (London): 20br, 21tl, 26b, 27t, 30cl, 31c, 43tl, 50c, 51b, 78b, 163t/l.

ORONOZ, Madrid: 22t, 43bl.

PICTOR INTERNATIONAL: 81t; PLODIMEX AUSSENHANDELS GMBH, Hamburg: 178cr/bl.

NATASHA RAZINA: 150b, 151t; REX FEATURES: V. Sichov/SIPA Press 30cr; ELLEN ROONEY: 53t, 79t, 83b, 138–9.

GREGOR M SCHMID: 50br; SCIENCE PHOTO LIBRARY: CNES, 1989 Distribution Spot Image 11cr; STATE RUSSIAN MUSEUM: 7cr; *Blue Crest,* Wassily Kandinsky (1917) @ ADAGP, Paris and DACS, London 1998 39br, 93tr, 104cl /bl/br, 105tl/br, 106tl/b, 107 (all 3), 110b.

TRAVEL LIBRARY: Stuart Black 85br.

VISUAL ARTS LIBRARY: 44b; State Hermitage, St. Petersburg *L'Homme aux bras croisés,* Pablo Picasso (1905) @ Succession Picasso/DACS 1998 91b; 123c.

Jacket: all special photography except GREGOR M SCHMID: front cover center.

Phrase Book

I N THIS GUIDE THE RUSSIAN LANGUAGE has been transliterated into Roman script following a consistent system used by the US Board on Geographic Names. All street and place names, and the names of most people, are transliterated according to this system. For some names, where a well-known English form exists, this has been used – hence, Leo (not Lev) Tolstoy.

In particular, the names of Russian rulers, such as Peter the Great, are given in their anglicized forms. Throughout the book, transliterated names can be taken as an accurate guide to pronunciation. The Phrase Book also gives a phonetic guide to the pronunciation of words and phrases used in everyday situations, such as when eating out or shopping.

GUIDELINES FOR PRONUNCIATION

The Cyrillic alphabet has 33 letters, of which only five (а, к, м, о, т) correspond exactly to their counterparts in English. Russian has two pronunciations (hard and soft) of each of its vowels and several consonants without an equivalent.

The right-hand column of the alphabet, below, demonstrates how Cyrillic letters are pronounced by comparing them to sounds in English words. However, some letters vary in how they are pronounced according to their position in a word. Important exceptions are also noted below.

On the following pages, the English is given in the left-hand column, with the Russian and its transliteration in the middle column. The right-hand column provides a literal system of pronunciation and indicates the stressed syllable in bold. The exception is in the *Menu Decoder* section, where the Russian is given in the left-hand column and the English translation on the right-hand column, for easy use. Because of the existence of genders in Russian, in a few cases both masculine and feminine forms of a phrase are given.

THE CYRILLIC ALPHABET

А а	a	**a**limony
Б б	b	**b**ed
В в	v	**v**et
Г г	g	**g**et (see note 1)
Д д	d	**d**ebt
Е е	e	**ye**t (see note 2)
Ё ё	e	**yo**nder
Ж ж	zh	lei**s**ure (but a little harder)
З з	z	**z**ither
И и	i	**s**ee
Й й	y	**b**oy (see note 3)
К к	k	**k**ing
Л л	l	**l**oot
М м	m	**m**atch
Н н	n	**n**ever
О о	o	r**o**b (see note 4)
П п	p	**p**ea
Р р	r	**r**at (rolling, as in Italian)
С с	s	**s**top
Т т	t	**t**offee
У у	u	b**oo**t
Ф ф	f	**f**ellow
Х х	kh	**kh** (like loch)
Ц ц	ts	le**ts**
Ч ч	ch	**ch**in
Ш ш	sh	**sh**ove
Щ щ	shch	fre**sh sh**eet (as above but with a slight roll)
ъ		hard sign (no sound, but see note 5)
Ы ы	y	l**i**d
ь		soft sign (no sound, but see note 5)
Э э	e	**e**gg
Ю ю	yu	**you**th
Я я	ya	**ya**k

Notes

1) Г Pronounced as *v* in endings -oro and -ero.
2) Е Always pronounced *ye* at the beginning of a word, but in the middle of a word sometimes less distinctly (more like *e*).
3) Й This letter has no distinct sound of its own. It usually lengthens the preceeding vowel.
4) О When not stressed it is pronounced like *a* in *a*cross.
5) ъ, ь The hard sign (ъ) is rare and indicates a very brief pause before the next letter. The soft sign (ь), marked in the pronunciation guide as ') softens the preceeding consonant and adds a slight *y* sound: for instance, *n'* would sound like *ny* in 'ca**ny**on.'

IN AN EMERGENCY

Help!	Помогите! *Pomogite!*	pama**geet**-ye!
Stop!	Стоп! *Stop!*	stop!
Leave me alone!	Оставьте меня в покое! *Ostavte menya v pokoe!*	as**tavt'**-ye myen**ya** v pak**oye**!
Call a doctor!	Позовите врача! *Pozovite vracha!*	paza**veet**-ye vra**cha**!
Call an ambulance!	Вызовите скорую помощь! *Vyzovite skoruyu pomoshch!*	viza**veet**-ye **skoru**-yu **pomash**!
Fire!	Пожар! *Pozhar!*	pa**zhar**!
Call the fire brigade!	Вызовите пожарных! *Vyzovite pozharnykh!*	viza**veet**-ye pa**zhar**nikh!
Police!	Милиция! *Militsiya!*	mee**leet**see-ya!
Where is the nearest...	Где ближайший... *Gde blizhayshiy...*	gdye bleezh**ay**sheey...
...telephone?	...телефон? *...telefon?*	...tye**lyefon**?
...hospital?	...больница? *...bolnitsa?*	...bal'**neet**sa?
...police station?	...отделение милиции? *...otdelenie militsii?*	...atdye**lyenye** mee**leet**see-ee?

COMMUNICATION ESSENTIALS

Yes	Да *Da*	da
No	Нет *Net*	nyet
Please	Пожалуйста *Pozhaluysta*	pa**zhal**sta
Thank you	Спасибо *Spasibo*	spa**seeb**a
You are welcome	Пожалуйста *Pozhaluysta*	pa**zhal**sta
Excuse me	Извините *Izvinite*	eezvee**neet**-ye
Hello	Здравствуйте *Zdravstvuyte*	**zdrast**vooyt-ye
Goodbye	До свидания *Do svidaniya*	da sveed**anya**
Good morning	Доброе утро *Dobroe utro*	**dobra**-ye **oo**tra
Good afternoon/day	Добрый день *Dobryy den*	**dobree** dyen'
Good evening	Добрый вечер *Dobryy vecher*	**dobree** **vye**chyer
Good night	Спокойной ночи *Spokoynoy nochi*	spak**oy**nay **no**chee
Morning	утро *utro*	**oo**tra
Afternoon	день *den*	dyen'
Evening	вечер *vecher*	**vye**chyer
Yesterday	вчера *vchera*	fchye**ra**
Today	сегодня *sevodnya*	sye**vod**nya
Tomorrow	завтра *zavtra*	**zaf**tra
Here	здесь *zdes*	zdyes'

There	там	tam
	tam	
What?	Что?	shto?
	Chto?	
Where?	Где?	gdye?
	Gde?	
Why?	Почему?	pachyemoo?
	Pochemu?	
When?	Когда?	kagda?
	Kogda?	
Now	сейчас	seychas
	seychas	
Later	позже	pozhe
	pozzhe	
Can I...?	можно?	mozhna...?
	mozhno?	
It is possible/allowed	можно *mozhno*	mozhna
It is not possible/allowed	нельзя *nelzya*	nyelzya

USEFUL PHRASES

How are you?	Как дела?	kak dyela?
	Kak dela?	
Very well, thank you	Хорошо, спасибо	kharasho, spaseeba
	Khorosho, spasibo	
Pleased to meet you	Очень приятно	ochen' pree-yatna
	Ochen priyatno	
How do I get to...?	Как добраться до...?	kak dabrat'sya da...?
	Kak dobratsya do...?	
Would you tell me when we get to...?	Скажите, пожалуйста, когда мы приедем в...?	skazheet-ye, pazhalsta, kagda mi pree-yedyem v...?
	Skazhite, pozhaluysta, kogda my priedem v...?	
Is it very far?	Это далеко?	eta dalyeko?
	Eto daleko?	
Do you speak English?	Вы говорите по-английски?	vi gavareet-ye po-angleeskee?
	Vy govorite po-angliyski?	
I don't understand	Я не понимаю	ya nye paneema-yoo
	Ya ne ponimayu	
Could you speak more slowly?	Говорите медленнее	gavareet-ye myedlyenye-ye
	Govorite medlennee	
Could you say it again please?	Повторите, пожалуйста	paftareet-ye, pazhalsta
	Povtorite, pozhaluysta	
I am lost	Я заблудился (заблудилась)	ya zabloodeelsya (zabloodeelas')
	Ya zabludilsya (zabludilas)	
How do you say... in Russian?	Как по-русски...?	kak pa-rooskee...?
	Kak po-russki...?	

USEFUL WORDS

big	большой	bal'shoy
	bolshoy	
small	маленький	malyen'kee
	malenkiy	
hot (water, food)	горячий	garyachee
	goryachiy	
hot (weather)	жарко	zharka
	zharko	
cold	холодный	khalodnee
	kholodnyy	
good	хорошо	kharasho
	khorosho	
bad	плохо	plokha
	plokho	
okay/fine	нормально	narmal'na
	normalno	
near	близко	bleezka
	blizko	
far	далеко	dalyeko
	daleko	
up	наверху	navyerkhoo
	naverkhu	

down	внизу	fneezoo
	vnizu	
early	рано	rana
	rano	
late	поздно	pozdna
	pozdno	
vacant (unoccupied)	свободно	svabodna
	svobodno	
free (no charge)	бесплатно	byesplatna
	besplatno	
cashier/ticket office	касса	kasa
	kassa	
avenue	проспект	praspyekt
	prospekt	
bridge	мост	most
	most	
embankment	набережная	nabyeryezhnaya
	naberezhnaya	
highway	шоссе	shasse
	shosse	
lane/passage	переулок	pyeryeoolak
	pereulok	
square	площадь	ploshat'
	ploshchad	
street	улица	ooleetsa
	ulitsa	
apartment	квартира	kvarteera
	kvartira	
floor	этаж	etash
	etazh	
house	дом	dom
	dom	
entrance	вход	fkhot
	vkhod	
exit	выход	vikhot
	vykhod	
river	река	ryeka
	reka	
summer country house	дача	dacha
	dacha	
swimming pool	бассейн	basyeyn
	basseyn	
town	город	gorat
	gorod	
toilet	туалет	tooalyet
	tualet	

MAKING A TELEPHONE CALL

Can I call abroad from here?	Можно отсюда позвонить за границу ?	mozhna atsyooda pazvaneet' za graneetsoo?
	Mozhno ostyuda pozvonit za granitsu?	
I would like to speak to...	Позовите, пожалуйста...	pazaveet-ye, pazhalsta...
	Pozovite, pozhaluysta	
Could you leave him/her a message?	Вы можете передать ему/ей?	vi mozhet-ye pyeryedat' yemoo/yay?
	Vy mozhete peredat emu/ey?	
My number is...	Мой номер...	moy nomyer...
	Moy nomer...	
I'll ring back later	Я позвоню позже	ya pazvanyoo pozhe
	Ya pozvonyu pozzhe	

SIGHTSEEING

castle	замок	zamak
	zamok	
cathedral	собор	sabor
	sobor	
church	церковь	tserkaf
	tserkov	
circus	цирк	tseerk
	tsirk	
closed for cleaning "cleaning day"	санитарный день	saneetarnee dyen'
	sanitarnyy den	
undergoing restoration	ремонт	remont
	remont	
exhibition	выставка	vistafka
	vystavka	
fortress	крепость	kryepost'
	krepost	
gallery	галерея	galeryeya
	galereya	

garden	сад *sad*	sad
island	остров *ostrov*	**o**straf
kremlin/fortified stronghold	кремль *kreml*	kryeml'
library	библиотека *biblioteka*	beeblee-at**ye**ka
monument	памятник *pamyatnik*	**pa**myatneek
mosque	мечеть *mechet*	myech**ye**t'
museum	музей *muzey*	moozy**ey**
palace	дворец *dvorets*	dvar**ye**ts
park	парк *park*	park
parliament	дума *duma*	**doo**ma
synagogue	синагога *sinagoga*	seenag**o**ga
tourist information	пункт информации для туристов *punkt informatsii dlya turistov*	**poo**nkt eenfarm**a**tsee-ee dlya toor**ee**staf
zoo	зоопарк *zoopark*	za**pa**rk

SHOPPING

open	открыто *otkryto*	atk**ri**ta
closed	закрыто *zakryto*	zak**ri**ta
How much does this cost?	Сколько это стоит? *Skolko eto stoit?*	sk**o**l'ka **e**ta st**o**eet?
I would like to buy.....	Я хотел (хотела) бы купить... *Ya khotel (khotela) by kupit...*	ya khat**ye**l (khat**ye**la) bi koop**ee**t'...
Do you have....?	У вас есть...? *U vas yest...?*	oo vas yest'...?
Do you take credit cards?	Кредитные карточки вы принимаете? *Kreditnye kartochki vy prinimaete?*	kryed**ee**tnye k**a**rtachkee vy preeneem**a**yetye?
What time do you open/close?	Во сколько вы открываетесь/ закрываетесь? *Vo skolko vy otkryvaetes/ zakryvaetes?*	Va sk**o**l'ka vy atkriv**a**yetyes'/ zakriv**a**yetyes'?
This one	этот *etot*	**e**tat
expensive	дорого *dorogo*	d**o**raga
cheap	дёшево *deshevo*	dyosh**ye**va
size	размер *razmer*	razm**ye**r
white	белый *belyy*	b**ye**lee
black	чёрный *chernyy*	ch**yo**rnee
red	красный *krasnyy*	kr**a**snee
yellow	жёлтый *zheltyy*	zh**o**ltee
green	зелёный *zelenyy*	zyel**yo**nee
dark blue	синий *siniy*	s**ee**nee
light blue	голубой *goluboy*	galoob**oy**
brown	коричневый *korichnevyy*	kar**ee**chnyevee

TYPES OF SHOP

bakery	булочная *bulochnaya*	b**oo**lachna-ya
bookstore	книжный магазин *knizhnyy magazin*	kn**ee**zhnee magaz**ee**n
butcher	мясной магазин *myasnoy magazin*	myasn**oy** magaz**ee**n

camera shop	фото-товары *foto-tovary*	f**o**to-tavari
delicatessen	гастроном *gastronom*	gastran**o**m
department store	универмаг *univermag*	ooneevyerm**a**g
drugstore	аптека *apteka*	apt**ye**ka
florist	цветы *tsvety*	tsvet**i**
grocer	бакалея *bakaleya*	bakal**ye**-ya
hairdresser	парикмахерская *parikmakherskaya*	pareekm**a**khyerskaya
market	рынок *rynok*	r**i**nak
newspaper stand	газетный киоск *gazetniy kiosk*	gaz**ye**tnee kee-**o**sk
post office	почта *pochta*	p**o**chta
record shop	грампластинки *gramplastinki*	gramplast**ee**nkee
shoe shop	обувь *obuv*	ob**oo**f'
travel agent	бюро путешествий *byuro puteshestviy*	byoor**o** pootyesh**e**stvee
bank	банк *bank*	bank

STAYING IN A HOTEL

Do you have a vacant room?	У вас есть свободный номер? *U vas yest svobodnyy nomer?*	oo vas yest' svab**o**dnee n**o**myer?
double room with double bed	номер с двуспальной кроватью *nomer s dvuspalnoy krovatyu*	n**o**myer s dvoosp**a**l'noy krav**a**t'-yoo
twin room	двухместный номер *dvukhmestnyy nomer*	dvookhm**ye**stnee n**o**myer
single room	одноместный номер *odnomestnyy nomer*	adnam**ye**stnee n**o**myer
bath	ванная *vannaya*	v**a**na-ya
shower	душ *dush*	doosh
porter	носильщик *nosilshchik*	nas**ee**l'sheek
key	ключ *klyuch*	kly**oo**ch

EATING OUT

A table for two, please	Стол на двоих, пожалуйста	stol na dva-**ee**kh, pazh**a**lsta
I would like to book a table	Я хочу заказать стол *Ya khochu zakazat stol*	ya khach**oo** zakaz**a**t' stol
The bill, please	Счёт, пожалуйста *Schet, pozhaluysta*	shyot, pazh**a**lsta
I am a vegetarian	Я вегетерианец (вегетерианка) *Ya vegeterianets (vegetarianka)*	ya vyegyetaree**a**nyets (vyegyetaree**a**nka)
breakfast	завтрак *zavtrak*	z**a**ftrak
lunch	обед *obed*	ab**ye**t
dinner	ужин *uzhin*	**oo**zheen
waiter!	официант! *ofitsiant!*	afeetsee-**a**nt!
waitress!	официантка! *ofitsiantka!*	afeetsee-**a**ntka!
dish of the day	фирменное блюдо *firmennoe blyudo*	f**ee**rmenoye bly**oo**da
appetizers/starters	закуски *zakuski*	zak**oo**skee

main course	второе блюдо *vtoroe blyudo*	ftar**o**ye bly**oo**da
meat and poultry dishes	мясные блюда *myasnye blyuda*	m**ya**sniye bly**oo**da
fish and seafood dishes	рыбные блюда *rybnye blyuda*	r**i**bniye bly**oo**da
vegetable dishes	овощные блюда *ovoshchnye blyuda*	avashshn**i**ye bly**oo**da
dessert	десерт *desert*	dyes**y**ert
drinks	напитки *napitki*	nap**ee**tkee
vegetables	овощи *ovoshchi*	**o**vashshee
bread	хлеб *khleb*	khl**ye**b
wine list	карта вин *karta vin*	k**a**rta veen
rare (steak)	недожаренный *nedozharennyy*	nyedazh**a**renee
well-done (steak)	прожаренный *prozharennyy*	prozh**a**renee
glass	стакан *stakan*	st**a**kan
bottle	бутылка *butylka*	boot**i**lka
knife	нож *nozh*	nosh
fork	вилка *vilka*	v**ee**lka
spoon	ложка *lozhka*	l**o**shka
plate	тарелка *tarelka*	tar**y**elka
napkin	салфетка *salfetka*	salf**y**etka
salt	соль *sol*	sol'
pepper	перец *perets*	p**y**eryets
butter/oil	масло *maslo*	m**a**sla
sugar	сахар *sakhar*	s**a**khar

Menu Decoder

абрикос *abrikos*	abreek**o**s	apricot
апельсин *apelsin*	apyel's**ee**n	orange
апельсиновый сок *apelsinovyy sok*	apyel's**ee**navee sok	orange juice
арбуз *arbuz*	arb**oo**z	watermelon
белое вино *beloe vino*	b**ye**laye veen**o**	white wine
бифштекс *bifshteks*	beefsht**ye**ks	steak
блины *bliny*	bleen**i**	pancakes
борщ *borshch*	borshsh	borscht (beetroot soup)
варенье *varene*	var**y**en'ye	Russian syrup-jam
варёный *varenyy*	var**yo**nee	boiled
ветчина *vetchina*	vyetcheen**a**	ham
вода *voda*	vad**a**	water
говядина *govyadina*	gav**ya**deena	beef
грибы *griby*	greeb**i**	mushrooms
груша *grusha*	gr**oo**sha	pear
гусь *gus*	goos	goose
джем *dzhem*	dzhem	jam
жареный *zharenyy*	zh**a**ryenee	roasted/grilled/fried
икра *ikra*	eekr**a**	black caviar
икра красная/кета *ikra krasnaya/keta*	eekr**a** krasna-ya/ k**ye**ta	red caviar

капуста *kapusta*	kap**oo**sta	cabbage
картофель *kartofel*	kart**o**fyel'	potato
квас *kvas*	kvas	kvas (sweet, mildly alcoholic drink)
клубника *klubnika*	kloobn**ee**ka	strawberries
колбаса *kolbasa*	kalbas**a**	salami sausage
кофе *kofe*	k**o**fye	coffee
красное вино *krasnoe vino*	kr**a**snoye veen**o**	red wine
креветки *krevetki*	kryevv**y**etkee	shrimp
курица *kuritsa*	k**oo**reetsa	chicken
лук *luk*	look	onion
малина *malina*	mal**ee**na	raspberries
минеральная вода *mineralnaya voda*	mineral'naya vad**a**	mineral water
мороженое *morozhenoe*	mar**o**zhena-ye	ice cream
мясо *myaso*	m**ya**sa	meat
огурец *ogurets*	agoor**y**ets	cucumber
осетрина *osetrina*	asyetr**ee**na	sturgeon
пельмени *pelmeni*	pyel'm**ye**nee	meat or fish dumplings
персик *persik*	p**y**erseek	peach
печенье *pechene*	pyechy**e**n'ye	biscuit
печёнка *pechenka*	pyech**yo**nka	liver
печёный *pechenyy*	pyech**yo**nee	baked
пиво *pivo*	p**ee**va	beer
пирог *pirog*	peer**o**k	pie
пирожки *pirozhki*	peer**a**shk**ee**	small parcels with savory fillings
помидор *pomidor*	pameed**o**r	tomato
продукты моря *produkty morya*	prad**oo**kti mar**ya**	seafood
рыба *ryba*	r**i**ba	fish
салат *salat*	sal**a**t	salad
свинина *svinina*	sveen**ee**na	pork
сельдь *seld*	sye'ld'	herring
сосиски *sosiski*	sas**ee**skee	sausages
сыр *syr*	sir	cheese
сырой *syroy*	seer**oy**	raw
утка *utka*	**oo**tka	duck
фасоль *fasol*	fas**o**l'	beans
форель *forel*	far**ye**l'	trout
чай *chay*	chai	tea
чеснок *chesnok*	chyesn**o**k	garlic
шашлык *shashlyk*	shashl**i**k	kebab
яйцо *yaytso*	yayts**o**	egg
слива *sliva*	sl**ee**va	plum
фрукты *frukty*	fr**oo**kti	fruit
яблоко *yabloko*	**ya**blaka	apple

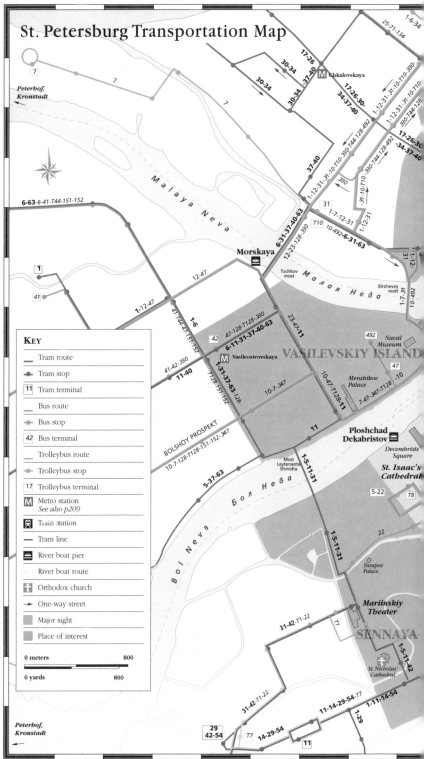